Centennial Tales and Selected Poems

An all-inclusive edition of the poetry of Watson Kirkonnell would run to some ten large volumes of original verse and translations. His original verse would fill two volumes the size of this one, and his translated verse—from Icelandic, Italian, Dutch, French, Magyar, Latin, Ukrainian and Polish—would fill 5,000 pages. No poet in the English-speaking tradition is more deeply grounded in world literature.

The original poetry of Watson Kirkconnell has been primarily narrative in character: first, the twelve philosophically slanted books of his Spenserian epic, *The Eternal Quest*; then the seventeen vivid narratives in *The Flying Bull, and Other Tales*, a sort of Western echo of *The Canterbury Tales*; and finally the thirty narrative poems of his new *Centennial Tales*, many of which were written in 1964. These are framed about the history of Canada, and are written in honour of the nation's Centennial in 1967. They range from the coming of the first "Amerindians" from Asia about 30,000 B.C. to a possible atomic holocaust in A.D. 2000, and include poems on the Quebec Conference of 1864, the Vimy Memorial, the Italian Campaign and the Canadians in Cyprus.

This volume also contains some lyrics from Dr. Kirkconnell's light opera, The Mod at Grand Pré, and the whole of his Greek-style drama, Let My People Go, with its setting in Egypt just before the Exodus and its issues in the present. The original poetry has been arranged in roughly the reverse of chronological order, while the translations are arranged according to the dates of publication.

WATSON KIRKCONNELL was educated at Queen's University and at Oxford. He taught at Wesley-United College, University of Manitoba, 1922–1940, and at McMaster University 1940–1948. From 1948 to 1964 he was President of Acadia University, and is now President Emeritus. Dr. Kirkconnell has written over forty books, chiefly in comparative literature, and more than one hundred smaller volumes. He is a Fellow of the Royal Society of Canada, and of some thirty-five other learned societies in many countries.

WATSON KIRKCONNELL

CENTENNIAL TALES

and

Selected Poems

WATSON KIRKCONNELL

Published for Acadia University by

UNIVERSITY OF TORONTO PRESS

TO HOPE

Preface

THE PRESENT VOLUME contains nearly one-half of my original verse and somewhat less than one-thirtieth of my work in verse translation. Having passed my first coronary and my seventieth birthday, I feel that at least this much of my poetic output ought to be placed on the pre-obituary record. The first 122 pages are almost entirely new work, written in 1964, while the remaining pages are a selective consolidation from some forty previously published books and brochures and from hundreds of items in periodicals.

A collected edition of my verse would total nearly ten volumes the size of this one and would serve no useful purpose. In any case, four of my latest works—*Pan Tadeusz* (from the Polish, 1962, pp. 388), *The Ukrainian Poets* (1963, pp. 500), *The Poetical Works of Taras Shevchenko* (also from Ukrainian in collaboration with C. H. Andrusyshen, 1964, pp. 563) and *That Invincible Samson* (from Latin, Dutch and Italian, 1964, pp. 218)—are still in print with the University of Toronto Press; and *The Flying Bull* (1940, 1949, 1956, 1964, pp. 154) is in print with Clarke, Irwin and Company.

The original poetry in this present volume is printed in roughly the reverse of chronological order, so as to put the freshest fruit in the top layer of the basket. The translations, on the contrary, are arranged according to the dates of publication. The first such volume, *European Elegies*, has been reprinted in full, since its organizing pattern would otherwise be lost; but only some sixty pages out of the remaining four thousand have been included.

I am grateful to Clarke, Irwin and Company for permission to include the major part of my *Flying Bull and Other Tales*; to the University of Toronto Press for permission to reprint items from *Pan Tadeusz, The Ukrainian Poets,* and *The Poetical Works of Taras Shevchenko*; to my collaborator, Dr. C. H. Andrusyshen, for permission to reprint from *The Ukrainian Poets* and *The Poetical Works of*

Taras Shevchenko; to the Macmillan Company of Canada for permission to use my "Manitoba Symphony" from *Manitoba Essays*; to the *Dalhousie Review* for "A Rime of Glooscap" and "The Gloomy Forest"; to *Saturday Night* for "Nova Scotia Suite," "The Trapper and the Bears," and "The Crow and the Nighthawk"; to the *Winnipeg Free Press* for excerpts from my *Manitoba Limericks*; to the *Regina Leader-Post* for a few of my *Saskatchewan Limericks*; to the *Canadian Forum* for my "Lay of Elijah" and "The Ayrshire Muse"; to the *Canadian Jewish Review* for "The Agony of Israel"; to the *Canadian Poetry Magazine* for "Foreword on Request" and to *Amethyst* for "Rain on the Waste Land" and "The Twa Muses."

I would also record my grateful thanks to Acadia University for consenting to sponsor the publication of this volume.

W. K.

Wolfville, Nova Scotia

Contents

[*xi*]

Selected Verse Translations

Selected Original Verse

Centennial Tales

THE ALASKA CROSSING
(35,000 B.C.)

This was the vanguard that from Asia pressed
Into the untenanted Americas,
That vaster Rub' Al Khali of the West,
A voiceless wilderness whose unknown jaws
Might swallow up forever all their quest;
Yet onward still they moved, from pause to pause,
And never dreamed that Time would see their way go
To Greenland and Tierra del Fuego

And all that lay between: the ocean fjords,
The snow-capped ranges and the pathless plains
(Thronged by the bison in their burly hordes),
The Eastern forests, and the tropic rains
On Amazonian swamps, Andean swards,
And the vast anaconda's dank domains,
Down to the pampas of the cooler South
And Golfo Nassau with its icy mouth.

For Man had never trod these continents.
Europe he knew, and Africa's deep Rift,
And Asia also marked his slow ascents
To fuller comprehension and the lift
To laws and culture as his brain invents
New concepts in his migratory drift,
Until this day he opened a new gate
To knowledge by transcending Bering Strait.

Across the cold Atlantic in that day
The stone age hunter followed on the track
Of fleeced rhinoceros or hid away
In caves of Solutré and Aurignac;
His skills the Amerind's could not outweigh
Save by his paintings in those shelters black,
Dramatic colours on the rocky walls
That topple beatniks from their pedestals.

Now on Alaska's coast two leaders stood,
As long ago stood Abraham and Lot
Before they parted company for good.
From this first beachhead, this rude beauty-spot,
They made their choice to wander where they would,
To eastward or to southward, cold or hot,
Tracking the reindeer, the Siberian sheep,
Musk ox and bear and elk along the steep.

And one band, marching eastward up the rivers,
After a season filtered through the ranges
To find enormous plains, abundant givers
Of game to hunt. Their leader then exchanges
Eastward for southward, since the east delivers
A glacier's frigid greeting that estranges
While all the south spreads grassy, warm and airy,
An evident infinity of prairie.

The other hunters spread along the coast,
Learning by boat to navigate the shore-way,
Daring the billows to the uttermost,
Rude, red-skinned Vikings down a vaster Norway;
And at the last a victory they boast
As by the sea they open up a doorway
Into a wonderland of tropic splendour
And fertile fields that to their tilth surrender.

Hundreds of plants they tame to human use,
Maize and potato, gourd and artichoke;
Peanuts and squash and chilis they produce;
Pumpkins and Lima beans their gardens cloak,
And others more conducive to abuse
In coca chewing and tobacco smoke,
So that to their discredit may be flung
The genesis of cancer of the lung.

Whereas the long house, wigwam, lodge or teepee
Might house the northern Indian from the storm,
Inca and Maya chiefs as they grew sleepy
Had great stone palaces to keep them warm;
Stone roads and culverts built through jungles creepy
Were monumental in their massive form;
And aqueducts and skilful irrigation
Upheld the culture of the dusky nation.

[4]

Astronomy they framed with careful mind,
Into time's reckoning a peerless window;
To mathematics they were much inclined,
Inventing zero long before the Hindu;
And Maya writing as an art we find,
For which they made bark-paper sheets and skin do;
But primal archery, from Asia brought,
Was helpless against guns, when Spaniards fought.

In short, the Empty Continents thus entered
They filled from end to end, from side to side—
A far-flung culture area, though centred
In Yucatan, Peru and all their pride.
And so the white man's travels, redskin-mentored,
From sea to sea with Indians to guide,
Called "exploration" in our white effront'ry,
Were "guided tours" through most familiar country.

SHEGUIANDAH, MANITOULIN ISLAND
(*ca.* 7,000 B.C.)

The land was haunted. As the little band
    Moved north behind the haunches of the ice
    That still retreated towards the hinterland,
The dusky hunters found, not once or twice,
    Inexplicable ghosts of earlier days,
    Of ancient toil and far-off sacrifice.
First, far to north and west, in great amaze
    They had encountered giant lizard bones
    When deep through blasted wastes had lain their ways;
So vast these fossils lay among the stones
    That, were their owners given flesh and blood
    To bellow hungrily in bestial tones,
Bigger than fifty wigwams had they stood.
    And do such mighty monsters yet survive?
    Can we, perhaps, far off still hear the thud
Of their colossal feet as, all alive
    And ravenous for food, they roam the plains?
    Such premonitions of disaster drive
The shuddering hunters eastward. None remains

To dangle screaming down from serrate jaws
    Or to be picked apart with hideous pains.
Eastward and south they press, with little pause,
    And reach at last a chain of sea-like lakes
    And a great cataract that overawes
Their humble spirits as its torrent breaks
    Over a rocky cliff and foaming pours
    Down a raw canyon, while its tumult wakes
The wooded wilderness with sullen roars.
    Then on the escarpment of that limestone trench
    And in the ragged rubble on its shores
They light on fish of stone; their faces blench
    At clams and snails likewise in stone imbedded
    Amid the cataract's unceasing drench.
How could these creatures to the rock be wedded?
    Do all things turn to stone in this weird place?
    And shall we too? This was the thought they dreaded.
Circling the last great lake, their way they trace
    To massive cliffs of clay that fronted south
    With broad lake-waters lapping at their base;
And half way up the slope, with open mouth
    They gape to mark a belt of dark debris—
    And as they probe the spot, in reason's drouth,
A mass of ancient trunks and stumps they see
    Beneath two hundred feet of glacial till,
    And each old log is from some noble tree
That grows no longer in these regions chill.
    Can these then offer proofs of warmer climes
    Before a later glacier came to fill
The land with layer on layer of frosty slimes
    And then move off to northward in its turn?
    Slowly this truth from deep reflection climbs
Up to convictions that they all discern
    As a clear principle, the fertile source
    Of many another lesson they may learn.
Northward they wander next upon their course
    And on a sprawling island there they find
    A quartzite bed from which their skill can force
Scrapers and arrowheads of every kind,
    Spearheads and knives to help them in the hunt.
    The ice had ground it clear but left a blind

Old rocky cave beside it, masked in front
　　With sand and gravel from the last moraine.
　　Under its drifted edges, with a grunt
The eldest hunter, following a vein
　　Of rock, unearthed a human artifact,
　　A neatly fashioned scraper that had lain
Under the sand and gravel, all intact.
　　He dug still further and with wonder found,
　　Deep in the till but formed with skill exact
Hundreds of tools and weapons underground.
　　Had his own tribesmen hidden them away?
　　There were too many in that sandy mound
And all upon the stone floor-level lay,
　　Not buried from above but fashioned there,
　　Authentic relics of an earlier day.
These with those buried trees he might compare
　　That in the cliffs of clay he had beheld,
　　Incomparably old he was aware.
His fellows gathered round, by awe compelled.
　　"Use magic, father," said a thoughtful lad,
　　"For you as a magician have excelled.
Swallow peyotl and then all unclad,
　　Save for these weapons we shall heap about you,
　　Slumber. Perhaps some vision may be had
As forces from the past may move throughout you.
　　This you have done before, your comrades know.
　　For wisdom, we could never do without you."
The old man gave assent, serene and slow,
　　And laid him down that night beside the fire;
　　The others on his flesh these weapons strow
Out of past ages as his sole attire;
　　Peyotl through his veins in flames ascends
　　And ancient forces with the drug conspire.
Watched from a distance by his anxious friends,
　　His face grows stony and his breathing still
　　As phantoms from the past he comprehends.
For dusky forms he saw, benign not ill,
　　Here in an open cavern, chipping flints
　　In friendly fashion and with ready skill.
Their speech he did not know yet lacked no hints
　　Of what they thought, communing mind with mind,

[7]

As each on each his inmost sense imprints.
"Who are you then?"—"Why, men of your own kind."
  —"How do you live?"—"To hunt we are intent."
  —"Whence did you come?"—"Long since we left behind
The borders of a far-off continent,
  Crossing to this and found no creature here
  Of human speech, no matter where we went."
—"In what age did you live, what far-off year?"
  —"The dating of our time we cannot tell;
  For life is timeless in this hemisphere
Save as the mighty glaciers shrink or swell.
  Great oaks and chestnuts bloomed above our head
  And summer wove for us a sultry spell."
He woke, and with his dream dispelled the dread
  Of his companions, having thus communed
  In peaceful converse with the deathless dead.

* * * *

This land is haunted: and a mind attuned
  Can conjure up the spirits of the past;
  For evidence that cannot be impugned
Attests antiquity supremely vast.
  The carbon-dating of the old chief's embers
  Over nine thousand years is backward cast,
While more than thrice as many cold Decembers
  Across the glacial clay and gravel span
  To that far epoch that his dream remembers—
So ancient is America's first man.

THE SERPENT-MOUND, RICE LAKE
(350 B.C.)

Out of the south they came, this gentle race
That from the forest hewed a dwelling-place,
East from Otonabees's broad, swampy mouth
And on a shelving shoreline, facing south.
Where only hunters in the past had ranged,
They brought the seeds of maize, whose kernels changed

(Along with squash and beans) the forest gloom
To fruitful fields, the tribe's rich dining-room.
And novel crafts they brought; a woman's hand
Would mould creative dishes for the band;
While men carved horn and stone with subtle skill
And moulded lumps of copper to their will;
Pipes of pure silver, conch shells carved with art,
All set them from the earlier tribes apart.

More than all else, among them there was rife
Preoccupation with the after-life,
A high religious faith that ever fed
Their deep affection for the noble dead.
Whereas their forest neighbours, stony-eyed,
Flung into open pits their friends who died,
This newer people, with devoted rites,
Burned them on pyres in the silent nights
And gathering up the bones from off the ground
Would place them tenderly within a mound,
With faithful gifts of copper beads and shells
And many a tool that their affection tells.
Over the funeral fires a priest would tower,
Crowned with stag-antlers in that sacred hour;
And his high benedictions, as they soar,
Are answered by the waves upon the shore.

The sign of their believing was a Snake,
Reared up with earth and stones beside the lake,
High on a promontory's grassy crest
With noble views to east, and south and west.
Well nigh two hundred feet from fangs to tail
The lordly reptile mounted from the dale
And just before its jaws an egg was set,
Built likewise out of earth by toil and sweat.
What serpent did they hail with reverent breath—
The snake of healing or the snake of death?
Great Quetzacoatl who was once adored
By Aztecs was, we know, a serpent-lord;
And in the Natchez Temple of the Sun
The rattlesnake was god to everyone.
That Aesculapius and Mercury
Paid tribute to the serpent, all may see;

And Moses' tale of Adam and sin's birth
Proclaimed the snake the subtlest beast on earth.
How shall we know the impulse that impelled
Men's hands to build this Thing we have beheld?
Though even greater serpent-mounds were reared
In far Ohio, there have disappeared
The race and tongue of those who might have glossed
The answer, and the evidence is lost.
Their brothers, by Rice Lake, more briefly stayed
And passed forever underneath the shade
Of things forgotten and uncomprehended,
Timely begotten and untimely ended.

    Long, long ago they lived; their campfires shone
Coëval with the rise of Macedon,
The wars of Alexander and the fame
That rang through shattered Asia as he came.
But these were men of peace; our thought avers
A race of Amerind philosophers—
Some redskin Plato wise debate begins
With Aristotle shod in moccasins,
Some Theophrastus herbal lore reveals,
Some sage Hippocrates their sickness heals.
Of these the solemn serpent sign remains
Under our summer suns or autumn rains,
Older than Hadrian's Wall or Mausoleum,
More ancient than the Flavian Colosseum,
The arch of Titus or of Constantine,
And all that makes the Roman name divine.

    How did its builders vanish? Some would say
They lingered on these shores for many a day,
Fading like Roman outposts, far from home
And cut off from the sustenance of Rome;
But some would give their faith a darker fate,
Butchered by neighbors who were full of hate
For alien rites and dreams not understood
As evil cannot grasp the mind of good.
So were the serpent-builders fiercely slain
With pangs unspeakable and hideous pain,
Sad martyrs of a gentle new religion
Cut down by some old cult still stark and Stygian,

Two thousand years before the torturous vogue
Would murder Brébeuf, Lalement and Jogues.

Along the mighty Snake upon the hill
The grass in summer winds is never still,
Until the cozened vision might attest
That the great Reptile wriggled towards the crest,
As the deep meaning that upheaved its earth
Writhes in our consciousness in quest of birth.
The Sphinx had once a riddle. Who can break
In this New World the riddle of the Snake?

LEIF SPEAKS TO FREYDIS
(At Brattahlid, Greenland, A.D. 1008)

Freydis, my wicked sister, I am sickened
By this your midnight act of massacre.
I have examined three among your crewmen
With stern duress, each man heard separately,
And all three stories tally to a jot.
You have befouled my fair retreat in Vineland
With black atrocity, lied to your husband
And stirred him up against the innocent,—
Finnbogi, Helgi and their thirty men.
You swore they had maltreated you by night
And that the insult of their loathed molesting
Must be avenged by death. He roused his men,
Seized on the guiltless victims while they slept
And led each man outside, securely bound.
At the house-door you stood and hissed your orders
To cut each Norseman down as he appeared.
Soon all the men were dead; but there remained
Five wives who shared the building with their husbands.
"Kill them!" you cried, but no one would obey you.
"Hand me an axe!" you screamed; then split their skulls
As fiercely as a weasel slaughters rabbits.
And all for what? For profit, my bad sister:
To carry all things in one vessel home
For you and yours alone in evil comfort.
    Our noble father, Eirik, had three sons—

Leif, Thorvald, Thorleif—and, to stain his name,
One base-born daughter who has shamed us all.
Eirik discovered Greenland, and his children
Each had a share in probing to the south
Where Bjarni Herjolfsson had glimpsed new land,
A mighty continent of rock and forest,
But had not stayed to search its secret out.
First of the sons I sailed, with Bjarni's ship,
And probed the barren flats of "Helluland";
Behind them rose steep mountains capped with ice
And no grass grew upon the slabs of stone.
Nothing was here to tempt a husbandman;
And so I southward fared past level coasts
With spruce in serried ranks of gloomy green.
Thereafter, league on league of sandy beaches,
White as a dream, shelved gently to the sea.
Then two days sailing with a northeast wind
Brought us in safety to a promontory
Projecting northwards from a mass of land.
My scouts found self-sown grain along the margin
And harvests of wild grapes; small blame is it
That from that circumstance I called it "Vineland."
Here I set up my booths, here built a house,
Here spent a winter in supreme content,
And with the spring came safely home again.
    A passion for discovery then seized
Our brother, Thorvald. With the self-same ship
He sailed to Vineland without incident
And spent, like me, a quiet winter there.
All the next summer went to exploration
Along the western shore of that new land,
Fair and well-wooded and without a sign
Of human habitation save a grain-rack.
The second summer saw him farther north
Along the wooded coast. There, in a fjord,
Surrounded by tall trees, they fell on Skraelings,
The natives of the land, and out of nine
They cut down all but one, who in his turn
Brought to the shore a quick, avenging host,
Armed with strong bows and arrows tipped with stone.
Thorvald received an arrow in his belly,

Died, and was buried on the sandy shore.
    When the sad crew reported home next year,
Our other brother, Thorleif, took a vow
To go by vessel to that far-off coast
And bring back Thorvald's body for the church-yard.
Him hopeless weather, storm on savage storm,
Battered all summer on the North Atlantic;
And having floundered home, he died of plague.
    The greatest venture out to Vineland came
When three stout vessels took some eight-score men.
Thorfinn Karlsefni led them; there were wives,
And many cattle for a settlement
That might endure as long as that in Iceland.
My father's base-born daughter also sailed,—
You, my dark sister. And when Skraelings came
And hemmed the colony by hundreds in,
First to trade furs and then to do it harm,
Karlsefni's party was too weak to prosper.
In one fierce fight, you won a name for courage—
Whetted a war-sword on your brazen breasts
And put to flight the astonished enemy.
But the fair land was clearly full of danger;
Against a warlike host, Karlsefni's men
Seemed all too few and feeble to survive,
And after three short winters they sailed home.
    And now ensued a fifth and final voyage:
Two ships went out with hope to trade in furs—
Helgi, Finnbogi and their crew in one,
You and your husband and another crew
Borne in the other; and from that dark venture
Only one ship and crew came mutely home,
Laden with dead men's wealth.
                                    I curse you, sister!
I cannot kill you, for our childhood's sake,
But execrate the deed and you the doer;
The doomed Norse corpses on that far-off shore,
Slain by your greedy hands, outnumber far
All whom the screaming savages have slaughtered.
Eirik's own children claimed this new found land,
Explored it, built upon its pleasant meadows,
And now have drowned the dream in gall and blood.

This is the end. The stately house I built
Must moulder into dust on Vineland's loam,
Guarded by Viking ghosts. No more I'll go,
Nor suffer any other so to travel.
Eirik's base daughter has defiled that shore;
And it, and she, are damned for evermore.

A RIME OF GLOOSCAP

(A CENTO OF MICMAC LEGENDS)
ca. A.D. 1400

I

In the morning of time, when the world was new,
Glooscap, the god-man, red of hue,
Set up his teepee—long since gone—
High on the summit of Blomidon,
For where on earth was a site as fine as
The bastioned gate of the Basin of Minas.
Great was Glooscap and vast his strength.
Often in summer he'd loll full length,
Trailing his hands in the Minas tide
And cooling his feet on the Fundy side.
The Wolf and the Loon were his faithful hounds,
And sometimes, too, as he went his rounds,
The Squirrel followed at Glooscap's heel,
Tackling all rivals with equal zeal,
And changed at times by his magic might
To a giant squirrel for a giant fight.
A Skunk had Glooscap, as big as an ox,
Who stood stern first on the Kingsport rocks,
Greeting his guests, in blasts of glee,
With super-teargas artillery;
But soon washed sweet, in the friendliest state
The guests were fed from a magic plate
Where a tiny sirloin of beaver meat
Could feed a thousand yet stay complete.
The arrows of Glooscap were swift as light;
They found their mark in unerring flight,

And pierced it through and returned straightway
To the hand of their Master. He wore, they say,
A wizard belt that endowed his arm
With omnipotent power against all harm;
While he was the first on all our planet
To make a canoe from an isle of granite,
Using its pines as the masts for sails
To bear him swift through the Fundy gales.
   Now giant beavers built of yore
From Blomidon clear to the Parrsborough shore
A mighty dam with a pond to fill
The Annapolis Valley from hill to hill.
Glooscap, out hunting, returned in ire
To find the flood at his wigwam fire,
While swimming near Kingsport and almost sunk
Was the draggled form of his gunner the Skunk.
Angry was Glooscap. He took his axe
And with a couple of monstrous hacks
A four-mile hole through the dam he slit
And the water sent pouring out past Cape Split.
Looking to eastward, Economy way,
He spotted a beaver across the bay
And flung some boulders across its path.
Even today they mark his wrath
For off the shore near Economy Highlands
His rocks remain with the name "Five Islands."
The beavers have vanished long ago
But we know that the tale of their size is so,
For their bones have been dug out, sure enough,
From the fossil grave-yard of Horton Bluff,
While entrails of moose that Glooscap slew
Are reefs along Fundy, plain to view.

II

   Unmarried was Glooscap, but not alone
In his Blomidon camp on the cliffs of stone,
For he brought to his bachelor wigwam there
An adopted grandmother, Madam Bear,
To broil his salmon and tend his tent
While out through the forest he hunting went.

[15]

An adopted boy, named Marten, came
To be a third by the hearth-fire flame.
These were the people who had a part
In the inmost love of great Glooscap's heart.
　So, when the sorcerer, Win-pe, sought
To wound the master, he straightway thought
Of kidnapping Marten and Mother Bear
While Glooscap was absent, hunting the hare.
Seizing his victims, away he went;
And Glooscap returned to an empty tent,
A silent hill and a cold camp-fire;
But as he stood there in fierce desire
To know what had happened, to serve his wish
He chanced upon Marten's birch-bark dish
From which he speedily could divine
Win-pe's offence and his course malign.
Then in pursuit their trail he scanned
From Blomidon clear to Newfoundland;
But many a year and many a throe
Remained before he could meet his foe;
For fierce in his path a sorceress,
Pitcher the Witch, or Pook-jin-skwess,
Made ambushed efforts to thwart the Master
And compass his death in complete disaster.
She took on a hag's appalling form
And pled with him to remove a swarm
Of venomous vermin from out her hair
And each, as his hand removed it there,
Became a porcupine or a toad.
He took no harm and away he strode,
Only to meet with her hate once more
In two fierce she-wolves, but these he tore
To pieces raw with his own two hounds,
Grown by his magic beyond all bounds.
Two amorous witches they also slew,
Who hung on his neck, which they sought to lasso
With smoky nooses of bear-gut wurst,
Magic with spells of a kind accurst,
That would have wasted his strength away
And left him at once as their easy prey.
At last he stood, with these perils o'er,
On wooded Cape Breton's farthest shore

And learned again from Marten's bowl
That Newfoundland's coast was next his goal.
Then he looked at the sea and chanted a song
Whose spell over whales has persuasion strong
And a female whale of the largest size
That ever was seen under human skies
Came steaming up with a foaming track
And took the hero upon her back.
Over the misty seas he sped
With one foot on her tail and one on her head
And landed dry-shod in an hour at most
On a rocky point of the Cape Ray coast.
And he asked Ma Whale: "What thing do you
                                    lack o' ?"—
"Give me a pipe and some strong tobacco,"
She answered straight. And he took his pipe,
Rich and reeking and juicy ripe,
And filled it and placed it, as was her wish,
Between the lips of the giant fish,
Then he lit it politely and off she sailed
And as she puffed on the pipe and exhaled,
She left adrift on the Northern wind
A wonderful cloud of smoke behind.
And Glooscap laughed as he saw her go;
Then turned to discover his ancient foe,
Win-pe the warlock. With footstep firm
He crushed him to earth like an evil worm,
And rescued Marten and Madam Bear
After years of hunger and slow despair.

III

Tales without number are told today
Of Glooscap's deeds and the tricks he'd play
To foil the wicked and help the good
In every way that a Master could.
Thus a sorcerer sought to assail his power
In a contest of smoking one evil hour
And burned out a pipe with a single puff
As being of mastery proof enough.
But Glooscap's pipe was ten times greater
Than that of this nicotine-gladiator

And he cleared it all in a single spasm
And blew in the mountain a smoking chasm.
And the sorcerer scuttled away in panic
At proof of a lung-power so titanic.
　　Then a lordly giant, as tough as nails,
Invited Glooscap to fish for whales.
They went by canoe and in the prow
Stood mighty Kitpoo-seeagunow,
With a spear in his hand, and his feet wide-straddled,
While Glooscap sat in the stern and paddled.
The giant's great spear was strong and sharp;
He speared a whale as you'd spear a carp.
But Glooscap smiled and he trimmed the sails
And murmured, "I mostly bait with whales."
And he took the whale and baited his line
And trolled with care in the heaving brine
Till right off the Continental Shelf
He caught the great Sea-Serpent himself.
　　Now the heart of Glooscap was wondrous kind
When men of the Micmacs became inclined
To seek him out and implore his aid
In granting some wish that their souls had made.
Three men of the tribe one day had gone
To visit the Master on Blomidon;
And the first besought him for peerless height,
To stand erect in his fellows' sight;
The second asked to stay always there
Amid Blomidon's beauty and fragrant air;
While the third man begged him for length of days,
Watching the centuries pass their ways.
Then the Master thought and the Master sighed.
And turned them to pines by the Minas Tide—
Tall and stately and plumed and still,
Daring the centuries do their will,
The noblest trees of the noblest cape
Fashioned by Glooscap to that fair shape.

IV

Glooscap had cleansed the earth of evil,
Cannibal-giant and warlock-devil,

But the hearts of all beasts and men grew bad
And in wicked deeds were exceeding glad.
Then was Glooscap oppressed in spirit;
Glooscap moaned till the moon could hear it:
"Wicked are all in the world today.
I cannot bear it. I go away."
Then the great Master of men and beasts
Gave to all living the best of feasts,
A final supper by Minas' shore,
Laid out on the beach in abundant store.
Then he spread the sails of his stone canoe
And out into Fundy he passed from view,
And they watched him go as he passed from sight
And they heard him sing in the gathering night;
Fainter and fainter the great song came,
Faint as a far-off candle-flame,
Till silence fell and beyond all ken
Had passed the Master of beasts and men.
Then all living creatures who once had spoken
A common speech, found their concord broken,
For every species, old or young,
Gave utterance now in a different tongue,
Braying and chirping and barking and mewing
And so on down to each age ensuing,
While chaos came upon human speech,
Marking the tribes off, each from each.
Glooscap's departure was met with woe.
Nature sorrowed to see him go.
And the Wolf and the Loon bewail their friend
Night after night till the world shall end,
While the Snowy Owl in the woods makes stir:
"*Koo-koo-skoos*, I am sorry, Sir."

v

Whither went Glooscap? None can tell
What far adventures his lot befell;
But legends linger about his name
That dream the ways of his after-fame.
Sailing, they say, to west and north,
He pushed his craft on a broad stream forth,

A mighty river, serene and fair,
Where he sailed with Marten and Madam Bear.
But the stream grew narrow and dark and swift,
Stony-bedded and shadowy-cliff'd;
Higher and higher arose each bank,
And then in a tumult the river sank
White over monstrous cavern-sills
And under the base of the ancient hills.
Swift as an arrow the small boat sped
With only the black of the cave o'erhead,
And the waters wailed as they swept in grief
By hidden boulder and unseen reef.
Marten and Madam Bear paled to hear
And their strong hearts died in their utter fear
At the risk of wreck by the slightest error,
The cold of night and the cold of terror.
But Glooscap still paddled erect and calm,
And sang in the darkness a dauntless psalm,
Sang through the eddy and cataract
Till the shadows paled and the current slacked
And the boat swept forth into sun at last
With the terror done and the danger past,
And a waiting wigwam beckon'd agleam
On the shining bank of a tranquil stream.
Glooscap turned to the corpses twain
Of his friends who had died in their panic pain:
"*Numchahse*, arise!" And forth they stepped,
And lo, they deemed they had only slept.
     There in that far remotest west,
Surrounded by those he loves the best,
He labours, they say, as the years glide by,
Storing up arrows, a vast supply,
Infinite arrows, made swift and keen
For a Day of Battle too well foreseen,
A terrible day when the evil dead
Shall rise from the grave for a purpose dread.
Then Malsum, his brother, fierce and strange,
Who slumbers now as the Shickshock Range,
Shall come once more as commander fell
Of all the vampire hosts of hell.

Glooscap that day shall return again
To fight for the lives and the souls of men,
And his arrows shall darken the midday sky
Where the good and the evil by millions die,
And the sun shall set on a waste of mud,
Moistened with flesh and a sea of blood.
But the field shall be won and the wicked destroyed
And the kingdom of evil be waste and void,
And the dawn that comes to the earth once more
Shall shine on the righteous for evermore.
Then Glooscap, the Master, once more shall rest
In his Blomidon wigwam, by all men blest,
Healing and teaching, redeeming, forgiving,
The bountiful Master of all things living.

JOHN CABOT
(A.D. 1497–98)

John Cabot was an Englishman—in Genoa born Cabotto.
When of his voyages we read, it seems that he was blotto.
He left Old Bristol for Japan and sailed directly west;
The track of his discoveries might seem a drunkard's test.
He landed at a mighty cape—Cape Breton *or* Cape North
Or Labrador *or* Signal Hill—the second and the fourth
Are tied for popularity among the Boards of Trade;
The Tourist Bureaux to and fro exchange fierce cannonade;
For Newfoundlanders vow with heat, they are his "new
       found land,"
And it must be their noble coast his eagle eye first scanned;
While Nova Scotians cry with rage that Cape North cannot fail
To be his landfall long ago—or why "the Cabot Trail?"
Even the grave *Britannica* between their claims is mired;
The Great Panjandrum, which, it seems, by many dons is sired,
Sub verbo "Cabot" says Cape North, with utter certainty,
But *s.v.* "Newfoundland" says No, Cape North it cannot be.
The Cabot Trail, with such a guide, will drive a body giddy—
You'll roll on down to Cheticamp by way of Quidi Vidi,
Or if you take the other shore, you'll have to make your way
To find the beach at Ingonish through Bonavista Bay.

A second year he came again, and landing on a shore
On icy Greenland's eastern rim, he called it "Labrador."
When all his sailors got cold feet beside that glacial highland,
He turned his vessels south and west and came to Baffin Island.
This, too, proved most unpopular; this, too, he left behind;
And ever southward steered his ship, to see what he could find.
The north wind blew, miraculous and steady in its force:
He passed St. John's and Halifax (which were not there, of
    course),
He sailed past Boston and New York (which still did not exist),
Saw on Atlantic City's beach the Redskins do the Twist,
But still no merchants of Japan with silks and spices came
To prove the expedition right and bring the skipper fame.
The latitude was thirty-eight, the edge of Old Virginia;
So far as poor John Cabot knew, it might be Argentinia,
Brazil or More's Utopia, and he'd no wish for these.
He'd found Virginia cigarettes—but nothing Japanese.
Old Henry Tudor would be cross (the king who sent him out),
But rations on the ships were scarce, this too he could not doubt,
And since the hunger of his crew was threatening as a pistol,
He turned his vessels round about and sailed back home to
    Bristol.

John Cabot was an Englishman of courage and of brains,
But of his brilliant voyages a muddled myth remains.
Five cities of the ancient world claimed Homer's place of birth,
Though many modern scholars say, he never lived on earth;
John Cabot really lived and sailed, vouched for by many men,
But London, Venice, Genoa, called him their citizen;
And mystery cloaks his voyages, the places that he found
Are either skewed like Labrador or set on challenged ground.
Perhaps he entered up his log in sad intoxication;
Perhaps the fault is not with him but with our generation,
Which tries to cash in on the past and seeks a specious image
To draw the summer tourist trade and win the dollar scrimmage.
Across the capes and centuries we skip him like a rabbit,
That every paying visitor may dream of Master Cabot.
A hundred years before Champlain, five hundred after Leif,
He stands with our discoverers, no doubt among the chief.
One only caution we must leave—that none should waste an hour
In riding down the Cabot Trail in search of Cabot Tower.

THE ORDER OF GOOD CHEER
(A.D. 1606–1607)

Old Henri Quatre, in sixteen-three,
    Proclaimed Sieur de Monts
The Governor of Acadie;
    And he set up ere long
A farm and fortress by the shore,
    A forest fastness strong.

In France's oldest colony,
    Set on Acadian soil,
The waning year of sixteen-six
    Brought slow returns from toil;
The kettles of Port Royal's cooks
    Had little left to boil.

No pleasant rations graced the board
    In that far, hungry year;
The store-room had no oil or wine,
    No sugar and no beer;
And so Champlain proposed to found
    The Order of Good Cheer.

Each member of that joyful Band
    Would sally out in turn
To comb the rivers and the woods
    With food as his concern,
And share with all the company
    Such game as he could earn.

Then Pont-Gravé brought down an elk,
    Biencourt shot a moose,
And Champlain brought ten partridge home,
    And Miquelet a goose,
And Hébert caught an angry skunk—
    Which wasn't any use.

Lescarbot brought twelve salmon back,
    La Taille a dozen plaice,
And Membertou devised a net
    And took a thousand dace,
But when he caught two bobtailed squid
    He ended in disgrace.

Still other huntsmen killed a bear
    Along the steep inclines;
Muskrat and rabbit, lynx and wolf
    Fell to their carabines;
One even took a spiny brace
    Of pudgy porcupines.

Each hunter got his exercise;
    De Monts got all the skins;
And every Frenchman round the board
    Got all his vitamins;
While Joy prevailed to warm at heart
    Those forest paladins.

The echoes of that epic hunt
    Roll on from year to year;
The birds and beasts and fish recall
    Its toll with shuddering fear,
As tourist bureaux re-invent
    The Order of Good Cheer.

HENRY HUDSON
(A.D. 1611)

His spirit haunts the Bay that bears his name,
That inland sea across whose roaring mouth
The rip-tide and the ice-floe reign supreme;
For many a sailor, bound for Churchill's port,
Has seen, or thought he saw, at dusk or dawn,
An ancient shallop sail athwart his course
In which a grey-haired master sits erect,
Rigid and mute, his young son at his feet,
And other seamen who, with outstretched hands,
Still plead for life across the centuries.
   It was the summer solstice in the year
When the Great Book that bears King James's name
Came from the press and Shakespeare shaped a
    Tempest
That burst in plaudits on the London stage.
Five thousand miles to westward, in James Bay,

Becalmed in heavy pack off Charlton Island,
A little ship of less than sixty tons
Festered towards mutiny and callous murder.
The master of the bark *Discovery*,
Old Henry Hudson, sought the Northwest Passage
But forced by ice fields and an unknown sea
Had wintered in the James Bay *cul-de-sac*,
And now, on Spartan rations, turned towards home.
   The *hubris* of a generous mind deranged
By toil and danger most intolerable
Had issued in intolerable wrongs:
Juet, the mate, had been replaced by Bylot
And Bylot by illiterate John King;
The honest carpenter, stout Philip Staffe,
Was cuffed and cursed to back untimely orders;
And having shielded his base favourite Greene
And given him a cloak, the wayward captain
Grew resolute too late and damned Greene's vices.
The rumour spread that hidden stores of food.
Were guarded by the master for his cronies;
And early on the year's most lengthy day
A bold cabal of Motter, Pierce and Thomas,
Wilson and Greene, laid hands upon the captain,
Even as he left his cabin; in the sloop,
That trailed behind the ship, they flung him down,
With the new mate (John King), the captain's son,
Pale Woodhouse, the unlucky scientist,
And four sick men who languished in their bunks.
These were to be abandoned without food
So that the mutineers might sail for home
With ample rations for their ruthless bellies.
Then Staffe, the carpenter, chose death with honour,
Vowing that only force would hold him back
From dying with the master who had wronged him.
His chest of tools, forsooth, must go with him;
To this they yielded, and he joined the sloop.
Then the *Discovery* at last made sail
And having towed the shallop from the ice
They cut her loose and left her to her fate.
   Rigid and mute the grey-haired master sat
And mused no doubt on this untoward end.

He traced again his earliest Arctic journey
Up Greenland's coast and east two hundred leagues
Along the Great Ice Barrier till he reached
Remote Spitsbergen and its spouting whales.
Next came two summers in the Barents Sea,
Seeking in vain an opening through the floes
Off Nova Zemlya, from whose frosts he turned
To temperate America and traced
The Hudson River, lured by the Pacific.
The *ignis fatuus* of a route to China,
Sought ceaselessly, had brought him to this pass.
The treacherous, the violent and the surly,
And his own pride and folly, had betrayed him
And cut him off beyond all hope or help.
    For murder had been done on that cold sea,
Murder that did not shed a drop of blood
But just as surely murder as the famine
By which grim Stalin slew five million peasants.
A few bleak days of thirst and mortal hunger
Would see the doomed men perish one by one,
And then the tossing hearse that bore their corpses
Would suffer shipwreck and oblivion,
Shouldered by wave and ice-floe to the shore,
Brayed in the mortar of a northern beach,
Till splintered timbers and abraded bones
Were blended with the gravel and the sand
As indistinguishable silt of death.
    What of the evil men who wrought their doom?
They found no bounteous store of hidden rations
To glut their appetites on board the ship;
And when they later, after five long weeks,
Set foot on shore in search of provender,
Eskimo arrows slaughtered four of them—
Greene the new captain, Thomas, Wilson, Pierce—
Even as longship Vikings out of Greenland
Six centuries before in Labrador
Had seen their leader, Thorvald Eiriksson,
Slain by an arrow from a Skraeling bow.
Of the five men who led the mutiny
Only old Juet, sour malcontent,
Remained to perish on the homeward voyage.

Eight sorry creatures brought the vessel home
And broke grim tidings to the port of London.
   Three other sailings sought the Inland Sea
But searched in vain for Hudson and his sloop—
All trace was irrecoverably lost,
For the braised atoms of his boat and bones
Are mingled with the shingle of the shore
And blown perhaps about the ambient air,
A deathless part of our Canadian North,
While the enduring spirit still survives
To visit an imaginative eye
At dusk or dawn along the silent deep.

THE DOWRY AND THE CITADEL
(A.D. 1629)

King Charles, he was a hungry man, and very short of cash.
He married Henrietta, for her dower-lands were fat;
But King Louis dropped the boom on him, his golden hopes to
      dash,
And the little princess, aged fifteen, came poor as any cat.

A righteous rage filled Charles's heart against his spouse's brother,
And presently he launched a war to balance the account;
His little queen and he might come to value one another
If gold were added to the match, a sizable amount.

Three Kirkes now mount a citadel, the summit of Quebec.
King Charles had sent the brothers out, to seize the fort from
      France.
The tiny, tattered garrison their onslaught cannot check;
Champlain must render up his fort in bitter circumstance.

The Admiral, Sir David Kirke, acclaimed the land with praise;
His brothers, Tom and Lewis, were enchanted with the spot;
With ardour for the future, the British flag they raise
And claim a vast half-continent as England's noble lot.

Six weeks at sea brought Champlain back in Kirke's most
    courteous charge
To walk the port of London and to see the ambassador
Of regal France beside the Thames, who had him set at large
And told him happy tidings of the closing of the war.

For King Louis had consented to lay money on the line,
A dowry for his sister that would warm King Charles's heart,
And the lordly land of Canada, beyond the Atlantic brine,
Would be the lot of Louis as it had been at the start.

The dowry that he paid him had been owing anyway;
A land the size of Europe was a bonus on the deal;
But so happy was the English king to see the Frenchman pay
That conquests were abandoned in an overflow of zeal.

Three hundred years and more have passed since Charles's
    generous fit
And even since in forty-nine his head rolled off in gore;
But thinking on his mighty gift, the sheer display of it,
One might presume he'd lost his head some twenty years before.

But queens are queens and cash is cash, and can we blame a king
Whose love for Henrietta was at last enhanced with gold?
The Commons kept him hungry—which he judged a heinous
    thing
And could he know that Canada was more than utter cold?

THE FRENCH NURSING SISTERS
(A.D. 1639, 1760)

Out of long centuries of grief
    The Nursing Sisters came,
From ages when man's breath was brief
And life was like a falling leaf
    That death would rot in shame.

They reared in France in days of old
    Their sisterhoods devout;
And royal hands their deeds uphold—
No Harry Tudor, bad and bold,
    Dared stamp their Orders out.

Less than four decades from the day
    When first a Frenchman reared
His forts upon Canadian clay,
Sailing the bleak Atlantic way
    French nurses too appeared.

Saint Thomas', Saint Bartolomew's,
    Bridewell's and Bethlem's wards
In London looked for graceless crews
Of drunken nurses out of stews,
    Recruited in their hordes.

But Nursing Sisters from Dieppe
    Came skilful and demure;
White-robed, black-veiled, the decks they step,
Unlike the dirty demirep
    In London's wards impure.

The Sisters to Quebec advance
    Their Order's mission small;
While through the efforts of Jeanne Gance
The skill and piety of France
    Are brought to Montreal.

Though waves of epidemics beat
    Upon Canadian shores,
As typhus rotted half the fleet
And smallpox blasted with its heat
    And pestilential sores,

And almost half the settlement
    Were slain by Iroquois,
And many a wounded innocent,
Scalped but alive, erect though spent,
    Came with his skull all raw,

The Nursing Sisters, skilled to heal,
    Would strive with pox and pain;
The hand of death themselves they'd feel,
But the survivors, tense with zeal,
    Their healing would maintain.

More than a century went by,
        And tides of far-off wars
In spreading eddies mounted high
Until New France undone must lie
        Before its conquerors.

Then Amherst in his victory
        Discovered with surprise
Canadian hospitals to be
Spacious and clean to a degree
        Unknown to English eyes.

Canadian nurses had been trained
        Through years of skilful care;
And gentle nuns in faith unfeigned
Healed French and English, and ordained
        Impartial treatment there.

Their sweet lay sisters reaped the love
        The nuns' soft care inspired,
And many a Scot went on to prove
Like some devoted turtledove
        A marriage much desired.

Two passing centuries and more
        Their passion cannot quench,
And those who search ancestral lore
Still find upon the Levis shore
        MacDonalds who speak French.

The nuns' bright Bridegroom reigns on high,
        But their devoted skill
In healing bodies could supply
A peace of soul to sanctify
        A home's bi-racial will.

And not the least of all their deeds
        Since sixteen-thirty-nine
Was thus in bringing to the needs
Of man and maid of rival breeds
        This clemency divine.

THE FRENCH ARMADA
(A.D. 1746)

Here stands the D'Anville Cairn, and between its mute plaque and
    the Basin
Flashes the flow of the traffic that seeks and returns from the city,
Clashes the steel of the freight-cars that marshal their loads for the
    journey.
Yonder on gay, blue billows the sun's multitudinous laughter
Joins the oblivious chorus that lives in the joy of the present,
Deaf to the groans of the past and the grim-voiced ghosts of affliction.
Here, two centuries since, when the fate of New France was at issue,
Hopes that were high met destruction, as pestilence, sad past
    conjecture,
Sank like a mist from the sea, overwhelming the ships and the sailors.
This is the tale that the monument, passed by the traffic unheeding,
Silently sighs forth in anguish and strains of profound lamentation.
    June was the month, in the year after Louisbourg fell for the first
    time
Into the farm-horny hands of the Puritan sons of New England;
Jubilant chanted the colonists hymns for invasions to northward,
Seeking to topple the French in their towns on the mighty
    St. Lawrence.
Meanwhile, in France itself, the loss of the notable fortress
Wounded men's pride past endurance, demanding an effort of
    honour—
Louisbourg must be retaken and Boston be rendered to ashes.
Half of the navy of France was forthwith to form an Armada,
Far the most powerful war-fleet that ever had crossed the Atlantic,—
Formed of eleven great ships-of-the-line and twenty-five frigates,
These with some thirty-four transports and veteran troops for the
    conflict,
Soon to be joined at Chebucto by four of the heaviest warships
Lately despatched to West Indian seas under valiant DeConflans.
Admiral over them all was the Duke, old D'Anville the hero,
Hardened in many a battle and full of incredible valour.
    June was the hope-filled month and rejoicing from Brest the
    flotilla
Sailed on its course to the westward, to alter America's future.
Ah, but the sky was against them, with battering squalls upon Biscay;
Near the Azores came a calm that for day after day kept them idle;

Volleys of lightning then smote them and ravaged their decks with
  destruction.
Then, when in mid-September, they groped for the shore in the
  fog-banks,
On them a hurricane fell that was spawned in the fierce Caribbean,
Swirling its fury to northward and rending the land and the ocean—
Waves ran as high as the masts, great vessel on vessel would founder;
Then when the morrow brought daylight and peace from the worst
  of the tempest,
There rolled the *Argonaut* helpless, bereft of her masts and her rudder,
Others had jettisoned guns in a desperate fight for survival.
Battered they gathered at last in the sheltering Bay of Chebucto,
Seeking to rally their forces for deeds that would ring through the
  future.
  Worse than all storms was a pestilence, smiting them first upon
  shipboard,
More were the sick than the well, as they journeyed across the
  Atlantic;
Now in the calm of the Basin they rotted and died by the thousands;
D'Anville himself, overburdened with bitterest grief for his shipmates,
Died apoplectic or plague-sick (the tales of his end are uncertain).
Next in command, D'Estournel, gave his order to turn again
  homeward;
Others deciding against him, he fell on his sword blade and perished.
Week after week of inaction brought week after week of contagion;
Crews were encamped on the shore, but the pestilence slew without
  mercy;
Autumn came early that year and the desolate rains of October
Fell on the withering leaves of the poplars and maples above them
(Yellow, malarial red or bespotted with death-blots of typhus),
Fell on these emblems of dying and carried them, sodden cadavers,
Down on the graves of the dead, on the pits of their hasty sepulture;
Fell on the pines and the hemlocks, that loomed like the shadows of
  Sheol,
Dark as the night over Egypt when doom walked abroad in the
  darkness;
Fell on the mouldering fleet and its storm-battered hulks in the
  harbour;
Out of the fighters of France but a pitiful tithe were survivors.
  Thus came disaster to Athens, when locked in its conflict with
  Sparta.

Carried by sea out of Egypt, the plague laid its hand on Piraeus,
Spread from the port, like a meadow that blazed, as it leaped on the
city.
Headaches came, fetor of breathing, with retching and pustules and
ulcers;
Bodies were burning within, as the pestilence spread through the
members;
Worst of the curse was dejection, despair as the onset grew potent.
Fugitives fleeing the Spartans came crowding the lodgings and
temples,
Only to perish, by thousands and thousands, along with the others;
Dying men lay with the dead and the rest lacked the logs to cremate
them.
Thus was Sennacherib smitten, the lord of Assyrian legions,
Bringing against Hezekiah an hundred, fourscore and five thousand
Warriors armed to the teeth, who beleaguered Jerusalem straitly.
Rabshakeh, ribald, robustious, came roaring out doom to the Hebrews,
Laughing their city to scorn in the path of the master of nations.
Him did Jehovah cast down, for the angel of pestilence met him;
Nothing but corpses remained of the host that had boasted of conquest;
Even great Nineveh's king had but scarcely escaped from the
slaughter.
   Death at Chebucto at last nerved the leaders to stern resolution:
Mustering all that was left of the fleet that was fit for the ocean,
Loading their ships by the healthy with all of the sick and the dying,
Westward they sailed for Annapolis, fortified seat of the English,
Only to sink to their doom in a hurricane close to Cape Sable.
   Here stands the D'Anville Cairn. But the graves of the plague-sick
have vanished,
Lost like that mighty Armada, the greatest to cross the Atlantic,
Lost like the dreams, the devotion, the valour of men now departed,
Slain by inscrutable fate and the onset of awful contagion.

THE BICENTENNIAL TWINS
(A.D. 1763)

When Louisbourg had fallen
And angry armies tore
Acadian bands from all their lands
Along the Fundy Shore,

Out of austere New England
    The Baptists roamed afar
And reached the dikes of Minas,
    The flats of Tantramar.

First, Ebenezer Moulton,
    A Brimfield pastor he,
In seventeen and sixty
    To Yarmouth came by sea;
And three short springtimes later
    Pursued his pious way
And shepherded a Baptist church
    By meadows of Grand Pré.

In that same gracious season
    Good Nathan Mason came;
From Swansea, Mass., they saw him pass
    With others of his name,
And on the fields of Sackville
    Rear up a Baptist cause,
Transplanting there with fervent prayer
    That version of God's laws.

Now Elder Moulton preached the Word
    To many in brief space;
He, from their pride, in Minas' tide
    Baptized them by God's grace.
Likewise did Pastor Mason
    Proclaim the word of truth,
And to baptismal waters brought
    The feet of age and youth.

Alas, the Devil drives away
    These shepherds and their flocks;
A silence drear for many a year
    Their field of labour mocks;
And yet the seed that they had sowed
    At last brought harvest fair;
Two hundred years since first they toiled
    Tall spires are standing there.

Still are those churches standing,
    Twin sisters from the past;
They raise the voice of worship,
    The faith their hearts hold fast;

And still their stately steeples
Salute the evening star
Above the dikes of Minas,
The flats of Tantramar.

NAPOLEON OPENS OUR FORESTS
(A.D. 1808)

Here was the forest primaeval, the murmuring pines and the hemlocks
Stood like a bountiful banquet to tickle the palates of bankers,
Spread on the table of Nature from Halifax clear to Vancouver.
Ages past number had reared it; stone tools of the Redskin were
    baffled;
Even the French and the Loyalist, armed with the steel of their axes,
Rendered tall trunks into potash in clearing new acres for tillage,
Rather than ship them as lumber to countries that would not absorb
    them.

  Wars, and Napoleon's fiat, first opened far lands to our lumber:
Seeking blockade of all timber to Britain from ports of the Baltic,
Bonaparte left to the British no source but Canadian forests.
Thus was our logging begun; squared timber untold was transported;
Felling and drawing and rafting white pine of the tallest and finest
Swept with insatiate hunger to gorge on the banquet of nature.
After some sixteen decades, the forest primaeval has vanished,
Save for remoter stands that are hid in Pacific-coast mountains;
All of the rest has been looted, and lost in the lumber-kings' fortunes.

  First came the square timber trade and the deals of the heavier
    planking;
Then followed sales of sawn lumber, descending at last down to
    plywood,
Woodpulp and paper and toothpicks, from saplings and still smaller
    saplings.
Britain first led the assault on the primal Canadian forest;
Later, American wood-kings came, having laid waste their own
    woodlands,
Turned to Canadian timber with havoc of new devastation,
Rafting Canadian sawlogs for open-mouthed mills to dismember,
Building broad gullets of railroads to carry such food to the gizzard,
Licking the forests away like fierce fires consuming a meadow,

Ravenous dragons of greed that would die when the prey was all eaten,
Leaving a wasteland of stumps, of dead sand and burnt-over granite.

What Herculean hero, sinewed like Cyclops or Samson,
Led on both sides of the Border the lumberjacks' legions of axemen?
Sing, O whiskey-jack Muse, hoarse goddess of shanty and bunkhouse,
Sing of the deeds of Paul Bunyan, with Babe, the Blue Ox, as his
      helper!
Out of the East he had come, from Maine or from Prince Edward
      Island:
Glooscap perhaps was his dad; the *News Tribune* (Detroit) was his
      mother;
Both of his parents find echo in most of his mighty achievements.
Down on the Big Onion River, a hundred square miles in a morning,
White pine was shorn by his broad-axe and laid like a hayfield in
      windrows.
Babe, the Blue Ox, without sweating, hitched to a string of great
      shanties,
Dragged them from campsite to campsite, with all of the loggers
      inside them.
Trouble Paul had, to be sure, in a drive on the mouthless Round River;
Trouble he had in that winter when blizzards came blue as the ocean;
Peasoup and flapjacks and prunes he could swallow in mighty
      profusion;
Lumberjacks all through the forest were proud to have worked with
      Paul Bunyan.

Tales of his marvellous deeds are the gleams of a fraudulent
      rainbow,
Drawing our eyes from the wrack of the storm that has ravaged our
      forests,
Millions of acres of stumps and the puny new growth of the brûlé,
Cloaking our eyes, moreover, to raids by Neanderthal chemists,
Scalding the woods from the sky with elixirs of death and destruction,
Rending the whole web of life—fish, mammal and bird in one murder,
Wrought in the name of man's good, but in truth as a rape upon
      Nature.

This was the forest primaeval, but still more primordial hunger
Gorged on its towering beauty and swallowed its wealth in a frenzy,
Turning its strength into gold for the gods of New York and Chicago.
Hark to the sighs of its wreckage, the murmur of grief in the saplings;
Listen again as in wistful woe the Canadian nation
Speaks, and in accents disconsolate answers the wail of the forest.

THE SEVEN OAKS MASSACRE
(A.D. 1816)

I

The tale begins in blood. From out the west
Some sixty half-breed horsemen rode in arms
The fences of Fort Douglas to invest;
And humble settlers, working on their farms,
Rushed to the stockade in a wild unrest
To stammer out the cause of their alarms:
"The half-breeds come! The half-breeds!" Sore dismay
Seized on the little settlement that day.

Beside a sea of grass Fort Douglas stood,
Looped in the windings of the muddy Red;
The soil beside its walls, fertile and good,
Two hundred miles to south and westward spread,
A verdant ocean, void of hill or wood,
Set in a vanished lake's prolific bed;
And here the Earl of Selkirk's kind humanity
Had planned for homeless men new life and sanity.

When Robert Semple, Governor-in-Chief
Of all the Hudson's Bay's far-flung endeavour,
Heard of the mounted troop, in disbelief
Of any slaughterous intent whatever,
He rode to meet them for a parley brief,
Nigh weaponless, as witnesses assever,
And with him five and twenty men whose amity
Was all too little armed to meet calamity.

Seven scrub oaks upon a little knoll
Had marked the spot at which the half-breeds halted.
At once they ringed around the small patrol
And raised their rifles in a mood exalted.
A scuffle started. In a thundering roll
The bullets in one blast the whites assaulted;
And from the sweep of that terrific round
A score of men lay lifeless on the ground.

Semple, though prostrate, wounded in the thigh,
Was finished off, a bullet through his heart.
Then the still-twitching corpses as they lie
The skinning-knives of foemen rend apart,
As the Métis, with a horrendous cry,
Revert to Indian warfare's ancient art
And desecrate with savage mutilation
The bodies of a murdered alien nation.

Next came an ultimatum to the fort:
Unless the colonists at once vacate
The prairies, bag and baggage, long and short,
They will be victims of the same dark fate.
No man or woman stays, such death to court;
At once to terror they capitulate;
And down the northward trail, along the Red,
Headlong the panic-stricken settlers fled.

II

The murders had been plotted at Qu'Appelle,
More than two hundred miles to west-north-west,
By a Nor'wester leader, Macdonnell,
A white man whose consuming interest
In making all the plains his citadel
Against all rivals made him plan with zest
A massacre that almost matched the shambles
Inflicted on Macdonalds by the Campbells.

"Good news!" he shouted, when the tidings reached him.
"Twenty-two Englishmen have been shot down."
Yet for that deed no angry court impeached him;
No judge on his malevolence would frown;
No scolding priest for his offences preached him;
Mists of forgetfulness his record drown.
What is still plain is that this sorry tale
Sprang from a conflict on a vaster scale.

Our annals start with fishing, on the banks
That fronted Acadie and Newfoundland;
But eager traders soon reformed their ranks
And journeyed farther from the fishy strand,
Seeking for peltries from the beavers' flanks,
Traded by Indians, an eager band

Who asked for iron kettles, guns and axes
And levied on the wild their furry taxes.

Our half of North America comprises
The half in which the beaver had his haunts;
The Shield's ten million lakes saw the demises
Of thrice ten million beavers; where now flaunts
The mine its slagheap in a thousand guises
And miner and promoter make their vaunts,
Was once the trapper's realm; the bounds he made
Are ours today, as witness to that trade.

After the Conquest, based on Montreal
The North-West Company was prompt to blend
The old French fur trade as a useful thrall
With British enterprise; supplies attend
From thrifty Britain for the westward haul,
Cheap yet well made; such traffic puts an end
To mortal pressure from a coterie
Of rivals in New York and Albany.

In time they spread their net from coast to coast,
And in the far logistics of their quest
Built on the native lore that linked each post
By birch canoe, and in the winter's test
By snowshoe and toboggan; they made boast
To push their journey to the farthest West;
And in the culmination of their hopes
Swept the sea otter from Pacific slopes.

Yet ever higher costs in this far trek
Enhanced the advantage of another rival
Who, based on Hudson's Bay, bade fair to check
The fierce Nor'westers in their dark connival
With tribes five thousand miles from old Quebec.
It was this menace to their firm's survival
That led the agents of these troubled folks
To shoot the settlers down at Seven Oaks.

The Trapper wed the Dame whose young he slew.
The Norns of Economics willed it thus—
To these there was no other thing to do,
Though shotgun weddings are not amorous.
To one great whole their patrimonies grew,
This breadth of continent they framed for us.

The old Nor'westers formed this northern nation,
Weaving its threads before Confederation.

III

Yet in those murders by the slab Red River
A strange new people struggled into birth.
While still the twitching corpses lay a-quiver,
The half-breeds heard one, Falcon, in his mirth,
A warlike anthem stridently deliver,
Announcing a new nation upon earth,
And calling all Métis to sing that day
"To the great glory of the *Bois-Brûlés.*"

"We are Métis!" This was the imperious cry
Echoed for decades down the forest trail,
By grasslands underneath a windy sky,
By hidden coulee and by salty swale,
Flung out the white Ghost Dancers to defy,
And then borne off to silence down the gale.
This was the dream the half-breed memory hallows,
Though ending in Regina, on the gallows.

Their blood was mixed. When first on Indian wives
The French *coureurs de bois* begot their sons,
They bred a race within whose baffled lives
A sense of deep rejection ever runs,
An inner conflict of genetic drives
That strains their living and their lexicons,
Unapt in tongue or discipline to be
A perfect Frenchman or a perfect Cree.

They were the wanderers of the wilderness;
They were the best of trappers, boatmen, guides;
They shared the Indians' culture and souplesse
Throughout the Western lakes and countrysides;
Some thirty thousand strong, they bore duress
In helping whites advance by ample strides;
Yet were rebuffed as an inferior race
By white men who would keep them in their place.

[40]

Canadian land-greed in a Great Partition
Was blind to every half-breed's honest claim.
When on a premature, possessive mission
A would-be governor, MacDougall, came,
Out of sheer folly and unslaked ambition
He forced an edict in Victoria's name
And told the half-breeds (on his own authority)
No rights were in their twelve-to-one majority.

John A., alas, was privy to the trip
And to the disregard of half-breed right,
But could not overlook MacDougall's slip
And ended his career in Stygian night.
Meanwhile hot soldiers came by trail and ship,
And the chief half-breed leaders took to flight.
Goulet, Guilmette, O'Lone, were stabbed or shot
For the court-martial death of Thomas Scott.

Fifteen years followed; and again John A.,
Having learned nothing as the years moved on,
Was prone in slow derision to betray
The half-breed settlers in Saskatchewan
With year on year of cotton-mouthed delay,
Their pleas unheard, their land-claims put upon.
Priests, Mounties, agents, urged consideration,
But he was scornful towards the half-breed nation.

The desperate Métis called in Riel,
Who in Montana lived in humble peace;
At first there was no purpose to rebel,
But John A. burked their rights with more police;
They pled for help—he swore to give them hell;
And in the bloody, martial afterpiece
Stupidity and arrogance destroyed
A humble folk and made all justice void.

That white men should invest the Western plains
And bring its ancient sod beneath the plow
Was doubtless fated; but the fact remains
That earlier settlers' rights to disallow,
Regardless of their age-old toil and pains,
Would be condemned were it propounded now;
But then, Confederation's impresario
Thought only of the voters in Ontario.

Treason, no doubt, was in that sad revolt,
But treason all evoked by Ottawa.
The troops who came as John A.'s thunderbolt
Admitted that the half-breeds' lot was raw.
Battleford and Batoche soon gave a jolt
To those who from official versions saw
These actions as small broils some knave incites—
Not the last stand of men who sought their rights.

IV

Well nigh a human century has passed
Since Wolseley marched his army to Red River;
Proud Middleton in turn his warriors massed
Eight decades since, a victory to deliver;
And the Métis, to cold oblivion cast,
Their fate accepted with a stoic shiver.
What do Canadians, full of hopes millenial,
Find here to celebrate their land's Centennial?

Today, four million white men throng the West.
Out from the skirts of seven cities sprawling,
Some threescore million acres manifest
A billion bushels for the year's outhauling;
Year after year, their wheat is of the best,
And golden honour crowns the farmer's calling;
Although an old man's gooseflesh grants, with shame,
That the subarctic winter stays the same.

Thus, when some office clerk, at Main and Portage
Waiting for streetcars in a howling blizzard,
Stamps on his numbing feet with sniff and snortage,
Sensing a torpor creeping through his gizzard
And good, warm heart-blood in appalling shortage,
He feels himself as naked as a lizard
And mutters hoarsely, as his features freeze:
"I vote we give this land back to the Crees!"

What would we give them back? The lands we took
(Without a word of thanks to those who held them)
We opened to erosion. Haste forsook
Manure and fallow, though discretion spelled them.

[42]

Men plowed the grassland with exultant look,
Mined it for profit as their greed impelled them.
And now in dwindling potency remains
The ancient virtue of the plundered plains.

From every continent the warning comes
And he who runs may read the haggard tale—
Tunisian fields filled Rome's emporiums
With wheat, but now are shifting sand and shale;
Broad Anatolia's slopes are rural slums
Where once the fertile harvest did not fail.
Even while earth's great birthrate shows explosion,
Its lands are disappearing in erosion.

The chemists have betrayed us in their turn
Through arrogantly spread insecticide
That soon originates a new concern—
New strains outstrip the poison in their stride,
While bird and beast and fish and mankind learn
That they are sickening from the toxic tide.
Unless we turn to natural controls,
The pests will rule the earth in hungry shoals.

THE MARCH ON LINDSAY
(July 12, 1846)

Bill Parker of South Emily
      By Crown and Throne he swore
That the great House of Orange
      Should suffer wrong no more,—
By this he meant the Order
      That locally he led,
For bitterness had filled its cup
Since Lindsay lads had roughed him up,
      The Lodge's noble head.

"Let the Irish by the Scugog
      Beware my wrath!" he cried.
"We'll mark the Battle of the Boyne
      With deeds by Scugog's side.

[43]

Let every gallant Orangeman
    Come join me in the fray,
For Parker of South Emily
    Is on the march today!"

The fife-men and the drummers
    Came pouring in amain
With muskets and militia swords
    To make their purpose plain;
They mustered at "Omemee"
    Beside Galbraith's distillery,
Then on twelve miles of corduroy
They sallied boldly, man and boy,
    Horse, foot and light artillery.

With irate resolution
    Their cohorts onward stomp,
Though some were mired at Stony Creek
    And some in Scully's Swamp;
The hottest sun of summer
    Was blazing in the sky,
But neither heat nor primal muck
Could melt their zeal or mar their pluck;
    For Parker, all would die.

Meanwhile beside the Scugog
    The dreadful news was heard
That Parker to destroy the town
    Had pledged his mighty word;
A flying sentry from East Ops
    Had heard the distant drumming
And gasped his frantic tidings out:
    "The Orangemen are coming!"

All who had muskets got them out
    And lined the river's banks;
Good Thomas Keenan from his store
    Supplied the other ranks
With scythe-blades, which, with handles wrapped,
    Could serve as wicked sabres,
And pitchforks that gave deadly threats

As all-efficient bayonets
    Amid their martial labours.

Then Lenihan and Connelly,
    Gillogly, Pyne and Greenan
Stood stoutly by O'Holloran,
    By Brady, Spratt and Keenan;
McBride, McHugh and Thatcher tall,
    Carlin and Leddy too,
And Bryce and Twohey, Dunn and Roach
Waxed valiant at the dark approach
    Of all the hostile crew.

Only one bridge the Scugog crossed
    To give the invaders entry:
If this were won, the town was lost,
    Averred the flying sentry.
Two cedar stringers spanned the stream,
    With shorter cross-logs laid;
Four men on the abutments stood
    To ply the axeman's trade.

Then out spake Patrick McEvoy,
    The parish priest was he,
From Mayo, Ireland, he'd come
    Across the hungry sea:
"Hew down the bridge, ye spalpeens,
    And I, bedad, shall go
A half-mile hence along the trail
Up to Lang's Corners, nor shall fail
    To parley with the foe."

Then out spake good John Sanderson,
    A Methodist was he,
A preacher who on William Street
    Was likewise dominie:
"Beside you, Father McEvoy,
    Set at your strong right hand,
I'll go, a Lindsay citizen,
And speak to these misguided men
    Who such a deed have planned."

Then out spake Alex Bryson,
    A Presbyterian he,
An elder who, on Francis Street,
    On Sunday bent the knee:
"I'm with you, Father McEvoy,
    Set at your strong left hand;
I, too, shall go on foot to-day
And shall have something stern to say
    To that misguided band."

And now the keen broadaxes
    Bite deeply in the logs
As with his straining muscles
    Each frantic axeman slogs;
Then with a rend of timber
    There comes the final slash
And with that last deciding blow
The bullfrogs in the stream below
    Are blinded by the splash.

Meanwhile bold Parker's army
    The heralds' voices heard.
To Bryson and to McEvoy
    They answered not a word.
Then spoke the gentle Methodist:
    "Boys, this was badly done!
Be sure the judge will pay a call
To hold assizes in the fall
And if you've killed a man at all,
    He'll hang you, every one!"

"You're right, bedad," said Parker then,
    "I never thought of that.
An Irishman may love a fight
    But hanging's rather flat.
The Battle of the Scugog
    Would at the last be hollow
When hanging for the lot of us
    Had made it hard to swallow.

"Comrades, I thank you for your trust,
    But home we'll turn our head.

The blood of Sixteen-Ninety's fight
    Must not again be shed.
Here in this strange new country
    Another day may come
When Irish of the North and South
    Will be less quarrelsome."

*   *   *   *

And now when Lindsay Rotary
    That ancient feud remembers,
Both Protestants and Catholics
    Are happy fellow-members;
And with weeping and with laughter
    The story still is told
How long ago at Lindsay-town
Two armies glowered, frown for frown,
And bullfrogs watched the bridge go down
    In the brave days of old.

WILLIAM HALL, V.C.
(A.D. 1857)

Here at the Hantsport crossroads,
    Where the transports pause and pass,
Rises a cairn of boulders
    And a plaque of enduring brass.

It tells of an old Hants hero,
    Born on the Cheverie Shore
In the days of the Fourth of the Georges
    In a home with a poor dirt floor.

This son of a black slave father
    Spent his boyhood at Horton Bluff,
But soon took to sea as a sailor
    And a life that was hard enough.

He served on the warship *Rodney*
    Through the long Crimean war;
Then shipped to the East with the *Shannon*,
    For that was what life was for.

[47]

He offered for special danger
 With a naval brigade of guns
To seek the relief of Lucknow
 Where the Gumti River runs.

There, by the winding Gumti,
 On the level plains of Oudh,
Brave Havelock was beleaguered
 By foes in a mighty crowd.

A scant two thousand British
 Endured in the heat and the drought,
And sixty thousand rebels
 Encompassed them round about.

At last, in a fierce November,
 Sir Colin Campbell came
To break their circumvallation
 With an onset of sword and flame.

Four thousand five hundred soldiers
 Were all of the force he brought,
But the navy's volunteer gunners
 With the strength of a giant fought.

"Who will be first for the gun-crew
 To blast through the rebels' wall?
For the fire of the foe is bitter,
 And many are sure to fall."

—"I shall be first," said the Negro,
 The man from the Cheverie Shore.
And his cannon through the gateway
 A mighty opening tore.

Through it, the column entered;
 Through it, the whole force heaved;
Through it, they joined the defenders—
 And Lucknow had been relieved.

And now in a Baptist churchyard,
 Set by the Queen's high way,
A quiet Canadian village
 Still honours his deed today.

The first of all Nova Scotians,
    The first of his dark-skinned race,
He won the Award of Valour,
    The Cross of Victoria's grace.

And as long as the hearts of heroes
    In our land shall remembered be,
Men shall speak of the deathless daring
    Of William Hall, V.C.

THE QUEBEC CONFERENCE
(A.D. 1864)

All pundits agree that the birth of our nation
Must date from the parleys that planned Federation
At Charlottetown, Halifax, then at Quebec—
The final divan of the delegates' trek.
All hearts were at peace on that tenth of October,
For George Brown was jolly, and John A. was sober,
And Tupper and Tilley and Gray all agree
To forget the cold dissidents down by the Sea.
The parliament house, where the conference met,
Erect on the edge of a cliff had been set,
And lofty arched windows looked out on a River
Majestic as Rhine or as Nile, the life-giver,
While blue, swelling mountains, their summits cloud-fleeced,
Looked down on its waves as they swept to the east.
    The chairman whose rulings they gladly obey
Was that gracious old doctor, Sir Étienne Taché,
With a round, friendly face and a halo of hair
As white as the soul of an abbess at prayer.
Next year he would die, at full threescore and ten,
Lamented by even the surliest men.
    Most notable there, as the prince of all friskers,
A clean-shaven man in that forest of whiskers,
Was John A. Macdonald, whose Caesar-like nose
Proclaimed him a leader to friends and to foes;
His dark, curly hair and his gay, friendly eyes,
His smile all-sardonic and genially wise,

His animal spirits that flowed like a brook,
Exuberantly gay in both gesture and look,—
These marked him the bold, all-convivial hero
To steer a safe course when the chances were zero.
"Soft sawder" he used and the phrase neatly tawdry;
He'd melt away scowls with a story of bawdry;
And ever moved forward, through sunshine and murk,
By a tireless penchant for masterly work.

There faced him at table a man who could probe
His laughter with rancour, George Brown of *The Globe*.
Impulsive and moody, with smouldering gaze,
The great press-dictator was grim in his ways;
But his sense that the country had reached a dead end
Impelled him to work with John A. as a friend.
His share in the Great Coalition worked best
For concurrence in wisdom by Canada West.

Not least of the party, the issue to con,
Sat Tilley (stout Leonard), the man from Saint John,
A neat little fellow, with glances so bright,
And sharp little features aflame with delight.
He feared that his province might think it a sin,
But he backed Federation through thick and through thin.
Defeated at first by electoral rage,
He came back to power on the very next page;
And later in life smiled at enmity's worms
In Government House for a couple of terms.

Then Doctor Charles Tupper from Halifax came
To enter New Scotland in leadership's game.
His round, youthful face ever cheerful appeared,
Enclosed in a framework of black hair and beard.
A gadfly to Howe in the Federal race,
He went him one better and carried his case.

John Hamilton Gray came as chief of the Island,
The premier of all, whether Lowland or Highland.
From nineteen to forty, strange coasts he had trod,
A cavalry officer serving abroad
With the British light horse on South African plains
And Indian hills in the droughts and the rains.
Retired by peace, he came home with his glories
And rose to be chief of the Islanders' Tories.

He gave Federation his praise and protection
And fell to defeat in the next big election.
   A tally too long for my tale it would be
To paint at full length all the Thirty and Three;
And merely to name all the great round that board
Will strain the just limits my yarn can afford.
From Newfoundland sauntered in Carter and Shea;
From Prince Edward Island there journeyed with Gray
Coles, journalist Whelan, and Palmer and Pope,
Macdonald and Haviland, mingled in hope;
New Scotland with Tupper had sent along Dickey,
McCully and Henry, in principles sticky,
And Adams G. Archibald, Colchester's pride,
Who stood like a rock on the Federal side.
New Brunswick with Tilley had chosen Charles Fisher,
And Mitchell and Gray, a Platonic well-wisher,
And Johnson and Steeves and the stout E. B. Chandler,
Who proved in debate a precarious handler.
From Canada, John A., George Brown and Taché
Were aided by Galt and George Etienne Cartier,
And Mowat, McDougall and D'Arcy McGee
(A poet and prophet, as all men could see),
And Cockburn and Langevin, Campbell, Chapais—
These filled out the list on that cardinal day.
   For almost three weeks they bent down to their task,
With great statements to make and small questions to ask,
Procedures to settle and rules of debate
And groundsills to carry a federal state.
Grave errors had shattered American unity—
These could not be copied with hope of impunity:
Unspecified powers must rest with the centre
In this the design that they purposed to enter,
And responsible government, British in mode,
Must hold the régime on a resolute road.
The members, moreover, in Commons and Senate,
Must vary in numbers (a logical tenet)
In some rough proportion to census-returns
In each province-range as the head-count discerns.
   But some of the "Fathers" were obstinate souls;
For Chandler and Dickey and Palmer and Coles

Were so much concerned with their provinces' rights
That most of their joy was in eloquent fights;
In debate, every sort of obstruction they fished for;
To "father" the scheme was the last thing they wished for.
Their worth at Quebec was to serve as reminder
That thousands of voters would prove even blinder
To all the advantage of federalism.
By this they gave notice of probable schism
When all of the ridings to east and to west
Would put the Great Plan to its ultimate test.
Yet the Maritime Union (they said they preferred)
Had just died a-borning for reasons absurd,
Since Prince Edward Island refused to play ball
Unless it were given the state's Capitol.
Nine years were to pass ere the Island came in
To this Federal state that they viewed with chagrin.
But Newfoundland looked with still more hesitation—
It was eighty-four years till they joined with our nation.

But back at the Conference, labour went on,
And ever the soul of the effort was John;
For countless suggestions still flowed from his pen
To clarify darkness to sceptical men.
And still on the lofty arched windows the rain
Relentless kept drumming, again and again,
A downpour autumnal that day after day
Monotonous music to lull them would play.
The sky cleared at last; and at last they were free—
This resolute band of the Thirty and Three.
Their labours had finished their great Constitution's
Full seventy-two well-approved Resolutions.

The task has been finished: and yet there remain
Two years and a half of distraction and pain,
Despatches and speeches and angry debates,
Elections made hot by electoral hates,
And the problem of gaining, by pressure and tact,
From the House at Westminster a relevant act.
At home and in London the aim of Joe Howe
Was to scupper the scheme with a terrible row;
But the Fenians' red raids made the task of defence
Too large for the provinces' soldiers and pence,

And the murders at Ridgeway made patent at last
The need of the hour; and the Great Act was passed.
Tantae molis erat—such toil and vexation
To rear up at last a Canadian nation!

RIDING SONG OF THE MOUNTIES
(A.D. 1874)

North of the Border and west of the Lakes
Gallop, my lads, across coulee and level,
Routing like Patrick a legion of snakes,
Flouting like Peter the gates of the Devil.

Two million square miles is the range we must ride;
Fifteen hands and a half stands our runtiest horse;
No rum-runner's cunning or Indian pride
Can frighten or flatter or wheedle the Force.

Scarlet our tunics, our breeches are black;
Only three hundred bold horsemen are we;
Westward we ride to the Rockies and back,
North to the Arctic, northeast to the Sea.

Down in Montana the trail of the viper
Leads to Fort Benton, the snakepit of sin;
Ever the harvest of licker grows riper,
Wrecking the Redskins for profit on gin.

Gallop then, comrades, the outlaws await you!
Ride to Fort Whoop-Up, the Curse of the West!
Round up the ruffian hoodlums who hate you!
Capture the spiders and wipe out the nest!

Up the Commissioner, Colonel George French!
Up the Assistant, our Major Macleod!
Winder and Walsh make the murderers blench;
Crozier and Potts cow the criminal crowd.

Indian tribes in the coulees are seething,
Murmuring waifs from American wars;
Rage at the white man's bad faith they are breathing,
Grief for the misdeeds their tepee abhors.

[53]

These must be met with bold hearts and clean hands,
Saved by our skill from the scum of the earth;
Thus shall new justice be known to their bands;
Thus a new nation may struggle to birth.

North of the Border and west of the Lakes
Gallop, my lads, across coulee and level,
Routing like Patrick a legion of snakes,
Flouting like Peter the gates of the Devil.

THE GREEN CURSE OF VAN HORNE
(A.D. 1889)

Oh, the mayor of Port Arthur was sulky;
    The councillors boiled in the shade;
For the C.P.R. taxes were bulky
    But never a dollar was paid.

The line might stretch west to the Ocean,
    But the costs had been high as the hills,
And its bosses were kept in commotion
    With trying to settle their bills.

The heart of the mayor of Port Arthur
    Was as hard as a mountain of flint;
And the councillors' faces grew swarther
    As they clamoured for coin from the mint.

So they sharpen officialdom's axes
    And when a fat freight-train rolls in
They seize the whole shipment for taxes—
    And straightway their troubles begin.

"Grass shall grow in the streets of Port Arthur!"
    Sir William Van Horne cried in rage.
"Let its neighbour grow faster and farther,
    And leave it to shrivel with age!

"To Fort William our office we'll carry;
    Our package-freight sheds we'll transport;
Our yards to the Kam we shall marry,
    And our shops we shall move to the Fort.

"Our taxes we'll pay—on compulsion—
    But the mayor is an impudent ass.
We shall move, in the utmost revulsion,
    And Port Arthur can go back to grass!"

Van Horne was as good as his thunder;
    He did what he threatened to them;
And for thirty long years the big blunder
    Left the hill-town to pine on the stem.

But Van Horne and the Mayor live no longer,
    And the grass that Port Arthur once got
On their two graves grows greener and stronger;
    Each town is a flourishing spot.

Each city swings wide on its axis,
    And the hill-town that languished in scorn
For that summary seizure for taxes
    Has outlived the green curse of Van Horne.

MOSES COMES TO CANAAN
(A.D. 1895)

In the fields of their Austrian Goshen
    Where landlords grew rich by their toil,
The suffering plowmen of Halycz
    Outnumbered the tilth of the soil.

But a Moses arose to relieve them,
    One Joseph Oleskow by name;
Ph.D. from the college of Pharaoh
    In the lore of the earth he became.

Post-doctoral studies he followed
    In farms and the science of wealth,
And he groaned as he saw all about him
    His land's economic ill-health.

Now some of these plowmen were boyars—
    Arsenych, Romanchych and others—
Once nobles who guarded the frontiers,
    Now mixed with their commoner brothers.

[55]

Impoverished, growing in numbers,
    Undigested in tongue by the Pole,
They jealously guarded their title
    And saved their Ukrainian soul.

But the cornland of Goshen was straitened
    And the eye of Oleskow was cast
On the far-away prairies of Canaan,
    Unhandseled, inviting and vast.

"I shall go," he declared with decision,
    "And shall spy out the land for my folk.
Perhaps in that Eden my people
    Can be saved from necessity's yoke."

His dark eyes flashed potent in promise;
    His bushy hair rose in a mane;
The tips of his big black moustaches
    Twitched fast with the zeal of his brain.

He journeyed from Dan to Beersheba—
    To wit, from Quebec to the West—
And he saw that the prairies could offer
    Uncounted new farms of the best.

His mind was on fire with emotion,
    So great was his hope for his kin;
Then he went back in ardour to Goshen,
    And there found new troubles begin.

For his trekkers must watch out for Pharaoh,
    Since Pharaoh had hardened his heart;
And reluctant was Canaanite Tupper
    To give them a loan for a start.

When his migrants rose up for departure,
    The landlords stood ready to foil them;
And the scoundrelly shipmen of Tarshish
    Were lying in wait to despoil them.

But now in our Canaan they flourish,
    A healthy half-million at least;
On farm and in city untrammeled,
    Spread out in the West and the East.

But when they consider their triumph,
    They reckon its source, beyond doubt,
As the time of Oleskow's Hegirah,
    The year that their Moses came out.

SIR WILLIAM OTTER'S TALE
(A.D. 1900)

Walking one day through the hospital lines,
Out on the veldt, where the Boer sun shines,
I noticed a tent with a note on the flap,
Penned by some victims of war's mishap,
A cry from the heart as in pain they lay:
"We are too sick to be nursed today!"

    Quite apart from the pangs they felt,
Why were Canadians here on the veldt?
Why the South African plains had they gone to,
Ten thousand miles from their dear Toronto?
Too little they thought on why they went
To bring a profit of fifty per cent
To millionaire dealers in gold and gems,
Though the Tenth Commandment the grab condemns.
But London had smiled on the hoped-for theft,
And what to colonial hearts was left
But a passionate leap to support the strong
Old Mother at war, though the war was wrong?
Moloch now stood by the side of Mammon,
But Canadian souls never smelt the gammon,
The great, superlative folly and sin
Of a war to gather the profits in.
Such questions of virtue they never knew.
They were just brave men with a job to do.
    We had raised our units and crossed the ocean
To take our part in the great commotion.
Our men in the field got their first big lift
In the desperate slogging of Paardeberg Drift;
For we led the charge on that final night
That ended old Cronje's part in the fight.

On we marched into Bloemfontein
And added the town to our Queen's domain.
But I was only a few days older
When I stopped a bullet with my right shoulder
And joined the thousands of British pals
Who lay in the vast field hospitals.
With enteric and bullets the lads were filled;
There were twenty patients to each man killed;
For our weakest spot in that rugged war
Was the British Army Medical Corps.
　　Later the nursing arrangements were better,
But nurses at first were a half-writ letter:
Their hearts were good, but their hands appalling
Had none of the skills of a nurse's calling.
A London lady, whose velvet cheek
Imperial Britain's all-Red mystique
Flushed with fervour for deeds of duty
Performed for the gallant by gentle beauty,
Felt much of the exaltation leave her
When faced with a camp full of typhoid fever.
A tender hand on a fevered brow
Or the tenderest talk that the laws allow
The needs of the sufferer scarcely meets
When what he most wants is a change of sheets.
Hence came that wail of sincere dismay:
"We are too sick to be nursed today."
　　The world is sick, and about its bed
The nurses of folly in thousands tread:
The Nurse of Glory, the Nurse of Greed,
The Nurse of Passion, the Nurse of Creed,
The Nurse of the merciless doctrinaire,
The Nurse of the grasping common share.
If these are the nurses that throng our time,
Blind to the horrors of war and slime,
It is no wonder that nations say:
"We are too sick to be nursed today."

THE VIMY MEMORIAL (for April 9, 1917)
(Elegiac couplets)

High on the summit it towers and gazes in silence to eastward,
  Over the plain of Douai, over the lowlands of France:
Based on twin ramparts of ashlars, upreared in a pile cyclopean,
  Flanked with cold figures of stone, worthy of Mizraim's prime,
Pillars of marble upsoaring, stupendous and touched with the sunrise,
  Speak of a battle of old, tell of a victory won.

Yonder to westward, far down, in the sheltering shades of the valley,
  Deep in the dark of the night, low in the slush of the spring,
Stirred a conspiring army of wakeful Canadian legions,
  Poised for the word of command, tense for the shout of attack.
Sudden the thunder of guns tore asunder the mists of the morning,
  Full in the face of the foe, first on the front of their line,
Then with relentless precision it swept the impregnable hillside,
  Rending its trenches to mud, churning its nests into shreds.
Back of that creeping barrage four divisions came shoulder to shoulder,
  Every man's bayonet fixed, every man's magazine filled,
Smashing the outermost hinge of the enemy's mighty emplacement,
  Storming the obstinate ridge, held through two years of despair.
Slopes were a slither of slush and a chaos of shell-smitten ramparts,
  Enemy fire was fierce, taking a terrible toll;
Thousands of khaki-clad figures lay dead in the wake of the onset;
  Thousands of field-grey foes littered the hillside in death.
Less than an hour was to pass till the troops of the foremost Dominion
  Stood on the crest of the hill, gazed in grim joy to the plain.
Here stands the noble Memorial, marking the place of their triumph;
  This was their greatest deed, this their most notable hour.
Here amid warfare titanic, and armies that massed in their millions,
  One great Canadian Corps moved as one man to its goal.
There had been bloodier slaughter of soldiers at Ypres and Givenchy,
  Bloodier still on the Somme, murder in oceans of mud,
Capturing water-clogged shell-holes and wreckage of derelict hamlets,
  Churning up cauldrons of clay, pouring in life-blood of men.
Climax of all of the pain was to come at the close of October—
  Thrown into Passchendaele's slough, countless Canadians died.
Months of incessant bombardment had shattered the countryside's
    drainage;
  Autumn's torrential rains had formed an impassable bog;

[59]

Guns were to sink to the axle, the artillery horse to his belly;
    Men were like clotted flies, caught in the glutinous ooze.
Generals, British and French, in their rivalry only for fame,
    Poured out the lives of their men, setting impossible tasks.
Borden and Currie made protest, and threats to withdraw from the
        contest
    Rather than lose of their best, slain at a field-marshal's whim.
Amiens yet was to come, and Arras and Cambrai thereafter,
    Victory followed at last, victory bought with a price.

Here on the hilltop at Vimy the monument stands in remembrance;
    Threescore thousand dead, these were the price that we paid.
Here will their spirits foregather, pale ghosts of our nearest and
        dearest,
    Thronging the steps of the plinth, thronging the platform of
        stone.
What will they dream as released from the clogging constraint of the
        body
    Over the flatlands they gaze, over the lowlands of France?
Will they rehearse all the battles that raged on those plains through
        the ages—
    Caesar assailing the Gauls, Attila's army of Huns,
Saracens sweeping in ardour to conquer the world for the Crescent,
    Norsemen who land from their ships, feudal despite to the
        Crown,
All of the sweep of the warfare that followed the French Revolution,
    Legions from over the Rhine, brought by the French on them-
        selves?

Such may the reveries be of the ghosts of our kinsmen departed:
    Deeds of a handful of dust, vanquishing valorous dust.
Will they be proud as they see, in our land that they laid down their
        lives for,
    Petty political spite, bickering selfish and crude?
Deathless their valour remains, to rebuke the small souls who come
        after.
    If we should founder in shame, ghosts of our great will be
        grieved.

IN PERPETUUM, FRATER

(To Walter Kirkconnell, killed in action, Amiens, August 8, 1918)

Athwart the sun, the autumn wind goes sighing;
Great grassy hills lie bare and desolate;
Yonder an empty highroad, stark and straight,
Runs northward muddily, where, darkly dying,
Shell-shattered Morgemont Wood stands bleak and torn;
No house remains, no hamlet left to mourn
The sons of earth; grey peace enfolds the spot
Where only wandering winds now weep their staves
Of lamentation, while the dead grass waves
Its drooping heads about this fenced-in plot,
This little line of graves.

Filled with fraternal grief I come, my brother,
Here beyond seas that sunder us from home.
As boys we loved before we learned to roam,
Born of one honoured sire and one sweet mother,
And now must say farewell for all the years.
You cannot hear my voice nor see my tears;
For you this wind is mute, and dark this sun;
Yet would I leave the tribute of my breath,
The words of one who also journeyeth
To this still goal, and when his march is done
Must lie, like you, in death.

Yours was a valiant ending; you are buried
With these, your comrades, who, that August dawn,
Tense with expectancy for night withdrawn,
Sprang to assault the foe in legions serried
And warred with flaming thunders of attack.
Fate blotted out your fortitude, alack!
Four years of war had spared you but to slay
At this eleventh hour; soon would have come
An end of strife; your ears knew not joy's drum
Nor the triumphant trumpets of that day.
Your boyish lips were dumb.

We little knew, my brother, what the curtain
Of unseen futures held for you and me,
In those far days of simple childish glee
When life was fair and nothing seem'd uncertain.

Children, we ranged the hills and raced the breeze,
Or play'd at redskin through the whispering trees,
Or paddled, barefoot, in the little stream,
Or with small fingers fed each cherish'd pet,
And fell asleep at evening but to dream
Of new adventures. Even now they gleam
Too perfect to forget.

The years brought new delight and new affection,
With swimming, boating, hunting in the wild;
And still the elder brother gladly smiled
When I besought your teaching or protection.
Often our parents' pride rejoiced to trace
Maturing beauty in your manly face
And ardent eloquence upon your tongue;
Often we laugh'd at all the quips you cast,
And shared with you, in ardour to the last,
The songs by sister play'd, by brothers sung,
In the unreturning Past.

Then duty call'd you forth; and love of daring
Cast lore of law aside and seized the sword.
Shameful it seem'd to your warm heart to hoard
The gold of youth when dangers were declaring
Their clamant challenge in the blood-red east.
And yet you did not go as to a feast
Of joyful jousting and deep-relish'd war:
Your eye could read its horror and its hate,
Yet shrank not from the uttermost of fate
If by your doom the curse would come no more
To spoil mankind's estate.

Thus did you pay the price, and pass the portal
Of man's Valhalla in the vast unknown;
Nor can our loving verse or sculptured stone
Do more to make your memory immortal.
Here have you left a legacy of trust:
You and your fellows in the silent dust
Will silently reprove us if we fail
To consecrate the prayers your anguish cried
For peace on earth; no other boons abide;
And boasts of victory will but avail
To mock the deaths you died.

And now, farewell, my brother, though my going
To you is as this wind that walks the hill,
And all my words and weeping wake no thrill
Within your heart, that has nor sense nor knowing.
We who are left will slowly wither out
To tottering senescence and a drought
Of youthful dreams, though touch'd to wistfulness
By memories of old springtimes and your face.
But you, years may not mar you nor disgrace,
Lying in timeless youth, unstirr'd by stress,
Eternal in your place.

1921

THE MAN WHO WRESTLED THE GRIZZLY BEAR
(Yukon, *ca.* A.D. 1930)

I opened the door of the small saloon,
And there by the stove, near a wide spittoon,
I saw him sitting, his face one leer,
A mountainous man with a chewed-off ear,
And known to all of the natives there
As the Man who had Wrestled the Grizzly Bear.
As I was a journalist, travelling light
And gathering copy for *Saturday Night*,
I sought him out as you'd seek for gold,
And this is the truthful tale he told:

"Back in the days of my youth, my lad,
A sailor I was, and a time I had,
Chiefly sailing the Eastern ports
And mightily crazy with wrestling sports.
Nobody finer could ever you meet
In English style in the merchant fleet,
And then I would study among the Japs
The slicker tricks of those Eastern chaps,
Ju-jitsu and Judo and all the rest
With which they baffle the brawnier West.

"Many years later I came this way
To hunt for nuggets among the clay.

The months went by and here I was stuck
With never a smile from old Lady Luck,
And of all my hardships I felt the worst
The penniless pangs of a mighty thirst.

"Simeon Sloan was the bar-keep here;
He was long on whiskey and short on beer;
But his pride and joy, his delight and care,
Was his giant pet of a grizzly bear,
Raised from a cub but at last full grown,
With a ponderous frame of stupendous bone
And muscles bulging in every bump
From his cunning nose to his massive rump.
Eight feet high when he stood erect,
He would weigh six hundred I half suspect.
He had mean little eyes and a crafty look,
And they called him "Belial" out of the Book.

"A notice was posted in Simeon's bar,
Announcing to all men from near and far,
Attesting to even the meanest scoffer,
A cast-iron, steel-ribbed, mighty offer
Of a case of Scotch and a rocking-chair
To the man who would wrestle his grizzly bear.
I fancied the chair and I wanted the Scotch;
The countryside all would be there to watch;
So I signed for the bout and the day was set—
A day that this Valley will not forget.

They roped off a ring in the village street,
And the folk thronged round in the summer heat,
I stood in my corner and thought of my Maker,
And back of me stood the undertaker.
Belial sat in the opposite corner,
Smiling his smile at this foolish scorner,
While back of him Sloan had displayed with care
The case of Scotch and the rocking chair.
They rang a bell and the bear advanced,
Ready to hug this man who danced,
But I knew some Judo, as I have said,
And pitched the fellow right over my head.
Round he turned with a grunt of pain,
And I tossed him over to Sloan again.

Pride, as they say, can precede a fall
And pride nigh finished me after all,
For I foolishly turned from these foreign schools
To beat the old devil by British rules.
It wouldn't work, for I found at length
That I had the holds but he had the strength.
I got my grips, but his nose was clear
And he playfully chewed off my starboard ear.
I roared with rage and my next wild fling
Cross-buttocksed the monster right out of the ring.

"That ended the round and we both retired
Back to our corners, where each perspired.
Ill fate then hinted to Sloan that whiskey
Would make his critter a bit more frisky.
Now the beast from the start had been reared on water,
As strict as a Baptist deacon's daughter,
And the sudden taste of the tingling stuff
Tickled his fancy sure enough.
His eyes were a-blink with enjoyment kind;
He patted old Simeon's broad behind;
Then stretched out his mighty arm a notch
And grabbed up Simeon's case of Scotch.
He opened the bottles and kept on drinking
Till the jag he developed was more than stinking.
Quart after quart of the stuff we saw
Vanishing down his greedy maw;
Slowly he sagged to the ring's dirt floor,
Falling asleep with a boozy snore.

"What followed next is the truth, young man,
Though the ways of Heaven are hard to scan,
But so to the muzzle had he been loaded
That all of a sudden the bear exploded
When a fellow lighting a cigarette
Had dropped a match that was flaming yet.
That street took hours to clean, I guess,
And all of our clothes were a hairy mess
But everyone swore I had fought right purty,
Though the Scotch was gone and the chair was dirty.

Simeon stood with a frown on his face,
But he gave me the chair and another case.

This chair that I rock on will testify,
With this chawed-off ear, that I do not lie."

This was the story I wired collect
To *Saturday Night*, but my hopes were wrecked
When they answered back with a sizzling wire
That I was a fool and my man was a liar,
Known to their janitor's lad, no less,
As a paragon of untruthfulness,
And his ear not lost to a bear at all
But chewed by a Swede in a tavern brawl.
The boy, they added, had lived out West
In the very town of my present quest,
And he knew the man and he knew the story,
And they both were headed for Purgatory.
I kept my peace in a righteous huff,
And two weeks later I sold my stuff
At more than double their regular rate
To the true-blue *Temperance Advocate*,
Thus proving the worth of a noble tale,
For Truth is mighty and will prevail.

THE LAY OF ELIJAH
(A salute to the Rt. Hon. R. B. Bennett, 1935)

CANTER ONE

Compute the Prophet

Of all the prophets raising hell
Throughout the coasts of Israel,
The loudest noise, the biggest shot,
The joker of the poker-pot,
The readiest of all to guide ye
Was that great man of God, Elijah.
He was a seer of portly build
With Bashan's beef and fatlings filled,
So crammed with vitamins and victuals
That life seemed always beer and skittles.

[66]

Hard times but made his heart more staunch
And bravely amplified his paunch.
Some have in error thought him thin
But hungry kine are prone to sin,
And none could venture to accuse
That saintliest of all the Jews.
Men crowded to the synagogue
To hear his pious monologue;
Or broke their Sunday golfing rules
To see him in the Sabbath schools.
He could quote Moses by the hour
(A proof of high prophetic power)
Or tell with unctuous eloquence
The why and where and what and whence
Of riches, temporal or holy,
As high ideals for the lowly.
    Born by the sea, he had a nose
As blue as when some match-head glows.
His father trained him for the law;
He practised; starved; then musing, saw
An ampler living loom for him
Near Foothills of Mount Ephraim.
There did he prosper mightily
In title and rotundity;
But since at last law's zest fell dead,
He turned to prophecy instead;
And learning how to make invective
A weapon slashing and effective,
He carved his way, and put it over
All other prophets of Jehovah,
Still more those liberal priests of Baal
Who gritted teeth and raised a wail
To see a zealot such as he
Direct the Jewish destiny.
Yet thousands greeted with acclaim
The crescent glory of his name,
Claiming his match could not be found
In those who eddy round and round.
That may be so; we venture here
To sketch the course of his career.

The Well-known Ravens

Back in the dim, unhonoured days
When foes and rivals dogged his ways,
Once to Elijah on his bed
A little bird, or angel, said:
"Arise, and go far off, Elijah!
The sons o' guns are goin' to ride ye."
The prophet woke; put on his pants;
And, moaning at his sad mischance,
Stole off in silence to the hills
To hide his head and dodge his ills.
Beneath a bush of juniper
He flung him down, and did aver:
"Woe to a land of grace bereft!
For I, alas, alone am left,
The one prophetic doctrinaire on
The mountains or the plains of Sharon;
And now they seek my wretched life,
Although I never had a wife
To make intriguing matrons swoon
In Judah's Land-of-Afternoon.
It is enough. I'd rather die
Than live an outcast such as I."
So had he starved, had not a raven,
Divinely sent to feed the craven,
Brought with his brothers (dusky legions)
From every corner of those regions
A menu with a hundred courses
Of tidbits from the land's resources.
They fed him there among the rocks
With rich preferred and common stocks
Of oil and pulp and steel and grain
That brought him back to faith again.
And ever after in affection
He gave the raven tribes protection.
He claimed such birds were sent to bless
The widowed and the fatherless:
They brought dead children back to health,
They cheered the widow reft of wealth,

And handed her, these faithful friends,
A cruse of deathless dividends.
He always stormed with thund'ring words
If other prophets blamed the birds
For plucking lambkins to the hide
And taking widows for a ride.
"Nay," he affirmed in frenzy strong,
"The raven tribes can do no wrong;
And we must guard them from their foes,
Egyptian choughs and Syrian crows.
Let migratory birds be banned
To save the ravens of our land!"
Thus was the prophet's breast imbued
With the rare grace of gratitude.

CANTER THREE

Hot Stuff on Carmel

There came a summer, hot and dirty,
'Way back in B.C. nineteen-thirty,
When stout Elijah did assail
The standing of the priests of Baal.
For nigh a decade had the latter
Been privy to King Ahab's platter;
They'd ruled the land for many a year;
Their leader was a plump vizier
So mild he could not be a hater
But starred as a procrastinator.
Now in those days great trouble was
On Ethiopia and Uz,
Elam and Ur and Gath and Phut,
On Sheba and the realms of Tut,
Mesopotamia and Goshen,
And all the lands beyond the ocean;
A period of deep depression
And economic retrogression
Had gripped them all, since each refused
To buy the goods the others used.
The Thracians on their cold savannahs
Tried hard to raise their own bananas,

While Ethiopians toiled with moans
To start a trade in ice-cream cones.
Only in Canaan did the folk
Grow rich as oil or duck-egg yolk,
Exchanging products of their labours
For manufactures of their neighbours.
Such was the Baalite policy;
But now Elijah sought to be
The first adviser to the crown
And damned free-traders up and down.
So vehement was his invective
That all the nation grew Protective,
Such is the force of lungs in season
Against the passive peace of reason.
"How long," said he, "in these Dominions
Halt loyal men 'twixt two opinions?
Raise high your tariffs! Make blockade!
And stop this treasonable trade!
Our native ravens will grow thin
Unless we check this deadly sin."
Such was his speech one day in June
On Carmel's Mountain, to impugn
The priests of Baal, who thronged the heights
With full ten million Israelites.
"Not so," replied the Baal-priests then,
Appealing to that host of men,
"Would you not sell your provender,
Especially to Chaldean Ur,
From which our grandsire Abram came
To settle in this land of fame?
Judean wheat will rot unsold
If you refuse all foreign gold."
Bright inspiration then was born
Within Elijah's brain of scorn:
"I promise you, beyond all doubt,
To keep our neighbours' products out
And at the same time sell our wheat,
For every nation has to eat;
And should some erring race refrain,
I'll blast a market for our grain!"

Then, for the people's admiration,
He staged a local demonstration;
He built an altar of compunction
And poured twelve barrels of oily unction
On faggots of explosive phrases
And campaign booklets, hot as blazes;
Still gazing as the day grew dark,
The people did not see the spark
Brought subtly by a wired cord on
A power plant upon the Jordan,
A recent venture, started there,
By a Baal-priest concessionaire.
The pyre blew up; the crowd went wild;
The priests of Baal were all reviled;
And the stout hero of my story
Won five safe years of power and glory.

CANTER FOUR

The Prophet Has his Day

Then was Elijah glad and great,
And might have lived in royal state
Had he been harnessed to a spouse
To insist upon a splendid house.
Instead of that, he chose to dwell
Unwedded at a grand hotel,
Scorning the ease of softer ways
And drudging through laborious days.
His letters (though the record varies)
Wore out a hundred secretaries;
His interviews were past all count;
His speeches were an endless fount.
His reputation issued forth
To east and west and south and north:
He sent his sister's husband out
As chief ambassador and scout
To Egypt and its mighty States
Just southward from Judea's gates;
Another legate went as guest
To distant kingdoms of the West;

And some declare his envoys ran
To sunrise coasts of far Japan.
To Conference at Jerusalem
Came all the kindred tribes of Shem,
And even Babylon's great city
Sent over a select committee.
The prestige of Elijah's power
Sank swiftly from that famous hour,
For export trade, foretold with pride,
Soon shrank away and almost died.
At first, poor fools just shouted louder
With blessings on his blasting-powder;
But all the people all the time
Can't be deluded; and the crime
Of muddy economic thinking
Had passed the stage of stupid blinking.
Thus provinces of Canaan grew
Bewildered, vexed, extremely blue,
Then started in to use their head
And ended up an angry red.
Two tribes of Israel in one day
Rose up in wrath to have their say,
And voted solid for a change
From policies so void and strange.
Elijah tried the ancient bluff
Of working thunderbolts and stuff
And when the folk commenced to bawl
Called fire down upon them all.
The day stayed fine; the sky was clear;
No sacred brimstone did appear.
"You've no more skill," they roared
      like comics
"In nature than in Economics."
The prophet turned a sultry pink,
And used his well-known brain to think:
"Beware," he shouted, "or, by Moses,
I'll leave you for a bed of roses
Aloft in heaven, my proper place,
And none will save this erring race!"
Then looking round, he raged to see
Their acquiescent jollity.

Elijah Goes Up

That day arrived, foretold and fated,
When he at last should be translated
Unto another, nobler sphere
With softer skies and beds than here.
There poet, sage, or scientist
May figure in a Holy List
As honoured baronet or knight
Forever in the realms of light;
While the terrestrial rich may come
To be a baron, bold as rum,
Or even, by some lucky fluke,
A marquis or a glass-eyed duke;
The killer of his kind may mount
Through war to be a ruddy count;
And many a profiteering churl
Basks blessed as an ermined earl;
But special rank, in spite of Tophet,
Is showered on the mighty prophet
Whose policies, like holy leaven,
Swell grateful in the sight of heaven.
So did the angels importune
Elijah one fair Third of June
Borne in their best Rolls-Royce to rise
And be a peer in paradise.
He bargained first, to serve his ends,
For kindred honours for his friends—
When they in turn should leave the earth
To revel in the realms of mirth—
Then posed, and cried in accents steady:
"Step on the gas! My soul is ready."
In stories that some people tell,
His mantle on Elisha fell,
Bestowing on that faithful follower
His greatness, only somewhat hollower.
What really happened was that Two
In frenzy at that raiment flew,
Each beating off the other's hands
With angry threats and hoarse demands.

[73]

One, eagle-nosed and glassy-eyed,
Had walked the Roads with stately stride;
An honourable speaker, he
Could match Elijah's dignity.
The other, though a rougher sort,
Could Harry him with many a snort,
Assisted by the sweated poor
Who hoped to make good wages sure.
While o'er the cloak they smote and sware,
The priests of Baal bumped off the pair.
　　What of Elijah, who had gone
To loll upon Elysium's lawn?
Though little's known to earthlings yet,
A cherub with my Muse once met
And told her of Elijah's smiles
On landing in the Happy Isles.
The seraphs gave him as a starter
A bath, a thistle, and a garter;
Then made him, with a thousand thrills,
The Viscount of Valhalla Hills.
He married with a holy dowry
A ruddy Happy Island houri:
Matches are made in heaven they say,
And there with joy we'll let him stay.

THE ITALIAN CAMPAIGN
(A.D. 1943–45)

"Quicquid delirant reges, plectuntur Achivi."

Mild came that morning in May to the fields below Monte Cassino,
　　Fields where the abbots had delved, fields where Aquinas had
　　gazed;
Crocus and daffodils blazed on the hillsides of yonder Arpino;
　　Cicero there had been born, these he had plucked in his youth;
High on the Apennines brooded the exquisite haze of the springtime;
　　Still the same sun as of yore gilded the river with gold.
How came Canadian legions to march here on roads of the Roman?
　　Why, on this morning in May, batter the lines of a foe?

Teeth of the dragon were sown long before by Lloyd George and
    Clemenceau;
    Now had the harvest come, millions of foemen in arms.
Over the Seven Seas, from the dawn of each day to its setting,
    Armies now fought to the death, treading the winepress of war.
More than four years had elapsed since the foe in a raid of September
    Started the awful campaign, opened the portals of death.
Save for the beach at Dieppe, where they poured out their lifeblood
    like water
    (Merely for Stalin's regard, gestured to prove our good will),
All the Canadian forces still trained in the meadows of England,
    Waiting the Channel Affair, waiting the onset in force.
Loud the Canadian press now called for some letting of lifeblood,
    Jealous of others' fame, deeds of the Commonwealth troops;
Cries of a war-eager public soon pushed on our Chiefs to decision,
    Sending Canadian troops, south to Sicilian shores.
Still was the madness of leaders a curse to descend on our armies,
    Stretching the war out by years, costing us numberless lives;
Roosevelt's senseless demand for surrender devoid of conditions
    Hung like an albatross corpse, foul on the neck of the West.
Only Old Stalin would win by our leaders' infatuate folly,
    Tyranny's dinosaur bulk lies on the deserts we made.
Clamour from Moscow, moreover, for Second Front onslaughts to
    aid them,
    Led to extravagant plans, turned to the waste of our strength.
Churchill's flamboyant new phrase of the soft underbelly of Europe
    Sought an Italian thrust, found there a crocodile's back;
Two long years of attrition, the loss of our men without number,
    Ground up our units to death, filled up stupidity's cup.
Meanwhile the route through the Balkans, to rescue East Europe from
    Moscow,
    Had to be cancelled forthwith, faced by a Communist Nyet.
Down at the tactical level, the tally of folly continued:
    Towns must be bombed into bits, quite blotted out from the air;
Ever the Germans, behind them, went free, while civilians were
    butchered;
    Ever the wreck filled our path, blocking our soldiers' advance.
Thus Regalbuto, Randazzo, Palermo, were wasted to rubble;
    Thus, in a climax of rage, Monte Cassino was smashed.
Though not a German was housed in this home of devotion and
    learning,

Though, by this gangster attack, strong points were made for
the foe,
Still the obsession with blasting outdid all the outrage of Jenghiz,
Fourteen hundred years of dignity vanished in dust.

Now the Canadian legions were brought as the point of a spear-thrust
Into the Gustav Line, up through the Liris Vale;
Losses were heavy as near Pontecorvo Canadian armour
Breached the opposing line, poured through the shuddering gap.
Such had their destiny been at Agira and Vinchiaturo,
Such at Ortona, too, bloody with Christmas fray.
Soon once again they were sent to the stern Adriatic campaigning,
Passed through Metauro Stream, forded the Foglia trench,
Thrusting the paratroops back in a pressure intent and relentless,
Breaching the Gothic Line, flanked by undauntable Poles;
Broke Coriano Ridge and occupied San Fortunato,
Opened the plain of the Po, ending the war of the hills.
Rimini now lay before them, famed for Francesca the hapless;
Then came Ravenna's streets, blessèd for Dante's tomb.

Nearly two years of such conflict, long thousands of miles from their
homeland,
Cost them a desperate price, fallowed the land with their bones,
Wrecking the culture of ages with more than barbarian outrage,
Leaving their thousands of dead, far from Canadian soil.
Blame not the steel of the hammer that swings in the hands of a
madman;
Blame not these valiant men, driven by fools to their doom.
Deathless their valour abides in the annals and hearts of their country,
Ageless the grief of their homes, wistful yet proud for their deeds.
Hard upon Hannibal's trail they strode through the land of the
Romans,
Close upon Caesar's track, Sulla's and Pompey's too,
Brave as those armies that marched in the centuries gone and
forgotten,
Worthy of tribute true, sure of our pride and our love.

THE CIPHER CLERK
(A.D. 1946)

The cipher clerk is working hard; he plans to take to flight;
He's filching from the cipher pouch a sheaf of dynamite,

The proofs of guilty citizens who had with Stalin dealt;
He stuffs his shirt with treason from the neckband to the belt.

Cold sweat is on his forehead as he saunters to the street,
But to leave that deadly Embassy is most surpassing sweet;
His heart is pledged to freedom but the risks are still to run—
Perhaps he will be dead tonight, his venture all undone.

He seeks a city editor, but finds a dunderhead;
He tries the Justice Building, but the Chief has gone to bed;
The Minister of Justice will not see him when he calls;
A timid Premier dodges, for the matter quite appals.

That second night his tattered nerves have come to be a wreck,
Because he knows the M.V.D. are breathing down his neck;
The bloodhounds of the Red police, with slaver on their jaw,
Are sniffing down his guilty trail through streets of Ottawa.

They seek his neat apartment out, an evil group of four;
No person meets their knocking, so they smash the sturdy door;
The bureau drawers are rifled and the writing desk is cracked,
But the ever-blessèd coppers come and catch them in the act.

Five years of Stalin-worship have besotted high and low,
But the evidence of treason gives the Premier vertigo;
He shares the truth with Truman and to Attlee tells the case,
And a thumping Royal Commission checks the papers for a space.

Our men had given Stalin all the secret of the Bomb;
Our little nest of traitors were the guys he got it from;
A thousand lesser mysteries on which our fate might hang
Were handed on to Russia by our precious little gang.

But none were shot for treason, as a Russian would have been;
A few were sent to prison as a punishment for sin;
Still others were acquitted, though the cause may seem absurd—
That their fellows would not testify, not even by a word.

But still the little cipher clerk deserves our grateful thanks
For bringing back to sanity our Stalin-muddled ranks;
And in our new survival-hope we all should bless the day
When Pavlov smashed a hallway door and gave the show away.

MY NAME IS LEGION
(A.D. 1939–50)

PROEM

All we like wicked sheep have gone astray
    And nibbled pastures in the pit of hell;
The world's mad politicians led the way,
    Abetted by the bankers' Jezebel,
But all the rest of us, we men of clay,
    Sinned savagely and loved our errors well.
We must confess, a darker fate to shun,
For none of us is righteous, no, not one.

When in the Bible tale the Galilean
    Broke straitly the demoniac control
Of a poor wretch and asked the Tartarean
    Indweller for his name, the reply came droll:
"My name is Legion in my boundless lien,
    A thousand devils in a single soul."
So we ourselves, by any true confession,
Have been the slaves of multiple possession.

We have supped full of horrors in our times,
    Horrors with which our hands are also red;
No other age of earth has seen such crimes,
    Such utter mountains of the guiltless dead;
We have sunk deeply in mendacious slimes
    And flouted Truth and Mercy without dread—
Fools played upon by monstrous propaganda
And hypnotized by "statesmen's" memoranda.

The snake of lies its length in history squirms
    (During my life) back to the war on Spain:
The President the need for war affirms
    To Congress, while the Spaniards plead in vain
Their full capitulation to his terms—
    Their note is in his pocket, clear and plain,
But he conceals it, arch-conspirator,
Because the New York press is wild for war.

The greedy years preceding World War One
 Saw Poincaré and Sazanov intent
On having German frontiers over-run
 And Germany's defenders quickly rent
By forces that outweighed them two to one;
 Then Grey and Asquith lied to Parliament,
Disclaiming secret pledges they had made
To join the aggressors in their swift crusade.

But when the coup took longer, we were told
 About a (non-existent) Belgian pact,
And of July War Councils, bad and bold,
 In Germany—that never met in fact;
The Russians first their army call-ups hold,
 Which made it clear who was to be attacked;
And it was later that, alarmed and tense,
The Kaiser mobilized in self-defence.

John Maynard Keynes was eager to confess
 That guilty victors worked their own vexations;
Professor Sidney Fay in time would stress
 The Franco-Russo-Serbian conjurations;
And Woodrow Wilson in cold bitterness
 Declared at last that we, the Western nations,
Instead of struggling for our own survival
Had been suborned to crush a business rival.

Europe was shattered in the monstrous folly;
 Russia collapsed in bloody revolution;
Vindictive treaties were the final volley
 That downed the Central Powers in destitution,
And in a sequel still more melancholy
 Brought World War Two in common retribution.
Mass propaganda and colossal greed
Had made us swine of Gadara indeed.

Though World War One watched men in millions dying,
 Its great successor brought a deeper pit
Of blood and death and journalistic lying,
 Stupidity and hatred infinite.
If we would shun hells still more terrifying
 And halt the jingo and the hypocrite,

Let us recall the devils we have known,
Including some choice demons of our own.

I   THE GERMAN DEVIL

First let us gird our loins to rail at Hitler!
    All patriots rake the dunghill of his crimes;
Though there were greater rogues and many littler,
    His infamies befit our clotted times.
His pals, the Russians, lead in damning "Gitler,"
    But in all far-flung continents and climes
The pharisees and scribes of every nation
Join in the universal execration.

Begotten by the Peace and the Depression,
    He rose, it seemed, to set his people free
From Allied legends of unique transgression,
    From loss of lands and utter poverty,
For unjust treaties were a black obsession—
    We would not yield an inch, for any plea,
But blocked revision with insane obliquities.
We bred the Monster by our own iniquities.

His passion was a theory of race
    Fermenting in his brain like brew-mash bubbles,—
Among all human stocks the foremost place
    Went to the "Aryans" in this Time of Troubles,
As rare as Ribbentrop in mental grace,
    As lithe as Goering and as blond as Goebbels;
And this fair lily's first-begetting tuber
Was the damp Austrian soul of Schickelgruber.

His deepest crime was hatred of the Jews
    (On whom he blamed the First War's tragic tort);
And these his Nazi henchmen would abuse
    With liquidation of the vilest sort.
Even acceding to the recent news
    That census-Jews are not six million short,
We find the savage murder of *one* million
A dreadful act, Satanic and reptilian.

This hatred was to prove his dark undoing—
    New York and Washington decreed his fate
Before the War. James Forrestal, eschewing
    All consequence, disclosed that early date
Of Britain's, France's, Poland's secret wooing
    When Hitler had not armed his feeble state
And Schacht's wise budgets practised due austerity
To give the Reich unparalleled prosperity.

Warned of his doom, the cornered wolf went wild
    And sought to slay before they pulled him down;
All thought of clemency was now reviled
    When the alternative would be to drown
The Reich in agony, Clemenceau-styled.
    Faced with this destiny's appalling frown,
One only principle he found commendable—
That men were power pawns and were expendable.

Thus, when he seized on Poland's western lands
    He drove a million helpless people out
From hearth and home by pitiless commands
    In stark mid-winter, and the helpless rout
Sans food, sans shelter, all despairing stands,
    Men, women, children. Such outrages flout
Humanity; and furious at his crimes,
I organized a protest in *The Times*.

Slav armies in the East a chance beseech
    To smite the Reds with weapons punitive;
He fenced them in with wire, their bones to bleach,
    For not an ounce of rations would he give,
And every blade of grass within hand's reach
    Was plucked and chewed in vain attempts to live.
The ground was bare: no grass remained to green it—
A Baltic witness told me he had seen it.

The Reich went down in ashes and in blood.
    Ten Germans died for every Jewish martyr.
The sequel buried deep in stinking mud
    The precepts of the smug Atlantic Charter;
And those who had released the evil flood
    Saw freedom swallowed by the Russian Tartar.

[*81*]

Chaos is come again and doom is nearer
Since F. D. R. resolved to smash the Führer.

II   THE RUSSIAN DEVIL

Worse than a blackguard is a doctrinaire,
    The God-Almighty complex in whose mind
Seals off all pity, deaf to man's despair,
    As he works out a blueprint for mankind.
Millions may perish, but he does not care;
    A stern Utopia has been designed,
And in that rigid pattern men must fit
Though half of them should die in doing it.

Across the world unnumbered "liberals"
    Were suckered into fools by Uncle Joe;
They saw in Bolshie programmes and cabals
    A role for Plato's guardians, and so
They set themselves on splendid pedestals
    As fit to tell all others where to go.
Had it not been for their ungodly pride,
They would have turned in shame from Stalin's side.

For Bolshevism rose by death to power:
    All leaders of the past were liquidated,
They toppled the Old Order's every tower,
    The chiefs of church and government they hated,
And every skilled profession saw its flower
    Picked by a ruthless hand and devastated;
When these by millions had in graves been folded,
All others were but putty to be moulded.

Whenever a new country was invaded,
    The same old lethal pattern was repeated;
I have the trim police forms, still unfaded,
        By which all Baltic leaders were deleted—
All judges, merchants, officers were raided,
        M.P.'s and bankers evilly entreated;
And having robbed these gentry of their lives,
Stalin wiped out their children and their wives.

He slew a quarter million clergymen;
     He stole nigh ninety thousand buildings, too,
From Russia's churches; only one in ten
     Is left for foreign addleheads to view
As evidence that Faith's as strong as when
     The Tsar still ruled and Communists were few.
Five thousand churches more away they chop
Since Khrushchev followed Stalin at the top.

A villain darker than the vilest Borgia
     Was Stalin, but a Southern pastor-swell
Brought him a Bible from "the other Georgia"
     And softly wished the bloody tyrant well:
"For guarding Russian Baptists I reward ye!
     Let my good will all bitterness dispel."
One Baptist church is left for Moscow's millions—
A showpiece for American civilians!

The tsars, you say, had camps for penal cases—
     But only a few thousand there were found.
With Stalin the vast GULAG trap embraces
     Some twenty million souls in pain profound
Of all the country's languages and races
     In scores of mighty camps on frozen ground,
From barbed-wire hells in the Siberian highlands
To dungeons on the Solovetzki Islands.

A refugee has told their awful plight:
     "Marching to labour in the bitter frost,
Filthy, in lousy rags, a dreadful sight,
     Swollen with hunger and in illness lost;
Those who fell dying in the snowfield white
     Were by unfeeling guards checked off and crossed—
Their hearts endured a bayonet's keen cut;
Their skulls were shattered with a rifle-butt."

Only the Communists, since Time began,
     Have sealed their borders against all escape:
Successive waves of troops and wolf-hounds scan
     The barbed-wire fence, the belt of soil they scrape
To show the print of an escaping man;
     Bullets and dogs' teeth rend his sorry shape;

And if perchance they find him still alive,
He dies by tortures that the guards contrive.

Perhaps you mutter: "Social engineering
    Exacts a present price for future good."
A sober answer from the past appearing
    Shows faster railway growth while tsardom stood,
And farm collectives, their exhaustion nearing,
    Import from Canada. The moral would,
Except to zealots, prove with bitter pain
That thirty million victims died in vain.

III   THE BRITISH DEVIL

Dear Dresden, town of dainty porcelain,
    Sweet ancient home of harmony and peace,
In memories of the past I dream again
    The student days in which I did not cease
To find your charms a solace to enchain
    My fancy, and from joy sought no release.
Six hundred thousand souls my spirit greet
In fair-haired children laughing in the street.

Here stood the gracious buildings of the past,
    Steeples and gables out of fairyland,
The palaces, museums, towers vast,
    The arching bridges that the river spanned.
The Court Church a rococo shadow cast
    And by the Neumarkt plaza, near at hand,
The Frauenkirche stood serenely tall,
A stately sister of the Taj Mahal.

No city in the world breathed less of war,
    Its craftsmen made perfumery and lace,
Gold ornaments and china were its store,
    And violins and chocolate gave grace;
No picture galleries were famous more
    Than those that spread throughout this glorious
        place;
I still remember, but with horror's shiver
Its sunny gardens and its shining river.

For this fair paradise no longer lives;
     This is the hapless spot that bears the brunt
In Forty-five of what our Air Force gives;
     This is the quarry that our harpies hunt
(Crowded with half a million fugitives,
     Women and children from the Eastern Front),
Defying strategy, in lust's black error,
With one Satanic act of utter terror.

England began the bombing of civilians
     In May of 1940 (*teste* Spaight);
For months she smeared the map with the vermilions
     Of children's blood before this British hate
Brought Hitler's answer; but we slaughtered millions
     At many, many times the German rate.
If you are still beneath the War's psychosis,
I give you General Fuller's diagnosis:

The air attacks that brought the War's fierce end
     Were all strategic, aimed at coal and oil;
Mass bombing of their homes, their will to bend,
     Quite failed to turn the Germans from their toil;
The architects of hatred sought to rend
     Soft, human flesh as their inhuman spoil;
This was but nightmare murder, grossly planned,
By the black bowels of our Air Command.

Vansittart's venom and Lord Bracken's lies,
     The daily poison ration of the Press,
Encourage these mad gentry to devise
     Still more appalling forms of frightfulness;
Hamburg they break and burn and pulverize,
     Cologne and Rostock feel the blazing stress,
And now for peaceful Dresden's homes they scheme a
Far more disastrous death than Hiroshima.

Three February nights and days they slew
     Women and children in a holocaust;
Two million fire-bombs our airmen threw
     And four-ton heavies as they still recrossed;
Sad, universal shrieks of pain ensue
     From mangled mothers and from babies lost,
As by the thousands, hemmed in one vast pyre,
They crackle to a crisp in flames of fire.

Germans have come to Coventry to mourn
    But not a single east-bound penitent
Admits the vaster wrongs by women borne
    And countless children on the Continent.
Such sanctimonious blindness springs from scorn
    And wartime frenzy that is still unspent—
York's own Archbishop blessed this hideous murder;
Had Mercy spoken, no one would have heard her.

Will no one rid your minds of this abuse?
    Will no one exorcise this evil spell
That still is strong your spirits to seduce?
    These are your gods, O British Israel—
Fair little Teraphim for family use
    And for your kinfolk, Furies out of Hell.
Can you in world religion play a part
With this red cancer rotting at your heart?

IV   THE AMERICAN DEVIL

This Devil was a total politician
    And an unmitigated egoist;
He sacrificed all truth to his ambition,
    And warped his language with an evil twist;
His policies have brought us to perdition
    And left us little reason to exist;
Beyond all other rulers doomed to damn it, he
Appears our century's supreme calamity.

For years ere Hitler's eastward sallyings,
    Sleek F. D. R. had set his mind on war.
Across the years he pulled his puppet-strings,
    And Briton, Pole and Frenchman did devoir
At his light-fingered bidding from the wings
    And made mad treaties that disaster bore;
For Hitler knew that F. D. R. was certain
With murderous intent to pull the curtain.

As for the Japs, he framed them into action,—
    In times of peace he built up war's substratum;
Cut off their oil in vicious malefaction;
    Rejecting Grew's and Stark's desideratum

Not to impose this murderous contraction;
    Stout Churchill helped him draft his ultimatum.
Pearl Harbour came by Roosevelt's inciting,
To force reluctant Yankees into fighting.

He interfered thenceforth at every turn
    Without the morals of a demirep;
Stalin's advantage was his sole concern—
    For this he staged our folly at Dieppe,
Invasion through the Balkans did he spurn,
    Held back his conquering troops at every step,
So that Berlin, Vienna, Budapest,
Should none of them be granted to the West.

Two evil plotters sold him, in his pride,
    A post-war German plan that they had mooted—
Part of the nation would be shot untried,
    Half the remainder starved to death imbruted
Because the Reich was stripped on every side
    And every German industry uprooted.
The infamy I leave to startled scholars—
But Churchill signed it for six billion dollars.

All this, and more, was implemented later
    In the great treacheries of Yalta's pact—
Handed by Roosevelt to the Red dictator
    Were several ancient nations all intact,
One-third of Poland; and the Yankee traitor,
    Seeking to justify the shameful act,
Gave the Red-conquered victim of his leers
Regions quite German for eight hundred years.

Ten million Germans from their homes were driven—
    Raped, bludgeoned, staggering starving towards the
        West,
Unnumbered victims, having vainly striven,
    Died hopelessly, by agony oppressed.
By him, moreover, were to Stalin given
    Or to the British, factories of the best,
And German workmen, into slavery shipped,
Were doomed to work for Stalin, chained and whipped.

By the same Pact, millions of fugitives
    From the Red Empire into Western lands
Were to be caught in military sieves,
    American and British, by whose hands
Thrust in such boxcars as occasion gives,
      They pass, with screams and tears, to Russian
        strands,
There to be shot in venomous hysteria
Or sent to slave-camps in remote Siberia.

Before these actions by the President,
    The battered Japanese had sought for peace;
To this his ears were deaf, because he meant
    In time to drop the Bomb in black caprice;
By bribes of Asian lands he sought the assent
    Of Stalin thus to share the loot's increase.
And so he made half Asia surely Red,
And added vastly to the toll of dead.

This man finessed the War, both West and East,
    And strove at every turn to toady Stalin—
Feeding him half the world, a horrid feast;
    Ready, it almost seems, to add us all in;
His wild devotion to the Bolshie Beast
    Has dug a monstrous pit for us to fall in.
His folly, pride and policy's deformity
Have wrecked the future by their sheer enormity.

EPILOGUE

Of all the devils in our catalogue,
    Three devils tried a fourth, sans precedent,
In "War Crimes Courts," a mighty pettifog
    Where they themselves did nothing to relent;
No evil of their own they sought to flog;
    Only on Germans was their fury spent,
As in sheer cruelty and obscene sport
The Yanks used torture of the foulest sort.

A Pact forbade the bombing of civilians.
    Britain had signed it and was closely bound;
But broke it grossly and assaulted millions.
    That she was first this treaty to confound

Meant that she led the Devil's own cotillions;
　　But on her crime no Nürnberg justice frowned,
For of "the crimes" the victors had been choosers
And "War Crimes Courts" were only for the losers.

Old Stalin murdered quite a million Poles:
　　By slavery or bullet these were slain.
He slaughtered Balts, two hundred thousand souls;
　　He killed off Cossacks in the sad Ukraine,
At least five million by the smallest tolls.
　　Both Katyn and Vynnitsia bore his stain.
But all these killings made no culprit blench,
Because the murderers were on the Bench.

The War was launched by Yankees' machination,
　　And they prolonged it by a needless year.
The enemy sought peace deliberation
　　But Roosevelt refused their pleas to hear;
He dropped his Bombs in needless conflagration.
　　The deaths of millions as his crime appear.
But none of this concerned the War Crimes judges,
Whose task was feeding all their own black grudges.

We smuggled weapons to the Underground,
　　Whose Terror slew a hundred thousand French;
We did the same by Tito, who was found
　　With Serbian blood the Serbian soil to drench;
We sold out Chiang to please the Bolshie Hound
　　And lost his world in diplomatic stench.
But none of this was tried. The Courts were aimed
At maiming leaders whom the Yanks had framed.

The price of this will come in like the tide.
　　Here stands fair notice that in future wars
All of the leaders of the vanquished side
　　Face tortured killing by the conquerors
And hence would blow the world up ere they died;
　　For they are left, with all their servitors,
No other choice but with their final breath
To fight in gutted cities to the death.

THE CANADIANS IN CYPRUS
(A.D. 1964)

High in the passes of Cyprus, the rocky Kyrenian mountains,
  Stands a Canadian guard, men of the dauntless Van-Dooze.
Far to southwestward there tower the snow-covered peaks of Olympus;
  Down on the levels between, speckled by patches of palms,
Lies Nicosia embattled, the capital town of the island,
  Torn between Greek and Turk, caught in the talons of war.
Nigh, to the North, beyond sea-waves, the vast-shouldered mass of the
  Taurus
  Looms like the Turkish power, anxious to succour its own;
Five hundred miles to the west, beyond sight but in fervent remem-
  brance,
  Lingers the coast-line of Greece, dear to the Cypriote heart.
Peace is the solemn assignment of air-borne Canadian soldiers,
  Here in this ancient land, tense with an age-old strife.

Five thousand years of conflict have tortured the life of the island:
  Men of Mycenae came; Thothmes of Egypt next;
Sargon the king of Assyria smote them with arrows of conquest;
  Persian Cambyses, too, added the isle to his realm.
Great Alexander, at Issus, gained Cyprus as well in his warfare,
  Left it to Ptolemy's kin, they in succession to Rome.
Many long epochs of warfare saw Christians and Muslims in conflict;
  Richard, the Lion-heart, seized on the throne for himself.
Dynasties of the Crusaders three centuries held it unconquered;
  Venice secured it next, vanquished in turn by the Turk.
Over three hundreds of years the Sultans were lords of the island,
  Planting their settlers there, striking revolters down.
Britain by treaty with Turkey at last held the land for eight decades,
  Yielding it freedom at length, after an underground group
Bloodily murdered their Greek-speaking kindred by innocent hundreds,
  Merely for living at peace, treating the English as friends.
Warned by that slaughterous programme that won independence for
  Cyprus,
  Turks of the island recoiled, fearing a similar fate.
Cypriote Greeks by the thousands had smuggled black guns to the
  island;
  Turks in their turn sought for help, fewer their numbers in
  strength.

[90]

Hatred from hundreds of years were aflame in the blood of the rivals,
    Shadows of ancient shame, death at their doorsteps was couched.
This was the cauldron of enmity found by Canadian soldiers,
    Sent by Assembly vote, keeping the foes at arms' length.
Thus had Canadians served in the Congo and Israel's coastland,
    Acting as global police, keeping the battlers at bay.

Yet, were we honest in judging this practice of vigilant action,
    We should be anxious at heart, weighing the chances of doom.
Though the Security Council was formed as the watchdog of justice,
    Five score Soviet "Nyets" baffled the will of the rest.
Eager to by-pass with guile this militant blockage by Russia,
    We the Assembly empow'red, giving it strength not its own.
Thus the police that it sanctioned, unbacked by the Charter of
        founding,
    Worked for a worried West, wrought for our obvious friends.
How can we levy subventions for forces that thwart Red advantage,
    Asking unlawful tolls, dues for campaigns they condemn?

Dangers more perilous still are involved in a concert of nations
    Only united by crime, sundered by conflicts in greed.
Lacking a moral foundation, the sill of a Rule that is Golden,
    Despots will govern our earth, tyranny rule at the end.
See a religion of death, with humanity marked as the victim,
    Science the dark high priest, Lenin the Levite who slays.
Given a stark world order, with Communists spread through its
        members,
    Given a world police, matchless in utter power,
This, the Praetorian Guard, will master the world for its Caesars;
    Legions of Russian troops, set on Canadian soil,
Ruthless will stamp out our freedom and leave us, like all of the
        nations,
    Mute as reptilian teeth, set in a crocodile's jaw.

THE TWA MUSES
(A.D. 1964)

One day in Canada I chanced upon
A pair of jangling belles from Helicon
With muddy sandals and with mantles stained
From trudging down our highways while it rained.

Sent by Apollo to spy out the land,
They had, they said, grown giddy as they scanned
Our echelons of art and tried to gauge
Parnassus' praise for any printed page.
The skinnier of the pair, in song more chirpy,
Admitted to the title of Euterpe;
While her more massive sister wheezed to me
That Homer knew her as Calliope.
Soon, as I sat upon a cold park-bench
Between the pair, each wan Hellenic wench
Poured in my startled ears, from left or right,
A diagnosis of our nasty plight:

EUTERPE

Why do some gentle poets trill their scales
To non-Canadian larks and nightingales?
Can their soft feelings only grow intense
In transatlantic frames of reference?
Why are these bards' bucolics not bestrewn
With lyrics from the mud-hen and the loon?
Are such men native to the least degree?
I wish they'd learn some ornithology.

CALLIOPE

These are pale echoes of a British past.
Others from laxer lands are learning fast;
For lo, the tavern rhymesters seem content
With fornication and with excrement;
Four-letter words and words for privies fitter
Will set their tippling circles in a titter.
Are there strong deities that mould and shape us?
Their stark, old gods are Stercus and Priapus.

EUTERPE

Unlike these rakehells with their lays obscene,
The realistic Marxists keep it clean;
Yet their chaste poetry grows saturnine
In clinging to the latest Moscow line.

[92]

Since to old Lenin's plots they lend their art,
Their Muse gives service as the Party tart;
For these would end the Age in lethal war
And tyranny, the final dinosaur.

CALLIOPE

I found Apollo's mission just as hard
In following the fervent *avant-garde*.
These have no faith at all, in fact would add
Their gloomy verdict that the world is bad,
That man is an enigma ripe for slaughter,
A lump of smutty carbon mixed with water.
These, as the chief of all poetic arts,
Haruspicate their own dear inward parts,
The liver of emotion, wildly specked,
The steaming entrails of the intellect;
Others mix manic type-fonts with a curse—
A sort of gabbled scrabble in reverse—
Or think themselves original to mimic
Some slicker whose one skill is just a gimmick.
Others the gulf of chaos cannot face,
And on a tight-rope thread of time and space
Balance above a void of murky seeming,
Intent on footwork, lest they topple, screaming.
No verse of value comes from such as these.
Ora pro nobis, Sancte Socrates!

EUTERPE

But some have toppled into an Abyss
Whose serpent-throat exhales a sulphurous hiss.
These are in hell, beneath a Stygian sky—
Quivi sospiri, pianti ed alti guai
Risonano per l'aer senza stelle.
This is no bestial belching of the belly,
No stallion's lust, no bitch's rabid rut,
But horror of the heart, forever shut
In the infernal darkness of a pit
Where hopelessness is black and infinite.

[93]

CALLIOPE

What message shall we take back to Apollo?
That the Land is Waste and all the Men are Hollow?

EUTERPE

He won't buy that. In fact, I'm sure he'll say
That this is just Canadian delay.
Time-lags of forty years we must allot
For poets here to march with Eliot,
Who wrote his *Hollow Men* in 'Twenty-five
And from that nadir quickly could arrive
At solid faith. It isn't every man
May rise to be a High Church Anglican,
But each in his own way might hammer out
Some credo to sustain him in his doubt.
To such a little surrogate of heaven
Perhaps they will arrive by 'Sixty-seven.

MAN IN THE MIDDLE

A plague upon you both for bilious bias,
You solemn sisters of old Ananias!
Are all men half-wits, if two dozen lack?
Are no sheep white, because a score are black?
I grant we have these bards, the breeds you say.
Must all our poets be as bad as they?
You've had your fun. You've twisted through the wringer
The lost colonial, the tavern-singer,
And all the addled bards whose art's infections
Grew septic from out-moded *New Directions*.
But we have grounds for pride, I tell you flat,
In Klein, Scott, Souster and the epic Pratt
And many more, a host of noble lads
Who have not bowed the knee to critics' Fads.
Acknowledge these, I say, or get you gone,
You scabby, scolding scuts from Helicon!

AFTER ATOMIC HOLOCAUST
(Altamira, *ca.* A.D. 2000)

Our failing flashlights flicker down a shadowy tunnel
Where skin-clad man once sheltered from the sabre-tooth
And scratched the mammoth's doom in ochre on the walls.

Out beneath venomed thunder-clouds of Armageddon,
The remnants of the race breathe death like gasping catfish
In a boy's basket. Every tower has toppled down

And every home disintegrates to bloody shards;
Moscow gapes Stonehenge now and Washington lies shattered
As desolate as Ilium or the Dead Sea plain.

Darkly along the currents of the sky's high ocean
Sweep virus tides of terror, tumbling all living things
In an ineluctable surf of strangulation.

The seventh Vial of the Apocalypse has been emptied;
And the Earth, as at the beginning, spreads out void and
    formless
And darkness is upon the Deep's disfigured face.

We only, like the household of Noah, have been saved—
If we, indeed, be safe; for it does not yet appear
Whether the poisoned ebb-tide will run out in time.

Seven we sit here. A week ago we descended
To explore the abysses deep beneath the mountains,
Leaving a world of peace and teeming life behind us.

Then the sky fell in frenzy; and when we returned,
After five days, the dying tremors of the wireless
Warned us of choking death if we should venture forth.

Seven we sit here: three are nubile college women;
Three, iron-thewed male students from my seminar;
And one, alas, a grey-haired archaeologist.

Does life end thus? Shall we, like some old Pharoah,
Find in the penetralia of a stony hillside
Our viewless tomb among the granites of the past?

Or shall we answer Gamaliel in unwonted fashion
And see that erring humankind is born again,
Here in the genial entrails of maternal Earth?

Our failing flashlights flicker down the ancient tunnel.
Our food can last a week. Then we must look to sorties,
One man at a time, and hope in mountain torrents

To snare some fish, survivors of the fatal ash,
Or pluck some upland vegetation, safe to nibble,
Or dig out cliffside conies free from strontium.

But if we stand as new progenitors of the race,
Let us avoid forever, as more lethal still,
The mental fall-out of the nations who have died:

The lust for power at the price of millions murdered,
Lies gross as hell itself, and Lenin's engineering
That treats the souls of men as fodder for the machine;

Or on the other side, the gilded appetites
That love the belly and the upholstered chariot
Above the liberties of themselves and others;

And, tearing up all blue-prints of the best of rulers,
The insatiable passion to progenerate
That must engulf all polities in endless hunger.

Help us, Great Father of all human hearts, to instruct
The humble dynasties of our children's children,
Saved as by fire, to cherish truth and holy justice,
Reason and simple love as cornerstones of freedom.

1958

THE STARKER ALTERNATIVE
(A.D. 10,000)

Two crumbling arches, ashen as pale bone
And lichened like gaunt granites of the north,
Bridge the dark waters of a nameless stream
Among forgotten hills. There, high above
The naked wastes, the wither'd promontories,
Where comes no foot of any living thing,
Chill wisps of wandering mist-wraith float and weave
Vague webs of weary shade and meaningless
Grey pageantry; but the sombre stream goes on,

Pouring its black length through the vaulted arches
As the slow sallies of a sullen snake
(Cold-blooded, blind, and full of brooding malice)
Might slide through the hollow orbits of a skull—
Once quick with living skill, but left long since
For cold, unseeing Time's reptilian sport
Upon the misty hills of mouldering death.

1940

* * * *

THE CORONARY MUSE
(Wolfville Hospital, February–March 1964)

I   THE GRATEFUL HEART

I lay as lonely as a cloud:
The doctor kept my friends away
For fear their conversation loud
Might make my coronary fray.
Week after week I lay inert
Obedient to the doctor's will,
To let old Nature heal the hurt,
Aided by stethoscope and pill.
But letters from the postal sky
Upon my happy desk were piled,
Warm sheets of paper mounting high
As snowdrifts in December wild;
And cards of greeting, short and long,
To make their entry did not cease
As in an ever-growing throng
They marched around my mantelpiece,
While flowers with their fragrant grace,
As gay as Wordsworth's daffodils,
Came filling all remaining space
From bureau top to window sills.
Hearts do not break with love, my friends,
But they can crack from overwork.
Life brings at last strange dividends
As old men learn to loaf and shirk.

And past all else an aging heart
Grows warm with pleasure to recall
What kindnesses have played their part.
Out of its depths, it thanks you all!

II SED. INDEX

The Index of Sedimentation
Brings sorrow or joy to the nation:
    If it goes up too high,
    You get ready to die;
But if low, you have sure restoration.

On this course, I am told I would par it,
Did not the "Sed. Index" still mar it;
    For the day I shall roam
    From this hospital home
Will depend upon stern Mrs. Starratt.

III THE 25TH DAY

Barnacle Bill had a heart attack—
    To the hospital he's gone.
Limp as an oyster he lay, alack,
Cautiously breathing, on side or back,
For fear that his ticker some more might crack,
    While the weeks crawled slowly on.

Barnacle Bill was a patient cuss,
    As the nurses will testify.
He wasn't the feller to raise a fuss
Though the days were long and the nights were wuss,
And he felt as low as a mote of pus
    In a mouldy tomcat's eye.

Barnacle Bill is happy at last
    As they loosen him from his log;
For the doctor has spoken; the die is cast;
He may sit in a chair, as straight as a mast,
From three o'clock to the full half-past.
    He's the merriest sort of dog.

[98]

Barnacle Bill has his lesson learned
     As he lay in his barnacle state:
That age is a legacy gently earned
By leisure cherished and stress well spurned,
That the candle at both ends must not be burned;
     The wise in their day will wait.

IV   DRINK TO ME ONLY—WITH MAALOX

The cocktail is white and the glass is petite;
I ask for no water, I take the stuff neat;
It kills stomach acid and keeps the thing sweet—
     And that is the way that I like it.

No belchings now wrench me, no gripings alarm;
The little white cocktail can act like a charm.
All hail to this draught that preserves me from harm—
     For that is the way that I like it.

V   THE ELECTROCARDIOGRAM

A sleazy squiggle on my E.K.G.
Can spell out weeks of bitter woe for me;
While stately marching lines in rhythmic grace
Speak glad reprieval to our stricken race.
Mindful of this, and hoping for good marks,
I leave the matter to the x-ray sharks.

VI   FIVE MILLIGRAMS ARE BEST

Prothrombin time, prothrombin time!
Your lore I celebrate in rhyme.
They pierce my veins day after day
And carry tubes of blood away
For secret rites in basement labs,
A subtle way of keeping tabs
How soon your vital juice will clot
If you are hacked or stabbed or shot.

Because my ticker was a clotter—
Its fluids more like glue than water—

They gave me, as the ill's abater,
A soft anti-coagulator,
Five milligrams of wonder drugs
Extracted from potato bugs—
The little varmints use the stuff
To soften up a leaf that's tough;
But nurses use it, in their art,
To loosen up a sticky heart.

One Sunday noon they gave me twenty.
Reaction rates were swift and plenty.
My blood grew so surpassing thin
That, had you stabbed me with a pin,
The spurting fountain of my gore
Had drenched the bed and fouled the floor.
The doctor came, and saw, and yelped—
A yellow pellet promptly helped.
And now I boast, to end my rhyme,
Exemplary prothrombin time.

VII   THE MUMMIES

In mighty Cairo, in the State Museum,
Stretched out in solemn halls for all to see 'em,
And bandaged tight, except for shrivelled faces,
A hundred mummies sleep in mummy-cases.
Some forty years ago I saw them lie,
But could not fathom how they came to die.
Why were they swathed with such cold calculation?
Why had their eyes that look of desperation?
But now at last, when I have shared their woe,
I sense their secret from the long ago.
These were the coronary lads who lay
Inert on white ward cots in Pharaoh's day.
Beside each victim stood an anxious nurse:
"Don't stir a finger, or you'll soon be worse!
We wash your face and hands, your toes and teeth;
We turn you over when you're sore beneath."
And there were rebel patients, past all doubt,
Who said bad words and threw their arms about,

Till honest indignation flared at last
Among the sisters of the nursing caste.
"Girl Guides of Egypt, rally to our aid!
Get us a mile of roller bandage made!
And for our purpose you may bring us too
A hundred gallon tins of liquid glue!"
I see the sequel, as the sticky bands
Hem in the kicking feet, the flailing hands,
Till each man is encased from heel to head—
The nurse triumphant and the patient dead.
Partners in heart attacks, from this take warning!
Obey your nurses without oaths or scorning.
The coronary programme may be tough,
But keep your tempers while the going's rough,
Lest wrapped in bandages from toe to face
You greet the future from a mummy-case.

VIII   THREE A.M.

Awake at three A.M., the anxious mind
Is filled with frenzied fancies, flying blind.
Imagination at that lonely season
Has all facilities but that of reason.
For every slightest ache it has the answer—
That gnawing in your bowels must be cancer;
Your vertebrae are sore, and you divine
Advanced tuberculosis of the spine;
Twinges affect your head—you sense with shock
A mastoid abscess and an antrum block;
Your right lung stabs you with a pain severe,
And lo, the pangs of pleurisy are here;
Your left lung answers with an equal shot—
Behold, another coronary clot;
Pulses of anguish from your ankles beat—
You grow aware of diabetic feet,
Rotting to gangrene; by your calculation
Tomorrow brings a double amputation;
Sciatica is tearing both your hips
And leprosy is starting on your lips;
Your mind collapses as you fight the demons
Of this *Delirium infantis tremens*.

One hope is left you as your case grows worse—
You pull the life-line and evoke the nurse.
A simple cure has cool Hygeia's daughter—
A touch of reason and a glass of water,
And just to make the remedy complete
She smoothes the wrinkles from your rubber sheet.

IX   THE MOPSTER

Alert and quivering as a timid lobster,
I await the advent of my morning mopster.
First comes her pail's loud clank, the oozy slosh
With which her sluicings set the floors a-wash;
Then comes the mopping up, the wringing out,
And lo, my floor is clean beyond a doubt.
But after her departure, tense I lie
In anxious trepidation till it's dry.
With reason do I fear this film of soup,
For dampish floors can throw you for a loop;
And many a speeding patient has upset
While rushing down a corridor still wet.
The older nurses on the morning shift
Wait wisely for the early dew to lift,
But reckless patients, for the bathroom bent,
Have met the downfall of the innocent.
Hail to the Mopster, for her deeds are good!
We could not spare the mopster sisterhood—
But what we need, to keep us from these falls,
Is highway signs along the morning halls:
"This road is dangerous when wet! Go slow!"
Wayfaring men, though fools, might learn to go
The hasty highway, and not err therein.
We ask no better in this world of sin.

X   THE BIRD WITH THE LEAKY BEAK

"Oh, what a flap for the final week!"—
Grumbled the bird with the leaky beak.
"One would have thought I was clear at last,
With all of the mites and the moulting past,

Clean as a whistle, one might suppose,
From my shiny eyes to my talon-y toes.
Sedimentation, prothrombin time—
Both had come down from their skyward climb;
Pectoral pains had completely vanished,
Gout from the gizzard was firmly banished,
When in at my open window crept
A virus-devilkin, while I slept,
And into me slipped as I lay unheedin',
As Satan entered the snake in Eden.
Now I must rattle the windowpane
With the crazy call of the whooping-crane;
Down from my beak there descends a sap
Like the steady flow of a leaky tap.
Four days more was Departure Day!
What will the frowning doctor say?
Oh may the patter of nasal showers
Soon subside through the tedious hours!
The knife cures cancer, and diabetes
Signs with insulin life-long treaties;
The octogenarian lightly shrugs
Pneumonia off with the "wonder drugs";
Vaccination the smallpox wheedles
Not to attack; and assorted needles
Keep some dozens of microbes off,
From cholera down to the whooping-cough.
Only one pesky virus-critter
Baffles Science and keeps us bitter,
Eternally ranging the Seven Seas
With a drip and a spit and a cough and a sneeze;
It mocks the wise and it flouts the bold,
This ornery curse of the common cold."

LET MY PEOPLE GO
A DRAMATIC POEM

The setting throughout is in front of the massive palace of Pharaoh
in Memphis, Egypt, the evening before the Exodus. Leading down
from the door is a flight of broad steps, at whose foot is a stone altar.
To the left of the palace there is a second exit, by street into Memphis.

The guards of Pharaoh seek to arrest Moses on this night of the Passover but cannot find him. In his place they bring to Pharaoh Moses' sister Miriam and certain other Hebrew women. As Pharaoh threatens them with torture, Moses appears and orders him to stop. Pharaoh indulgently permits Moses to engage in a lengthy argument on the importance of freedom—for body, for mind, and for soul. The death of Pharaoh's first-born son turns the scales and the Hebrews are permitted to depart.

DRAMATIS PERSONAE

Pharaoh

Pharaoh's wife

Miriam, eldest sister of Moses

Moses

Sergeant

Child, the son of Pharaoh (mute)

Chorus of Egyptian guards

Chorus of Hebrew women

Pharaoh's guards, a Sergeant and fifteen privates, march out in two files and face inwards towards each other. As Pharaoh appears on the top step, they all turn to face him and greet him with a straight-arm, Nazi-style salute.

PHARAOH

Where is this man that still defies my rule?
Go, summon Moses! Call him to my presence!

(The Sergeant salutes and goes off stage, left.)

We live, my trusty men, in nightmare times
And dine on darker horrors every day.
First the great River flowed in eddying blood,
The fish all died, the clotted margins stank,
And we dug pits to find out drinking water.
Then frogs innumerable thronged our homes
And died upon our beds and in our kitchens,
And reeked abominably; then the dust
Turned into crawling lice on man and beast;
Next swarms of flies corrupted all the land
Save Goshen only, where these Semites dwelt;
A grievous murrain fell on Egypt's cattle;
And ashes from the kiln, to heaven cast,

Infected man and beast with hideous sores,
Bubonic pustules that were swift to slay us.
Then bolts of lightning blended with such hail
As this our blessed land had never known;
And every living thing that walked abroad
And every herb and tree throughout our fields
Was lost in devastation from the sky.
Then an east wind came blotting out the sun
With inky clouds of locusts; ravenous
They fell upon our battered countryside
And ate up every shred the hail had left.
Then for three days a darkness came upon us,
Darkness that could be felt, that chilled the hearts
Of many of my subjects. Yet I still
Am unconvinced that this is not mere chance.
Some would persuade me that our land has felt
The finger of some god, called up by Moses,
But I would still insist that all these plagues
Are but a flood of infamous misfortunes,
Fortuitously foul, and that this Hebrew,
In claiming to have brought them on my people,
Is but the luckiest of charlatans.
Such fortunes cannot last. I now declare
That darkest hours are just before the dawn
And golden times will soon return again.

  Then, with my queen Hatshepsut and our son,
The little prince we love, we'll take our ease
Once more in gracious gardens by the Nile,
While hail and blood and locusts are forgotten
In radiant sunshine in a land of spring,
And artisans shall fashion pleasure-houses
For our delight out of the bricks of Goshen,
Baked by these Hebrews, who shall serve us still.

  The Minister who heads up our State Planning
Would not consent to lose these labourers,
Even if their demand to saunter out
Some three days journey in the wilderness
And there make sacrifice to please their god
Were not a subtle ruse to leave the country
And never come again. They prate of freedom!

The wretches must be mad in what they say.
To east and west lie wastes of sterile sand
While here in Egypt is a paradise,
The world's most fertile valley, rich and sweet.
Free! Is the man who dies of hunger free!
This maundering Moses would be free to starve,
To lead besotted Hebrews sheeplike forth
To perish in the scorching wilderness!
Such a mad enterprise is an affront
To social engineering. Here in Memphis
The corporate wisdom of our socialism
Has planned the economy to bless mankind
With earth's considered bounty for us all.
All farms are now collectives, from whose fields
The grain comes dutifully to the state;
My commissars in turn distribute it
To every humblest table in the land.
So too the artisans of every trade
Have been arrayed in mighty factories
Where each man's output must attain the norm
And each man's housing, food and privilege
Are graded to the measure of his output.
These Hebrews know not Joseph, that vizier
Who in the long ago laid the foundations
Of this our state economy; who drafted
A seven-year plan of thrift in times of plenty
And yet another such to bridge a famine.
From him, their far-off grandsire, comes forsooth
The very system that makes great our country
Beyond all other lands beneath the sun.
Midsummer madness must have touched their brains
To make them want to leave so fair a realm,
A heaven in which the wisdom of their rulers
Ordains a competence for every man.

CHORUS OF GUARDS

We hail the social state, where all engage
In mutual labour for the common weal.
This is the wonder of Earth's final age
Where every citizen is made to feel

His children's fortune in a heritage
Of tasks and duties and abundant zeal.
This is the land where every man is great
By sharing in the duties of the state.

We hail the affluent state, from which outpour
The golden harvests of the nation's fields,
And every table has abundant store
Of all the produce that the garden yields,
And every city, from glad shore to shore,
Joys in the welfare that great Pharaoh wields.
Behold the land where all rejoice to see
The bounteous wealth of our prosperity.

We hail the People's state. Here none may own
A privity of dwelling or of land
But all share gladly in the fields they've sown,
And in the tenements so spruce and grand.
All men are equal, subject to the throne,
And turn to face the future, hand in hand.
Here lies our loyalty in faith ecstatic—
The climax of all nations democratic.

SERGEANT

(*Enters and salutes*)

My lord, he will not come!

PHARAOH

You say, he will not?
Take then these lusty guards where Moses dwells
And bring the blackguard back by force of arms.

(*Exeunt all of the guards.*)

The insolence of the Hebrew grows apace.
How can he brave the State's omnipotence
And hope to prosper? Sure, his errant folk,
The contumelious guild of brickyard potters,—
Unweaponed, inexperienced, unequipped,—

Are helpless in the face of my police
And my abundant troops. The mere logistics
Of leading out a whole community,
Women and men, horn'd beasts and little children,
With food and clothing and crude tools of war
And all the implements of settlement,
Could well frustrate the boldest general.
How can these vermin dare to affront the State,
And hope to challenge the impregnable?

Enter Pharaoh's Wife, leading their small son by the hand

PHAROAH'S WIFE

My husband! O my husband! Anxious fear
For us and ours has compassed me about.
I dread some fatal stroke, I know not what,
To rend the fabric of our happiness.
This Moses whom you scorn appals me most,
For I have suffered many things this day
In dreams because of him. Were it not wiser
To show the man and those for whom he speaks
The fullest measure of your clemency?
I know not what I dread, yet fears appal me!

PHARAOH

What! Can a wife of mine be superstitious?
Dreams have no meaning but as clues to explore
The labyrinthine crypts beneath the mind,
Where monsters of our childhood panicks lurk
And ghosts of the affections wrestle darkly.
These Hebrews are a brickyard labour union
That does not know its duty to the state
In loyal emulation to produce
More ample blessings for the common good.
High fences, bloodhounds and a wall of troops
Make firm our frontiers. Our police are staunch.
How can bare-handed artisans prevail
Against the terror of such fearful odds?

If reason were my mind's totality,
I might endorse your boldness. But alas,
My intuitions are of equal force
And blanch my cheeks. Therefore I counsel mercy.

PHARAOH

I grieve to see your fear, but cannot share it.
Our firm Utopia is based on reason
And grounded on the mighty sills of science.
There are no spirits loose upon the earth
To meddle with the onward march of matter
And halt the dialectic of our progress.
Therefore, dear wife, I counsel you, be calm!
Return to our soft chamber. Let our son
Be gently laid to rest, so that tomorrow
His eyes may sparkle in the light of dawn.

  Exit Pharaoh's Wife and Child
 Enter presently from the left, Pharaoh's guardsmen,
each clutching the arm of a Hebrew woman. The
Sergeant holds the arm of Miriam, eldest sister of Moses.
They salute.

SERGEANT

Most noble lord, we could not find the man
Although we found his trail where, house on house,
He had been smearing ugly gouts of blood
Upon the horrid side-posts and the lintels:
But none would tell us where the fellow lurked.
Now in the man's default we bring his sister
And other women of his house and clan.
The touch of torture to their shrinking bodies
May bring the Master Rat to taste your trap.

PHARAOH

You, woman, yonder by the Sergeant's side,
What is your name?

[*109*]

MIRIAM

               They call me Miriam.
I am the eldest sister of our Leader.
Nay, it was I who many years ago
Preserved his infant life by guarding him
In a reed basket by the riverside
Where Pharaoh's daughter found him and with grace
Reared him to manhood in the deepest wisdom
That Egypt's wise men could communicate.
My old, grey hairs are honoured for my act.

PHARAOH

Not by my people, whom your deed has troubled.

MIRIAM

Yet all the Hebrews are therewith content.

PHARAOH

What are you seeking in your insolence?

MIRIAM

We seek, like every nation, for our freedom.

PHARAOH

What is this freedom that you prate about?

MIRIAM

The right to rule ourselves, unvext by any.

PHARAOH

This is the very principle of chaos.
Interdependence is the fact of life
On which our human welfare all depends.
Where scores of little nations live alone

And scrape a niggard living from the soil,
Proud Isolation mates with Penury
And what can they beget but Indigence?
And to what purpose? What is patriotism?
All races are but mixtures. Jacob's sons
Were borne in part by slaves of alien race
Who gave no grounds for racial snobbishness.
You seek for fragmentation of mankind
While men in truest nature are but one.
All workers of the world are closer kin
Than those who claim the bond of race or tongue;
And all men should be workers. We proclaim
The coming age when all men, as in Egypt,
Are citizens of one economy,
A world-wide state where all shall share alike,
According to their needs, from all men's toil.

MIRIAM

These are the dogmas of a doctrinaire,
The blueprints that a zealot would impose
Upon mankind's intense diversity.
Most men would rather dwell in poverty,
And badly ruled, provided they had freedom,
Than live in comfort in a human anthill
Where every act is ordered from above.
The Ethopian, though dark of skin,
Knows love of liberty as passionate
As Greek and Hittite and the far-off folk
Of Scythia and Tarshish and the Isles.

CHORUS OF HEBREW WOMEN

Across the earth, from sea to farthest sea,
No matter what the time or place may be,
Mankind is still in love with Liberty.

CHORUS OF EGYPTIAN GUARDS

In this our Egypt, affluent and great,
All workers are as brothers who create
In harmony the welfare of the State.

[*111*]

CHORUS OF HEBREW WOMEN

This is but propaganda that you speak,
A vast mendacity that hides the bleak
And grim oppression of a ruling clique.

CHORUS OF EGYPTIAN GUARDS

Your insolence is worthy of restraint.
How have your spirits this mysterious taint
That stirs you ever up to foul complaint?

PHARAOH

O wicked women of the Hebrew race,
Restraint is far too mild a regimen
For the disease that preys upon your minds.
The gentle cellars of my state police
Will use the subtle surgery of torture
To probe the cancer of your discontent.
My flesh mechanics will pluck out your secret,
Muscle by muscle, nerve by quivering nerve.

(*During this speech, Moses has entered unnoticed and
stands behind Miriam and the Sergeant at the altar.
As he speaks in thundering tones, all fall back in stunned
amazement, leaving him a solitary figure there.*)

MOSES

Lay not a hand upon these Hebrew women!
The wrath of the Almighty is at hand
To vindicate the freedom of my people.

PHARAOH

Nay, my good guardsmen, do not seize him yet!
Let the man rant awhile. It will amuse us
To hear his superstitious arguments
And empty threats from non-existent gods.
Our dialectical materialism

[112]

Is proof against the arrows of religion,
For they are headless and unfeathered shafts
From a cracked bow. There will be time enough,
After his mouthings, to dispose of him
And all his women too.
                              Come, tell me, Moses,
How can a starving Bedouin know freedom?
Your ancient grandsire, Jacob, and his sons,
Would beyond doubt have starved in liberty
In Palestine's parched fields, in utter famine,
Had they not freely joined our corporate state
And saved their lives in Egypt. Now, forsooth,
You would opt out again, again go free
To die of hunger upon Zion's hill.
Was not old Jacob's wisdom more than yours?
Would you reverse his choice of destiny?

MOSES

When Joseph stood by Pharaoh long ago,
Humanity prevailed throughout this land
And equity and truth maintained the throne;
But justice hardened into tyranny
As pharaoh followed pharaoh down the years.
All power corrupts and power absolute
Works absolute corruption in the ruler.
Such is the fate of Egypt. All the land
Groans with the grim perversion of all good.
Now Pharaoh's iron plans o'ermaster mercy
And every worker is a tortured toad
Beneath the harrow of some Ministry.
The corporate state becomes the veriest Hell,
Over whose portal one may read in blood;
"All hope abandon ye who enter here!"

PHARAOH

That they have hardships may be understood.
This is the present price that we must pay
For future benefits beyond description.
But if you now should lead your people out,

[*113*]

What future can you have? Many will die,
Starved in the wilderness of Sinaï
Or stung by desert vipers as they march.
You will face murmurings and foul rebellions;
Men will cry out in longing for the leeks
And fleshpots they have left. Security,
Not Freedom, will seem sweet to all of these
Whom you have led away to die in vain,
In liberties hard come by, quickly lost.
Perhaps no soul who leaves with you from Egypt
Will tread the land you seek, and only children,
Born starvelings in the desert, will survive
To seize the soil and occupy the land,
Stolen from other nations by the sword.
If, centuries hence, your people build a kingdom,
It will be torn in twain by jealousies,
For king will murder king and tribe slay tribe.
Dispersion and captivity await you
As mighty neighbours smite your citadels
And tumble down your temples, stone by stone.
Weak little nations cannot hope for freedom
Except by careless sufference of the strong,
And that comes seldom. One brief generation
In twenty is the measure of your hope;
And at the last you shall be cast abroad
To murmur in the shadow of all states.

MOSES

An evil glimpse you give! Is Pharaoh also
Among the prophets in these stirring times?
Yet even such a fate I should prefer
To servile suffering in Pharaoh's stye—
Reared up like hogs or oxen by the state,
Vile bodies in the abattoirs of labour,
Regarded as expendable by those
Who have lost long since the sense of human pity
And any motive but their greed for power.
You preach commitment to the people's state,
To socialist responsibility
And stark devotion to the common task.

This has become the sugar in the poison
With which you drug the masses of your workers
To acquiescence in their servitude.
But even human bodies must have freedom
If they would keep the dignity of men.
The bowel-worm and thread-worm once were free
But tethered in the intestine or the flesh
They have grown monstrous in deformity.
This were the final fate of man's poor race
If pinioned in the slave state's iron stalls
By heartless bureaucrats and doctrinaires.
A prison-house of peoples lies your land;
To north and south the captive nations groan;
And where intrepid patriots bar your path,
You make a wilderness and call it peace.

CHORUS OF HEBREW WOMEN

It is iniquitous to dam the course
Of freedom in the stream of history
By shameless guile, unmitigated force,
And arrogance towards all who would be free.

Egypt its hand of rapine has extended
To murder peace and fetter every nation,
While mouthing pious prayers with blessings blended
To sanctify its evil usurpation.

The socialist may talk of grace and pity;
Yet freedom finds him ready to suppress
Its spirit as he wreaks in field and city
The frightful deeds of Pharaoh's righteousness.

Justice and empire cannot coëxist;
Man's greed for wealth and power writes in blood
Colonial conquests in an endless list
And tramples truth and mercy in the mud.

Men worship vulgar greatness in those leaders
Who bring still other tribes beneath the yoke,
While visiting dark fate on the seceders
Who to old freedoms would restore their folk.

[115]

Strange myths acclaim as heroes men of battle,
The conquerors who have ploughed all freedom under,
And treated humankind as hapless cattle.
May God speak out against them with his thunder!

PHARAOH

Silence, you surly hags! Have you not heard
The fine, rhapsodic ballads of our poets
And the glad music of our brave new age?
Have you not gazed on Egypt's mighty art,
The paintings and the sculptures that proclaim
The glory of our state? These give the lie
To your black charge of servile degradation.
Socialist realism guides the spirits
Of those who hymn the wonders of our kingdom.
All other cultures are degenerate;
They serve reaction and the rottenness
Of bourgeois egoism. In their music,
The cult of novelty and dissonance
Reeks of decay—the avantgarde's thin conceit
Postures its trivial folly and says nothing.
Meanwhile our stage, our novels and our poems
Condemn as worthless the pernicious rubbish
Of sex and horror with which bourgeois art
Betrays its last extremity of death.
Rather we hymn the greatness of our state,
The universal culture of a type
Beyond all precedent, new principles
Of culture that our workers all possess
As gracious bulwarks of our social system.
And underlying all this heritage
Is Science as the foundation of our thought.
In other lands than ours, the tree of knowledge
Bears poisonous flowers of idealism,
With a mystifying reek of mathematics
Condensing in an indeterminate fog
At physics' very heart. This we disclaim,
We have no place for doubt or scepticism,
For matter is the one reality
And lies within the range of human thought.

No Spirit fills the earth. No God transcends it.
We are the masters of our destiny;
And in the glad achievement of our glory
All writers, artists, scientists rejoice.

CHORUS OF EGYPTIAN GUARDS

Hail, Pharaoh, leader of all men's alliance!
Father of all our people and their friend!
Hail, coryphaeus of Egyptian science!
To your wise throne be glory without end!

MOSES

Your arts are all corrupt through lack of freedom.
The Politbureau tells the Writers' Union
What each may write; and if one should resist
Or differ from the letter of the edict,
A dagger in the ribs will soon amend him.
An iron curtain hems the country round
To keep out all ideas from abroad;
And sleazy slogans that exalt the rulers
And cast a halo round your slavery
Are spawned in stale profusion. Every writer
And artist, scientist or sad composer
Will publish at his peril. Ruthlessly
The Party moulds all minds by social myths—
Cool calculation on a monstrous scale,
With facile ambiguity of jargon—
And in this evil process all the arts
Must dance in leaden boots of propaganda.
Out of this mental slavery no greatness
Can ever hope to come. The human mind
Must seek the conquest of reality
By its own insights and its sense of form;
And this pursuit of truth perpetually
Goes on and on within each consciousness,
An existential search that every artist
Must wrestle to encompass by himself.
Art is the bold expression of man's freedom
To set the world before us as he sees it,
And thus redeem his soul from nothingness.

[117]

The slavish turning out of propaganda
Dictated by the state is sheer frustration,
The black denial of life's very purpose.
You issue gilded images of glory
But all are counterfeit and damn the coiner.
A core of evil lingers at the heart
Of all existence, and the greatest artist
Is most aware of human tragedy.
If you should force him to belie his vision
And falsify his art, you have betrayed
The very essence of his living mind.

As for the glittering image of your science,
Your ruthless plans to stamp out heresy
Have stabbed the breast of science to the heart.
The goal of real science is the truth,
The basic facts research may bring to light
Interpreted by rigours of the reason
Regardless of all interests whatever.
But you have made your dogmas absolute
And hacked away research's head and feet
To make it fit the bed of your design.
In such a system, scientific truth
Is not arrived at by the scientist
But by some shallow Party bureaucrat
Sitting in dullard judgment on his betters.
You have no place for doubt, you say indeed,
But not because the voice of science says so.
The Father of All Lies is Pharaoh's self,
Who has ordained the measure of all "truth"
To buttress up the power of his throne.

You have disdained the sense of mystery,
Denied all thought of spiritual design
Within our lives and in the universe.
For you, both men and women are but cattle
To pasture for your purposes of state,
To rear, to feed, to kill if need may be,
In the sure confidence they are but matter
Which you may twist and shape without a qualm.
But I proclaim the Wisdom that adores
The incommunicable name of God.

I have loved Wisdom above strength and beauty,
I chose her leadership instead of light,
For Wisdom is the hope of incorruption,
The unspotted mirror of the Almighty's power,
The brightness of the everlasting Light.
All just men's souls are in the hands of God,
For God created man to be immortal,
An image of his own eternity.
Here is a reason for the mind of man
To claim its freedom in all human ways;
But this you have befouled and desecrated.

CHORUS OF HEBREW WOMEN

Rise up, O God, and let thy power be known!
Rise up, O Lord, and vindicate thy reign!
For clouds and darkness are about thy throne
And sinful eyes may search for thee in vain.

My soul has been a pelican in grief,
A desert owl, a sparrow on the roof;
My heart was smitten, withered past belief;
I wept before the heathen's dark reproof.

Let the sea roar and let its fulness speak!
Let heaven rejoice and let the earth be glad!
Because God cometh to uphold the weak,
Because his judgment will console the sad.

O sing unto the Lord a brave, new song,
The voice of people waiting to be free.
For deeds most marvellous to him belong;
His holy arm will gain the victory.

The poor man's soul shall be a watered garden,
The captive soul regain its heritage.
No more, O God, thy heart towards Israel harden,
But bless our souls in liberty's new age!

PHARAOH

You talk in idle verbiage of the soul
As if each had a private universe,

[*119*]

Unseen and vast, in which his spirit-self
Was acting out a mighty destiny.
I am a realist. I deal with men
As social animals, who must be fed,
Doctored and taught, employed, manipulated,
So that the greatest good of every man
May be accomplished. In these human masses
I have found laziness and spite and greed
And suffering and anguished loneliness.
All this were more intense if I permitted
Each little ego greater liberty.
The units must be merged within the mass,
To lose the sense of solitary torment
By working with, and for, their fellow men.
That is the dream of our Apocalypse
To which we seek by sacred guile and force
To bring the sorry tribes of all the earth.

MOSES

And thereby damn mankind! I have set forth
The freedoms of the body and the mind
As fundamental reasons why I ask
That you should let my Hebrew people go.
A greater lies behind, a mightier reason
Rests in the freedom of the human soul.
You doubt the soul and laugh at its survival
And flout its part in personality.
Yet in the sure experience of the soul
Is found life's secret. All of us are slaves
To appetites of body, flaws of mind,
And all this inward agony is heightened
By the frustrations of your brave new order
And all the lies by which it is maintained.
This Deity we worship has revealed
A measure of deliverance from sin
By due obedience to his prohibitions
Exhorting to a life of purity.
We trust in our devotions to find peace
Like sheep in pastures green, beside still waters.

Yet it is difficult by such recourse
To cleanse the muddy springs of human motive.
I can foresee, in moments of deep insight,
That from our race across the centuries
Will come a deeper answer to man's need.
Our people's exile in captivity
Will teach the role of suffering atonement;
And later still I see a Hebrew son,
Hanged on a darkened hill between two thieves
To lay his life down as a price for evil
And give believing souls new liberty
From Sin and her dark daughter, carrion Death.
This is the far-off freedom for all men
That is the purpose of our pilgrimage.
God will descend to hallow human life
And in his own stark death deliver man
From slavery to Sin.

                  All seek for freedom,
All men of every race and every age
Yearn for their liberty of mind and body
And most of all for freedom of the soul.
And yet the price is bitter. That far death
Is but God's consummation of a series
Of payments for the freedom of mankind
In every age—commencing here this night.
The grievous price of freedom will be paid
And you must help to pay it. Even now
A messenger of death has passed unseen
Into your inmost courts and will not pause
In his swift work. His hand will likewise smite
The home of every soldier of your guard.
This is the hour of darkness for your land.
Pharaoh, I charge you, let my people go!

*As Pharaoh points to Moses and is about to order his
arrest, there is a shriek from within his house and more
distant wails from farther in the city. After a pause,
Pharaoh's wife appears, carrying the dead body of their
little son. She places him in Pharaoh's arms. There is
prolonged silence. Then Pharaoh speaks to Moses.*

Go, take your people hence! Your god has conquered.

One by one the guards hurry citywards in dismay.
Pharaoh and his wife totter back into the palace. Moses
and the Hebrew women are left alone.

CHORUS OF HEBREW WOMEN

The ways of God with men are manifold
And our own eyes this night have seen him act.
The judgment that our Leader had foretold
Struck down through time to consummate the fact.

Our people may go free to worship God.
To a sweet Land of Promise they will go.
May all in every age who feel the rod
And yearn for freedom be delivered so.

And may our Leader's words to this blasphemer
At last come true in days beyond our ken—
Bringing at last the death of a redeemer
To free the captive souls of sinful men.

MOSES

Come, we must leave our homes without delay!
Tomorrow we are on the march to freedom.

(The women file off the stage, left, with Miriam and
Moses, side by side, coming last.)

From THE MOD AT GRAND PRÉ

Hail, genealogy!
Blest fruit of ancient times
Shining upon a tree
That to the future climbs!

Hail, holy lore of race,
Guilding the path we tread
With an ancestral grace,
Names of the noble dead!

Hollow the lives of men
Witless of whence they sprang;
All years before their ken
Viewless and voiceless hang.

He who in ignorance
Names not his ancient sires,
Lacks half the circumstance
Feeding the future's fires.

Hail, genealogy!
We in thy strength would stand,
Equal to destiny
Here or in any land.

* * * *

CHORUS OF ACADIENNES

We're allergic to you English in the morning,
We're allergic to you English, noon and night,
    We are giving ample warning
    That our hearts are full of scorning
And we hate you dreadful beasts with all our might. . . .

CHORUS OF ENGINEERS

Your indictment of our people is amazing;
We are startled that you speak of us as brutes;
    We must marvel at your notion
    Of a wicked Nova Scotian
Who is English to the bottom of his boots.

For the Truro and the Onslow men are Irish;
The Cape Breton and the Pictou men are Scots;
    While in Lunenburg a sermon
    Is a special kind of German,
And in Dartmouth there are cultured Hottentots.

Up in Cumberland the settlers came from Yorkshire
Half of Shelburne came from Harvard long ago;
    While Acadians are found
    On ten thousand plots of ground
From Old Yarmouth to the Cove of Belliveau.

[*123*]

For there isn't persecution any longer;
We are brothers now and fellow-patriots;
　　If you ask *us* for *our* notions
　　Of the modern Nova Scotians,
They're a very special breed of blended Scots.

*　*　*　*

I'm looking for Mimi this late afternoon,
A cow quite unequalled my verses attune,
Her breath is as sweet as an orchard in June—
　　Mimi, my Gaspereau cow.

CHORUS

　　Mimi, my Gaspereau cow,
　　Mimi, my Gaspereau cow,
　　No task can compare
　　With my privilege rare
　　Of milking my Gaspereau cow.
　　Co-bos! Co-bos! Co-bos!

Her milk is as white as her forehead is black;
Her temper is gentle: she never kicks back.
Today I have lost her, alas and alack,—
　　Mimi, my Gaspereau cow!

She cannot be far, for our fences are good.
She cannot get out to chase skunks in the wood,
Although there's no reason on earth why she should—
　　Mimi, my Gaspereau cow.

*　*　*　*

　　The Thirteenth Louis reigned in France
　　　　And Charles was Scotland's king
　　When fruit-trees to the Valley brought
　　　　Their snowy blossoming.

　　A son of France brought out the slips
　　　　In sixteen-thirty-three
　　And gave them in the Valley's earth
　　　　Fair immortality.

For kings may come and kings may go,
  They linger but a breath
And pass in silence to the still
  And dusty hands of death;

But ever through the Valley sweep
  The blossom-tides of May,
As fair as in that ancient time—
  That farthest yesterday.

When we in turn at last grow old
  And to the graveyard pass,
And when our children's children sleep
  Beneath the Valley's grass,

These white, eternal tides of spring
  Through every farm will flow
And spread across these deathless fields
  Their surf of living snow.

*   *   *   *

Along the tides of Minas swam a little gaspereau,
A-looking for a flapper-gate beneath an aboiteau;
He wanted warmer water in a brook that wanders slow
  By the Minas Basin Shore.

DOUBLE CHORUS

Glory, glory to the Valley!
Glory, glory to the Valley!
Glory, glory to the Valley!
And the Minas Basin Shore!

He started up the river in a silly sort of fret,
But with a thousand others, sure we caught him in a net;
We taught them all a lesson that they never will forget
  By the Minas Basin Shore.

We cleaned them with a gully-knife and washed them in the
  creek;
We salted them securely in a keg without a leak;
You really have to salt them or they wouldn't last a week
  By the Minas Basin Shore.

The moral of my story can be very plain and brief—
For all the little fishes and for human folk in chief—
Just keep away from danger and you'll never come to grief
　　By the Minas Basin Shore.

* * * *

Gie us a platter o' haggis,
This is the dish for your odds.
Gie us a ration o' heavenly passion:
Gie us the food o' the gods.

Wash out the wame o' a hoggie,
Fill it wi' tripe o' the best,
Mix it past reason wi' suet and season—
Yon will be sweet to digest.

Stir in oatmeal till it thickens,
Slice in a pickle o' leeks,
Call on a kimmer to gar the pot simmer
Ower the hearth till it reeks.

Brunstane may pleasure auld Clootie,
Fillin his neb wi' the lunt;
Rich effervescence o' haggis's essence
Wad nat the angels affront.

Sweeter is haggis than paitrick,
Sweeter than roast frae the paunch,
Never a pechan in all Ecclefechan
Trades it for venison-haunch.

Lunnon may boast o' its beefsteak,
Dublin may boast o' its stew,
Scotland's chief brag is the lordliest haggis
That ever swat nectar and dew.

So gie us a platter o' haggis,
This is the dish for your odds.
Gie us a ration o' heavenly passion:
Gie us the food o' the gods.

* * * *

Miscellaneous Poems

FOREWORD ON REQUEST
(Written for the *Canadian Poetry Magazine* at the request
of its editor, Leo Cox)

The Winter Zodiac is loath to curse,
But Leo rages and demands my Verse.
Why must a rampant Lion ride so hard
A senile Prexy and a spavin'd Bard?
I take my Pen. May this discourse I dread
Debase his Title-page and harm his Head!
   First, to the Matter: As the thankless Heir
Of all the Great who once adorn'd my Chair,
I scatter Benisons, in Mercy dipp'd,
On those who scratch true Verse on Manuscript,
Spinning their mental Entrails into Webs
Until the Tide of Inspiration ebbs.
Peace to your grey goose Quills, or fountain Pens,
Or stubby Pencils, in those Muses' Dens
From which, in time, like Star-groups of the North,
Your glittering Hieroglyphs come marching forth.
   I care not in what School your Hope is found—
In Pope, in Pater, or in Ezra Pound;
Let rapt Dodecaphones like Schoenberg play,
Or duodenal Ulcers tune your Lay;
Mix it with Stardust or with Dynamite;
The Test is, have you anything to write?
What tragic Episode, what Gulf of Tears,
What Irony that stains the brazen Years,
What glimpse of Infamy or Glory shines
Inevitable in your perfect Lines?
This is an Age when Magyar Hearts declare
Unmeasured Valour and untold Despair;
Within the Mutterings of the threatened Field,
The Atom's Calibration is concealed;
In Zeal insensate or in Honour high,
We drift to unknown Gulfs across the Sky;
If Verse can build upon that Future's Wraith
The Sills of Doorways for tomorrow's Faith,

[127]

Is not the Gospel great that Poets speak?
Is it not Shame to rest in mere Technique?
What will you leave, in Words that Men recall,
To prove that you were Poets after all?
What can you write, if Earth's last Age be done,
As ageless Trophies of the setting Sun?

1956

THE RETURNING

Here, by the Christmas hearth, the heart remembers
    The loved ones, now no longer in the flesh,
Who shared with us the joys of far Decembers,
    Whose glances, in the fancy, shine afresh.

Their shadowy forms surround us in our musing;
    Their unseen hands upon our shoulders rest;
The sense of their affection comes suffusing
    The unforgotten anguish of the breast.

I see their dim, familiar faces smiling
    Upon our children whom they never knew,
Thus by their benediction reconciling
    The years that flow between us as they do.

It may be to their eyes' untroubled dreaming
    The youthful figures yonder are our own
As once we were, there in the firelight seeming
    Unchanging effigies from days now flown.

But no, these presences are not unwitting,
    In the high realm of their ongoing life,
Of all that passes with the ceaseless flitting
    Of time in our low world of finite strife.

We cannot see them, but their eyes are on us;
    We cannot touch them, but they touch us still;
Through joy and sorrow their deep glances con us;
    They watch our lives in love through good and ill.

Are these the spirits who have shared our living?
    Then still more close must be the Heart of Love
That in the climax of Creation's giving
    Came as a Babe, in pity from above,

The birth of God Himself in human fashion
    Hallows this season beyond word or thought,
For in His Birth we also see His Passion
    And an Atonement for his loved ones wrought.

And so enfolding all the glad endeavour
    In which, with the departed, we take part,
We feel God's living presence bless forever
    The peace of Christmas to the human heart.

1951

THE ROAD TO BETHLEHEM

Above the road to Bethlehem
    When I was very young,
A twilight sky of tender blue
    With golden stars was hung;

And kneeling at the stable-door,
    I happily confessed
My humble worship of the Child
    Who slept at Mary's breast.

But now the road to Bethlehem
    Seems cold and steep and far;
It wanders through a wilderness
    Unlit by any star.

The earth I tread is frozen hard;
    The winter chills my breath;
On either hand rise evil shapes
    From valleys dark with death.

The air is tense with moans of pain,
    Mingled with cries of hate,
Where bloodstained hills and shattered stones
    Lie black and desolate.

How can the sacred heart of God
    Heal all this guilt and grief?
Lord, I believe. And yet, this night,
    Help Thou mine unbelief!

Purge Thou mine eyes, that they may see
    Thy Star across the gloom!
Touch Thou my heart, that it may lose
    These agonies of doom!

Now in the darkness guide my feet,
    Give holy strength to them
To walk with childlike faith once more
    The road to Bethlehem!

1944

NOVA SCOTIA SUITE
GRAND PRÉ

Adagio

The grass is green along the gleaming meadows
    Beneath the sun, beside the shining sea;
Not even random cloudlets cast their shadows
    On these fair fields and their serenity.

Along the dykes of old Acadian annals
    The soft-eyed cattle graze and wander slow
Beside the tidal brooklets' oozy channels
    And ghosts of gardens vanished long ago.

In this domain the living present slumbers
    In solemn sleep, and dreams an ancient dream,
And hears across the years in timeless numbers
    The still-returning tides of Ocean's stream.

BLOMIDON

Allegro con Brio

Blow me down, Blomidon! (What is so fine as
College-crowned slopes by the Basin of Minas?)
Blow me down, Blomidon! (Let the wind blow
Over the Ridge to the green Gaspereau.)
Blow me, and blow me, and blow me, I pray,
Fragments of dreams of a far yesterday:
Sunshine and shadow and laughter and love,
White halls that soar to the heavens above,

[*130*]

Dreams of the spirit and dreams of the brain,
Dreams of the heart with its rapture and pain . . .
Blow me down, Blomidon, blow from the deep,
Acadie's dreams to ennoble my sleep!

ANNAPOLIS VALLEY

Allegro Vivace

Sally lives 'mid apples in the Valley of Annapolis;
Rosy-cheeked as apples in the fall is pretty Sally;
Prim she walks on Sunday where the snow-white Baptist chapel is;
Neat and sweet and slender, she's the pride of all the Valley.

Sally has a suitor whom she smiles upon most tenderly.
Few there are who know him. 'Tis the lad she hails as "Willy."
There is much decorum in that maiden made so slenderly:
Open exhibition of their love she'd think was silly.

Willy sits beside her and they sip soft cider happily;
Just to be together is a little taste of heaven;
Not a word of wedlock has been spoken, slow or snappily:
Sally is but six, you see, and Willy's only seven.

SOUTH SHORE

Scherzo

Here of old a man would sooner
Sail a lugger or a schooner
As a fisher or harpooner
    Than have castles by the score,
For a ship was all their glory,
Whether privateer or dory,
And with ships they wrote their story
    On the Old South Shore.

Out of Lunenburg or Chester,
In the wake of a Sou'wester,
They would sail her just to test her
    Or to implement their store,
And they'd sail a little quicker
If the fog was getting thicker—
Or the cargo was of liquor
    For the Old South Shore.

And the Shore folk still go faring
In pursuit of cod and herring,
And they do their deeds of daring
    As their fathers did of yore;
Here the deep is still auspicious,
And they dine on clams and fishes
For there's nothing more delicious
    On the Old South Shore.

CAPE BRETON

Adagio

Here, as of old, the misty mountain rises
    In solemn state beside a Northern sea;
Here, as of old, blue loch or firth surprises
    The eye with beauty or sublimity;

Here, as of old, men joy in honest labour
    By land or sea or deep within the mine;
Here, as of old, they dance, and toss the caber,
    And pipe the airs that stirred their fathers' line.

Here, from the headlands of this vast grey island,
    Our children gaze on grey, familiar foam:
If, as of old, the pulsing heart is Highland,
    The heart of Scotland shares a vaster home.

1949

KIRKCONNELL, GALLOWAY, A.D. 600
(Visited A.D. 1953)

How did they keep their ancient Yule in Scotland
    Amid the Solway's mists and Nithside murk,
In the rude valley in the dim, forgot land
    Where the old Culdee, Connell, built his kirk?

There, under Criffell, by the Polchos-water,
    Close to the Roman campsite on the hill,
Rose the low roof of the young Church's daughter,
    The abbey fane that praised God's holy will.

With what glad reverence did the grey Galwegians
    Welcome the birthday of the Infant King!
What exultation filled those simple regions!
    What descants touched December skies with spring!

Here man and matron knelt before the Manger;
    Here little children bowed the humble head;
Even their beasts breathed awe before the Stranger,
    As once at Bethlehem, in its lowly shed.

Saint Connell's kirk has mouldered past all token
    Beneath the loftier shrine the Balliols reared;
Even that brave New Abbey now lies broken;
    All but its shattered walls has disappeared.

Yet, as a symbol of a faith unchanging,
    The changeless mountain towers to the sky;
Across the flats the unwearied tides go ranging,
    Like human souls that pass but do not die.

Here Pict and Gael and Angle have been blended
    With Norseman and with Norman through the years;
Nor has war's bloody bludgeon ever ended
    The Christmas season's triumph over tears.

Nay let us turn like them and still recapture
    From fourteen centuries of human pain
The spirit of our ancient sires' rapture
    And kneel before our newborn God again!

1953

THE HILLS OF REMEMBRANCE

Unto the hills I lift mine eyes:
    The mountains I have known
Stand glorious under cloudless skies
    In memoried vistas shown.

The Ganaraska upland bids
    My boyhood bliss return;
The Rockies and the Cobequids
    In flames of beauty burn.

The pine-clad Adirondacks give
    The bristling Shickshocks hail;
And mountains in remembrance live
    That guard the Cabot Trail.

Across the sea the memory scans
    Old ranges' rocky sills—
The Juras and the Grampians,
    The Hellaspontine hills.

From Munich or Milan I mark
    An Alpine rampart rise;
I hear a Transylvanian lark
    Athwart Carpathian skies.

The Polish Tatras glitter clear—
    Tumultuous snowy hordes;
Dark granites to the sky mount sheer
    Above Norwegian fjords.

Vesuvius' smoking summits greet
    The Bay that Vergil knew;
The hills of Hellas and of Crete
    Stand stark against the blue.

Mokattam's tawny palisades
    Confront the brimming Nile;
Across tall Taurus' rim still fades
    Paul's proud, approving smile.

Broad-shouldered Lebanon looks west
    Along the Tyrian shore;
The snows of Hermon's lofty crest
    In quiet splendour soar.

From Carmel's grassy ridge I gaze
    Towards humble Nazareth;
From Olivet, in awed amaze,
    I mark where God knew Death.

All of these summits stir my heart
    With witness from the past;
Each of these peaks with timeless art
    Its spell on me has cast.

Yet this December night my hopes
    Find still more dear than them
The gentle, blessed, sheep-grazed slopes—
    The hills of Bethlehem.

1954

AESOP UP-TO-DATE

A kindly farmer one cold morning found
A frost-bit rattler stiffening on the ground
And would have passed him by, had not the snake
Appealed to him for help, for Justice' sake.
"You've carried in your arms," the serpent said,
"Lambs, kittens, puppies. Here am I, half dead.
Take me and warm me. A refusal slights
The Serpents' League for Democratic Rights."
The farmer raised the critter from the dirt
And tucked him tenderly inside his shirt.
You know the rest. Thawed out by body heat,
The rattler's strength and venom grew complete.
He stung the man, and in his dying ear
Hissed a triumphant message, sharp and clear:
"You are to blame that you have perished thus.
It is my nature to be poisonous."
The Communist brings peril such as this.
He is Democracy's antithesis.
His basic rule is to exterminate
All other parties in the modern state.
"When I am weak," he says, "you'll help my plight;
It is but just, for I am in the right.
But I shall wipe you out when I am strong;
It is but right, for you are in the wrong."

1944

AGONY OF ISRAEL

Bow your heads, all ye nations,
And humble yourselves, all ye peoples,

In the presence of sorrow unspeakable
At the sight of anguish beyond measure;
For the sons of Israel are slaughtered all the day long,
And the daughters of Jerusalem are violated and slain,
And the synagogue is burned in the fire,
The place of the congregation is utterly destroyed.

These are the people of Jehovah,
The folk of the Ancient Covenant,
Who were spread throughout the earth
And were scattered among the nations—
Sojourners among many peoples
And dwellers in kingdoms far from Zion.
Yet they rendered good to the alien
And comfort to men of many races,
Seeking out cures for the ills of the flesh
And healing for the bodies of mankind. . . .

But the hangmen of Haman have risen up,
And a greater than Haman has come,
A man whose heart is filled with darkness,
Whose veins run evil,
And he has purposed to destroy them all,
To cause them utterly to perish. . . .
Therefore let the nations gathered against Haman,
The peoples who war against the Agagite,
Swear mightily to avenge the blood of the guiltless,
To serve Haman as he has served Israel.
And let us offer refuge to a remnant,
Even safe refuge to the fugitive from slaughter,
That the guilt of his death be not upon us also,
The mark of his death upon our doorsill;
For we are all bound up together in the bundle of life,
And the Lord God will require the blood of the guiltless
Both from him that slays and from him that stays not the
        slayer
In the day of blood,
In the day of the desolation of Israel.

Printed in the *Canadian Jewish Review* for June 11, 1943, with the following
"Editor's Note": "This poem was written for the English-language Jewish papers
of Canada by Dr. Kirkconnell 'out of life-long sympathy for the Jewish people and
keen distress over our government's attitude towards the refugee situation'."

[136]

MANITOBA SYMPHONY

I. THE HERITAGE

Andante

Province of plain and wood and Arctic seas,
Scant is the share of thee we yet have won—
Here on the prairie's bright immensities
Where, under breezes that are never done,
Thy rippling tides of grain in glory run
To break round island-bluffs, jade-cliffed and high,
Poplars green-gold athwart the evening sun,
And homesteads in the wind-break warmly lie
With evening spires of smoke that seek the sapphire sky.

Broad streams, deep-valleyed in thy fertile clay,
And fringed with stately cottonwoods, move slow
And muddy-bosomed on their turbid way
By towns and teeming cities, on below
Bridges and causeways, gliding to bestow
Their silty tribute in some shining lake,
Wide as Nyanza or Ontario,
Where billows that the hither winds awake
On far-off, unseen rocky coast-lines surge and break.

To northward sigh thy forests, twice as far
As Hebron to Aleppo, leagues untold
Of spruce and pine, whose gloom crepuscular
Is paved with moss and fern, beneath whose mould
Sleeps a deep store-house of primordial gold
Hid in the granites of a timeless past,
A heritage of treasure that was old
Before the white Himalayas reared their vast
Sky-piercing pinnacles to flout the Monsoon blast.

Beyond thy farthest forests yet, there spread
Bare, treeless wastes of marsh and lichened stone,
With frost forever torpid in its bed
Of pallid sphagnum; and there comes the moan
Of barren Arctic waves forever blown
To drench the crags of coasts without a name;
While high across the northern night are flown
Slow, ghostly banners of Auroral flame,
Lighting a formless land eternally the same.

Throughout this realm, the Redskin used to rove
In south and north; here came the questing Scot
In search of peltries, and in season strove
With jealous voyageurs; till time begot
The tilth of fertile plains, an ampler lot
That from the farthest coasts of Europe drew
Teuton and Slav and Magyar, doubting not
That them the unhandselled Prairie would endue
With homes as brave as aught that our first parents knew.

II.   WESTERN FARMER, NEW STYLE

Allegro

On prairies wide as steppe or veldt
A hard, frost-bitten farmer dwelt,
John Smith by name, a man as gaunt as
The John that fondled Pocahontas,
And grim in visage as a cliff
Wave-carved with Arctic hieroglyph.
His farm lay (when I start my ditty)
Six muddy miles from Rapid City,
In which sad hamlet he would sell
His harvest if the year went well.
He had a wife, a cheerful dame
Whom no adversity could tame.
No sons had she; the years had brought her
No children but a single daughter—
Valeria, a mournful vestal
Whose life was anything but festal.
Two hired men the home complete,
With grizzled heads and miry feet.
Big Bill and Oscar had been barmen,
Consule Roblin, out in Carman,
Well-read, in days before the smash,
In campaign literatures of cash,
But drabber days and dryer neighbours
Had brought them down to rustic labours.
    John Smith had gained, by indirection,
The ownership of one whole section,
But all the harvest he could get
Could scarcely keep him out of debt;

For rust and weeds and hail and drought
Conspired to wipe his profits out.
Wheat was his passion, wheat his pride,
On wheat each year his hopes relied
To pay his bills and make him wealthy,
Instead of which, though dourly healthy,
He saw some plague each season stop
The promise of his one big crop.
Undaunted, faithful to the soil,
John still maintained unceasing toil;
Sheer native courage kept him sweet,
Though dogged by fear of stark defeat,
Lest he should end, for all his grief,
Bankrupt, in Brandon, on relief.
  But moods of threatening and slaughter
Arose within his ill-clad daughter,
Who slipped away to Winnipeg
With all the dollars she could beg
From a reluctant mother's purse,
A mother fearing ways still worse.
Henceforth, more cheerful is my tale;
Our heroine is far from frail;
And in the course of time, Valeria,
Working in Eaton's cafeteria,
Grew in acquaintance day by day
With a sagacious B.S.A.,
A Highland red-head, Saul MacTavish,
Homely and honest, far from lavish,
But keen in zeal as any vulture
In scientific agriculture.
In scarcely any time at all,
Valeria was Mrs. Saul,
And touched with filial affection
Asked him to give her dad direction.
  Then he, with all his shrewd devices,
Studying trends of crops and prices,
Foresaw that farming, blind and lax,
Would bring a world-wide dearth of flax
And raise such prices, high and thrilling,
That men with flax could make a killing.
"Six hundred acres, strong and healthy,"
Said he, "would make a farmer wealthy.

Just get your pa to take this tip:
He'll come through like a battleship!"
   John put his whole farm into flax,
Scorning his neighbours' witty cracks
About the ignorance of scholars—
And cleaned up eighty thousand dollars.
Laughing, not far from sudden tears,
His first real laugh in forty years:
"Friend son-in-law," said he to Saul,
"For downright brains, you beat us all.
But now I'm rich, what shall I do
With all this cash? I'm asking you."
   Once more the youth took time to ponder.
"A man," quoth he, "with cash to squander
Should put it all in nickel, for
I smell a European war."
   At once John hastened to invest;
A city broker did the rest.
He placed his dollars all in pickle
In preferential shares to nickel;
And lo, on the ensuing Monday
They split the stock six ways for Sunday.
   John's agricultural days are over;
Out at the coast he lives in clover,
Plays golf with prim Victorian friends,
And banks unfailing dividends.
The moral here need not be pressed.
Throughout the history of the West,
Often, a balance, frankly struck,
Would find cupidity and luck
And ignorance in close alliance,
Unleavened by the light of science.
Had wisdom been less transitory,
The West might tell a different story.

III.   UNDER THE DOME

Scherzo

The hall they met in, like some classic fane
Was reared majestic by that prairie stream:

[*140*]

Vast fluted pillar, sculptured colonnade,
And arches of white marble thrust aloft
To where upon a dome's high crown stood poised
A golden Hermes. Through cool corridors
Of jacinth and chalcedony, by stairs
Of porphyry, with candelabra decked
And stern bronze bison, strode the Conscript Fathers
In milky togas to their grave debate.
About their chamber hung rich tapestries
Adorned with many a scene: In bracken coverts
A lion couchant, while across a brook
Stand lush young willows and the angry stubs
Of thunder-smitten oak, defiant yet.
   But if that Senate-house should open wide
Its ponderous and marble jaws to broadcast,
What accents would men hear? Sure, noble words
From some lush throat, and, as it stopped for breath,
The comments of its weary auditors
Like linnets in the pauses of the wind—
Bitter half-truths, unjust *in vacuo*,
But blending justly with the panegyric:

"No province, Mr. Speaker, can compare
In soil and mines and men with Manitoba,
The rarest jewel in the British crown.
Our wheat is rated first in all the world,
The paragon of cereals; and our butter
Eclipsed the universe at Toronto Fair . . ."
         ("The hard wheat country's well-nigh petered out,—
         What between drought and drifting and the years
         The exploited fields have gone unfertilized.")

"Our Northland is an Eldorado, rich
In gold and silver ores, beggaring description!
Yes, Mr. Speaker, Milton's gorgeous East
Showered upon no kings such treasures rare
As Flin Flon, Sachigo, and White Mud Falls . . ."

         ("He names some paying mines, but plenty more
         Were merely framed to rook the gullible.")

"Here is the future centre of the world,
The destined capital of one great state

For all who utter English. Here the best
From God's Imperial Islands came of yore,
With sapient Yankees out of Massachusetts
Seeking in faith the true North strong and free;
And Bluenose heroes wrought here side by side
With kingly souls from Huron, Grey, and Bruce. . . ."

("The latest census shows the Anglo-Saxons
Not half our population, and their births
So few they'll vanish in a century.")

"Consider further, gentlemen, how great
Are all our industries! Our flour and lard,
Bacon and native beer and furniture,
Gas-engines, sewer-pipes and sauerkraut
Here blossom into wealth and affluence,
Nursed by the cheapest power in the world! . . ."

("We're losing population steadily.
Ten thousand families are on relief
Right here in Winnipeg, and we have thrown
Well over eighty millions in that pit
Since '29. If Ottawa keeps on
Shirking its duty towards a federal problem,
This town will soon be dead as Casey's cow.")

"Oh yes, I nigh forgot another thing:
We know we have a university
Second to none on earth in reputation.
Our faculties regale the service clubs
With noble thoughts, confirm the Board of Trade
In its grand projects, and instruct the young
With all the inspiration of a staff
Whose names are known from China to Peru. . . ."

("Our best men always leave us. Loss of funds
Was bad enough; but plots in real estate,
A generation back, so prejudiced
Our counsels that a fateful choice of site
Will dog the institution for all time.")

And so the voice goes on into the night,
Its unctuous honey slashed with gouts of gall,
Half-truth with half-truth mingling, hour by hour,
Until the Dome's high light no longer blinks
And even orators must yield to sleep.

Adagio

The Red Man passes like the lordly bison
That once he slaughtered with exultant cry;
Nothing endures except the dim horizon,
The vast, green steppe-lands and the high blue sky.

Assiniboine and Sioux are vanished faces,
And now the Celt and Saxon likewise wane,
Passing away and leaving other races
To rule the ancient Marches of the Plain.

The pioneers depart; they yield to nations
Whose loins have not forgotten to beget;
Until our fading names and generations
Are one with Bohun and Plantagenet.

What shall we leave to those who follow after?
Shall we be laughing-stocks of stupid greed?
Shall we be thought of with derisive laughter?
Condemned by those we cheated in their need?

Shall we be known in shame as those who hasted
To gut the mine and loot the fertile soil?
Shall we be cursed for forests we have wasted,
Preferring headlong gain to patient toil?

Shall we be called Philistians, fat and venal,
Whom God at length demolished in His wrath,
Deserving by our pride His justice penal—
Dull, heedless lords of Askalon and Gath?

Or shall we leave here, when our day is ended,
A spiritual flame that cannot die,
Traditions of the mind devoutly tended,
A torch for other hands to carry high?

Shall we, for love of truth intensely burning,
In zeal for good and beauty for mankind,
Further that ancient quest for higher learning
That is the noblest effort of the mind?

For thus men yet unborn might still remember
With grateful hearts the builders of the West;
In many a far-off April and December
Their lips would name the leaders of that quest—

Who sought to know and utter light and sweetness,
To cleanse the mind and set the conscience free,
To nurture human life in its completeness,
Led by a virile university.

And only by such ardent legionaries
Can thought's emergent empire be made good,
Blending the threescore races of our prairies
Into a stream of living nationhood.

RAIN ON THE WASTE LAND
(With apologies to Mr. T. S. Eliot)

But yesterday, with weak and bloodshot eye,
Red like the ghunghchi seed,
God's maere tungol slowly sah to setle
Along the westlin hill,
Sehet-k am en, most truly, neter nefer,   5
And Sweeney's ruddy corns began to ache,
Sure sign of rain, from China to Peru.

In utter drought all dumb we stood,
Stille Nacht, nicht heilige,
Die Ruhe eines Kirchhofs!   10
Narade ya yuki no kare obane
Og á hjarnið ískalt stjarna blikar
Et nullae dulce queruntur aves;
Yume wa kare no wo,
Zimna i twarda, sucha i plugawa,   15
A dismal Situation waste and wild
Sans breath of Vernal Air
βλήχρων ἀνέμων ἀχείμαντοι πύδαι.

Can Spring be far behind? Was wettet Ihr?
Fagaim ar m'fhallaing gur fada liom uaim . . .   20
Still broods the winter of our discontent.
Hir yw 'r haf ei harofyn.
But Sweeney marked the labouring cloud afar,
Toppling, a looming bastion fringed with fire,
And thogte, "Alas! now comth Nowelis flood!   25

Comme une onde qui boue dans une urne trop pleine—
A barca, á barca, hou lá!—
A little water clears us,
But enough's enough."
An' broodin' care come roostin' on 'is dile.   30

A note of going in the oak-holts moan'd:
Italianità!
Th' Empire of Negus and the antique lands
Ring to the roar of an aëro-onset:
ἄνεμος κατάρης δρύσιν ἐμπέτων   35
Liang-fung ch'ui ye-yü, siau-se tung han-lin.
Le'ummim kishe'on maim rabbim yishsha'un,
S vér csurog a földön
Per sozzo mistura dell' ombre.
Da vordic ar c'hoajo, where the winds   40
Dreht jeder sich in engen Zirkeltanz.

But kneeling in an empty wayside Shantih,
Poor Sweeney has gone Sadhu—Model "A"—
His flippant scherzo softened to andante
And mute the strident strings of yesterday.   45
There in secluded thought encyclopaedic,
Cleistogamous with Essences of Light,
He listens to the thunder gargling Vedic
Up in the noisy bathroom of the night:
Lhude sing da-DA, a learned note,
And Adolf and Benito win the pot.   50
But no!
Jinkoari eskerrak, hortarik libro niz!
Out of this nettle danger cometh
Not by wars only nor by prayers alone   55
In terra pax hominibus bonae voluntatis.
While some destroy
And some, with eyes turned inwards, wail the drought,
Still others toil and toil and toil and toil
In the drencht fields   60
Under the rain
That new creative harvests may arise:
And lo!
Pien-chin-shu ko lien-ji tung
Florum sidus   65

Safir 'an badri
Goude bladen met perlen van de lucht, den zilvren
  dau, geladen,
Aus Duft und Glanz gemischt;
And sustenance for man, tovarish—
nahamu, nahamu, 'ammi!   70
Caeruleus cucumis tumidoque cucurbita ventre . . .
And the Saviours of the new world
Hearing the jeremiads from the Shantih
Shall cry in exasperation:
A truce to Erudition!   75
σπένδε τῷ Κοαλέμῳ!

                                                          1938

NOTES

line
2. From the Hindi of Sur Das.
3. The Anglo-Saxon *Battle of Brunanburh.*
4. Hogg's "Kilmeny."
5. Egyptian, from the Stele of Panchesi: "Thou makest light there, beautiful god!"
6. Cf. *The Waste Land*, line 182.
7. Cf. Johnson's *The Vanity of Human Wishes.*
8. Coleridge, of course.
9. Joseph Mohr.
10. Schiller, *Don Carlos*, III, 10, 220.
11. Japanese of Basho: "All dead and withered lies the grass that lately waved so tall."
12. Icelandic of Guðmundur Guðmundsson: "And on the frozen ground the ice-cold stars glitter."
13. Ovid, *Heroides*, XV, 152.
14. Japanese of Basho: "In dreams I trudge the wild, waste moor."
15. Polish of Adam Mickiewicz: "Cold and hard, dry and dirty." (*Dziady III*, vii. 228).
16. Cf. *Paradise Lost.*
17. Cf. *Samson Agonistes.*
18. Alcaeus, *Fragment 165.*
19. Shelley; and Goethe's *Faust*, "Prolog in Himmel."
20. Douglas Hyde, *Abhrain gradh chuige Connachta* (Dublin, 1893), p. 74: "I'll bet my cloak that I'll have a long wait."
21. Shakespeare.
22. Welsh of Dafydd ab Gwilym: "Long is the waiting for summer."
23-4. Tennyson, *In Memoriam.*
25. Chaucer, "Milleres Tale," line 632.
26. Victor Hugo, *Légende des siècles.*
27. Portuguese of Gil Vicente's *Auto of the Ferryboat of Hell.*
28. *Macbeth.*
30. Cf. C. F. Dennis, *The Sentimental Bloke.*

31. 1 Chronicles, 14: 15.
33. *Paradise Lost*, XI, 397, and "Ozymandias."
34. Tennyson's "To Milton."
35. Sappho, *Frag. 54*: "A down-rushing whirlwind, falling on the oaks."
36. Chinese of Chang Shwo: "The cold blast blows, the night rain comes down; a
    desolate moaning shakes the wintry woods."
37. Hebrew of *Isaiah*, xvii, 13: "Nations as the crash of vast waters are crashing."
38. Magyar, from Géza Gyóni's "Csak egy északára": "And vomits blood on the
    earth."
39. Dante's *Inferno*, vi, 100–101: "Through filthy scum of shadows."
40. Breton folk-song. Cf. F. M. Luzel and A. le Braz, *Soniou Breiz Izel* (Paris,
    1890), Vol. I, p. 206: "At the edge of the forest."
41. Goethe's *Faust*, I, 5, 94.
42. Cf. *The Waste Land*, 11, 388, 433.
48–9. Cf. *The Waste Land*, Part V.
50. "Sumer is i-cumen in."
51. "When icicles hang by the wall."
53. Basque folk-song: "Thank God, I'm free from all that."
54. Shakespeare, *Henry IV, Part I*, ii.3.10.
56. Cf. Vulgate, *Evangelium secundum Lucam*, ii, 14.
57. Cf. *Gulliver's Travels*, Part III.
64. Tu Fu's famous poem "To the Academician Chang Sz-ma, going to Nan-hai to
    erect an epitaph." Translate: "In the hostelries of the wilderness, thick flowers
    shoot forth."
65. From the fifth-century Roman epigrammatist, Luxorius.
66. From the Arabic of Ibn Khaldun: "More resplendent than the full moon."
67. Joost van den Vondel, *Lucifer*, ii, 29–30: "The golden leaves, laden with pearls
    of the air, the silver dew."
68. Rückert, "Die Sterbende Blume."
69. Lenin, of course.
70. Hebrew of *Isaiah*, xl, 1: "Comfort ye, comfort ye my people."
71. Propertius, IV, ii, 43.
76. Aristophanes of course (*Knights*, 221, "Pour out a libation to Dulness!")

TO HORACE

(Verses composed for the Horace Bimillenary Celebration, held under
the auspices of the University of Manitoba, December, 1935).

I SCHERZO

Horace, two thousand years have gone
Since first you gazed upon the light,
Yet still your spirit lingers on
And in our Boreal town to-night
Brings warmth like wine and wishes hearty
To this two thousandth birthday party.

[147]

Our festal zeal were still more fresh
If you could greet us in the flesh,
And talk with as much ease between us
As once with Vergil and Maecenas!
How we would clasp you by the hand
And vow that in this far-off land
Where Eskimos and Redskins wandered
Your deathless lines are loved and pondered!
A thousand questions crowding in
Would almost deafen you with din:
You would be asked to end debate
For all the professoriate,
By settling with transcendent ease
The readings of the codices;
Perchance your judgment then would spurn
Even the manuscript of Berne,
And ruin, cheerily and gently,
The toil of Vollmer, Klee, and Bentley,
Ruling with light but final rod
The subject-hosts of "qui" and "quod".
But faster still would come our queries
About your ancient Roman dearies:
That red-head Pyrrha, timid Chloë,
Chloris, Neaera, Leuconoë,
Sweet Glycera, Pholoë tidy,
And laughing Lalage and Lyde,
With Cinara you loved the best,
Lyce and Phryne and the rest—
Did you indeed embrace them all?
Or do their pretty names recall
Your wistful fantasies of yore,
The day-dreams of a bachelor?
Still others here would like to know
Your wartime record long ago:
Did you fling down your shield and fly
The stricken field at Philippi?
Or did you still contest the fight
Till rescued by the shades of night?
Such are the questions we'd extend
To one who has become a friend

To every classic-nurtured man
From Tokio to Yucatan;
And you, I'm sure, would want to chat
About our age in this and that,
And many things of interest
Since, with Maecenas, you "went west."
From habit, you no doubt would ask
To wet your throttle from a flask
Of Massic, but would find it gone to
A brand of grape-juice from Toronto.
Unmoisten'd but not melancholy,
You'd start a conversation jolly;
And we would talk by fits and starts
Of Hepburns and of Aberharts,
And how a praetor, bold and gallant,
Has promised every man a talent
Paid down each month in every year,
A golden age of cakes and beer.
We would expound the present fuss
Which Caesar Mussolinius
Has stirred up by his ruthless plans
Against the Ethiopians,
Cursing betimes in rage unruly
The far-off Britishers from Thule
Whose iron triremes have been sent
To watch the Afric continent.
"What!" you would ask, "Have fifty legions
Made war in those infernal regions?
The air-force of the tropic jungle—
Mosquitoes—make the act a bungle.
Some Cleopatra of ambition
Has lured this Caesar to perdition!"
"Quite right, my friend!" we would reply.
"Each day a hundred rookies die
In filth and fever, far from home,
To serve the arrogance of Rome.
May Jupiter such rage restrain
And bring us all to peace again!"
Thus would we chat in interchange
With one whose person is not strange

To students of a noble tongue
Acquired when our years were young;
But since we cannot have you here,
Your friends have gathered, full of cheer,
To celebrate, with wagging jaw,
Your birthday in absentia.

II   ADAGIO

All, all are gone: those comrades who with laughter
Joined in your jesting and convivial mirth;—
Silent their voices, and their lips hereafter
Ashes in silent earth.

Vergil went first; his great soul could not save him;
Fuscus the gay, and gallant Pollio,
And Varius and the fame that fortune gave him
Are lost like last year's snow.

Maecenas and his wealth have long been banished,
With Plotius, from life's melancholy shore;
Messalla and Numicius have vanished
Two thousand years and more.

You only, Horace, of those friends consorted,
Passing like us to join the shadowy dead,
Still linger on in spirit where they sported,
Though centuries have fled.

Long-headed, tanned, in spite of grey hairs merry,
Plump and well-favoured, we still see you sit
Beside your hearth, in Sabine uplands airy,
And laugh with mellow wit.

Sweet-tempered master of the art of living,
Loving alike the lovely and the good,
And courting with your nature's amplest giving
The Muses' sisterhood,

How have our lives through you gained richer reaping,
Age after age, since Rome your verses knew!
God grant, hereafter, in your kindly keeping
Our sons may love you too!

1935

THE AYRSHIRE MUSE

(Robert Burns, in life an ardent and convivial Mason, returns for the
Burns Night banquet of a Canadian lodge, in January, 1935.)

Maist worshipful an' festal sir,
What gars ye make sic' awfu' stir
To fetch me frae my sepulchre
    Each January?
Why seek my banes tae disinter?
    Brithers, how dare ye?

Yet since indeed we're unco dry
Amang the grave-stour where we lie,
A thirsty rhymester such as I
    Wad still be frisky
An' gladly climb the cauld, toom sky
    If promised whiskey!

Aiblins ye've naethin' half sae hot
To please a drouthie brither Scot;
There's watery joy in mony a pot
    These sair, douce days;
But I'll no glunch at what ye've got,
    Nor stint my praise.

An' first I wad be orra civil
Tae a' my feres o' square an' level;
I ken nane such tae drink an' revel,
    Their dool tae dodge,
Though I hae visited the Devil
    In Hell's Grand Lodge.

The Master there is e'en Auld Clootie,
Wi' horns an' tail an' hurdies sootie;
The Senior Warden's no a beauty
    Tae girn an' ogle,
But just a naked owre-graun cootie,
    A big black bogle.

Fecks, ye should see the deacons toddle
About yon lodge o' brimstane model!
It's little they're inclined tae coddle
    A candidate;
But whang a' brithers on the noddle
    That gang that gate.

Enough o' hell. Let's seek a change
In regions just as fierce an' strange
Amang yer chiels wha maun arrange
                    The next election;
Nae lousy collie wi' the mange
                    Has mair dejection.

Auld Cloots o' Calgary ye ken
Is farst amang the sons o' men
For bleezin hot wi' tongue an' pen
                    An' blastin-powder,
An' when elections come again
                    He whoops still louder.

Wi' tones that deave an' words than stun,
He broadcasts like Euroclydon,
An' vows that he's the only one
                    Can save the nation,
Wi' braw New Plans frae Washington
                    That beat Creation.

Lean Comrade Jim frae Winnipeg,
That Woodsworth carl sae gash an' gleg,
Maun wag his beard an' slap his leg
                    In snirtlin shock
Tae see a new-laid Marxian egg
                    Frae sic a cock.

But wae is me for Wullie King,
Wha's too weel fed to wark or sing;
The Fat Lad winna do a thing
                    But sit on 's bum
And trust that wi' anither spring
                    His turn will come.

Much ither news ye've had tae con, too,
Five bairns at ance were a' born pronto,
An' Hepburn an' his pals hae gone to
                    The South Seas blue
To shun the Tories o' Toronto,
                    An' Tim Buck too.

Take yon Dionne. A ferlie is he,
Wha one lang nicht was unco busy
To get five weans from one fair hizzie,
                His ain dear wife;
I' fecks, they make the gudeman dizzy
                Wi' yowlin strife.

Puir Mitch was sair fatigued, o' course,
For guillotinin jobs by force
Is waur nor feedin hog an' horse
                Doun on the farm;
An' tae prevent undue remorse
                He's keepin warm.

But golfin larks on Southern greens
Are far frae Tim Buck's ways an' means;
He's glad tae be wi' wife an' weans,
                An' hopes wi' reason
He'll sit nae mair in prison jeans
                Through shootin season.

An' now, gude sir, my thanks I'm speakin
Tae wardens baith an' either deacon,
May a' their noses like a beacon
                Forever shine
Tae testify they never weaken
                When offered wine.

Come, chaplain, scribe, and stewards braw,
An' peepin Tyler but the ha',
An' Inner Guard, an' brithers a',
                Gie owre yer nappy—
Let's pledge the Craft in usquebaugh,
                An' gang hame happy!

My rantin rhymes hae a' been said.
An' sae, gude nicht! But I've nae dread
Afore I seek my dusty bed
                As dark as ink
Ye'll aiblins gie the thirsty dead
                Anither drink!

1935

HOLY JOE
(Written for Burns' Birthday, 1949)

Warst of all fools beneath the ban
O' folly is a clergyman
Wi' Pinkish maggots in his pan,
      The sort we know
Fulfillin Satan's sootie plan
      As "Holy Joe."

What deil has blastit altogether
This brain o' bran, this saul o' leather?
Just name in any kind o' weather
      The Red slave-nation,
And lak a sheep he'll start to blether
      In adoration.

Heels ower gowdie see him sprawlin
To kiss the stinkin feet o' Stalin.
He winna smell the bluid-draps fallin
      Frae Stalin's looves,
Nor see that Stalin's feet appallin
      Are cloven hooves.

Oh wae is me that sic a blight
Pits consecrated brains tae flight,
That ane wha vowed tae do the right
      And sarve it well
Should thus forsake the God o' light
      Tae worship hell!

In Stalin-land the Kremlin-knave
Destroyed the pious and the brave;
He shot the half and starved the lave,
      And hell thus furdered;
But Holy Joe his blessing gave
      Tae him that murdered.

In midden-filth and ragged claes,
Millions in slave-camps end their days;
But show our holy friend sic ways—
      He winna waver
But scoffs it aff wi' smirkin face
      As clish-ma-claver.

He winna blat a holy eye
At Red police-force infamy;
He swears they are a blessing high
   And not a curse.
"Th' R.C.M.P. and F.B.I.
   Are far, far worse."

It is the law o' Stalin's land
That he wha murmurs shall be banned
From his ain ingle out o' hand,
   Wi' empty wame,
By factory-bosses, wha hae planned
   The deed o' shame.

The Russian workers fare still waur
Than even underneath the Tsar,
A palace has each commissar
   And piles o' siller;
But Holy Joe applauds from far,
   His praise is shriller.

Slow hunger is the workers' lot:
If three times late, in jail ye rot,
And gin ye strike, ye're aiblins shot,
   But the erratic
Auld loon declares this wrang, this blot,
   Is "democratic."

Five million honest peasant folk
Were starved tae death beneath the yoke.
Tae Holy Joe it was a joke
   O' far-off hearsay:
He blethered, in each word he spoke,
   O' Stalin's mercy.

All native worth by him is hiss'd;
All praise and virtue here are miss'd;
Alane upon his honour-list
   The Kremlin messan,
Red Moscow's master-atheist,
   Receives his blessin.

It maks a wise man unco weary
Tae see a spectacle sae eerie:
The staumrel sumpf gaes tapsalteerie
   And hails a scant
Ramgunshoch randie as his dearie,
   His patron saunt.

But baukie-birds and hoodie-craws
And vultures black wi' carrion claws,
All things in nature foul and fause,
   Befit the deil
This coof has chosen without cause
   And serves him weel.

The pious skull should be trepanned
Of ane wha Satan wrang has scanned
And sair misca'd his ain fair land
   Wi' creeshie lee
And kiss'd auld Stalin's bluidy hand
   Wi' doun-drapt e'e.

Nae special coof the name I call,
But gin upon the type ye fall
In Ayr, New York or Montreal,
   Ye'll no be slow
Tae greet the oily gommeral
   As "Holy Joe"!

A BALLAD OF SAINT ANDREW

Saint Andrew was a fisher, and he lived beside the sea;
 His brother's name was Simon and his father's name was
 John;
And he loved to take the herring just as well as you or me,
 And to talk about his catches in the seasons that were gone.

Saint Andrew met the Baptist and was taken to the Lord.
 He took the Lord out fishing, and a storm came on the sea;
But Jesus checked the tempest in his love for all on board,
 And a calm as sweet as heaven fell on heaving Galilee.

Saint Andrew gave up fishing for the herring in the deep;
    He fished for men for Jesus as he'd fished for cod before;
Till the Devil's servants took him as he lay in holy sleep,
    And they hung him like a haddock on a cross beside the
      shore.

His deeds are lost in legend, but of this we may be sure:
    His spirit still is homesick for the smell of net and line;
His heart is with all fishermen in all that they endure,
    And he haunts them in affection in their perils of the brine.

And since the Scots are fisherfolk, he claims them as his own;
    He wakes beside their dories from the Tweed to Scapa Flow,
From the Forth to far-off Fundy, wherever Scots are known,
    And he walks the waves beside them as his Lord did long
      ago.

1950

A WESTERN IDYLL
Prologue at Christmas

In dark, distressful days like these,
When nations die or fight for life,
And earth's fate, for long centuries,
Hangs on the outcome of the strife,
A simple scholar feels, aghast,
How small and flickering is the flame
That at his Christmas hearth is cast
On boys and girls that bear his name,
And how a single home's romance
Is lost in insignificance
In the vast flux of worlds amiss
Now eddying in Time's abyss.
Yet since in spite of storms of ill
Faith, hope, and love are living still,
And friendships shine more precious yet
Amid black whirlwinds that beset,
I send this greeting, true and warm,
Across the darkness and the storm,

And, as a Yuletide gift, this study
Of sturdy Bill MacGillicuddy,
A trivial yarn in simple rhyme
To wish you well at Christmas-time.

I

Bill was a true-bred farmer's son,
Reared on a fertile quarter-section
Near Minnedosa, where the run
Of rolling country won selection
From his Scotch dad, who came from Bruce
And wanted land for life-long use.
Both had a passion for the land,
And both could dimly understand
The symphony of dawn and spring
That the returning Aprils bring.
From the back door-step, looking down,
They'd see the ploughed fields, warm and brown,
While clouds, like ships, were riding high
Across the blue gulfs of the sky
And crows' glad cawing swelled sonorous
The prairie chickens' morning chorus.
Into their nostrils, too, would pass
The fragrance of the springing grass,
And through their veins would steal a sense
Of some pervading Influence
That caused the crops to bud and swell
And moved in human lives as well.
Hence came a mood of deep content
As through the barn-yard straw they went
In greasy denim overalls
To tend the horses in the stalls,
Or milk a dozen Holstein cows
And gladly scan from out the dairy,
From under bushy Scottish brows,
The undulations of the prairie.
The father dreamed that there might be
Such life in perpetuity
For scions of the flesh and blood he
Prized as the pure MacGillicuddy;

Yet Bill, the son, while quite prepared
To implement a dream he shared,
Was first intent on gaining knowledge
Down at the Agricultural College,
That he in future might fulfil
A farmer's tasks with greater skill;
And as for girls, he vaguely knew
That on the next farm, blue-eyed Sue,
The daughter of old Philip Pratt,
Was very good for looking at
And very sympathetic too
With all the things that farmers do.
No word was said between the pair
About their chance of getting married,
But in his absence, her one care
Was lest that future be miscarried.

II

Bill did quite well at M.A.C.
When he went in to take his course.
He knew just what he hoped to be
And toiled with unremitting force,
Just as at home he once had done
In rain and mud, in dust and sun.
He had no eyes for city girls,
And passed as many-coloured comics
The dainty flock in skirts and curls
Who majored in Home Economics.
They, for their part, were more observant
Of the tall, handsome, thick-browed lad,
And one young creature, growing fervent
About the qualities he had,
Resolved before the year had flown
To have him as her very own.
She was a vivid, red-haired hussy,
Known to the frats as "Necking Nell";
In inhibitions far from fussy,
She painted like Queen Jezebel,
Smoked like a furnace newly fed,
And dyed her nails a dazzling red.

Yet she was trim, as neat a wench
As ever made a shy man blench;
And while her dad, an auctioneer,
Found that his daughter cost him dear
In silken clothes of fancy makes,
She had the figure that it takes.
Obliging friends lured Bill to con
This ravishing phenomenon;
And though at first she got a snub
From one who faced his first frat party
Mad as a tomcat in a tub
At manners fresh and over-hearty,
Yet frequent meeting dulled his sense
Of all unhealthy difference
And roused a keen appreciation
Of her technique in osculation.
So, by the spring, he saw no harm
If she should visit at the farm
And really see the sort of life
That would await a farmer's wife.

III

Thus, one June day, his amorosa,
Taking her father's Hudson car,
Drove swiftly out by Minnedosa
And turned, with greetings jocular
And even tenderly profane,
Into MacGillicuddy's lane.
Bill's father's wrinkled face of leather,
Seasoned by years of wind and weather,
Looked on discerningly as Bill
Welcomed the girl; his glance was chill,
And one could place a clear construction
Upon his mood at introduction;
But neither Bill nor Nellie saw
The tightening of his iron jaw
Nor how his eyes grew still more bleak
On learning she would stay a week.

As things turned out, she'd had enough
Before a single day was through;
And though she staged a steady bluff,
Her mind indubitably knew
That farm life, drab and unromantic,
Would very quickly drive her frantic.
The hens' weird, raucous monotone
Beat on her hearing all day long;
Through sleepless hours by night would drone
The crickets' never-ceasing song,
Mixed with the barking of the dogs
And the loud chorus of the frogs.
And when at dawn she sought to doze,
Pajama'd in Italian silk,
A clamour in the orchard rose
From young calves bawling for their milk;
Or she would listen, swearing badly,
To small, lost turkeys, piping sadly;
And smells she never could forget
Were plug tobacco, pigs, and sweat.
The fourth day, about half-past three,
A still enamoured Bill had brought her
Where a great field of timothy
Moved like a lake of purple water,
And round the margins of the field
The hawks in airy circles wheeled.
While drinking in that scene of charm,
He asked her how she liked the farm.
"I hate it, Bill!" she answered hotly,
Venting her words in sudden passion.
"A circus clown, in all his motley,
Would scorn to live here, farmer-fashion.
In heat and grime, from day to day,
Hard work brings just starvation pay.
Surely a fellow's nerve must crack
In toil that slowly crooks the back
And life so brutish and so mean
In rural slums, unkempt, unclean.
Come, leave this place while there is time!
You've brains and force enough to climb

Into big money, worth your while."
She ended with a hopeful smile.
Bill was dumbfounded; bitter, too;
And in his heart enraged clear through:
"This is my life," he answered slow.
"And of its value I am sure.
Cities and towns may come and go,
But still the country will endure.
The city wastes its folk at length;
It rots away their moral strength
With easy lives and dissipation
And would disintegrate the nation
Did not the virtues of the farm
Preserve the race from final harm.
Our life is hard, I will admit,
But dangers lie in living soft.
This farm world is no counterfeit,
At which you have so roundly scoffed.
You, if you like, can go your way;
But here I am and here I stay!"
And go she did, that very night,
In sulky, disconcerted flight.

IV

Sue, meanwhile, had full news of Nell,
For neighbours were alert to tell
All that each one had seen or heard
Of the fine-feathered city bird.
Thus, when a fortnight later Bill
Called Sue by 'phone to know if she
Would meet him on a nearby hill
Beneath an old, familiar tree
That night at seven, she made haste
And dosed her nails with scarlet paste
That she had got by mail to swell
Her chances to compete with Nell.
That night Bill viewed with sober eyes
And just a shade of glad surprise
The winsome, blue-eyed girl who waited
Upon the hillock he had stated.

But when he saw her nails were red,
He lost his temper. "Sue," he said,
"Don't use that red stuff, or, by heck,
I'll wring your silly little neck!"
Sue gave a sigh of pure relief
At that possessive declaration,
Yet staged a sudden show of grief
And simulated indignation:
"My nails are mine. What right have you
To tell me what I have to do?
If you are set on giving orders,
Just try it on your lady boarders!"
"The lady boarder's gone for keeps.
I don't mean maybe," answered he.
"I'm like a man who rashly sleeps,
And wakes to the reality.
For years and years, my heart's been true
To one girl only. Kiss me, Sue!"
So through the evening, side by side,
They sat there with their hearts at rest,
And watched the sunset spreading wide
Its glories in the flaming west.
Illimitable snowy clouds
Grew crimson with celestial fire
And faded into ghostly shrouds,
And still sweet mutual desire
Wove its enchantment round the pair
That side by side were sitting there.
The mighty sequence of the seasons
And ancient earth with all its power
Told to their hearts a thousand reasons
Why, in that tender, fleeting hour,
The rhythm of their human fate
Was blended with a vaster will
And plans immeasurably great
Included little Sue and Bill.
As universal as all space
Yet simple, was the faith they found:
It is the soil that makes the race,
And love that makes the world go round.

1940

THE CROW AND THE NIGHTHAWK

For any golfer of resource,
The most exhilarating course
I know of has been bedded down
Beside an old Ontario town.
Along the links, the player sees
A motley grove of ancient trees,
While near them, on ungodly ground,
An old distillery is found.
Back in the days when first I knew
The joys of stance and follow-through,
That course was crowded with delight
From summer dawn to summer night.
Players were many, but still more
Were all the wild birds, score on score,
Who thronged the grove and thronged
        the green
And every fairway in between.
Wherever sprinklers wet the ground,
The hungry robins marched around
And, with their black beaks making passes,
Dragged juicy worms from dewy grasses.
Yet some there were who said the birds
Were given to unkindly words,
For meadowlarks were far from nice
In jeering at each hook and slice,
And every golfer in the rough
Heard cheeky blackbirds give him guff.
Now two outstanding birds there were
To give the place strong character.
One was a crow, as tough and black
As any fierce demoniac
That ever haunted cave or tomb
With accents hoarse and face of doom.
The startled golfers, every one,
Knew him as "Satan," for his fun
Seemed based on murdering the neighbours
Amid their friendly sports and labours.
He seemed to think the raven race
Entitled, for its living space,

To all the world, and thought it good
To slay the feathered brotherhood.
And so his kids, the little yeggs,
Were fed on larks' and bluebirds' eggs;
And young song-sparrows, all alive,
He took to make his youngsters thrive.
The master-race of black-plumed devils
Thus loved to murder in their revels.
The other bird of whom I spoke
Was "Hank," the nighthawk, one whose joke
It was with swooping wings to zoom
Above us in the gathering gloom,
Intent to see our golf-balls roll
Through twilight to the eighteenth hole.
He was a harmless sort of critter
In handsome uniform of feathers,
Playful in pleasant times and bitter,
And cheerful in all sorts of weathers.
Yet he had thoughts too deep for words,
A loyalty beyond all proof—
It was a nest of baby birds
Upon the old distillery roof.

II

Now, in that summer I recall,
We saw a sort of madness fall
Upon all birds of every sort
In that green-carpeted resort.
The golfers were all heavy smokers
Of every brand of cigarette.
One day the sparrows—always jokers—
Picked up some butts, left burning yet.
The smoke inhaled was good, they found,
And so they passed the word around
Till every bird on every green
Was crazy over nicotine.
A butt was scarcely tossed away
Before some feathered scavenger
Had seized the treasure where it lay
And with his little wings a-whir

Flew with it to some branch, to sit
And puff the fag out, bit by bit.
Satan, of course, performed his share
In this new prank, so tough and rare,
Yet he had scorn for little pets
Who only took to cigarettes.
For he would choose, as regulars,
The solid butts of black cigars.
Hank liked the smaller, milder smoke,
But practised, as a kind of joke,
Dive-bombing with his fag, and roaming
With trailing sparks across the gloaming.

III

Satan grew tougher every day,
And once, when Hank was far away,
He sought the nighthawk's nest, to kill
The little nestlings, thus to fill
Himself and all his greedy brood
With raw, dismembered flesh for food.
The raid succeeded. Hank came back
Too late to stop the dark attack.
And when, with Mrs. Hank, he went
To call on Satan at his nest
In a tall pine-tree, there to vent
The anger of a heart distressed,
They found the crow, with happy croak,
Having an after-dinner smoke.
Making contemptuous grimaces,
He blew cigar-smoke in their faces.

IV

It was the first day of July
That saw this dirty deed of blood.
Homeward they turned, with many a sigh,
When Hank was startled by the thud
And loud report of fire-crackers
From crowds of gay, young bivouackers
Who sought with noise to celebrate
The happy birthday of their state.

His bright eyes flashed. He did not loiter,
But cruised about to reconnoitre;
Then hurtled down without a pause
And picked up in his bony claws
A lighted cracker, from whose fuse
The sparks were spitting to amuse
Small boys at play. Up soared the bird
One, two, three hundred feet, and heard
The boys and golfers roar surprise
At the strange sight before their eyes.
His ceiling reached, he turned to dive,
With sputtering bomb-load all alive:
Straight at the crow's nest and its crew,
Down, ever faster down, he flew,
And with a bang would fairly scare ye
Hit squarely on the target area,
While he, with skill of wing and eye,
Veered off in safety to the sky.
The bursting cracker filled the air
With croaks and corpses and despair.
Down from the pine we saw them go—
Scorched chunks of old and baby crow,
A rain of feathers, beaks and legs,
And wreckage of once rifled eggs.
Satan, too tough to blow apart,
Fell shrieking down, and with a start,
We saw the battered crow expire
Four minutes later, spitting fire.
Some folk who marked him as he fell
Proclaimed this as a sign of hell;
The truth is that the blitz's jar
Had made him gulp a lit cigar,
And then in anguish writhe and hop
With poisoned flames inside his crop,
Ending a life of utter sin
With fierce heart-burnings deep within.
Then peace returned to bless the earth,
A peace unknown since Satan's birth;
And every nest in bush and tree
Was blest with sweet serenity.
Appalled by Satan's end obscene,
The birds abjured all nicotine.

(No nestlings, since that awful death,
Complain about their parents' breath.)
Since then, through all the feathered nation,
The proudest theme of conversation
Is the stout nighthawk's swift reproof;
While on the old distillery roof
Successive broods of little Hanks
Rise up to give their father thanks.

1943

From MANITOBA LIMERICKS

There was a young man of Elm Creek,
Who kissed a fat hen on the beak;
    So she laid him an egg
    As she stood on one leg
And vainly endeavoured to speak.

There was a young lady of Gimli
Who sought to walk slender and slimly.
    She won her heart's wish
    On a diet of fish—
And the gravedigger smiled rather grimly.

There was a young man of High Bluff
Who cried out: "I'm tough, boys, I'm tough!"
    But his linings grew thin
    On a diet of gin;
Now he's pushing up daisies, and stuff.

There was a young fellow from Lundar
Who made a most exquisite blunder:
    When he once in the park
    Snatched a kiss in the dark,
'Twas his grandma in knickers, by thunder!

There was an old dame of Miami
Who said to her husband: "Now, damn 'ee!
    Ye've fleas like a dog
    And a kiss like a frog—
By the Lord, I've a notion to lam 'ee!"

There was an old person of Russell
Who battered his wife on the bustle.
  In a hospital cot
  He remarked: "I'll be shot
If I thought that our Jane had such muscle!"

A person in fair Sainte Agathe
Had features as sharp as a rat;
  His whiskers they matched,
  And his nose was all scratched
From fighting the family cat.

A young boxer out in Swan River
Tried courting his girl in a flivver;
  But she broke up a clinch
  That he thought was a cinch
With a wicked left hook to the liver.

There was a young girl of Waskada
Who only milked cows when they made her;
  Her spirits would fail
  At the sight of a pail—
Yes, her parents would cheerfully trade her.

There was an old person of Winkler
Who washed all his kids with a sprinkler.
  He summoned his frau
  With the bell from a cow;
How she ran when he tinkled that tinkler!

An old man in Winnipegosis
Had a son with pronounced halitosis.
  He remarked with a sigh
  As he mixed up some lye:
"Well, I'm glad that I know what the dose is!"

A kindly old person of Zant
Gave a couple of crumbs to an ant;
  Then patting the head
  Of the creature he'd fed,
He bemoaned that the meal was so scant.

1933

There was an old dame from Regina
Who asked for some fruit in the diner;
    When they told her that Bennett
    Had tariffs agen it,
Ten constables couldn't confine her.

A giddy young girl of Govan
Gave her sweetie a kiss, and then ran;
    He caught her (not coldly),
    And married her boldly,
And that's how the trouble began.

There was an old person of Kelliher
Whose barnyard grew smellier and smellier;
    But he sang, full of glee:
    " 'Tis our North, strong and free!"—
Which enraged all the folks around Kelliher.

A kindly old person of Morse
Gave a bucket of beer to his horse;
    But the nag, getting frisky,
    Then whinnied for whiskey,
And tried to secure it by force.

There was a young bridegroom of Young
Who swore by the gods he'd been stung:
    "Sure I thought at the start
    She was all eyes and heart,
But I find that she's three-quarters tongue!"

1933

ODE ON THE DEATH OF MARSHAL JOSEPH PILSUDSKI

I

Out from the mighty town
That once his valour saved,
No smile or shadowing frown
On his pale face engraved,

Surrounded by a nation's grief and pride
The mighty Marshal goes on his last ride.
Son of the silent North,
He now goes south to sleep
In timeless peace henceforth
With the great dead who keep
Their vigil upon Cracow's storied steep.
Across the Polish plain
He rides a road of steel,
And myriad thousands kneel,
With myriad flaring death-fires in the grass
And myriad mournful torches in the rain,
At every league to see their Leader pass
And moan the pain they feel
That he they greet, that way, alas,
Will ride no more again.

II

O Pantheon of Poland, ancient fane
On Wawel's Gothic height,
Enlarge thyself this night
To house the holy dust of one who brings
To thy still reign
More grandeur than the mightiest of thy kings!
Now let Sobieski and great Stanislaus
Acclaim the cause
That straitens the dim cloisters where they lie;
Now let Slowacki and Mickiewicz speak
Their sorrowing pride in him
Who joins their company;
And let Kosciuszko's long since faded cheek
Flush at this meeting with his mighty peer!
About Pilsudski's bier
Cluster the noble ghosts
Of all the vanish'd hosts,
Statesmen and heroes, warriors and bards,
Whose bones Religion guards
Within this sacred place;
And living thousands in mute sorrow walk
By that dark catafalque
Where lies the lordliest patriot of their race.

[171]

Slowly the bell is toll'd,
Softly the censers sway,
Silence and grief enfold
The kneeling multitude while bishops pray
For that great spirit who for years controll'd
Poland's high destiny in peace and in the fray.
Hark, 'tis the Church's voice
Hailing her rebel son,
First by a nation's choice
Of those whose hand has won
Freedom for martyr'd millions upon Earth.
Some have been born in ancient liberty
And kept it well;
Others have fought like gods to make men free,
Yet fruitless fell;
But this man brought to birth
Out of the prison-grief of hopeless years,
Out of the bloody travail-pangs of war,
A nation to outsoar
The proudest vauntings of an earlier age,
A Poland meet to mingle with her peers
On history's stage.
Who then is this, a land unites to own?
A man of granite he, a corner-stone
Quarried by pain from Vilna's valiant stock.
A living rock
On which succeeding centuries may plant
A state of adamant.
No cold self-seeker, he was all a-thirst
In freedom's cause his heart's best blood to give,
One who in all things placed his country first,
Ready to die that Poland's self might live!
Whether in war his legions held in check
The fierce Red Hordes that beat at Warsaw's gate,
Whether in peace he wrung dissension's neck
Nor left embrawl'd assemblies to their fate,
He claim'd for Poland, amid time's caprice,
That he who gave her birth must give her peace,
Regardless of men's blows and frenzied blame
If, by his act, he saved his country's name.

IV

Then give this man sepulture with the dead
Who sleep in honour upon Wawel's crest;
Hew tributes out of marble to the best
Of all whose blood for Poland has been shed,
Even this uncrown'd king, who sought instead
Of sceptred pomp, a citizen's behest,
And now at last, when he must take his rest,
Finds a whole nation sorrowing by his bed.
And though their deep affection should upraise
A funerary mound of earth as high
As Cheops' rocky tomb, and mark his praise
With solemn summit pointing to the sky,
Nothing could match its timeless counterpart—
Its vast, unmarr'd memorial in the Polish heart.

PILSUDSKI'S HEART

I

His body lies in Cracow, where the voices
Of holy bells ring out their benediction
Over the arm that ruled, the hand that wrought;
And patriots come, remembering old affliction,
And standing pensive there in grateful thought
Mingle a mood that sorrows and rejoices
Beside the stately crypt that hides his glory.
Around him sleep the bones of kings and queens
And all the lordly great of Poland's story,
There in the vast Cathedral's grave demesnes.
Noble as any Pharoah lies he thus,
Lapped in the solemn peace of his sarcophagus.

II

Ay, but his heart was fond of simpler things.
Pomp he despised, and though he lent at death
His body to that burial-place of kings,
He gave commandment with his ebbing breath

That men should lodge his heart in simple earth,
Deep in the native soil he lived to free,
And laid in filial humility
Low at the buried feet of her that gave him birth.

III

Thus has that loyal heart come home to rest,
Home from the strife, the shattering of nations,
Prison, and palace, and men's acclamations,
To pledge the dearest homage of his breast
To her he loved the best;
And she will sleep content to know him safe at last,
Safe in the Polish earth she also loved,
Safest of all because his manhood proved
Supreme devotion to the Polish past.
This was the faith she taught his boyish heart;
And lo, that faith returns in love and trust,
For, having played the nation-builder's part,
He asks naught else, to make his grace complete,
But to sleep here, and at her holy feet
Moulder to Polish dust.

DRAŽA DIES A MARTYR
("Facit indignatio versus")

The cheeks of every honest man
    Are wet with tears today;
And everyone, at murder done,
    For justice kneels to pray.

The evil deed that Tito did
    Smells foul to honest men;
The world will weep at Draža's death
    Till freedom comes again.

Tito a triple traitor was,
    A life-long cheat and knave,
Who sought through Russian tyranny
    To make his land a slave.

While Stalin kissed with Hitler,
    Tito kissed Hitler too,
And blessed the bloody Nazi band
That raped and sacked his native land.
The Serbs and Draža made a stand
    But Tito was untrue.

And when the Russians joined the war
    And Tito turned to kill,
He fought not for his countryfolk
    But fought for Stalin still.

When Draža won a victory,
    Black Tito claimed the credit.
A radio on Russian soil
    In noisy clamour said it.

In vicious folly the Allies
    Then bowed to Stalin's orders,
And gave to Tito countless guns
To join the fight on Hitler's Huns;
But Tito murdered Serbia's sons,
    Who guarded Serbia's borders.

Cold Stalin's orders must be served;
    The Serbs must not be free:
Convicted by a mighty lie,
Draža Mihailovich must die
    Who stands for liberty.

Five hundred Yankee airmen
    Give Tito back the lie;
They know the truth of Draža
    Whom Tito dooms to die.

But Tito will not hear them speak;
    Foul murder is his aim;
Three of his bloody generals
    Conclude a court of shame.

And as the summer sunshine dawns
    Upon white Belgrade town,
The guns of murdering Communists
    Shoot noble Draža down.

At last the Yanks and English see
    No deed is on the level
That sells the saints and heroes out
    To please a bloody devil.

The lying clamours of their press
    And radio have ceased,
And men and nations now begin
To see the folly and the sin
Of hoping by foul means to win
    The friendship of a beast.

Pale Churchill gnaws his black cigar
    To hear of Draža's doom;
The haggard ghost of Roosevelt
    Is restless in the tomb;

But in the reeking Kremlin
    Where bloody Stalin stands,
The tyrant laughs in bloody glee
And cringing servants shrink to see
    Fresh blood upon his hands.

But all shall speak of Draža,
    And all shall tell his worth,
Long after bloody autocrats
    Have vanished from the earth.

For through all lands and nations
    His name shall glorious be
When, to the comfort of all souls,
Serbs, Balts, Ukrainians and Poles—
    And Russians—shall be free.

Then let us pray for Draža,
    That he with God may dwell,
His tortures done, his warfare o'er,
Among the saints for evermore,
    While Tito rots in hell.

1946

THE FLYING BULL AND OTHER TALES

THE DROVER'S TALE OF THE FLYING BULL

Caught by the blizzard, as it fell,
In that old Manitou hotel,
We sat and smoked around the fire,
Watching the birch-wood flames leap higher,
And told tall yarns to while away
The dull, interminable day.
We were a miscellaneous lot
Who thronged that parlour, wide and warm,
And deemed the place a pleasant spot
On such a stressful day of storm,
When all the roads were drifted high
And even trains had ceased to ply.
We were a dozen at the least:
A cattle drover, and a priest,
Two farmers, and a country teacher,
A Lutheran Icelandic preacher,
The driver of the Grey Goose bus
(Whose stoppage caused uncommon fuss),
Two Mounties (both extremely tall,
A Sergeant and a Corporal),
A wholesale "drummer," pale and wan,
And I, a bashful college don.
Still others drifted in and out
From the small village round about,
For work that day was standing still
And they, like us, had time to kill.
There was a merchant, sleek and fat,
Likewise a lawyer, thin and seedy,
A doctor with a red cravat,
A clerk whose voice was high and reedy;
A butcher reared on brewers' nectar,
And a lean, wrinkled school-inspector,
While keeping all our talk in motion
With breezy jest and fertile notion
Was the hotel-man, Michael Casey,
A big, stout fellow, free and racy,

Whose native Irish *savoir faire*
Had freshened in our Western air
Into a bluff and hearty way
That made his guests delight to stay.
   He and the drover had been cronies
For many a year in Winnipeg;
Together they had played the ponies;
Each loved to pull the other's leg;
And each in his own virile fashion
Could tell a tale of manly passion.
So, as with breakfast done we sat
About the fire in quiet chat,
He hailed the drover with conviction
And tried to stir him up to fiction:
"Patrick," he said, "you're much the least
Of all men living given to lying.
Tell us the truth about yon beast,
The Angus bull that took to flying!"
   The drover dusted off his vest,
And spat, and gave his pipe a pull,
And then began with quiet zest
His story of the Angus bull:

I

"The toughest bull I ever saw
Was on a farm near Neepawa,
Where an old cowhand, Dave MacMeans,
Kept a big herd of Aberdeens.
Dave was a rough and wrinkled Scot,
With bulbous nose and sunset whiskers;
He liked his whiskey neat and hot—
When young he'd frisked among the friskers.
And sixty years had left him cursed
With stomach ulcers and a thirst.
Two things he'd loved in life's long battle:
Theology and Angus cattle.
And while the Calvinist in him
Waxed fervent on predestination,
He'd argue long with equal vim
That black bulls were the farm's salvation.

"The pride of his own dusky herd
Was 'Mumbo-Jumbo,' bull supreme—
The biggest, grimmest, blackest-furred
Of all the brutes of Pharaoh's dream.
He was as black as Satan's dam,
And nigh as tall as Pilot Mound;
The rumblings of his diaphragm
Made thunder thirty miles around;
His ribs were like a Roman arch;
His back was level as the prairie;
His massive legs in stately march
Made a small earthquake through
        the dairy;
But of his eyes no words can tell—
Within them glowed the fires of hell,
Two lamps of livid yellow, lit
With anger from the nether Pit.
His cows had always found him kind,
But hatred smouldered in his mind
For all our human jacks and queens
Except his master, Dave MacMeans.
Yes, Dave he loved, beyond a doubt,
For the old sanctimonious sinner
Would often give his mammoth snout
A snort of whiskey after dinner;
And so a spirituous bond
Kept beast and man uncommon fond.
    "Now in the spring of '35
David was gathered to his fathers.
On Sunday he had been alive;
On Monday, fierce internal pothers
Brought on that final, fatal quiver
That ends cirrhosis of the liver;
And so by Wednesday night he lay
Dead sober in the graveyard clay.
    "Then distant heirs and lawyers, dark as
The vultures at Gehenna's gate,
Came flocking in to share the carcass
Of Dave's unfortunate estate.
Farming they held in cold derision;
So, to facilitate division

[179]

And settle up with one clean slash,
They auctioned everything for cash.
One August morning, hot and clear,
A leather-larynx'd auctioneer
Stood in Dave's farmyard on a table,
Half-way between the house and stable;
And there, amid a throng of buyers,
He bawled the merits of each chattel,
From combines down to common pliers,
And last, not least, Dave's Angus cattle.
The cows and calves were sold with ease
In tempting lots of twos and threes.
('Twas known to every farmer there
How often, at the Winter Fair,
Dave's feeders carried off the Cup,
And with what golden-handed itch
The abattoirs had snapped them up
To grace the banquets of the rich.)
But offers were not plentiful
For Dave's notorious black bull,
Whose most unmitigated choler
Was reckoned dear at half a dollar.
In vain the auctioneer avowed
That any farmer might be proud
To own so vast a thoroughbred,
Most famous in his progeny—
For looking in his eye with dread
Each vowed he'd let the monster be.
Just when it seemed the day would end
Without a bid for the old devil,
One quiet voice agreed to spend
A hundred dollars, on the level.
And thus was sold the brute unruly
To Deacon Williams of Plum Coulee,
A man as good as he was strong
And pious as the day is long.
But when at last each buyer sought
To drive away what he had bought,
A streak of dark satanic strife
In Mumbo-Jumbo came to life.

Perchance he blamed on all these men
The loss of his beloved master.
Perhaps there came into his ken
Some dim foreboding of disaster,
Or some distaste for dreary travel
By prairie trail or highway gravel,
Far from familiar scenes to stay,
Southeast, a hundred miles away.
Whatever maggot in the brain
Stirred him to frenzies of disdain,
He pawed the ground, he snorted fire,
And one could see him in his ire
Fiercely and visibly determine
To rid the farm of human vermin.
Straight at the human throng he charged,
Straight at these puny things of shame;
And frantic lanes of fear enlarged
To leave him passage as he came.
Over the fences did they leap
Grasshopper-like by tens and scores;
Shunning the bull's terrific sweep,
Awed by the bull's appalling roars.
Against such cars as had been left
Within the yard he turned his spite,
Venting on them his two-ton heft,
A thunderbolt of Hate and Night.
A dozen Fords were overturned;
He tore the fenders off ten Nashes;
Sparks from his onset lit and burned
A score of Pontiacs to ashes.
When nightfall closed the day's wild session,
It found the bull in full possession.
   "But hours later, far from thence,
Good Deacon Williams, sad but trusting,
Invoked the aid of Providence
To give the Devil's bull a dusting:
'Humble his spirit to the earth!
Give me my hundred dollars worth!'
Then with an 'Amen' loud and deep,
In simple faith he turned to sleep.

"After a night of breathless heat,
There dawned the hottest day that any
Had ever known. Rays seemed to beat
As from a vaster sun; and many
Thought of that final Day of Ire
When all should be destroyed by fire.
The leaves and grasses quickly wilted;
Cracks opened in the baking soil;
On homes that slowly warped and tilted,
The blistering paint began to boil.
Men took to drinking by the keg;
Dumb beasts cried out with moan and mutter;
And thirst-crazed dogs in Winnipeg
Drank melted asphalt from the gutter.
Small wonder was it no one went
On such a day to Dave's old farm
To see the bull's dark discontent
Or seek his frenzy to disarm.
Parched but triumphant, hour by hour,
He stood there in insensate power.
Alone, unchallenged, black as ink,
He scorned to bellow for a drink.

"Two hours past the gasping noon,
A dark cloud rose to west-northwest—
Slowly above a world a-swoon
It reared with thunder in its breast,
A roaring, swirling, cloudy funnel,
Black as the entrails of a tunnel.
But though the 'twister' nearer swept,
The Angus bull remained defiant;
Dauntless he stood to intercept
The black, intruding, cloudy Giant.
But all in vain: its mighty force,
Seizing him swiftly from the ground,
Propelled him on a skyward course,—
A heavenly bull, southeastward-bound.
And with him went the shattered hulk
Of Dave's best barn, and sped from sight
Revolving round his darker bulk
Like some infernal satellite.

"An hour later by the clock,
The storm near Deacon Williams' passed,
So close to all his barns and stock
That the good brother stared aghast.
Then 'mid the tumult of the storm
He saw a black, Satanic form
Swoop down, as though on hidden wings,
And light upon the prairie clay,
While with diminished thunderings
The great tornado ebbed away.
    "Not fifty yards from Williams' door
There lay a miry open slough.
From it now came a mighty roar.
Out rushed the Deacon, swift to view;
And there, by heck, stood Mumbo-Jumbo,
Up to his belly in the gumbo,
By 'act of God' delivered duly
To his new owner in Plum Coulee.
    "What thoughts had thronged his heavy mind
During that epoch-making flight
No one can tell; but I'm inclined
To think he got a thorough fright.
For all the rest of his black life
He was most mild—most timid, maybe—
And often Deacon Williams' wife
Would leave that bull to mind the baby."

THE CLERK'S TALE OF USQUEDUNK, THE FROG-KING

Prologue

"That was a bull," the clerk admitted,
And mused in silence for a space.
"It seems he met with taming fitted
For one of his infernal race.
He brings to mind an old tradition
Told me by Indians, as a child,
About a frog, whose disposition,
Though usually very mild,
Once woke to rage as fierce and full
As would do credit to your bull.
The Netley Marshes were his dwelling,
And there he fought a giant pike.

[*183*]

It is a yarn that's worth the telling:
I'll give the story, if you like."
Around the room entreaties ran,
And so the little clerk began:

I

"Eight miles due north of Selkirk town,
Great marshes slow the river down
And almost lose its turbid tide
In mazes where its waters glide—
A labyrinth of lakes and channels
And reedy fens and bogs spread forth,
Formed through long geographic annals
By the Red River of the North,
Across whose delta reeds and logs
Now shield a teeming world of life,
Insects and birds and fish and frogs,
In Earth's eternal ways of strife.
　"Here in the summer twilight rises,
Out of ten million lurking-places,
A living mist that agonizes
Throughout the endless marshy spaces,
Mosquito-hosts that surge and swell
Like choking gases breathed from hell,
An ambient element of voices,
Thin, piercing, and incessant wails—
The song of hatred that rejoices,
The cry of wrath that never fails,
Relentless disembodied tides
That beat against all living things
Like myriad ghosts of parricides,
Fierce vapours formed of unseen wings:
And ever and anon the swarm,
Emerging to material form,
Condenses, as to hellish rain,
In tiny poisoned points of pain.
Yet high above that insect chorus
An utterance more loud, sonorous,

Comes fluting in melodious notes
Out of a million velvet throats,
The descant of the frogs that tread
The marshy delta of the Red.
"The Master Minstrel of them all
Was Usquedunk, a mighty frog
Whose basso chant at evenfall
Outdid all others in the bog.
Yes, Nature could not boast his fellow,
He was so huge and stout of limb,
And in his hue so bright a yellow
That gold could not compare with him.
His yellow face was mild and placid,
The spots upon his massive back
Might have been etched with nitric acid
Upon a king's memorial plaque.
His thighs were thick and lithe and long,
His toes were tough, his muscles strong;
Yet this gigantic, yellow frog
Was gentle as a pollywog,
For all life's highest joy he found
In ceaseless harmonies of sound,
As if all values life could quote
Were gargled in his golden throat.
A bullfrog, in the sign of Taurus,
He deemed it his supreme delight
To lead the wide batrachian chorus
In dulcet flutings to the night.
Loud in the evening there arose
His trills and his arpeggios;
Sometimes he boomed a deep staccato,
A sort of vast and virile shout,
And sometimes sang an obligato
That almost drowned all others out.
True candour would admit, perforce,
His voice was very harsh and hoarse,
And yet it was so deep and loud
That every frog for miles was proud
To hear him every time he spoke
And hail him Emperor of Croak.

"For years he reigned without dispute
Among the marshes of the Red;
Mudhen and bullfrog, fish and newt,
Acclaimed him as their chosen head;
And every night his ringing voice
Made all the marshy host rejoice.
Only one vicious, wall-eyed pike
Conceived a venomous dislike
For Usquedunk, and vowed, the sinner,
To have the mighty frog for dinner.
    "One August morning, Usquedunk
Sat calmly on a hemlock trunk,
His favourite throne, beside a pool,
And put his royal brains to school
In fashioning new orchestration
For the sweet-voiced batrachian nation.
Thus waiting for the tune to hatch,
He sat there like a lifeless hummock,
And only stirred at times to scratch
A few mosquitoes off his stomach.
Low in the pool the pike lay hid,
Gauging the distance up the log
To Usquedunk; then nearer slid,
And made a lunge to seize the frog—
But just in time, a flash of grey
Showed the assassin to his prey.
The bullfrog did a high jump,
        standing,
Giving it all the strength he had,
And made a perfect five-point landing
Upon a nearby lily-pad;
And though his sudden massive weight
Half-sank the leaf and bent it badly,
It still bore up its yellow freight
And saved the vocal monarch gladly.
Alas, the pike, beneath the scene,
Marking the pad's frog-heavy hump,
Rose like a finny submarine
And nipped a morsel off his rump.

The bullfrog gave a roar of pain,
And vaulted to his log again.

III

"Each nature has its own reaction.
One might have looked for such as he
To seek melodious distraction
In strains of plaintive elegy,
Lamenting, like a flower in frost,
The tail-piece that he'd loved and lost.
But sudden anger, hot and harsh,
Gripped the great frog of Netley Marsh
And galvanized his mighty frame
Into a leaping yellow flame.
What right had any voiceless fish,
A mute, malicious, mud-brained pike,
To seek to make a breakfast dish
Of him, the Monarch? Thus to strike
Out of the depths without a warning
On such a perfect August morning?
His bosom heaved. His eyes turned black.
He tensed his muscles for attack.
Then like an arrow from a bow
He drove and swam to find his foe,
Who, unsuspecting such intent,
Was idling, slow and insolent.
Three times around the startled fish
A yellow vortex madly raced,—
A streak of frenzied frog a-swish,
A meteor of hate and haste.
Then, with a lamprey's grip, he seized
The breast-fins with his angry jaws;
His front feet round the fins were squeezed;
While farther back his hind-foot claws,
Worked by the pistons of his hips,
Tore the soft belly into strips.
In vain the pike in anguish churned
The water in a burst of power;
In vain in mighty curves he turned
In spurts of eighty miles an hour;

[*187*]

The yellow bullfrog kept his hold
With jaws and hands, and still he tore
The pike's flesh with his toes of gold
And dyed the marshes with his gore,
Until at length, eviscerated
From stem to stern by such attack,
The carcass of the foe he hated
Lay floating lifeless on its back;
And with disdainful strokes the frog
Swam proudly to his hemlock log.
Then the great Monarch, Usquedunk,
Sat long in fervent meditation
Upon that high, familiar trunk,
Upon his simmering jubilation
Boiled over in triumphant song
Proclaimed in accents hoarse and strong.
'I've won!' he croaked. 'My foe is sunk!
I've won! I've won! The pike is junk!
So perish all who steal a chunk
From off the rump of Usquedunk!
Chunk o'rump, chunk o'rump, chunk o'rump!"

THE DOCTOR'S TALE OF THE CAPTAIN'S CAT

Prologue

Our host threw on another log;
Sparks from the hearth in crackling higher
Roused the young doctor's spotted dog
That dozed beside him near the fire.
"Down, Marmaduke!" the young man said.
"That's a grand name," said Casey, smiling.
"I took it from a cat now dead,"
Replied the youth, "and if beguiling
The hours with most surprising tales
Of bulls and bears and moose and whales
Beside the hearth is your design,
Perhaps you'll lend an ear to mine—
The wildest, weirdest yarn, I'd say,
That ever came from Hudson Bay,
Although no region on this earth
Brings more uncanny tales to birth."

"Tell us your tale," we urged in chorus.
"Tell us," the drover cried, and spat.
And so the doctor laid before us
His story of the Captain's cat:

I

"Vaster than Caspian or Black,
Bering or Red or Caribbean,
Or where Okhotsk with storm-lashed back
Chafes at its barriers cyclopean,
Hemm'd by our shores there stretches forth
That *mare nostrum* of the North,
Mediterranean but cold,
Which Manitoba's coasts enfold
And bleak Ungava, white with snow,
And tundras of Ontario,
While to the north its path is spanned
By glacier-fjords of Baffin Land—
A wan and eerie inland ocean
Of which the world has little notion,
Leaving to tracts thus far asunder
Its width and wealth and wizard wonder.
Perhaps a century may come
When many a proud emporium
By Churchill, Nelson, Fish and Moose
Shall garner for Canadian use
The sea-borne riches of the world
Beneath Auroral Flags unfurled,
While coastal cities glitter bright
Far through the chill subarctic night;
Yet even now the great ships ply
Old Hudson's waters without fear,
Braving the grey subarctic sky
To bring Old Europe yet more near
By straits where in the Vikings' day
The gulf of primal chaos lay.
On such a steamship once I went,
A student with a load of steers,
To seek that far-off Continent—
A job Canadians of my years

By thousands gaily undertake
For fun and the adventure's sake.
The fun is always problematic.
It may be rough. And who would care
To be nurse-maid acrobatic
To cattle down with *mal de mer?*
But we were lucky. Not a breeze
Troubled a sky serene and cool
Across three thousand miles of seas
From Churchill clear to Liverpool.
But memory's pangs will never lack
The luck that struck us coming back.
Yes, for a time, it seemed that Hell
Was playing funeral odes in 'Largo'
For all aboard the *Nancy Belle*
And all the cook-stoves of her cargo.
But first of all I must rehearse
How we incurred a sort of curse.

II

"The captain of our sooty craft
Was Jock McBride, a Glasgow skipper,
A dour old man, a trifle daft,
But strict as Pole-star to the Dipper
In all the rules of navigation
That did not need imagination.
No wife had this dull autocrat;
The only living thing he cared for
Was his black-pelted, one-eyed cat,
A beast that pillows were prepared for
And extra mice in cages kept
In quarters where the Captain slept.
I am not squeamish in my ways,
And yet in all my living days
I never felt so strange a quiver
As when that tom-cat gorged on liver;
For he would toss it up and grab it
The way a lynx might rend a rabbit,
And gnaw off chunks and gulp them down
With throaty snarl and evil frown.

Even a vampire might rebuke
The horrid greed of 'Marmaduke'.
   "With such a cat and such a captain,
We started back from Liverpool—
Two thousand heavy cook-stoves clapped in
Our vessel's hold. The days were cool,
Even for August, but the sea
Was bright and calm as it could be.
Westbound, we'd passed through Hudson
        Strait;
Our longitude was eighty-four;
And Cape Southampton stretched in state
To starboard from Coats Island shore;
When suddenly a school of whales
Appeared beside our vessel's rails—
Not the big sperm or cachalot,
But gentle beasts, three fathoms long,
That often haunt that lonely spot,
A kindly, almost human throng,
Suckling their babies in the deep
Or drowsing on the waves asleep.
We slackened speed to watch the sight;
The cat sat on the Captain's shoulder;
I swear his one eye grew more bright
And his rapacious gaze still bolder
Just where a baby whale at rest
Was nuzzling at its mother's breast.
Black Marmaduke let out a mew
Into the Captain's shrivelled ear.
'Eh?' says McBride, 'What's that to you?
You'd like some liver? Ay, that's clear.
I'll not deny you such a trifle.'
And getting out his heavy rifle,
He shot the whale-calf as it suckled,
Then brought the little corpse on board,
And as he ripped it up he chuckled,
Finding fresh liver for the adored
Black-whiskered fiend, old Marmaduke,
By such an unexpected fluke.
But all the crew were not content
To share the Captain's merriment.

The purser was part Eskimo,
Versed in their lore of long ago,
And in a panic he made free
To tell McBride calamity
Would put us all past human aid
Unless atonement should be made.
McBride was wild: 'You silly fool,
I'll put you in the clink to cool
If there is any more such talk.
Off to your bunk, you rascal! Walk!'
And then he turned without a quiver
To stuffing Marmaduke with liver.

III

"The baby whale was killed at noon;
All other whales then disappeared;
But on the far horizon soon
To westward rose low clouds that reared
The promise of a bitter gale,
And each was fashioned like a whale—
A phantom whale of wind-blown mist
That towered high with rage, and hissed,
And darkened towards catastrophe
The grey abyss of sky and sea.
'The curse has come,' the purser said;
'In half an hour we'll all be dead!'
And certainly I never saw
Death open half so dark a maw.
Like some black chamber of the deep,
Where two miles down old galleons sleep,
Became that Arctic waste of waters
Through which we ploughed—some pit of slaughters
In which doomed victims gasped for breath
Under the strangling hands of Death.
Then almost as the purser spoke
The swift, tempestuous tumult broke,
And with abrupt, appalling din
A noon-day night rushed roaring in.
Over our reeling bulwarks swept
A frenzied drift of seething foam;

The steamship staggered, swayed, and leapt,
Heading defiantly for home.
But ever slower grew her thrusts
Against the sea's tremendous blows;
Ever more feebly she arose
To face the breakers and the gusts
That wrestled with her horribly
Like some relentless enemy.
Over her decks from stem to stern
A ridge of hissing whiteness poured;
Laden with wreckage did it churn,
And all our boats went overboard.
With bulwarks smashed and flooded deck,
The *Nancy Belle* was half a wreck,
Driving the Captain to conform
And make atonement to the storm.
Out of the pilot-house he stepped,
And with a curse that almost wept,
He took his tom-cat by the tail
And heaved him headlong to the gale.
Like some be-whiskered meteor
Or old King Arthur's hurtling sword,
Shot Marmaduke, and yet he wore
A grin that curdled all on board,
And purred so loud that we could hear it
Above the storm's indignant spirit.
Then out of seas like boiling milk
Rose a black whale and gulped him down,
As if determined thus to bilk
The waves that merely sought to drown.
The tempest ceased. The only stir
Was just a low, Satanic purr,
Deep in the waves, that slowly died
Beneath the fast subsiding tide.

IV

"Three mornings later, just at dawn,
We glimpsed the Manitoba coast
Far to the west. The storm had gone
With Marmaduke, but, like a ghost,

[193]

Hour after hour, old Jock McBride
Kept gaping from the vessel's side,
Leaving the first and second mate
To mend the steamer's battered state
And steer her on towards Button Bay,
Cape Mercy, and the rocky, grey
Old point where once Fort Prince of Wales
Stood guard above white British sails.
Gone was his wrath; his confidence
Had shattered in an hour intense;
And when we reached the Churchill quay
He solemnly abjured the sea.
  "He lives not far from Brandon now
With twenty acres and a cow,
Also a wife, and she has brought him
A son, John Solomon, and taught him,
Against his fuddled will, the way
To be a father day by day.
Yet sometimes, by a wayward fluke,
He calls his offspring 'Marmaduke,'
And even, with defiant shiver,
Stuffs the poor youngster full of liver."

THE MERCHANT'S TALE OF THE TRAPPER AND THE BEARS

Prologue

Outside the window howled the storm,
And made the room seem yet more warm.
Then said the drummer: "Days like these
Would make the bears and bison freeze.
Sometimes I think it would be best
To let the Red Man keep the West."
The merchant boomed expostulation:
"This weather is not cold," he said.
"Such climate makes a hardy nation.
Rough weather breeds the thoroughbred.
But I have known such cold as makes
This winter, in comparison,
Seem like a summer at the lakes,
A picnic day for everyone."

Expectant silence greeted this.
"Listen," he cried. "My tale is truth."
And so he told with emphasis
A trapping story of his youth:

I

"The coldest day I ever knew
Was New Year's, back in '22,
Out in the bush near Kapuskasing,
Where, as a trapper, I was facing
The grimmest prospect I had known
Since first I started on my own.
I had no money, to begin with,
And just the clothes upon my back,
Guns, traps, an axe, a knife to skin with,
Four snarling huskies, and a shack.
The spot I'd chosen was the worst
From Porquis Junction west to Hearst—
At least it seemed that way to me
As rations gave out steadily
And in my traps I failed to find
Much paying fur of any kind.
To make things worse, it was my dream
To get some cash, to cease to roam,
To form a matrimonial team,
And have some kids and rear a home,
Back in some thriving little town;
For I was keen to settle down.
    "Christmas brought neither cheer nor smiles—
The dogs and I were facing hunger
Unless I trekked in thirty miles,
To beg some food. When one is younger,
So piteous a case no doubt
Can blot the sun completely out,
And so, for four days I debated
This course of action that I hated.
    "Next morning, I was just departing
When heavy weather checked my starting.
The day began with flakes of snow
That fell in droves by half past seven,

Flooding a silent world below
Out of a dark and windless heaven.
They fluttered down, a flood of fleece,
Filling the morning sky completer
Than if ten billion big white geese
Were being plucked by old Saint Peter—
Thus sending, from the sky's high crown,
An avalanche of eiderdown
That soon had mounted, heap on heap,
To a white blanket, four feet deep,
And bent the branches of the spruce
Until it almost snapped them loose.
Towards evening, snowfall slackened off,
But a wild gale then smote the cabin
With shriek and sob and wail and cough
And through each cranny seemed to stab in
With icy daggers of derision,
While through the window-pane my vision
Saw in a maddened maelstrom go
A streaming flux of blinding snow
Torn from the spruce-trees' tossing boughs
And from the ground. In wild carouse,
Earth seemed to shatter, fuse, and fade,
And in white frenzy to disperse,
As if some cosmic Hand had made
A milk-shake of the universe.

II

"For six and thirty hours the wind
Raged madly on, and kept me pinned
There in my cabin, where my cupboard,
Like that of well-known Mrs. Hubbard,
Was grimly scant of food to feed
Me and my huskies in our need.
So, when the third day dawned at last
And all the storm was plainly past,
I went outside to find my sled
And mush to town to get some bread.
My little shack was almost hid
Under a mighty drift of white;

Smoke from my chimney upward slid
High in the frosty morning light,
A slender column, pale and wan,
Athwart the sundogs of the dawn;
But I had little time to gaze
On winter's strange and eerie ways.
Giving each husky as a treat
A cast-off moccasin to eat,
I chewed in haste my last cold bannock,
And, with a certain sense of panic,
I started in a hurry, tracing
The shortest trail to Kapuskasing.
  "A frozen creek off Woman River
Was windswept clear of all its snow.
My lead-dog here stopped, all a-quiver,
And when I tried to make him go,
He scratched the ice and gave a bark
That sounded like a curt remark.
I came to look. The little creek
Had frozen solid in its bed,
And in the ice, not far to seek,
Were six fresh pickerel, frozen dead.
Thus I had chopped, five minutes later,
From this first-class refrigerator,
A savoury dinner for my dogs
And for myself. I split some logs,
Built up a fire and fried a fish
Finer than any king could wish.
But the delay and bitter frost
Persuaded me to stop and camp,
Counting the time as safely lost
In such a long, exhausting tramp.
And so, with sleep my chief desire,
I lay down near the blazing fire.

III

"When I awoke, my dogs had vanished,
Leaving no trace that I could see
Beyond the heaving drifts that banished
All thought of stalking them for me.

[197]

The fire was out, and nature dealt
Such cold as I have never felt
In all my life, before or since:
It made my aching eyeballs wince,
And seared my anguished lungs and throat
As if some hidden fire smote
My tissues, mingled in my breath,
And doomed me to a gasping death.
My brows and lashes slowly froze,
My cheeks felt cut in tingling strips,
And the slow trickle from my nose
Formed icicles along my lips.
Yet in a crisis so terrific
My first desire was scientific,
An urgent impulse to be sure
About the present temperature.
I should have told you, in digression,
How, as a highly prized possession,
I took with me where'er I went
A very handy instrument—
A Fahrenheit thermometer,
To which I daily would refer.
Nor would I leave it at my shack,
For fear, before I happened back,
Some thirsty, wandering Cree would call
And drain it of its alcohol.
So, now, I quickly got it out,
And looked, and looked—and tried to doubt
My eyes' own evidence, but no!—
It stood at ninety-eight below.
    "I tried to start a fire, but found
My hands too numb to light a match;
And not an ember on the ground
Remained, on kindling wood to catch.
I shouted for my dogs. Amazed,
I heard no sound of my own voice.
My shouts were mute; and standing dazed,
I felt my one remaining choice
Was to keep moving down the trail
To town before my strength should fail.

"I had not gone five hundred feet
Before the cold began to get me.
I could not push on nor retreat:
My faltering snowshoes would not let me.
But just when hope was almost gone
I saw a wisp of breath-steam flow
Out of a fissure in the snow
Where a deep drift had formed upon
A cliff-base that in summer gave
Low access to a shallow cave.
Slipping my snowshoes off, I used them
As frantic implements to dig;
And with a vigour that abused them,
I reached the cave. It was not big,
But body-warmth was waiting there
To save me in my chill despair,
For two fat black bears in a heap
Were gently snoring in their sleep.
They were too drowsy to awake,
For when I snuggled down between them
One merely gave his paws a shake
And one growled slightly. I had seen them
Late in the autumn, by the river,
And never dreamed they would deliver
My body from a frosty fate,
But now, in a most friendly state,
I lay between them on my back
And dreamed about my dogs and shack.
How long I dozed, I cannot tell,
But presently I knew right well
That further warmth my veins caressed,
And found, accounting for the heat,
Some fourteen rabbits on my chest
And two fat beavers at my feet,
While every corner round about
That my dim vision could determine
Was packed with squirrels, plump and stout,
And fox, and lynx, and Arctic ermine.
The most unprecedented weather
Had brought these creatures all together,

A timid, cowering set of friskers,
With frozen toes and frosty whiskers.
Of hate or rage they showed no spark,
But proved as mild in disposition
As if the beasts of Noah's Ark
Had tried an Arctic expedition,
And I, a sort of Gulliver,
Had crashed the berths reserved for fur.
In circumstances such as these,
I was, however, rightly grateful
To beasts that would not let me freeze
And meet a death forlorn and hateful.
The only lingering fear of mine
In that uncanny, beast-filled place
Was lest some thoughtless porcupine
Should make a mattress of my face.
  "The hours passed by. I must have slept,
Although the air grew still more frigid,
And one by one the beasts that crept
About my frame were growing rigid,
Until at last the bears and I
Alone were left that did not die
Under that furry coverlet
That warded off the winter's threat.

IV

"Next day it thawed. I ventured out,
And was surprised to hear a shout
Raised in my own stentorian roar
Where I had called my dogs before.
The cold had chilled my voice, you see,
And left the air-waves all congealed,
And with the rising mercury
My yells thawed out, and as they pealed
Across the snow, before my eyes
I saw my huskies all arise
Out of deep burrows they had dug
To use the snowdrifts as a rug.
I had a busy time that day,
Carting the fur-beasts all away

From that old cave where they had died
While I was on the under side.
I left my friends, the bears, in slumber;
But from the small beasts without number
I got such pelts that, freed from fret,
I cleared two thousand dollars net,
And gave up trapping altogether
Because I didn't like the weather.

"All these things happened long ago.
Since then I've wandered to and fro,
And finally have settled down
Here in this quiet little town.
I've married, too, and have acquired
Such children as I long desired:
Five boys and girls, all under ten,
Make me the happiest of men,
With pity for the senseless drone
Who has no offspring of his own.
Yet sometimes, when in January
Cold winds by night sweep off the prairie,
And five small kids, in search of heat,
Come to my bed to warm their feet
On me, their father, I recall
That far-off, coldest day of all.
Then at those little girls and boys
I make a sleepy, bear-like noise,
And urge them (growling hoarse and strange)
To try their mother for a change."

THE DRUMMER'S TALE OF A LATTER-DAY JOB

Prologue

Loudest of all in mourning summer
Among our hearth-side company
Was the glum-eyed, dyspeptic "drummer,"
A sort of sad-faced chimpanzee,
Whose line was wholesale groceries
From custard-powder down to cheese.
He, as a constant traveller,
Faced every winter with demur,

Sadly averse to going places
Across the wind-swept prairie spaces.
"You grouse as loud as Job with boils,"
Said Casey crossly. "Sure it spoils
A social circle, hale and happy,
To see you so depressed and snappy.
Cheer up!"
    "Ay, that I shall," he answered,
"And since you mentioned Job just now,
I shall inform you, true as Hansard,
Of an acquaintance, who, I vow,
Has undergone in Winnipeg
Such woes as poached the Uzzite's egg,
And yet, like him, could take the rap
Without a blink."
    "Lead on, old chap!"
Said Casey and we heard intent
A salesman supercharged with slang
Explain in detail what he meant
By citing Job in his harangue:

I

"In Manitoba-Uz there dwelt
A grain-man Job, surnamed MacCammon,
Who every day devoutly knelt
Before his god, the mighty Mammon
Whose temple in the Grain Exchange
Was his delight, for he would range
Along its halls, his grey eyes lit
To serve the Spirit of the Pit.
    "Job was a perfect man and just,
Kindly and generous in his ways;
And Mammon, for his friendly trust,
Had prospered him throughout his days.
He had a mansion on the Crescent
And a fine cottage at Minaki,
Where his plump wife was effervescent
In summer days, supremely cocky,
Forgetting black-flies, heat, and midges
In cocktail-parties, teas, and bridges,—

While Job, her goose with golden egg,
Was sweating back in Winnipeg.
　"A gilded son and heir had he
Who went to University;
And though it vexed him that his son
Had flunked three times in Latin I,
Yet he was made to understand
That social circles of the land
Decreed that beer brought honour high
When drunk with Sigma Alpha Pi.
He had a lively daughter Lou,
Who also parked around the 'U',
And though her grades were rather meagre,
She was a knock-out Junior Leaguer,
Ready to run hotels and stores
And save the world by social chores.
But Job was forthright and old-fashioned:
With him there were no 'ifs' or 'buts';
He kept his rum austerely rationed;
In golf, he always played his putts.
It was his wife who put the skids
Of easy cash beneath the kids.

II

"Now Satan, or the Moral Law,
Patrolling Winnipeg one day,
Became aware of Job, and saw
The even tenor of his way;
And, just to test him, turned with glee
To his weak wife and progeny.
Hence was it that a slim, sleek youth,
Hector MacCammon, hot and twenty,
Oblivious to the simple truth
That he had drunk much more than plenty,
Into his father's Lincoln climbed
To drive Lou homeward, cocktail-primed,
From a late dance, where maid and stripling
Had mingled 'swing' with open tippling.
Hector was doing sixty-five
When, reaching Osborne Street on Broadway,

A cruiser-car saw him arrive
And plough through red lights. 'That's an
        odd way,'
Said Sergeant Koyle, 'to drive, bedad!
I think we'll follow up the lad.'
    "While turning southward on two wheels
On Sherbrook, Lulu grew aware
That the police were at their heels,
And told her brother to take care.
'Phooey!' said Hector, 'Watch me, matey!'
And shoved the Lincoln up to eighty.
The chase was on: and Koyle looked bland
When Hector, with drunk smile seraphic,
At Wolseley swerved up Maryland
Northward against the one-way traffic.
Half on the boulevard he raced,
Nine blocks careening up to Portage;
Of drunken zeal he had no shortage,
For he turned right with dauntless haste
And sought, with automotive roars,
The canyon of the down-town stores.
Just at the Bay, he gave a laugh
And shot south past the Cenotaph;
But Lou let out a maudlin wail,
For Sergeant Koyle was on their tail,
While at his back, ignoring stops,
Came eight fat motor-cycle cops.
Heck swung the Lincoln out of bounds
Across the Legislature grounds
Through flower-bed and grassy ridge,
And headed for the Osborne Bridge.
Just as he reached the narrow way,
A north-bound street-car beat him to it;
The speeding Lincoln could not stay,
But crashed the railing, hurtled through it,
And drowned the screeching son and daughter
Deep in the river's turbid water.
    "When their two corpses came home later,
Each face beneath a handkerchief,
Mute sorrow smote their grey-haired pater
But Mrs. Job grew loud in grief:

'I want to be where Hector is!'
She wailed—when suddenly, to please her,
A prompt *angina pectoris*
Stabbed like a knife in Julius Caesar,
And the plump spirit from her breast
Went gasping forth to be at rest.
  "Job's troubles were not over yet:
The morning *Free Press*, that next day,
Told how his lawyer, faced with debt,
Had wasted trust-funds quite away,
And all that Job had laid aside
Had gone with the embezzling tide.
Of children, wife, and cash bereft,
Poor Job had very little left,
And was inclined to sit and blub
Down at the Manitoba Club;
Yet no rash word escaped his lips,
Admitting grave paternal slips.

III

"There, to bring comfort to his bones,
Came Bildad White and Zophar Jones
And Foster, christened Eliphaz,
Who was a man that loved to razz;
And deep in chairs of padded leather
They sat and talked, discussed the weather,
Till soon all three began to wheeze
Of Job's abrupt calamities.
Quoth Eliphaz: 'It's very sad
To have investments turn out bad.
But it's your fault. I often told you
To watch this pirate who has rolled you.
If you had let me handle things,
Your wealth would not have taken wings.
You were a guy who knew it all,
But you were riding for a fall.
At the smug phiz of Eliphaz
Job looked in scorn: 'You fool, whereas,
In years, you haven't saved a dollar,
Are you the man to raise a holler

[205]

About that lawyer, who, it's true,
Was not an all-wise owl like you,
But who, before bad luck began,
Had all the makings of a man?
I'm not the sort that shies at folk—
I'd rather trust them, and be broke.'
   "Then, with hands clasped on his big paunch,
Bald-headed Bildad turned to launch
A subtle thrust to make Job halt,
And weaken, and confess his fault:
'Your young 'uns would be living still
If you had shown a firmer will;
For when a lad is drunk, I'm thinkin',
You shouldn't let him have the Lincoln.
You spared the rod and spoiled the child:
Just blame yourself if he was wild!'
   "Job groaned at this, but did not weaken;
His grim eye shone like any beacon:
'Who would have fancied such a creature
As "Baldy" Bildad turning preacher!
Your wisdom is no gushing fountain.
For you've a son in Stony Mountain,
And daughters out in Hollywood
With reputations far from good.
Come clean! Admit that both our lives
Have been bedevilled by our wives;
For when your own wife won't play ball,
You haven't got a chance at all,
And any hope of discipline
Among the kids is mighty thin.
I really tried to raise my son,
But Mrs. Mac. just let him run.'
   "A wavering light of triumph woke
In Zophar's eye, and up he spoke:
'If she was silly to the core,
You fool, what did you choose her for?'
   " 'Numskull!' said angry Job to Zophar,
'You've no more gumption than a gopher!
It's plain enough you never married,
And that your heart was never harried—
One minute hot, another frozen.
I didn't choose her. I got chosen!'

"Then the three friends of Job were mute,
Because they couldn't faze the brute.
And were provoked, beyond a doubt,
To see, before the year was out,
A buxom widow, named Malvena,
Come as a *deus ex machina*,
And take her place, without ado,
As Job's fair consort Number Two.
She set him up with cash in scads
And seven step-sons, all good lads,
As nest-eggs for a family
That soon had daughters, one, two, three.
Thus his last state was far more blest
Than any other's in the West.
And as a tribute to the spectre
Of his lost lad, the errant Hector,
He founded, named for that dull son,
A scholarship in Latin I,
Which his bright step-sons in succession
Win in industrious progression."

THE SERGEANT'S TALE OF THE MANITOBA STONEHENGE

Prologue

The tightest-lipped of all who sat
Beside that fire and smoked in peace
Was that steel-jawed aristocrat,
The red-coat Sergeant of Police;
So Casey led our talk about,
And tried to draw the Sergeant out.
"I've often heard it claimed," he said,
"That in the West, since Time began
And Adam's kids began to spread,
The Mounties always got their man.
Is it the truth the spalpeens speak,
Or are their facts a trifle weak?"—
Like sunrise on a foggy cliff,
The glimmer of a smile awoke
Behind the Sergeant's mighty whiff
Of eddying tobacco-smoke:

"You say the Force is never wrong;
But though the Law's red arm is long,
And though few men escape our hand
From Morden north to Baffin Land,
Yet there are cases, I'll admit,
That buffalo the boys a bit.
Sometimes sheer luck—or Providence—
Is all that cleans up an offence,
And credit for a crime's solution
Comes from uncanny retribution
That overtakes the wicked, when
They think their crime unseen by men.
I call to mind a baffling case
Up in the northern mining region,
Back in those first prospecting days
Just before Flin Flon brought a legion
Of hard-boiled, strong-arm miners in
To curse the wilderness with din.
Except for Fate, I question whether
The Force had not been bound to fail;
For later, piecing things together,
We got a most amazing tale
From the last member of the gang,
Who died too soon for us to hang."
The Sergeant halted. No one stirred
While he lit up a fresh cigar
And went on, weighing every word,
To tell how, up in wilds afar,
A higher Vengeance came to show
The murder of a sourdough:

I

"Up where the line of travel crosses
From Footprint Lake to Nistowasis,
Two hundred miles from Norway House,
Northward by portage-trail and river,
Where Arctic foxes prowl for grouse,
And where the mossy muskegs quiver
By moose-ponds lying cool and black
Through endless spruce and tamarack,

[208]

The wealth of milky reefs of quartz,
Ribbing the wilderness of granite,
Now brings prospectors of all sorts
Who hope for gold and come to scan it.
    "Twelve years ago, before the rush,
Three sourdoughs, one summer day,
Came by canoe, their brows a-flush
With hope that fortune might repay
Their present toil a hundredfold
With rich discoveries of gold.
Bill Smith, Jack Lloyd, and Pete MacLeod,
These unkempt, bearded sons of Chance,
Had left The Pas beneath a cloud
Of most suspicious circumstance
And fogs of dark unproven blame
Arising from a poker game.
Deserved or not, bad fortune dogged them:
A storm on Lake Athapapusko
Upset their boat, and muskeg bogged them
Along a trail near Lake Wekusko;
Most of their grub-stake thus was gone,
But still they struggled grimly on,
Hoping to reimburse their losses
By striking gold near Nistowasis.
Fly-time was at its very worst:
Out of dank woods and bogs accurst,
Blood-hungry blackflies came to fare
Behind their ears and in their hair,
While yellow-banded moose-flies bit,
Raising red welts where'er they lit,
And thick mosquito-clouds would drone
A maddening, murderous monotone.
    "But blood-gorged pests and rations'
        shortage
Were for a moment quite forgot
When the men sighted at a portage
A big bull-moose, a perfect shot.
Pete raised his rifle silently,
But the mere movement stirred the bull
To turn for flight past rock and tree,
Just as his finger crooked to pull.

The rifle barked. The great beast lurched,
Then lumbered off.—'I've hit the brute!
Come on!'—And eagerly they searched
Through jack-pine thickets, where his route
Lay clear in hoof-prints in the mud
With broken twigs and flecks of blood.
Then, on a sudden rocky slope,
They found the moose, whose blood's dark streams
Dabbled the quartz-reef of their hope,
The golden out-crop of their dreams!
Ten rods to left and right it spread—
That broad, white vein with gold encrusted—
And the great beast there, lying dead,
Was naught to this, for which they lusted
With all the raw, primaeval greed
Of gamblers in their time of need.
Kneeling there, joyous beyond measure,
They gloated on their new-found treasure.

II

"Two evenings later found them camped
Far back upon the homeward trail.
By portage short-cuts they had tramped
With their canoe, intent to scale
The brief, abrupt, basalt divide
Out to the Nelson River side
And with all haste record their names,
In Winnipeg, to clinch their claims.
At nightfall, glad to break their trudge,
They camped, and sheltered by a smudge
From ravenous mosquito-hosts,
They ate fried moose and made their boasts
How they would live at highest pitch
Of revelry when they were rich.
Then, by ill fortune, Pete MacLeod
Took from his battered dunnage-pack
A crock of whiskey, and he vowed
He wouldn't wait till he got back:
'Now is the time for celebration!
I am so dry, I know right well

I'd face the Devil and damnation,
Just for a drink!' And all three fell
To boozing in a noisy choir
Around their murky little fire.
Then, as the fumes of whiskey mounted
Up from the belly to the brains,
Drunk Jack to drunken Bill recounted
How much more rich would be their gains
If they should stab drunk Peter through
And share the mine between the two.
'Listen,' he whispered to his mate,
'Get out your skinning-knife, and wait;
And while he snores beside his pack,
We'll stab the rascal in the back.'
    "Such was their deed, but hands unsteady
Wounded but did not kill their man.
Up leapt poor Pete, half slain already
By streaming wounds, and staggering, ran
Along a little forest-path,
While after him, in drunken wrath,
His comrades, each with dripping knife,
Came lurching on to take his life.

III

"Wan moonlight lit the path they took;
And haggard Pete in hopeless terror
Soon slackened pace, with knees that shook,
For he had stumbled in his error
Into the weirdest rocky glen
E'er gazed upon by mortal men.
    "Hemmed in by high, sheer walls of black,
Steep as the ramparts of a crater,
A treeless, rocky pit stretched back,
Shaped like a grave but vastly greater,
And on its phosphorescent floor
Some human tribe of ages gone
Had ranged huge boulders by the score
To form a giant skeleton—
A Manitoba Stonehenge, set
With symbolism grimmer yet.

"Into that pit, Pete sickly gazed.
The butchering pair were close behind him,
And on he staggered, horror-crazed:
Down in that gulch they might not find him.
But soon he sank upon the stones
Beside those vast, symbolic bones,
Exhausted, and with swimming eyes
Looked at his slaughterous allies.
'Dead men,' said Bill, 'are slow to quote,
Especially after due cremation.'—
And drew his knife across Pete's throat
With murderous deliberation.
'Now let us build a fire,' he said,
'The blasted gulch is off the trail.
We'll burn this rascal who is dead,
And not a trace will tell his tale.
When we get back to Winnipeg,
We'll say he drowned in Fiddle Lake;
And not a person there will beg
For further details for his sake.'
Under the wan, uncanny moon
They dragged down wood into the chasm;
Pete crackled on his pyre soon,
But Jack Lloyd almost took a spasm
When by the light of that foul fire
A tall, dark stranger seemed to stand
Among the stones beside the pyre
And hail them with uplifted hand.
He looked like some old Indian priest,
But towered nine feet high at least;
And when he spoke, his accents fell
Like organ-music played in hell:
'Do not expect,' he said to Bill,
'To go unpunished for your crime.
Though human law prove not your ill,
Yet rest assured that in due time
You, who have merited such blame,
Shall perish here in penal flame;
And your ally shall earn his hire
In lingering death, but not by fire!'
But Bill in drunk derision cursed:
'I'll see you on this bonfire first!'

And a wild rain of slugs was dealt
From the revolver at his belt.
As moon and firelight seemed to dim,
They saw the stranger's form dislimn
And fade among the mammoth bones;
And all they found among the stones
Was half a dozen tiny pocks
Where Bill's discharge had chipped the rocks.

IV

"Five years passed by. The death of Pete
By drowning had been put to question,
But all our efforts met defeat.
There was no corpse. And the suggestion
That something was extremely wrong
Was proofless, though belief was strong.
Meanwhile the mine at Nistowasis
Was pouring out a golden store
Of bullion for its two grim bosses,
And still they darkly craved for more.
Air transport companies had brought,
To loot that shining reef of quartz,
All of the tools that modern thought
Has fashioned: there were sundry sorts
Of stamp-mills and amalgamators
(Each with its own peculiar failings),
With mercury in stamp-box craters
And cyanide for 'slime' and tailings;
And towering mounds of refuse rose
Where Pete MacLeod had trailed that moose,
While the incessant stamp-mill blows
Rang through the silent miles of spruce.
Since neither road nor railway ran
Into this realm of Smith and Lloyd,
And since the plant—machine and man—
Had come on wings across the void,
Bill Smith, who frequently had flown,
Soon bought a biplane of his own,
And having earned his pilot's papers,
Grew constant in his aëry capers.

[213]

"One August morning, he and Jack
Had put in eighteen holes of golf
At Deer Lodge, before starting back
To see the mine. The pair took off
Just as the Air Field clock struck noon;
At full speed they expected soon
To cross five hundred miles of sky
To where the mine would cheer their eye.
But engine trouble held them stalled
At Norway House for several hours;
And to Jack Lloyd, Bill seemed enthralled
By dark, infuriating Powers:
His tongue lolled like a dog's in drouth,
His blood-shot eyes were wild and staring,
And nervous twitchings at the mouth
Made his fierce glance seem yet more glaring;
While his remarks, as day decreased,
Seemed like the snarls of some wild beast,
    "The long, slow twilight of the North
Had merged with darkness when at last
The plane was ready to set forth;
And as the light was fully past,
Jack urged it would be wise to stay
At Norway House till break of day.
'You coward!' Bill began to mock.
'The moon comes up at ten o'clock,
Just past the full and plenty bright
To show our way across the night.
You'll get into that plane, you blackguard,
Or learn how lead can cure a laggard!'
More nervous over Bill's wild mood
Than any hazards of the dark,
And feeling that some trouble brewed
From a mad fit so strange and stark,
Jack, in slow silence, got on board;
And just at moonrise, off they soared.
    "A sea of shadows lay below them,
Silvered with soft, unearthly light;
Only vague outlines served to show them
Their northward way across the night.

Onward they hurtled, flying low;
When suddenly Jack's blood ran cold—
For there before them, all a-glow
With hellish glare as bright as gold,
A sunken, treeless valley shone,
Upon whose floor, outlined with fires,
A grim titanic Skeleton
Leered upward at the gaping fliers.
'That is the place you murdered Pete!'
Said Jack to Bill. 'No, it was you,'
He answered with demented heat;
'Who killed the rascal? Tell me, Who?'
Just at that moment, from the gloom
A huge, white owl, with skull-like eyes,
Swooped like a messenger of doom
And with infuriated cries
Of 'Who? Who? Who?', attacked the pair.
Bill lost control, and through the air
Fell yelling with the twisting plane.
Jack leapt out clear. Bill tried in vain,
With parachute too badly tangled.
The plane took fire. Alive but mangled,
He perished screeching in the fire,
Near where the ashes of Pete's pyre
Still lingered, hideous, moist and gray,
Though five long years had passed away.
   "We learned all this next day, for Jack
Bailed out too low and broke his back,
But lingered long enough to tell
The truth about their deed of hell,
When fire-rangers, who had sighted
A sudden, flaming plane come down,
Went there at dawn, looked and alighted,
And flew me promptly in from town.

   "Much of the tale is hard to credit,
But though the yarn is weird and gory,
It was a dying man who said it
And he believed his own dark story;

And when we found charred bones of Pete,
The bloody record seemed complete,
Proving, as said when I began,
That Fate can help us get our man."

THE CORPORAL'S TALE OF THE MEN WHO VANISHED

Prologue

The lean-faced Corporal nodded slow
His confirmation of the tale:
"Yes," he remarked, "I also know
A case where Heaven did not fail
To interpose its Justice, when
A ruthless pair of wicked men
Transgressed the laws of man and God.
But if the Sergeant's case was odd,
This one, I think, was weirder still.
Let me rehearse the tale of ill."
We puffed approval, though unneeded,
And the gaunt Corporal proceeded:

I

"The precious pair of whom I spoke
Were 'One-eyed Mike' and 'Scarface Dan',
As reckless, evil-hearted folk
As ever harried mortal man.
Perhaps some thugs are still more black,
Like those chill connoisseurs in crime
Who send your kidnapped children back
One severed finger at a time;
But Mike and Dan were beasts at best.
There were no worse in all the West.
Both were Bulgarians by birth;
As youths they had been jailed for murder,
And might have hanged and slept in earth
Had not a policy absurder
Than all unreason, being fed
By bounties of so much a head

[216]

For Western settlers in the raw
Transferred them out to Canada.
By just such tactics of perdition
Canadian agents earned commission,
And left the sequel for our nation
To bear in bitter tribulation.
Mike was a stocky sort of guy,
With glances fiery as a rocket,
Though through a fight his fierce left eye
Was missing wholly from its socket.
Dan, unlike Mike, was lean and bleak,
With grizzled stubble on his chin
And a long scar across his cheek
That gave him an unearthly grin.
After six months of pioneering
Up near The Pas, they tired of clearing
And faded out to Winnipeg,
Where each soon flourished as a yegg.
Then, when police hunts grew too hot,
They sought a less frequented spot,
And hit on a deserted shack
Out in the Rockies, north of Yakh.

II

"From this new base of operations,
They started on fresh depredations,
And often vexed with thievish sally
The humble Slovaks of the valley.
Emboldened by the latter's mildness,
They soon went on to greater wildness,
And dared one Sabbath day to search
And rob the entire Slovak church.
The priest was half-way through the Mass
When the two Bulgars, bold as brass,
A six-gun poised in either hand,
Came striding in, with sharp command
To face the walls and raise their arms;
Then, breathing threats of grievous harms,
They quickly took, with ribald mirth,
All each possessed of any worth.

[217]

Mike's one fierce eye was full of scorn
And Dan's scarred grin was bleak and pale,
Watching the old priest stand forlorn
Beside the little altar rail.
He lifted up his hand; and lo,
The pair, who were about to go,
Halted in silence as his wrath
Burst in a thundering aftermath.
He cursed their souls to lowest hell;
He cursed their worthless flesh as well;
He cursed their waking hours with pain;
He cursed their sleep with horror's reign;
He cursed their skins with tick and louse;
He cursed the safety of their house—
'On you shall surely come,' he cried,
'A far worse fate than if you died.
With all your human senses keen,
You shall subsist on food obscene
And snarl and howl with beastly breath
In anguished eagerness for death.
Within this day your work of sin
Its penal torment shall begin.
Go! Or, before it is too late,
Kneel down and pray for your sad state!'

III

"Giving a laugh, the scornful pair
Strode out and left him standing there,
Mounted their nags and rode away,
And called it a successful day.
Of this affair we Mounties heard
For several weeks no single word;
For Slovak folk, devoutly odd,
Preferred to leave such things to God,
And saw no need to tell police
About such breaches of the peace.
At length the Winnipeg command
Trailed the two miscreants to the land,
And one day I rode out from Yakh
To seize the men and bring them back.

Then, at the village in the valley,
The old priest told me stoically
About the Sunday when his flock
Were rudely robbed and set at mock,
Yet said there was no need to send
For villains who had met their end:
No one had seen them since that time;
God, he was sure, had marked their crime,
And had been pleased on them to vent
Unprecedented punishment.
When I insisted on my ride,
He sent a Slovak as my guide,
Who, with his face a trifle pale,
Soon led me up the mountain trail.
    "It was a bleak November day
As we rode up that rugged way.
Borne by a piercing autumn wind,
Grey clouds in drifting ribbons thinn'd
Across tall crags of naked stone
That shone as cold as polished bone,
And colder still behind them rose
Fantastic summits white with snows.
I am not a religious sort,
Yet I can candidly report
I sensed upon that mountain path
God's purity and awful wrath.

IV

"Around a corner of the trail,
We met the cabin suddenly—
A wooden shack, unkempt and frail,
Beneath a thunder-smitten tree,
A pine whose green had turned instead
To haggard, fateful hues of red.
A battered stable stood behind it
In ruinous dilapidation;
As with the house, we seemed to find it
A thing of utter desolation.
Hemmed round by shining peaks of morning,
They lay beneath a sense of night,

As if the spot, in awful warning,
Were smitten by some nameless blight.
The shack's one door was open wide
Upon a sagging pair of hinges,
And as we slowly stepped inside
I felt my hair-roots stir with twinges
Of some unutterable awe
Scarce called for by the thing I saw.
For there was little to be seen
In that uncanny, dusty room—
Two empty beds, a stove unclean,
Two upturned chairs, a broken broom,
Two suits of clothes, half torn to shreds,
That lay on the dishevelled beds,
And on a table, neatly stacked,
As if to satisfy our search,
The booty we had duly tracked,
The plunder of the Slovak church.
And then I saw, with one glance more,
That all along the cabin floor
Were countless wolf-tracks in the dust,
And marks where, in some fierce disgust,
Wild teeth and claws, their frenzy spreading,
Had gnawed the bed and clawed the
        bedding.
But of the Bulgars, Mike and Dan,
No single sign was there to scan:
Yes, though we searched on every side,
We could not find them, hair nor hide,
Nor even bloodstains anywhere
To show that wolves had killed them there.
Here were their clothes, and fruits of theft,
But the two men themselves had left,
And, without leaving any trace,
Had simply vanished into space.
    "Going out back to search the shed,
We found its door was open too,
And there, repulsive to the view,
Two saddle-horses, long since dead,
Were lying on the earthen floor,
While at their mangled haunches tore

Two mangy wolves, two cringing beasts,
Who seemed to loathe such carrion feasts.
Then, as I made a sudden sound,
The wretched creatures turned around
In snarling anger to unsheath
From haggard lips their yellow teeth.
I drew my gun. The Slovak checked me,
And crossed himself in pious awe.
Then, with his finger to direct me,
The thicker, stockier brute I saw
Had glances fiery as a rocket
And one eye missing from its socket,
While his companion wolf was bleak,
Lean as the famine-curst are thin,
With a long scar across his cheek
That gave him an unearthly grin.
They did not fight but only cowered
Back in the corner of a stall;
And there I left them as they glowered,
And did not harm the brutes at all.

v

"I'm sure my face was very pale
As we rode back along the trail;
At any rate, I know my mind
Was reeling, and I could not find
An answer to the uncanny sights
Up at that homestead on the heights.
Under the cold November skies,
Beneath those awful mountain summits,
I thought of man as one who dies,
A feeble beast, whose reason plummets
Only the surface of a sea
Of spiritual mystery.
What I had seen I scarce could tell,
Yet somehow knew a moving swell
From holy seas beyond my ken
Had washed the sin-stained shores of men,
And sweeping up along the beach
Had touched a spot beyond the reach

Of common tides and common reason
To punish evil in its season.
Yet when I turned in my report
I gave no version of that sort.
My humble Slovak guide and I
Could never hope to satisfy
A Philistine intelligence
With tales that somehow had no sense.
So to my chief I merely said:
'The men are missing. Likely dead.
We found the homestead wolf-infested.
No doubt the pair are now digested.'
That's what I told him. But I know
That after all it wasn't so,
And that it was my privilege
To stand upon the outer edge
Of a stupendous mystery
Beyond the guess of you and me."

THE BUTCHER'S TALE OF THE FORT HENRY TUNNEL

Prologue

The butcher shivered, and a trace
Of melancholy nightmare spread
Across his plump Teutonic face,
While in disquietude he said:
"There are conditions that appal
In tales so supernatural,
Yet I am certain, without error,
That there is more of mortal terror
In purely physical affright.
I can't forget one dreadful night
When, without ghosts or ghouls hell-painted,
I faced such horror that I fainted.
Since themes of terror are your dish,
I'll tell the story, if you wish."
As no one ventured to comment,
He took our silence for consent;
And with a shudder of his own
He told his tale in halting tone:

"The worst experience of my life
Was at Fort Henry, long ago
During the War, when bitter strife
Estranged our countries. Then, although
The sentence was but slightly earned,
I found myself at last interned.
The trouble was that Hermann Klein,
An old compatriot of mine
Back home in Baden, came to me
One autumn night in Napanee,
Where I was working in a mill,
And lodged with me. It was a thrill
To meet good Hermann once again.
I was the happiest of men,
Until he urged me, turned adviser,
To cross the sea and serve the Kaiser.
He then was on his way, he said,
But I refused, and claimed instead
That I had found in Canada
Congenial work and life and law.
He was arrested two days later,
Trying to reach the States from Bath,
And I, alleged collaborator,
Likewise incurred official wrath,
Although my sole offence, he swore,
Was housing him two nights before.
　　"Crumbling Fort Henry, cold and
　　　　damp,
Became our concentration camp,
Along with several hundred others,
Who hailed us as Germanic brothers.
It was a fortress, old and chill,
Sunk in the summit of a hill
That westward looked on Kingston town
And to the east sloped slowly down
To a deep inlet, bleak and grey,
That bore the name of Dead Man's Bay.
Southward, the broad St. Lawrence reeled;
North, lay the plains of Barriefield.

The fort, I learned, had been erected
A century since, but, long neglected,
Had mouldered with the frost's abuse
Until war claimed its sudden use,
Disturbing, in their dank abode,
Spider and beetle, slug and toad.
When Klein and I were landed there,
There'd been scant effort at repair,
For moss was thick upon the roof
And ancient doors were foul with rust
And tottering battlements gave proof
That mortar had dissolved to dust,
While deep along the great dry moat
That hemmed the 'Lower Fort' around
Whole strips of wall had lost a coat
Of ashlars, tumbled on the ground.
But high above, the sentries walked,
Patrolling all the wind-swept hill;
And we, within the ruin, talked,
Or dreamed that we were free men still.

II

"The oldest legend of the place
Was that a secret tunnel lay
Under the fortress' deepest base
And down the hill to Dead Man's Bay.
Just where it was, no person knew.
Even the guards had no idea.
In daydreams, when our minds were blue,
That tunnel was a panacea;
For thus in many a magic vision
We fled reality's derision
And slipped by ceiling, wall, or floor
Into that wondrous corridor,
Under the moat and down the slope,
An avenue to life and hope.
   "The ground floor casemate farthest east,
A darkened cell, as black as ink
And hardly fit to house a beast,
Was known to guardsmen as 'the Clink',

A prison cell where men unruly
In close confinement suffered duly.
Here Hermann Klein and I were placed
One late November day in haste
For having dared, with restless skill,
To make a sturdy home-made still
And boil a mash, high-proof and keen,
With makings from the fort canteen,
In hope to pass the waning year
With some resource of liquid cheer.
But soon the nosey adjutant
Had rooted out our little plant,
And so, instead of Schnapps to drink,
We had a sudden dose of 'Clink'.
   "Once in the dungeon, Hermann Klein
Professed to me he liked it fine
To have a chance to check the place
And in the floor to find a trace
Of that old tunnel. Other men
Had told him, ever and again,
That near the north wall, under test,
One spot rang hollower than the rest:
A shaft was underneath the floor
If only they could find the door.
He had come ready, you perceive,
For he was clever and designing—
With tallow-candles in his sleeve
And matches in his trouser-lining—
And with the aid of such a light
We searched the casemate half the night.
It seemed in vain. The floor rang hollow
In one spot, but it did not follow
That it would open at our will.
For hours, the whole result was nil.
Klein was undaunted, and at last
A still more searching gaze was cast
On three brass spikes spaced fairly wide
Breast-high upon the northern side.
We'd thought them clothes-pegs, but
        now Klein
Supposed them part of some design

To lock the stone beneath our feet,
And so he tried, in ways discreet,
To pull them slowly farther out
(A trick which failed), and then with care
To push them in. With sudden shout
He grabbed me, for a winding stair
Was at our feet, where one huge block
Swung on a pivot in the floor
And showed a shaft of limestone rock
Gape downward fifty feet or more.
'At last!' cried Klein. 'The tale was true!
Friend Wagner, we're as good as through.'
And so, with hearts as light as air,
We started down the winding stair,
Fresh from the tools of long ago.
But as we hurried on below,
A sudden thud above my head
Told that the stone had closed once more
And numbered us among the dead
Unless the path lay clear before.
'Mein Gott!' said Hermann. 'That is bad.
But we shall soon be out, my lad.'
"The staircase-shaft sank vertical,
For fifty feet, as I have said,
There then began a narrow hall
To east-northeast that overhead
Was dank with seepage from the hill,
Blotching the ceiling, low and chill.
The floor sloped steeply, it was clear;
It was the passage of our dreams;
Perhaps our liberty was near!
And so by two small candles' beams
(For each of us now bore a light)
We hurried on in happy flight.

III

"I shudder in remembrance yet
At the dark horror that we met

As we drew near to Dead Man's Bay
By that dank, subterranean way.
For first a rank, reptilian smell
Rose like a sudden blast from hell,
And then, almost at once with this,
A sleepy, thousand-throated hiss
Filled all the place from side to side
And set us gaping, horrified.
Just at our feet, as we descended,
The honest limestone pavement ended,
And the whole passage, two feet deep,
Was filled with vipers half asleep,
A monstrous, writhing, reptile mass
That here had crept in swarms to pass
The winter, kenneled in the dark;
While far beyond them, like a spark,
A low, dim exit we could see,
Cluttered with mouldering débris,
For half the roof had fallen in
Where once a way for men had been,
And only left a gap in view
Where rats or snakes could wriggle through.
Such was our plight. Far back, behind,
Cold limestone barred us from our kind,
Sentenced to starve, without a doubt,
Unless we found some passage out;
And now before us writhed and hissed
Such horror as no moralist
In dreams of grimmest resolution
E'er planned for sinners' retribution.
Then as I paused and, gaping, gripped
My candle tighter, Hermann slipped
And with a scream would wake the dead
Dove open-mouthed, with arms outspread,
Like some raw diver at the lakes,
Full in the heaving mass of snakes.
Aroused to fury by his fall,
They bit him fiercely everywhere
And over him began to crawl—
I could not even see his hair.

Then a last, dying flurry smote
My friend. I saw him rise and stand
With twenty serpents round his throat
And snake-teeth fleshed in either hand.
But though a single viper's bite
May seldom serve to kill a man,
The venom of such hosts had might
To poison a leviathan;
And Hermann sank to rise no more,
While hordes of hideous weavers wove
Their woof above him on the floor
Until his strength no longer strove.
  "One of my life's near-worst mistakes
Was waiting, gazing there, in terror,
For an approaching wave of snakes
Almost destroyed me in my error.
I saw them coming, just in time,
And turning round, began to climb
With frenzied haste from that abyss,
And still behind me heard them hiss.
My flickering candle sputtered out
As I raced madly up the steep,
Yet still I groped my way about
Like some wild madman in his sleep,
And blundered on in my despair
Until I reached the spiral stair.
Then up the dusty steps I sped
Until at last, with hope nigh dead,
I crouched beneath that massive stone
That held me prisoner. With a groan,
I sat, and marked my spirits melt
And all my fancies seethe and rankle:
I heard no sound, and yet I felt
A viper coiling round my ankle—
But when I went to kick it free,
My foot encountered vacancy.
In spite of all, I had the sense
Of snaky presences. Suspense
Clutched at my bursting heart and brain
Until I fainted with the pain.

"How long I swooned, I cannot say;
But all at once the stone gave way
Above me there; the fresh air blew
Upon me, and a face peered through.
'One of them's here,' a sharp voice said,
'It's Wagner, and he looks half dead.'
I knew the voice too well, I grant—
It was that nosey adjutant—
And yet to me he looked so good
I could have hugged him where he stood.
Finding the prisoners in the Clink
Had vanished, he begins to think
Of some old tunnel, closely checks it,
And so, like us, he finds the exit.
Half-crazed, I stammered out my tale,
And ten men down the backward trail
Went armed with hip-boots, clubs and rakes
And got Klein's body from the snakes.
　"Next day at ten I was paraded
Before the Commandant, to whom
I told (my face with horror faded)
The story of my comrade's doom.
He listened grimly till I ceased,
Then asked me, in a tone of warning:
'Why seek escape? You've been released.
The order came through just this morning.
And though your gaol-break needs rebuff,
I think we'll pass the whole thing over.
You must have suffered quite enough—
You didn't spend your time in clover.'
　"And so I left the Fort behind;
But till I die, within my mind
A secret shaft is hidden deep,
And often, waking or asleep,
A stone will move, dark steps descend,
And through black tunnels without end
I walk and hear once more, aghast,
The hissing horror of the past."

Prologue

The quietest of all the party
That sat and talked around the fire
Was a pale lawyer, far from hearty,—
A man who looked as if some dire
And sinister experience
Had harried him with pain intense.
"Believe in ghosts?" the drover laughed:
"Not I, my lads."
                    The lawyer frowned:
"If you are right, then I am daft;
Because I've seen one, I'll be bound!"
A sudden eerie silence fell,
There in that Manitou hotel.
Some disbelieved, but all could see
He had a story. Therefore, we,
Avid for tales of mirth or woe,
Urged him to tell of it, and so
The local lawyer, grim and pale,
Told quietly his ghostly tale:

I

"It was the worst year of the drought,"
The lawyer said, and looked more grim,
"That Jacob Beynon-Jones came out
To find his lost twin-brother Jim.
I still can see his hawk-like face,
Its unforgettable design
With brow of most excessive space
And nose grotesquely aquiline.
It was a scorching August day
When he arrived in Manitou
By taxi, and was forced to stay
When the rear axle cracked clean through.
He was a most impatient cuss
And kicked up an ungodly fuss,
Demanding, furious and profane,
To go at once to Deloraine.

As I was going out that way
On business, in my Ford coupé,
I asked the man to come with me
The hundred miles, for company.
  "Feeling the obligation strong,
He told me, as we drove along,
The reasons for his present trip;
For he had just arrived by ship
From England, and had come out West
Upon a most surprising quest.
'My name is Beynon-Jones,' he said.
'I have a lost twin-brother, Jim.
So like myself, from heel to head,
That none can tell me quite from him.
Back home in Devonshire as youths,
Black rivalry in love estranged us.
Through ten grey years of lies and truths,
In that, at least, Time has not
              changed us.
I wed my blue-eyed Susan, Sir,
But Jim one night, as I had feared,
Impersonated me with her
As husband, and then disappeared,
Taking my honour and my cash
To distant lands in one fell smash.
The shock of fortune so unkind
Unsettled my poor Susan's mind
And broke my heart. For many a day
I brooded on the runaway.
No trace of him was found abroad,
And ten long years of sorrow gnawed
My heart in silence. Susan died
Only last May, and it is queer
That day a cable from this side—
I SHALL BE WAITING FOR YOU HERE—
Reached me from Jim. The place, I saw,
Was Deloraine, in Canada.
Business took time to clear away—
Ties are not broken in a day.
And now I trust I'm not too late
To meet the brother that I hate!'

Then suddenly, as breezes flapped
His coat aside, with some alarm
I saw a black revolver strapped
Securely underneath his arm.

"We had a hundred miles to go;
And as we neared the range of drought,
All vegetation ceased to grow,
The starveling harvests petered out.
Till fields by Deloraine were just
A lifeless waste of hot, grey dust.

"We sought the station to enquire
About the sender of the wire.
The agent of the C.P.R.
Smiled as I brought my caller in;
Then almost dropped his black cigar
Half-smoked, and checked his friendly grin,
Staring at my companion's face
Like one who could not quite define
That brow of most excessive space,
That nose grotesquely aquiline.
'My God,' he said, in sober tones,
'I thought it was Jim Beynon-Jones.'
'I am his brother,' was the answer.
'Tell me, as quickly as you can, Sir,
Where I can find him.'

                                'I suppose
He's on his farm near Vulture Nose,
Southwest of us nigh forty miles.
Three months ago he called in here,
Excited-like and full of smiles,
To send a cable; but I fear
He hasn't been in town since then.
He's one of the unluckiest men
You ever saw. This cursèd drought
Has dried the plains completely out.
Most of the farmers out his way
Have left their farms this many a day;
Then both of his young children died
Of "flu" last autumn, more's the pity;
His wife then took a one-way ride
Back to her folks at Crystal City;

But Jim refused to leave the spot;
He lives alone there on the farm,
Feeding himself on God knows what.
I hope he doesn't come to harm.'
    "Sardonic satisfaction came
Into the brother's hawk-like eyes:
'Come, Mr. Jukes, and join my game!
Let's give old Jim a real surprise!
It's just an hour or so past noon.
Your car will get us out there soon.'
There was a menace in his tone
That thrilled me with a nameless fear.
I did not like him. That was clear.
And yet I could not hold my own
Against his dark, hypnotic eye
That mastered me, I knew not why.
And so, with feelings vaguely chill,
I started off against my will.

                    II

"As we pushed on from Deloraine
Into the endless, treeless plain,
A slow, hot wind began to rise
And stain the sunlight in the skies
With weird apocalyptic gloom
From stifling clouds of livid grit,
As if the smoke of final Doom
Were breathing from the nether Pit.
Like ashes on the floor of Hell,
Grey dust kept sifting ceaselessly
Across the half-hid parallel
Of buried fence and ditch, as we,
Turning our gaze from side to side,
Gaped at the blasted countryside.
In bald expanses, left and right,
The marl from which the soil had blown
Shone sterile in that lurid light,
The colour of decaying bone.
No honest desert was this land—
Where prickly pear and cactus grew

[233]

In smiling sunlight in the sand—
But the grey corpse of plains I knew,
Plains where strong men had won with toil
Abundant food from fertile soil;
But now a dead community
Lay stifled there in dust and heat,
Shrouded, with grim diablerie,
Under a dusty winding-sheet.
  "Warm dust was in my eyes and hair;
It clogged my nostrils and my mouth;
And ever hotter grew the air
Out of some furnace in the South.
By dun, deserted homes we passed,
Into the suffocating blast,
And saw the leeward roofs all draped
With drifts of dust; and underneath,
The homes' dark doors and windows gaped
Like cavities in dead men's teeth.
  " 'The road-gauge there reads thirty-five
Since we pulled out of Deloraine.'
Said Beynon-Jones. 'If Jim's alive
And at his place, I think it's plain
We're near him now. I wish the Devil
Would help us find him, on the level!'
As if it heard the thing he said,
Our engine coughed, and passed out dead.

III

"For hours I tried to start once more—
Checked up on spark-plugs, gas, and water.
She wouldn't budge. And Jacob swore
That Hell itself had surely bought her.
Leaving her there beside the road,
We set out for the nearest farm.
Over the drifted fence we strode,
Straight to the house; and in alarm
I saw the sun's infernal light
Was darkening to actual night.
The farmyard was a gruesome place
Under that failing light of day.

I wished myself, without disgrace,
A good five thousand miles away.
Nigh buried in the dusty waves
Were ploughs and harrows, rakes and
                    waggons,
Projecting from their sandy graves
Like skeletons of primal dragons.
But the gaunt house was still more eerie,
Bleak and unutterably dreary.
The drifting sand-blast from that home
Had worn away all paint, and left
A desolate grey monochrome
Of leprous planking, warped and cleft
By baleful heat; and at the door
The dust lay three feet deep or more.
    "We walked around to see the back
Of that grim house, but marked no sign
Of any life. The rooms were black.
'Well,' said my comrade, 'I decline
To walk to Deloraine to-night.
You get that hamper and a light.
Beds on deserted farms are cheap.
At least we'll have a place to sleep;
And when the morning comes, no doubt
We'll promptly find our way about.'
    "The back door yielded at a touch,
And with electric torch in hand
We carried in our lunch: not much
For hunger's clamorous demand,
But welcome fare. Without delay
We spread it on a dusty table,
And stowed our bread and cheese away
With such poor cheer as we were able.
It was a melancholy room
In which we sat on creaking chairs
And turned our flashlight on the gloom
From dusty stove to dusty stairs;
And though most obvious to see
Were signs of utter poverty,
I seemed to sense, I must aver,
Some presence far more sinister,

And shuddering smelt, with pale dismay,
A nameless fetor of decay.
    "Just off the kitchen where we sat,
A bedroom, with a double bed,
Stood waiting. 'I am ripe for that,'
Said Beynon-Jones. 'Me too,' I said.
So, without stopping to undress,
We lay down in our weariness
As simply as a pair of sheep,
And fell into a troubled sleep.

IV

    "When I awoke, it still was night.
Through eastward window panes the moon
Was pouring an unearthly light.
But not for this had I so soon
Wakened from sleep. Unearthly talk
Came from a Figure by the door,
A towering Form that seemed to walk
With shambling feet across the floor,
And point impatient to the stairs
And gibber loudly and rejoice.
My startled bedmate said his prayers:
'By Heaven,' he said, 'I know that voice!'
Then, as if caught by some dark force,
He rose up quickly from the bed.
'I've come!' he cried, in accents hoarse;
And followed where that Something led.
    "Armed with the flashlight, I came too,
Drawn by the strangeness of it all.
Up the dark stairs they passed from view
Into a bare, unfurnished hall.
There came a burst of crazy laughter
From Beynon-Jones; and then I saw,
Before us, dangling from a rafter,
With sagging neck and grinning jaw,
A corpse, half-rotten, to supplant
Our recent ghostly visitant.
And even in that greenish face
My gaping horror could divine

A brow of most excessive space,
A nose grotesquely aquiline—
A diabolic parody
On him who had come there with me.
This was the end of our strange ride:
To be alone at midnight there
In that dread house with such a pair—
A madman and a suicide.
Redoubled laughter chilled my ear;
Then Beynon-Jones became more grim
And beckoned with a maniac leer:
'Come, Mr. Jukes, meet Brother Jim!'
   "My trembling fingers dropped
      the light,
That jarred to darkness as it fell.
My hair rose up. I turned to flight;
Groped to the stairs; and with a yell,
Went stumbling down the steps like mad,
Out of the house and towards the car;
And then, behind me, heard the pad
Of running feet. It was not far
To where the car stood; but my knees,
Turning to water, left me lame.
My very heart-blood seemed to freeze
As through the moonlight towards me came
My crazy comrade, weirdly black,
With the cadaver on his back,
And on his face such hate and scorn,
Such hideous likeness to the other
In livid hue, I could have sworn
The corpse was carrying its brother.
'Lend me a hand,' the figure said.
'The rumble-seat's the place for Jim.'
So there we propped his nodding head
And made the cushions soft for him.
Into the front seat then we climbed;
Somehow or other, in my heart,
I knew Hell had that engine primed
And that the car would surely start.
   "At my first touch she gave a bound.
Quickly I turned her nose around,

And started back across the plain,
Racing, hell-bent, for Deloraine.
My nerves in no time were a wreck;
For how could sanity keep sweet
With mania's breath upon my neck
And carrion in the rumble-seat?
On, ever faster, past control,
We neared the town across the prairie,
And crashed into a Hydro pole
Beside the civic cemetery.
 "When consciousness returned again—
A whole week later, so they said—
I found myself laid up in bed
With every muscle full of pain
And forty stitches in my forehead
And both my arms done up in splints,
And a vague sense of something horrid
That I'd been through, until from hints
The doctor made, the whole weird, black
Night of appalling fear came back,
And then I learned that when we spilled
Against that pole, my man was killed,
And one grey grave had served to bury
Both brothers in one cemetery.
How I escaped is far from plain.
I'm glad that I'm alive and sane."

THE FIRST FARMER'S TALE OF THE DRIFTING CORPSE

Prologue

Right in the centre by the fire,
A farmer sat, a stalwart Swede,
Who looked as if no toil could tire
A man of such a virile breed.
Unmoved, he heard the lawyer tell
His story of the haunted farm.
"Still worse than that," he said, "befell
A woman, with the grim alarm
Of Hell, right at my neighbour's place.
Through all the course of all my days,

I never knew of anyone
Who faced such things as she has done
And still retained a stable mind
For intercourse with humankind."
    "I still am dubious," said the drover,
"About these yarns of eerie terror.
Perhaps your tale will win me over
And quite convince me of my error."
    "One's faith," he answered, "must go far.
I shall persuade you if I can."
And with a puff at his cigar,
The massive, blue-eyed Swede began:

I

"The setting for the affair malign
Was on the farm just next to mine,
Where fields and whispering poplars join
Along the broad Assiniboine
Just where its course runs full and freely
A few miles north and east of Elie.
Here Ivan Bykoff lived alone
In a low cottage of his own
Where poplar leaves forever shiver
Along the margin of the river.
Ivan was Russian, stout and squat,
His lips were full, his eyes were hot,
His straight black hair was thick and sleek,
His mouth professed a smirk oblique,—
A bold, insinuating smile
As if his heart were full of guile;
And certainly all through a life
Much marred with interludes of drabbing
He was too handy with a knife
And was a dirty man for stabbing.
    "He had a younger brother Paul,
Who lived six hundred miles up-stream
Just where a little waterfall
Broke the dull river's muddy dream
Near Binscarth—for though crows might fly
Between them through the clear blue sky

In upwards of two hundred miles,
The river's curving course beguiles
Three times that distance as it swings
Through countless slow meanderings.
Paul had a buxom Polish wife,
A warm, deep-bosomed, blue-eyed blonde,
But though he loved her as his life
And she of him seemed just as fond,
No fruit of little children came
To bless his union with his dame;
And so at times there was a trace
Of hunger on her handsome face
And fits of moody discontent
That vaguely came and slowly went.
Into their Eden, Ivan broke
One day in spring, and though he spoke
Of harrows, ploughs, and new seed grain,
Somehow to Marja it was plain
His hot, moist gaze was always prest
Upon her brow and throat and breast.
In brief, by ways obscurely human,
Within a week he won the woman,
And when she had agreed to flight,
He took his knife one stormy night
And stabbing Paul with eyes a-gleam
Sank his dead body in the stream.
Then by the C.N.R. genteelly
He took fair Marja down to Elie,
And in his shack, as man and wife,
They lived without a hint of strife.
When Binscarth learned that Paul was
          gone,
The people put the Mounties on
The pair that went by C.N.R.,
But no enquiry could get far.
There was no body—hence no murder.
'And what,' said Ivan, 'is absurder
Than worry over live men's fates?
Paul's on a visit to the States.
And is it a police concern
If his good wife, till his return,

Should come and visit with his brother,
The offspring of a common mother?'
No matter how police might frown,
They couldn't break that story down.

II

"Two months of guilty love went by,
More mad through mutual sense of sin;
But one warm evening in July
As Ivan, with a happy grin
Sat beside Marja on the bank
And watched the radiant sun that sank,
While his plump paramour beside him
With pensive gaze of passion eyed him,
A drifting Something slowly rounded
The upper bend of poplars sweet
And in unerring onset grounded
In the low shallows at their feet.
A quick grimace of horror warps
The woman's face: it is a corpse,
A naked body, white and bloated,
That in the muddy stream had floated,
Furnishing food to fish and leeches
Along the river's slimy beaches.
They rose and gave a closer look.
Then Marja screamed, turned pale, and shook,
Till Ivan caught her, lest she fall.
'Ivan,' she shrieked, 'it's Paul, it's Paul!'
For even in the rotting face
A recognizing glance could trace,
Plain for all humankind to scan,
The likeness of the murdered man.
Ivan looked black. 'By Heaven,' he said,
'He comes to plague us though he's dead.
And if that face were recognized,
Our guilt would soon be advertised.'
Then furious, but with nerves of steel,
He raised his heavy, hob-nailed heel
And stamped upon his brother's face,
Seeking thus harshly to erase

All human semblance that might be
A clue to his identity.
Then, to dislodge him from the shoal,
He took a sturdy ten-foot pole,
Pushed off the body from the shore,
And gave it to the stream once more.

III

"Meanwhile, across the western sky,
Fierce clouds of thunder mounted high,
Blotting the sunset's rosy light—
And with the tempest came the night.
Snug in the cabin lay the pair
With windows locked and door close-barred,
And watched the lightning's dazzling glare,
And heard the thunder rolling hard,
While on the roof the wind and rain
Beat out a clamorous refrain.
Protected in strong Ivan's arms,
Marja had lost the day's alarms;
When suddenly, with sense of shock,
They heard a loud though muffled knock
That even above the tempest's roar
Kept pounding on the bolted door,
And groping fingers seemed to snatch
And rattle at the metal latch.
A sudden, speechless horror gripped
The pair, and kept them frozen-lipped.
And now the rapping came again—
This time upon the window-pane
Leaving the bed, they came to see
Who the strange visitor might be
That on a night of wind and storm
Came rapping thus. They saw a form
That in the murky shades of night
Reached, as by touch and not by sight,
Inhuman hands that thumped abuse
And tried to pry the window loose.
There came a livid lightning flash,
And by its glare, beyond the sash,

Their staring eyes could clearly trace
A mangled, rotted, sightless face
And pale, disintegrating hands
Stretched in importunate demands.
'It's Paul, by Heaven!' Ivan said.
'Why can't he die when he is dead?'
Then wildly from the wall he drew
A small repeating .22,
And sent a stream of leaden rain
Exploding through the window-pane;
Yet saw that horrid figure stay
Though half one hand was shot away,
Nor did it falter or depart
With forty bullets in its heart.
Minute by minute, hour by hour,
Impelled by some unholy power,
It beat upon the bolted door
And tried the window-sash once more
And even thrust an arm in vain
In through the shattered window-pane.
By midnight, Ivan's nerve was broken;
And though no further word was spoken,
He tore his hair with laugh inhuman,
Took up a knife and stabbed the woman,
And with his face one twisted leer
Slit his own throat from ear to ear.

IV

"Such was the story Marja brought me
Early next morning, when she sought me
Across the sodden fields of mud,
Faint with fatigue and loss of blood.
Sobs of repentance racked her too;
Her prayers to heaven were warm and true,
Invoking holy aid to save
Her spirit from a sinner's grave.
All through the night, in much distress,
She had maintained her consciousness,
And would have sought me, sure as sin,
But her frail courage, past a doubt,

Could face the bloody dead within
But not the pale, white dead without,
Who still assailed the little shack
From side to side, from front to back,
But, when at last the first sun shone,
Turned to the river and was gone.
That same day, helped by the police,
I tried to give that body peace,
And found it grounded on some sand
Out in the river, close at hand.
   "It was a case that seemed to stir
The Mounties and the coroner;
But I maintained, (and proved a winner)
Marja was victim more than sinner.
Both Paul and Ivan sleep in earth
And walk no more; but far from mirth,
When'er I see the aspens shiver
Down in the copse along the river,
I think of that unearthly night
That changed a woman's hair to white,
And waking, too, an inner sense
Of all-consuming penitence,
Made her, until her days are done,
A shrinking, wan-faced, black-robed nun,
Who in a convent lives in prayer
And penance, out at St. Norbert."

THE SCHOOL-INSPECTOR'S TALE OF THE COURTING OF OLGA KARG

Prologue

Our host had thrown a log or two
Of birch upon the blazing fire;
In silence for a space, we drew
Upon our pipes, and seemed to tire
Of telling stories by the hour.
But interest returned with power
When Casey, as our talk's director,
Turned to the wrinkled school-inspector:
"You know this country pretty well,"
Said he, "and possibly can tell

Whether our fifty races blend
Into one nation. Do they end
In this new land their ancient woe
And bitter feuds from long ago?"
The school-inspector smiled: "I guess
The answer's neither No nor Yes.
But there are changes. As a rule,
They issue from the local school.
But sometimes . . . . Well, a tale of sorts
Is worth a bushel of reports."
He paused, with glances promissory.
To check him had been rude or mulish.
And so began his little story
How Olga Karg taught out a Kulish:

I

"East of the long Duck Mountain range,
Just where its high morainic ridges
Drop steeply down, and mad brooks change
To long, slow rivers, thronged with midges,
A Slavic hamlet, Kulish, lies
Among the stunted birch and spruce,
And with its hay fields occupies
The haunts of beaver, bear, and moose.
A narrow road of miry dirt
Leads eastward, out to Ethelbert;
But otherwise, broad forests bound
The small community around.
Humble Ukrainians and Poles—
In all, about a hundred souls—
Have there hewn out a small domain
And built their homes, white-washed and plain,
With low-thatched roofs and stacks of hay
Piled in the ancient Slavic way.
Out near the borders of the clearing,
A small Canadian school-house stands
To din into small children's hearing
The language of our Western Lands
And some slight modicum of learning
To make them citizens, discerning

A wider world of human good
Beyond that hamlet in the wood.
    "Here, one September, came as teacher
Young Olga Karg, aged twenty-two—
As plumply ravishing a creature
As Wesley College e'er put through—
With voice as luscious as a melon
And the ripe curves of Spartan Helen.
Her eyes were blue as summer pools,
Her curly hair was chestnut brown;
And sudden interest in schools
Smote the chief bachelor in town—
A tall young Pole named Zygmunt Janik,
Whose charms and eager interest
Might well induce delightful panic
In any normal woman's breast.
    "But to the hamlet's blank surprise
She looked on him with scornful eyes,
And would with bitterness disparage
His merest hint of love or marriage.
'You are a Pole,' she'd say with scorn,
'And I, a pure Ukrainian, born
In straight descent from that great Hetman
Who once beat Poland. Don't forget, man,
The old injustice of your race!
To me it would be black disgrace
To sell my true Ukrainian soul
In marriage to a tyrant Pole.'
    "But Zygmunt in remonstrance said:
'Surely the old feuds of our clans
Are now, in this new country, dead,
And we are both Canadians—
Born here on Manitoban soil
And freed from all that Old World broil!
Perhaps you think you have been foolish
To come and teach out here in Kulish,
And do not want to settle down
In such a tiny backwoods town;
Or, since you have such stores of
            knowledge
And in the city went to college

[246]

For four proud years, you feel above me,
And so won't condescend to love me.
This is the truth, and not some hate
Traced back to 1648!'
   "Olga was furious in denials
Of such provoking accusations,
And poured upon his head the vials
Of her soft-voiced recriminations;
But flamed so radiant that he swore
He wished to be her mate the more.
   "All winter long he wooed in vain;
His honest courting only seemed
To stir up more intense disdain:
Yet there were moments when he deemed
A softer light was in her glance
While she dealt out some verbal whipping,
As if she stormed, because, perchance,
She felt her resolution slipping.
Thus he still kept his courage up
Till spring brought back the buttercup.

II

   "It was a sunny day in June
That settled Olga's fate at last.
From the school-windows came the croon
Of learning's one enthusiast
In Kulish, as she gently sought
To get the daily lesson taught.
Across the road was Zygmunt's place.
That afternoon, he patched the roof
Of his old barn, yet kept his face
Turned towards the school, where, so aloof
From all his passionate regard
A girl taught—soft, and yet so hard.
   "Just down below the school-house hill,
Wild strawberries grew ripe and thick,
Tempting the little folks to fill
Their hungry mouths. Arithmetic
And history could not compete
With provender so fresh and sweet.

[247]

And many a little pupil's brain
Strayed sadly from the appointed book,
While Olga struggled on in vain
To win attention, for his look
Told that the mind beneath his thatch
Was absent in the berry-patch.
    "When four o'clock released them all,
A tousled score of girls and boys
In sudden, loud recessional
Went whooping forth. Their merry noise
Receded in a breakneck rush
To where the fruit grew low and lush.
There followed silence for a space . .
While berries at a headlong pace
Were slipping down each little throat
From Nature's one-course *table d'hôte*;
For hungry children, beyond doubt,
Would even rather eat than shout.
    "But all at once a piercing scream
Brought Olga rushing to the door.
She looked: it seemed some evil dream
Had cursed a day so fair before.
Among the frightened children ran
A baby bear; and, just beyond,
A tall, black she-bear rose to scan
The little black-furred vagabond;
Then, sensing peril for her cub,
She shambled out in angry error,
As fierce as black Beëlzebub
To all those children in their terror.
Appalled at their impending doom,
The teacher seized the school-house broom;
And with her own risks quite forgot,
She ran undaunted to the spot.

III

"Zygmunt had likewise heard their shriek
Of panic from the berry-patch,
And saw their peril, from the peak
Of his log barn, then rushed to snatch

A hasty axe up, on his way
To hold the wrathful bear at bay.
'Run to the school-house, all of you,'
He shouted as he reached the scene.
Swiftly, on feet of fear, they flew,—
All except Olga, who, with mien
Transformed by horror, love and pride,
Remained to battle by his side.
   "Then, in dull rage at all things
       human,
The she-bear first attacked the woman,
Who slammed her broomstick on the snout
Of the black monster, while the man
Swinging his axe up, with a shout,
Slashed at its head, but struck a span
Beneath its ear and gashed its shoulder.
Then, as blood spurted, growing bolder,
He drew near for a second stroke.
But frenzy in the bear awoke:
Roaring with pain, it reared and struck
The wheeling axe and sent it flying.
Zygmunt then turned, with desperate pluck,
And took up Olga's broom, relying
On its frail strength in time of danger;
But the grim bear, with one fierce bound,
Hurled its black bulk upon the stranger
And threw him headlong to the ground.
With bear above and man beneath,
His left arm felt those mighty teeth;
But Olga meanwhile had retrieved
His missing weapon and perceived
His peril. With her arms a-strain,
She sank the axe in Bruin's brain,
And panting, watched the enemy
Topple and die convulsively.
   "Half across Zygmunt's body lay
The mighty carcass; and in haste
She tugged it feverishly away.
Zygmunt was groaning, pale as paste;
And bloody currents, bright and warm,
Were gushing from his mangled arm.

In anguish at that savage hurt,
Whose blood-flow bore a mortal threat,
She tore quick strips from off her skirt,
And fashioning a tourniquet
Held back the fatal tide, then dressed
The arm with grief but ill suppressed.
Still pale, but with a wistful smile,
Zygmunt lay looking at her, while,
With strong but trembling hands, she finished
Her task with sorrow undiminished.
'Olga!' he murmured. At her name,
And at the hunger in his eyes,
Alternate white and scarlet came
Across her cheeks. She went to rise;
But, kneeling yet, with gaze grown tender,
She gave a sobbing little moan,
And pressed in sudden, soft surrender
Her quivering lips upon his own.
Then, in recoil from all alarms,
She fainted outright in his arms.

IV

"Love works His will in ways tyrannic.
Olga became, eight years ago,
A very happy Mrs. Janik,
And since then, every year or so,
Love's never-failing fires have sent
Her home some infant increment—
Some girl or boy, to grow and play
On Christmas Eve among the hay
Beneath a Slavic Christmas-tree,
And having gorged on *pierohi*,
Kutya, and fish, at length to pass
Out to a solemn midnight Mass.
But still, in fashions hard to scan,
They also grow Canadian:
Seven-year Olga, sweet and cool,
Takes six-year Zygmunt by the hand
And goes across the road to school,
Where a new teacher, plain and bland,

Builds up a slow Canadian nation
On patient sills of education.
Old hates die hard? Perhaps they do.
But love may help us muddle through!"

THE BUS DRIVER'S TALE OF THE MAGYAR VIOLINIST

Prologue

The long-faced driver of the bus
Grew restive at this tale of love,
And in impatience turned to us
And crossly said: "By Heaven above,
Some people have the notion still
That every Jack must have his Jill
In this imperfect world below;
But I have found it isn't so,
And many a case of adoration
Ends in sheer heart-break and frustration.
I call to mind a tragic case
In which a lad of parts and grace
Was destined to a tragic end.
I knew him somewhat, as a friend,
And so can vouch for every fact,
And saw, myself, the final act."
      The merchant roused a bit at this.
"Speak on!" he said with emphasis,
"For while there is no use pretending
We don't prefer a happy ending,
Yet we aren't children. We can face
The fact of suffering, in its place."
And so that melancholy man,
The driver of the bus, began:

I

"When I was young, I used my muscle
Out with a big construction gang
Building a railway north of Russell,
And came to know the bitter pang

[*251*]

Of winter frost, likewise the pain
Of summer suns that bake the brain.
We were a sturdy group of roughs,
Busy (on hash and pork-and-beans)
In gouging gravel from the bluffs
And filling in the deep ravines.
We slept in bunk-cars on a siding,
Sun-blistered box-cars, rudely fashioned,
And there the Chinese cook, dividing
Such provender as had been rationed,
Kept all content on copious fare
Who through the months were working there.
Yet sometimes, when, just in the offing,
I heard the big steam shovel coughing,
It seemed a lonely life to me,
Though on the prairie I could see
A village throng of furry loafers—
Those chirping kibitzers, the gophers;
But, by and large, the friends we made
Were in our own hard-bitten legions,
Though snorting freight-trains on the grade
Gave us a glimpse of outer regions.
     "As weeks went by, I realized
That every man of all our lot—
Magyar, Ukrainian, Pole, or Scot—
Had some deep vision that he prized,
And that behind each one there lay
Some tragic cause that made him stray
Beyond the parish of his birth
To this bleak corner of the earth.

II

"As neighbour to my bunk I had
A slender, brown-haired Magyar lad,
Young Imre Szabó, harshly torn
From the far land where he was born
By woes of war and revolution
That brought him down to destitution
And placed some millions of his folk
Under an iron foreign yoke.

He had been born in Transylvania,
At Kolozsvár, among the hills,
But ragged armies of Roumania
Brought to the land a thousand ills,
And both the parents he adored
Were slaughtered by the hostile horde.
He had been trained as a musician
At Kolozsvár and Budapest,
And had secured a good position
At the Liszt College, when the crest
Of revolution reached its height
And killed his prospects over-night.
Hence, of all work and wealth bereft
In the sad country of his kin,
After some hungry months he left
Another chapter to begin
With indescribable emotion
In western lands beyond the ocean.
But even here no work was found
For a superb first violinist.
The theatres used films for sound,
And so his living was the thinnest,
Until by quick degrees he came
To join the rough construction game
And warp his fine artistic hand
In lugging ties and tamping sand.
One warm, deep passion moved
      his life—
Love for a girl, his blue-eyed Sári,
Whom he proposed to make his wife;
And she as well seemed keen to marry
As soon as he, by eager toil,
Could bring her to Canadian soil.
Thus, as by day he worked near me
In trousers of old dungaree,
With knotted rope-strands for a belt,
And somehow smiled, I knew he felt
That all this hardship, though severe,
Would bring his Sári yet more near.
Or when at evening he would lie
Upon his bunk, and smile, and sigh,

I knew his thoughts were far away
Envisioning a happier day.
In time, he told me all his hope
And all the story of his past;
And though the young lad did not mope
About those days that could not last,
Yet memories were his existence
And his poor soul found its subsistence
In recollections sweet and far
Of summer nights in Kolozsvár
When the acacias were in bloom
And through the tender twilight gloom
The babbling Szamos whispered low
To the two lovers wandering slow,
Till starlight touched their happy cheeks
Beneath the Transylvanian peaks.
Or he recalled, beyond the rest,
One magic night in Budapest,
When high upon the Gellért heights
They sat and watched the myriad lights
In jewelled radiance illumine
The city like a sleeping woman.
Far down, the Danube eddied fleet
Dark, velvet waters at their feet,
And gypsy music floated still
Across the silence of the hill,
Stirring the heart in poignant fashion
With deathless hope and hopeless passion.
He was to seek, at dawn of day,
Another country far away
Beyond the salt, soul-sundering sea,
That there, with thrift and energy,
He might create an Eden fair
And bring his blue-eyed sweetheart there.
And so that night in Budapest
Before he sought an alien West,
They sat and talked the whole night through,
And kissed and cried, as lovers do,
And vowed that though harsh fate might sever
Their paths awhile, yet, blocked by none,

Their faithful love would last forever,
While hills should stand and rivers run.
With such remembrances enshrined
Imperishably in his mind,
He bore harsh toil and pain and ache,
And deemed them light for Sári's sake.

III

"One August day, a letter came,
A cold, brief message from her mother,
To say, without a word of blame,
That Sári had espoused another.
Had she been there, and I had heard her,
I would have told her it was murder;
For Imre never smiled again
In that rough world of working men,
And it was plain, with no word spoken,
The mainspring of his life was broken.
The end came soon. For when, that fall,
An onset of pneumonia faced him,
He did not fight the thing at all,
And six days later we had placed him
In a low grave of prairie clay
Along the lonely right of way.
   "Few of our people realize
How countless railway tracks and ties
Are laid with human blood and sweat,
And those who know it, soon forget,
While all the voiceless, toiling lot—
Magyar, Ukrainian, Pole, and Scot—
Go on their humble, tragic ways
After the rough construction days.
As for the many who remain
Beneath the grasses of the plain,
Like that young lad of dreams and sighs,
Only the coyotes' mournful cries
As dusk comes on, express to me
The sense of all their tragedy."

Prologue

Farthest of any from the fire
Of all who yarned and puffed in peace
Was an old priest who smoked a briar,
A Manitoba-born Métis
Whose heart had never wished to sally
Beyond the old Red River Valley.
"In blends of Indian and white,"
Exclaimed the lawyer, "I am sure
The Indian seems to pass from sight;
At least the type is never pure.
I doubt if the authentic strain
E'er comes in spirit back again."
The old priest murmured contradiction:
"I have a story from my youth,
And though it sounds like wildest fiction
I can assure you it is truth,
For with my boyhood eyes I saw
A man revert and be as raw
And fierce a savage, past restraint,
As ever fought in battle-paint."
We held our peace; we did not fear
A feeble tale from such as he.
And so we heard with eager ear
An old Red River tragedy:

I

"The dark Red River never pauses
In moving on its northward course,
Inscrutable as primal causes
And as relentless in its force;
Through level leagues of plain it passes,
Across a green infinitude
Of springing grain and prairie grasses,
In endless progress, still renewed,
Past Aubigny and Letellier,
St. Jean Baptiste and Ste. Agathe,

White St. Adolphe and white Cartier,
Where, by the River and the flat,
Frenchman and Cree, in mingled strains,
Are domiciled upon the plains.
Centuries since, before the French
Had mated with their dusky daughters,
The Red Men had been wont to drench
Deep in the River's turbid waters
A yearly human sacrifice
To the grim spirit of the flood,
Who would be friendly at the price
Of duly offered human blood.
    "Led by the shaman, one spring day,
They would assemble on the shore,
Standing in ranks upon the clay,
And while the sorcerer went before
Through all his holy rites and charms,
Would copy, as in mute kotow,
His solemn flexures of the arms
And three times beaten breast and brow
As silent prelude to the death
Of one who still drew living breath,
But who, when marked by the magician,
Died freely, of his own volition.
    "An Indian teepee-village stood
Just at the present Aubigny,
And there, beside a little wood,
The sacrifice was wont to be—
A solemn service to placate
A Spirit capable of hate.
No other spot that Red Men knew
Commanded equal reverence
Except the Straits of Manitou,
On His great lake, where confluence
Of flooding waves dread sounds awoke
As if the Chief of Spirits spoke.
But ever since bold French begot
On Indian wives a mingled race,
Their sons, as Christians, have forgot
The ancient horror of the place,

Save as an undertone of feeling
Scarce realized or worth concealing.
The steepled church beside the Stream
Lifts its triumphant cross on high;
No pious villager would dream
That he could flout it, or deny;
And yet in this small town befell
The startling story that I tell.

II

"When I was but a little boy,
The prettiest lass in Aubigny
And fittest for some lover's joy
Was Paul Couture's big girl Marie.
She was as supple as a willow;
Her hair was black, her lips were red;
Her budding bosom was a pillow
On which a king might lay his head;
Her voice was like a quiet brook;
Modest she was from head to feet;
And every man would turn to look
When she went shyly down the street.
    "Two men were rivals for her love:
Adolphe Dufresne and Jacques Bazin,
Each of them well equipped to prove
Her model of a fine young man.
Jacques was a trifle under size,
With beetling brows and brooding eyes,
But he was handsome in his way,
Lithe as a panther when he walked,
And a great 'cello seemed to play
Deep in his throat where'er he talked,
Voicing, for anyone to sense,
A nature tender and intense.
But young Adolphe was tall and straight,
With Scipionic brow and nose,
Born to command, in love or hate,
Imperious even in repose,
And his clear voice would mount and soar
Like trumpets summoning to war.

[258]

Both men were French in name and training;
Both to the holy Faith held fast;
Yet in their features, without straining,
One saw, four generations past,
How Indian fire and arrogance
Had mingled with the blood of France.
    "Howe'er Marie made up her mind,
Make it she did: and it was clear
That with the months her heart inclined
To hold Adolphe as much more dear.
But Jacques Bazin grew pale with moping;
Ever he racked his tortured brain,
Through labyrinths of passion groping
For some dark answer to his pain.
    "I was a boy, as I have said,—
A little, black-haired lad of nine;
And even yet I thrill with dread
In thinking what a sight was mine
One day in spring, with knees a-shiver,
Hid in a thicket by the River.

III

"I had been playing in that wood
Where shamans long ago had stood,
When, at a sudden voice, I shrank
Among the hazels by the bank,
And, peering through them fearfully,
I saw Adolphe and his Marie
Stand side by side; in threatening fashion
Jacques faced them in a towering passion.
Short breaths his heaving breast expelled,
And in his twitching hands he held
A one-barrel shot-gun, half-uplifted;
Then, with an oath, the gun was shifted
Up to his shoulder, thus to cover
The heart of the successful lover.
'Ah, mon Dieu, non!' cried out Marie,
And flung herself upon the breast
Of her Adolphe with loyalty
Just as Jacques' trigger-finger pressed

[259]

And the gun gave a murderous roar
That echoed on from shore to shore.
Thus, as her fragrant body clung
One quivering moment to her lover,
Black buckshot tore through back and lung
A wound whence no one could recover.
Blood spurted. With convulsive moan
She kissed him, and her soul had flown.
    "Adolphe stood staring one brief space,
Then laid the warm, dear corpse aside,
And in pale fury turned to face
Him who had robbed him of a bride.
Jacques used his spent gun as a club;
Adolphe had but a pocket-knife,
But would have slain Beëlzebub
In that grim fight of death and life.
For though again and yet again
Jacques' blows broke ribs and collar-bone,
He seemed impervious to pain,
And, stabbing fiercely, claimed his own
In streaming wounds on face and throat
Till Jacques grew feebler as he smote
And sank at last upon the clay,
Gasping his frenzied life away.
Then his foe helped the soul depart
With savage knife-thrusts through the heart,
And, in a weirder spectacle,
Grappling the hair of him now dead,
He drew the knife-blade round the skull
And wrenched the scalp from off the head.
Erect he stood then, French no more
But purest savage, scalp in hand.
All dabbled with his foeman's gore,
Upon the corpse I saw him stand
And raise with shrill intensity
The war-whoop of the ancient Cree!

IV

"As when dark clouds, as night draws on,
Succeed a lurid sunset-flame,

[260]

A bleaker, sadder mood anon
Over the suffering lover came.
Dropping the scalp with sudden loathing,
He turned with tears to his Marie,
Patted her hair and smoothed her clothing,
And took her gently on his knee.
 "Then, as I watched him from my thicket,
I saw how yet another mood
Entered his grieving mind, to prick it
Out of its tearful lassitude.
It was a mood as primitive
And pagan as his scalping-fit:
All of the years that I may live
I shall recall the thrill of it.
Lifting her body up, he strode
A few short steps and seemed to greet
The deep Red River's waves that flowed,
A turbid torrent, at his feet.
As in a trance, he laid her down
And faced the River, grim and brown.
He wove before it gestured charms—
No Sign of Cross to seal a vow,
But solemn flexures of the arms
And three times beaten breast and brow
As if in prelude to the death
Of one who still drew living breath.
Then, with Marie in his embrace,
He cast himself without a quiver,
But rather with a Stoic grace,
Deep in the eddies of the River.

v

"Near Ste. Agathe, some two weeks later.
The bodies, side by side, were found;
And but for me, the sole spectator,
A place in consecrated ground
Had been forbidden to a man
Whose suicide seemed plain to scan.
But I, the only witness, swore
That as he staggered, well nigh spent,

To bear her home along the shore,
He'd tumbled in by accident.
And so, still dubious and loath,
In one green plot they buried both.
But if my falsehood was a sin
And God is vexed to have him in,
I know that with efficient plea
Her soul will intercede for me
As well as him for whom she died
In springtime, by the River's side—
That broad Red River, dark, sublime,
That, on these prairies, seems to me
Our turbid human stream of Time
Through prairies of Eternity."

THE PARSON'S TALE OF THE GIMLI PRODIGAL

Prologue

We watched the hearth-fire for a time
In silence. Then the drover said:
"I wonder if a youth of crime
Has ever turned to good instead?"—
"Sometimes it has," the parson ventured.
"Sometimes a lad to hell indentured
Has proved a hero, fit for glory.
Yes, I am thinking of a story."—
"Go on," we urged him. "Tell your tale."—
"Granted," he answered. "That I shall."
And so he traced for us the trail
Of the young Gimli prodigal:

I

"There was a youth," he started primly,
"Whose habitation was in Gimli,
That bleak Icelandic fishing-village
From which the boats go out to pillage
The waters of Lake Winnipeg.
He was a badly addled egg:

For when you questioned anyone
About young Olaf Helgason,
A sadly shaken head would mourn
The utter shipwreck of his days,
And mothers used his name to warn
Their children from ungodly ways.
He was good-looking, tall and fair,
Blue-eyed, with Scandinavian hair,
And with that Irish nose, perforce,
That marks his nation from the Norse;
Yet all his gifts of form and face
Served but to heighten his disgrace.
His boyhood had been strict and stern;
His father, Helgi, as I learn,
Had been the grimmest, soberest liver
From Selkirk north to Berens River.
But when the old man's fishing-yawl
Was lost in a September squall,
Paternal thrift bequeathed the boy
A tidy fortune to enjoy.
Scorning his widowed mother's pleas,
He plunged into a gulf of ease
And grew expert to guzzle rum
With swinish males and female scum
In dark resorts of evil fame,
Dishonouring an honoured name.
But when these rats had picked him clean
Of all his little patrimony,
They coached the wild young wolverine
In devious ways to catch a coney;
Yet though he tried all forms of swindling
His hopes to side-step work kept dwindling,
Till desperation led in time
To fiercer, bolder forms of crime.
One night, with 'Slimy' Popovitch,
Who also had a thievish itch,
He paid a well-armed midnight call
On Gimli's Bank of Montreal,
Made entry, and began assault
Upon the safe within the vault.

[263]

The golden crib was well-nigh cracked
When Mounties caught them in the act.
'Put up your hands!' a red-coat said.
'What are you doing here, you bummers?'—
'Lay off!' says Olaf, turning red.
'We're just a helpful pair of plumbers.'—
'Then come with me,' the Mountie lours
'For working after union hours!'
Since Olaf had an automatic
Ready for action on his hip,
The magistrate was most emphatic
In giving him a five-year trip;
And so he settled the account in
A steel-barred cell at Stony Mountain.

II

"A sadder and a wiser man,
Young Olaf was turned loose at last,
Telling the Warden that his plan
Was bravely to live down his past
Back in the little fishing-port
Where he had been condemned in court.
His white-haired mother welcomed him
With faltering step and eyes grown dim,
But the community at large
Was hostile over his discharge:
'This mouldy jail-bird from the Pen,'
They said in scorn, 'should go on West,
And not compete with decent men
Where once he fouled an honest nest.
Why should he hope to find a job
Here, where he loafed, a thieving snob?'
In vain for weeks he looked about,
Till Walter Kvaran, full of pity
For the old mother, tried him out
In gutting gold-eyes for the City.
It was a job that stank supremely,
A bilious task and hard to stomach,
But he endured the stench unseemly,
The dripping knife, the reeking hummock

Of fishy offal and the rest,
Because he dared not fail the test.
Under the summer sun he toiled.
Though blistering dog-days almost
        broiled
The fish on which he plied his blade;
And still all Gimli, man and maid,
Looked with suspicion on the lad,
Regarding him as wholly bad.
    "August the Second duly came,
And an Icelandic celebration
Was held at Hnausa in the name
Of their renowned ancestral nation.
Thither in zest came everyone
From Arborg and from Riverton
And all the coast-folk, near and far,
From Gimli up to Sandy Bar.
Then children of the Arctic Isle
Upheld their old inheritance:
Some wrestled in Icelandic style,
And some led out the Viking dance,
And there were poets, old and young,
Grey Stephan G. and Guttormur—
Iceland and Canada were sung
In odes that made the heart-strings stir.
But to young Olaf one fair scene
Caused every other view to fade—
It was the crowning of the Queen,
The white *Fjallkona*, 'Mountain-maid':
For Sigrun, Gimli's fairest lass,
His school-mate in a day gone by,
Was deemed that season to surpass
All others for this honour high.
Serene and lovely, tall and sweet,
She sat upon her Viking throne—
A simple girl at whose shy feet
The tribute of a day was shewn.
Her eyes the glance of Olaf crossed:
He looked, and loved her, and was lost.
That night with hopeless, throbbing head
He lay upon his humble bed:

For how could he, who toiled in squalor
Under the shadow of a crime
And needed every hard-won dollar
To help his mother, hope in time
That she, the fairest queen of all,
Might wed the Gimli prodigal?
He knew, moreover, that his boss,
Big Walter Kvaran, whose good heart
Had saved his life from utter loss,
Had sought to play the lover's part,
And that, unless all plans miscarried,
Another year would see them married.
Walter was forty, to be sure,
A widower and plain of face,
But he was rich, his life was pure,
His name unspotted by disgrace.
Olaf had noted with surprise
A kindly light in Sigrun's eyes,
And yet he felt his hopes were barren
Compared with those of Walter Kvaran.
   "Day after day, amid his toil,
Her peerless face possessed his mind.
The foulest labour could not soil
A week in which her glance was kind.
And yet he held himself aloof,
Fearing the scorn of swift reproof,
And sought to mitigate the curse
Of hopeless love by setting down
In measures of Icelandic verse
The passion that he could not drown:
      'Sigrun only do I sigh for,
      Sadly moan my low estate.
      Sick and lone, true life I cry for.
      Love atones my evil fate!'
Such were the ring-rhymes that he fashioned
After the rules of ancient metre,
Feeling their permanence impassioned
Must somehow make his love completer.
But still he kept his verses hid
And breathed to no one what he did.

"Hard frosts came early that November,
Rimming the shores with shining ice.
Few of the settlers could remember
A colder fall. And since the price
Of fish was high and times were hard,
No fear the fishermen debarred,
After the coastal waters froze,
From netting whitefish through the floes.
Foremost among them, Walter sought
With three bold men to take his store;
And every night on sleds they brought
A silvery harvest to the shore.
And there, the scaly bellies ripping,
Salted the fish for early shipping.
    "One Friday, when the morning broke,
A heavy east wind rose and blew
Out of a sky of leaden hue
And to tumultuous life awoke
The twenty miles of open water
Beyond the ice-floes. But the slaughter
Of precious whitefish did not cease,
Although beneath the gleaming floes
A heaving ground-swell's strength arose
And groaned, and gave the ice no peace,
Cracking it clean in many a spot
With uproar like a cannon-shot.
At two o'clock, the east wind fell.
At half past four, a wild north-wester
Swooped, like a blizzard loosed from hell,
As if relentless to sequester
Some hapless fragment of the floe
And drive it to the open lake—
Nor swooped in vain. With movement slow,
Under its impulse, a great cake
Broke from its mooring near the shore
And on it, unsuspecting, bore
Big Walter Kvaran and the three
Who shared his daily industry.

Too late they startled and looked back
And saw between them and the land
A lane of water wide and black,
And frantic watched that lane expand:
No voice could pierce that snow-filled gale;
They waved their arms to speak their plight;
But every effort seemed to fail
Across the deepening dusk of night.
Dimmer and farther grew the town,
With lamplit windows in the gloom.
Ever more certain seemed their doom
As ever mightier waves bore down
And battered fragments from the floe;
They knew they had not far to go
Before their ice-isle would be tossed
To nothing and be wholly lost.
Then, on the waves, they seemed to mark
A blacker black within the dark.

IV

"It was a boat, with Olaf in it,
Tossing upon the icy waves.
Now some great billow seems to spin it,
And now once more the skiff behaves
As if in dogged bravery
It sought their rescuer to be.
    "In Gimli, when the blizzard broke,
Olaf was in the packing-sheds,
Intent on shovelling whitefish-heads
Into the refuse-vat. Then spoke
A frantic voice beside his ear:
It was old Hrefna Helgason,
His mother, who beyond the pier
Had marked the drifting ice-floe run
Into the heaving, storm-lashed lake
With the four men, and for their sake
Had rushed to gasp the message out
In Walter's fish-sheds. With a shout,
Olaf ran quickly to the beach
And gazed across the gathering night
To where, a mile beyond their reach,

[268]

The fated four had passed from sight
Others soon gathered by him there
And spoke in counsels of despair:
'The schooners are laid up for winter.'
'Walt's rowboat is the only thing.'—
'In storm and floe that boat might splinter;
And it's so small one man would fling
His life to chance in rescuing four.
That boat takes five and not one more.'—
'A man were mad to risk that fate!'—
'Who'll go?'—'Not I! It's now too late.'
    "Olaf stood silent as they talked;
Swift thought made tumult in his brain:
Walter was gone, the man who baulked
His love for Sigrun. Not in vain
Hereafter might his wooing prove.
He might aspire to Sigrun's charms.
Already, in a dream of love,
He held her warm within his arms;
And riches too in fancy came
To add their glamour to his name.
    "Then out of unguessed deeps of thought
A starker, sterner mood arose—
A man's strong purpose, making taut
His muscles, while his young face froze
To icy resolution. Surely
Out of his far Icelandic past
Heroic impulse now beat purely
To argue him a man at last.
His father, Helgi, once had taught him
His lineage of a thousand years;
And now, perhaps, remembrance caught him,
Perhaps that roll-call filled his ears—
Helgi and Axel, Sveinn and Bjarni,
Gisli and Kolbeinn, Páll and Gest,
Snorri and Sigurbjörn and Arni,
Gunnar and Oddur and the rest—
And in his heart he heard them speaking,
Those generations in his blood;
Dim in his mind he saw them seeking
Greatly their sea-borne livelihood.

[269]

Along that misty Arctic island
He saw their fishing-vessels tossed;
By skerry, reef, and craggy highland,
Their lives, but not their souls, were lost.
Thus, as he stood there in his place,
He quenched all thought of love or pelf,
Uplifted on a tide of race
That made him greater than himself.
    "Into the lake he rowed alone,
Into the darkness and the storm
Until at last the boat's frail form
Was lost to sight, and with a moan
Old Hrefna sank upon the snow,
Unable to conceal her woe.
    "Thus, in their need, the four lost men,
Their garments stiff with icy scurf,
Beheld him sweep into their ken,
Seeking their floe across the surf.
They cheered; then felt their joy withdraw
And turn to horror, as they saw
The skiff against the floe capsize
And Olaf sink before their eyes,
Never to reappear. In vain
They sought him, and at last in pain
They turned the boat's prow to the shore
And with two men on either oar
Into the storm they battled grimly
Over the billows back to Gimli. . . .
    "There's really not much more to tell.
Walter was laid up for a spell . . .
Pneumonia . . . And Hrefna found
The songs to Sigrun, and went round
And called on Sigrun with a view
To finding whether Sigrun knew
Olaf had loved her, and the price
And measure of his sacrifice.
Whether she did, I can't unfold;
For neither woman ever told.
But when in time she wed with Walter
And a male baby duly came,

She knew her mind, and did not alter
Her choice of Olaf as his name.
And in the Gimli graveyard, where
Drowned Olaf by drowned Helgi sleeps,
Through thirty years her tender care
A quiet vigil often keeps."
   The parson ceased. A silence fell.
Then said the lawyer: "It appears
That story lives on mighty well
In detail, after thirty years."—
The answer came back, soft and slow:
"With me, his memory is not barren,
Though born but thirty years ago.
My name, you see, is Olaf Kvaran."

THE SECOND FARMER'S TALE OF THE JOBLESS GAOLBIRD

The second farmer's past was Norse.
He was a thoughtful sort of chap,
Fair-haired, as husky as a horse,
And a fine backer in a scrap.
"I like the West," he said. "It's true
I'm a Canadian through and through,
And yet it is a grief to me
That with the country's boundless wealth
We have so failed to guarantee
The welfare, happiness, and health
Of every growing lass and lad,
But often send them to the bad
Through lack of work and lack of care
Until they crack in sheer despair.
Even our houses of correction,
Which ought to save them for their time,
Are sometimes centres of infection
And doom the young to lives of crime."
   "I scent a story," Casey said.
"Go on, and tell it, without fail!"
And so he willingly complied,
And told a tragic penal tale:

When I was young, I was a guard
Out in the Gaol at Headingly.
The duties were not very hard
For a big husky man like me,
Yet nearly everyone who serves
In such a place develops nerves—
And when I longed to be at large,
I asked, and got, my full discharge.
It's hard to analyse the mood
Of such a place. We liked the food;
And I can give a *bona fide*
I never saw a place more tidy.
But bricks and concrete, brass and steel
Are hard, cold things for men to feel,
And give an atmosphere of gloom
To every cell and cage and room.
Along the concrete floors one's tread
Goes echoing fit to wake the dead,
And steel on steel grates harsh and hard
When keys are turned and bolts are barred.
Yet more depressing still, I think,
Is tending men whose hearts are ink,
The human misfits whom the court
Has banished to this grey resort.
Two types are there, split fifty-fifty:
The one is earnest, kind, and thrifty,
But through weak impulse or bad luck
Has fallen headlong in the muck;
The other lot are bad at heart
And only foul a second start,
Compounding each successive time
The brutal baseness of their crime.
But to a thoughtful man, the worst
Is that the last type and the first
Are mingled here in cell and cage
Without regard for crime or age,
And many a likely lad begins
To learn a sordid list of sins

From vicious lags who never tire
In dragging others in the mire.
Release then means but more offending,
Which all too often has its ending
When in that fatal southwest room
The hangman works his act of doom:
Then, with a clang, the steel trap falls
And echoes through the shuddering halls.
   A tragic case that I remember
Was young Jim Tingle from Toronto,
Who rode the rods out one September
Because his work and cash had gone to—
Well, to that hopeless, hungry void
That swallows up the unemployed.
Jim was a winsome sort of boy
With light blue eyes and curly hair,
The sort a father would enjoy
In rearing as his son and heir;
But as an orphan, he was bound
To find his own hard way around.
To make his path more stony still,
The lack of all co-ordination
Between our provinces worked ill
In letting labour, in our nation,
Drift aimlessly from spot to spot
In search of some more active town
Or else in dull stagnation rot
When local industries shut down.
And thus, with many another drifter
Who sought for work and would not beg,
Jim thought of no solution swifter
Than riding freights to Winnipeg.
At first his luck seemed better here,
And for the space of half a year
He worked unloading wholesale meat,
And had a room on Hargrave Street.
In spring, alas, a lay-off came,
And Jim, aged twenty, had no claim
Compared with many a married man
With wife and children's needs to scan.

By summer, all Jim's cash was spent.
His boarding-house, with sundry oaths,
To guarantee arrears of rent,
Then seized his coat and winter clothes.
Hunger grew dire one August day;
And in a mood not felt before,
He tried to smuggle food away
Out of a big department store.
A lynx-eyed clerk was quick to see.
Jim got five months in Headingly.

II

When we first put him under lock,
The lad was dazed with shame and shock.
He had been reared with grace and knowledge,
And had a year or two of college,
When both his parents' deaths had thrown
The youngster wholly on his own.
Week after week, I looked at Jim
And watched the workings of his mind
To see if gaol had curdled him
And turned his soul against his kind.
I saw the old lags at their game
Of urging him to put off shame
And find revenge in hateful glee
In war upon society.
But Jim was made of better stuff—
A day or two before he left
He told me he had had enough:
He'd die before he'd stoop to theft.
When January closed his stay,
The gaol truck took him in to town,
And, with a chilly 'Well, good day!',
Pulled to the curb and let him down,
Dressed only in the summer suit
That he had worn at his arrest,
Of overcoat quite destitute—
No hat, no underwear, no vest,
And in his pocket not a cent
To feed or lodge him where he went!

He sought his former boarding-place,
But Mrs. Gooch, who met his ring,
Just slammed the front door in his face
And vowed he had not left a thing.
He sought his old employers out,
But found the boss refused to see him;
From firm to firm he trudged about,
But none from his distress would free him;
And if he chanced to beg a dime,
They cried that begging was a crime
And threatened him with the police
If the black practice did not cease.
In zero weather, thinly clad,
He shivered on from shop to shop,
A hungry and disheartened lad
Who saw no place where he could stop
There on the icy winter street
Down which the north wind wailed and beat,
Till Hop Lee Ching, whose bedroom lay
Above his little frame café,
Shared food and bed that night with Jim
When every door was barred to him
And all the Christian city stood
As heartless as a winter wood.
Next morning, with a stifled sob,
He started out to find a job;
But all men asked him, without fail,
How he had left his last employ,
And when they heard about the Gaol
They simply would not hire the boy.
To make it short, within a week
Of starting his unheeded plea,
A bobby found him, staggering weak,
And ran him in for vagrancy.

III

This time we got him back defiant.
All the old-timers in his flat
Now found in him a willing client,
And at their wicked feet he sat.

They taught the lad in easy stages
At talking-time along the cages,
And he would learn with bitter zeal
The way that steel can bite on steel
In drilling safes, and what expense
Would fix one's takings with a fence,
What lawyers were the best for crooks,
And how to fake a set of books.
Then he was taught by 'Stinky' Bates,
An old past master at the game,
To pinch a car and change the plates
And file the numbers off the frame.
Then a sleek Russian, Ivan Bunin,
Was always sure to come and tune in,
And urge on him, as his solution,
A glorious time of revolution,
When all the Workers would arise
And make this Continent their prize:
'The turnkey and the Governor,
Would then,' he muttered, 'scrub the floor,
While we, exultant to condemn,
Prepared the hangman's drop for them,
And shot the boorzhoys, days and nights,
Through all their homes in River Heights.'
But the most voluble of all
Was an old burglar, 'Butch' McColl,
Alias Brown, Brock, Bryce, and Vales,
A seasoned connoisseur in gaols.
He claimed he'd been in every one
From New Orleans to Edmonton:
'And some were very bad,' he'd say,
'And some were good, and this to-day
Rates on the whole as pretty good
In style and quality of food,
Except that Ivan, the big dope,
Once dosed the soup with laundry soap
To start a riot, for he likes
The raw, red violence of strikes.
I fear that if in time the stars
Bring all his fevered plans to birth,

The Comrades and the Commissars
Will make our life a hell on earth;
For ruthless Red minorities,
With acid in their veins for blood,
Would do with people as they please
And trample freedom in the mud.
Don't listen when his mad dreams fizz!
Just take the country as it is:
And though we sometimes get our lickings,
A clever crook can have his pickings.'
Such were his mentors, week by week;
And when they were released before him,
They gave him an address to seek,
As proof of the good will they bore him—
For when at last he too was free,
He planned a life of burglary.

IV

That very morning he set out
To look for Ivan, Butch, and Bates,
And found the trio just about
To pull a job. 'At equal rates,'
Said Butch, 'come in and work with us!
I think you'll be a useful cuss.
Meet us to-night at half-past-ten.
Here is some cash to last till then.
In the big safe we're going to crack
There's plenty. None of us will lack!'
Then 'Stinky' vowed, with many a nod,
That Jim would have no vain regrets;
And Ivan handed him a rod
And marihuana cigarettes,
Those hashish-fags that fill the mind
With killer's lust against mankind.
That evening, in the streaming rain,
He walked with frenzy in his brain,
Born of the deadly murder-weed
That nerves the heart to any deed.
As luck would have it, the detectives
Had been tipped off to Butch's plot

To crack the safe; and two effectives
Were there in ambush on the spot.
When Jim and the old-timer trio
Had just begun to ply their tools,
The bobbies challenged them *con brio*,
But when, in keeping with all rules,
The old lags ducked and ran away,
Jim with defiance turned to stay
And shoot it out with the police
In murderous mood and mad caprice.
Then, in a swift and fatal start,
His first slug found one bobby's heart.
His second bullet chanced to plough
A crease across the other's brow
And drop him likewise, as if dead,
Although it had but grazed his head.
Jim paused, and gasped, in sudden fright,
And hurried out into the night—
A night less dark, with storm and rain,
Than the black tumult in his brain.

▼

With six big prowl-cars on his trail,
A roused police force tracked him down,
And as the dawn was turning pale,
Found him, the sanest man in town,
A pale and penitent offender
And more than ready to surrender.
Out in a gaol-cage once again,
He sat and brooded, in such pain
That Hell could never hope to see
More utter, hopeless misery.
It was too dark, the thing he felt,
For that next night, to find surcease,
He hanged himself with his own belt,
And so, at last, poor Jim had peace,
There in that gloomy concrete den
That altered him, a simple lad,
Into an enemy of men
And slowly changed the good to bad.

Who killed Jim Tingle? It's my claim
That he himself was not to blame,
But you, and I, and all the rest
Who in this wide, abundant West
With all our wealth have failed to give
Each man a chance to work and live.
To me, the case was most alarming;
And I resigned and took to farming.
Close to the soil, it seems to me,
One faces a reality
In life and labour past compare;
And that is why I'm staying there."

THE POET'S TALE OF THE DARKENING DREAM

Prologue

At last the hour was growing late.
Some talked of bed. Said Casey: "Wait!
This quiet fellow in the corner,
Like well-known Master Jackie Horner,
Has had his finger in the pie
By way of listening, but is shy
In speaking out, for he alone
Has told no story of his own."
Then with a smile he turned to me.
"Round off the evening, Sir!" said he.
"I swear by Joseph's coloured coats,
I've watched you all day taking notes
There in the corner, and I'm sure,
Though you look timid and demure,
You have some stirring tale to tell
Will please our group almighty well."
Confronted thus by his intent,
I wriggled with embarrassment:
"If I were wise, I would decline,
For stories are not in my line;
But lest I seem, with thankless heart,
Unwilling to play out my part,
I shall tell briefly of a dream
From which I wakened with a scream

Only last night. As I'm a sinner,
It was not due to Casey's dinner—
I would not be misunderstood,
For this hotel is mighty good—
But some distemper in my veins
Produced in me these psychic pains.
Whether the vision had a meaning
Some one of you perhaps can tell.
I only know it has a leaning
Towards agonizing pangs of hell."
The rest were silent, so anon
I cleared my throat and thus went on:

I

"I dreamt I saw a marshy plain,
A scummy waste of stagnant rain,
And from it, like a sloping roof,
An eastward hillside drew aloof.
Up that broad mountain, countless men,
Emerging from the dismal fen,
Walked bravely upwards towards the height,
Their brows a-glow with morning light;
For high above the eastern rim,
Brighter than hosts of cherubim,
A blaze of glory had begun,
At times a cross, at times a sun.
Slowly the human army climbed,
With marshy traces still beslimed,
While each was faithful to the other
And helped him upward like a brother.
It was a soul-inspiring sight
To see kind faces gleaming bright
And see reflected in each eye
The holy glory in the sky.
    "After long ages, as it seemed,
It was a darker thing I dreamed.
For some no longer faced the sun,
But from earth's iron entrails spun
Fantastic types of cold machine
Such as mankind had never seen—

Machines for sport and recreation,
For government, and education,
To heal man's body and restore him,
And do his very thinking for him.
And as man's trust, through such abettal,
Was less on faith and more on metal,
The radiant light of heaven grew dim
And earth seemed merciless and grim.

II

"I saw my dream grow darker yet,
And all the heavens overset
With a miasmic fog of night
That choked and hid the earlier light.
Across the land, in horrid zeal,
Crawled giant dinosaurs of steel,
Churning the hillside into mire
And belching lead and gouts of fire.
Before them maddened thousands fled,
And thousands in their path lay dead.
From lairs of concrete in the hills
Slid pterodactyls, broad of wing,
With leaden murder in their bills
And in their throats loud muttering,
Demanding horror in a flood
And mighty draughts of human blood.
With hideous roars they swept the skies
Or ranged the fields like monstrous flies;
And those who fled the dinosaurs
These flying creatures killed by scores.
    "Some remnants of the race of man
Then down the slope in frenzy ran,
And after them steel monsters came
With gullets belching smoke and flame,
Driving them, furious and harsh,
To stifle in the ancient marsh.
Just as they sank beneath the scum
And I stood gaping, crazed and dumb,
A pterodactyl swooped at me,
And I awoke in agony . . ."

*　*　*　*

After an interval of quiet,
Said Casey, "Such a dream of doom
Is no reflection on the diet
I serve you in my dining-room.
Nor has it meaning. That is flat.
In such things, I'm perfect sceptic.
To have a nightmare such as that,
You must have been a born dyspeptic."
The teacher grinned: "Your dream was all
Quite palaeontological
And might provide a 'horror classic'
With setting in the Mid-Jurassic.
If dreams like that are writ in stone,
I'd leave Geology alone.
I fancy that your recent reading
Has had a hand in nightmare-breeding,"
But the old priest, his hand half-shaking,
Said slowly, with a sigh or two:
"My guess is, that he dreamed it waking,
And that its trend is all too true."

THE ETERNAL QUEST

"Sunt bona, sunt quaedam mediocria, sunt mala plura
quae legis hic. Aliter non fit, Avite, liber."

This poem presents a pluralistic approach to life. Its twelve parts
adumbrate twelve varieties of human experience, each with its own
virtues and limitations.

Dante, in the early fourteenth century, could expound a universe
harmoniously integrated by the scholastic philosophy of St. Thomas.
Since then, man's intellectual explorations have so extended the hori-
zons of knowledge that one mind can scarcely reduce macrocosm and
microcosm to any inevitably unified pattern. Mathematics and physics
lead a Bertrand Russell to metaphysical realism; biology directs a
Bergson to irrationalism; idealists strive for sanctification through the
blessed word "personality"; while sectaries and artists stand devotedly

on their emotions and insist of the reality of religious and aesthetic experience, regardless of epistemology. In the meantime, the great mass of mankind seeks inarticulate self-realization by such major modes of conation as sex, adventure, friendship, athletics, worship, acquisitiveness, altruism, and craftsmanship. Without denying that reality may conceivably be One, the present poem merely sets forth, in narratives more or less allegorical, an "eternal quest" after vital experience in keeping with twelve human types. These types are not exhaustive, and the treatment is admittedly fragmentary.

PROEM

Hard by a golden navel of the world,
Twelve pilgrims stood in anxious discontent;
And saw before their feet twelve roads unfurl'd
Which from that gleaming axle spoke-wise went
By field and forest, valley and ascent,
In winding wonder to the bounds of time—
Beckoning onward to some far event
That might transcend futility and crime
In some divine delight, some solacement sublime.

A restless fever burn'd within their breasts,
A sense of tears and misery that dimm'd
Their eyes in spite of dawning, still'd their jests,
And made their youthful souls, celestial-whimm'd,
Fierce-drunken with a nectar that o'er-brimm'd
The cup of their content. They'd stay no more
In idle childhood's playing, but, strong-limb'd,
Would seek to sate the hunger that they bore
In ardent quest for life and living's inmost lore.

And so they hail'd each other, and set forth;
Each by a separate path pursued his way
To spacious east or westward, south or north,
Beneath the radiance of the opening day;
And long they holla'd greeting, but the grey
Vast sundering distance grew between them still,
And smaller seem'd each comrade to survey,
Until at last the eye's most earnest skill
Mark'd nothing but the haze across the far-off hill.

1 The Hall of Mirrors

Upon a peak of granite, solemn-hued,
A lofty-window'd hall of strange design
Stood silent in majestic solitude.
The cliffs, from plains below, in beetling line
Rose naked, but a rock-hewn stair did twine
Its adit upward. On an April day,
A young man labour'd up that steep incline,
Step after chisell'd step, and made no stay
Until he reach'd the mansion, vaulted, vast and grey.

Its high dome seem'd a brain; its windows, eyes,
Into whose hollow gaze he peer'd, to guess
What lay within; and as he made surmise,
A maiden stood near by in sober dress,
A girl of chaste and grey-eyed loveliness,
Who gave him greeting thus: "In this retreat
We think on wisdom. If thou wilt, address
Thy thoughts to this; leave action's dust and heat,
Ev'n for a day; and view life steadily, complete!"

"Yea, that I will!" said he. "For all things flow;
And I, poor Desiderius, now vex
My soul for something that shall never go.
Vain dreamers yearn for Luck, or Strength, or Sex,
Or Wealth, or Law, or Implements complex,
Adventure, Science, Healing, Creeds, or Art—
But these are but as shadows, shining wrecks
Upon the rocks of death. Instruct my heart!"—
"Come!" was her gentle answer. "Join our life apart!"

A coil'd snake, wrought in gold, the Ring of Life
And token of eternity, was placed
Above the iron portal. "Staunch all strife
Forever, by that sign," she said in haste,
"The Worm of Wisdom!"—Gravely on they paced
To where a mighty mirror, poised awry,
Bore on it, through a skyward window traced,
A vision of the outer world and sky—
The hill, the slumbering plain, and cloud-shapes drifting by.

"Behold," said she, "the semblances of earth—
So firm to seeming, yet so fugitive!
Here shalt thou learn to test their fleeting worth
In this, the Hall of Mirrors where we live."
Thrill'd, he beheld the radiant pier-glass give
Reflection towards a mighty gleaming prism,
Passing its beauty through that crystal sieve
In sunder'd light, thence casting all that schism
Of colour to a consort mirror-mechanism.

He gazed upon this second sheet of light;
He watched his world resolving, flake by flake,
To rainbow glories, ranged from violet night
Through green to dawning scarlet. "Hark," he spake,
"These colours laugh, breathe perfume, throb and
    shake.'"—
"Yea," said his guide, "these are the garbs of sense
In which we clothe perception. Here we take
The illusive raiment off, to seek intense
The stark reality within intelligence.

"Below the spectrum, and above, we find
Two essences that cheat the naked eye.
The grey, vague universals of the mind
Spread ghostlike here; in yonder darkness lie
The imponderable *Ding an sich* and shy
Shapeless hypostases of utter things.
And now, mark well the art by which we try
To win for life the lore this mirror brings,
Yielding the heart of man immortal nourishings!"

Just where the consort speculum drew line
Between dim dark and colour, craft had bent
Its glassy face, keen-angled to decline
The darker unseen essence, while it sent
All colours and the phantom element
Of concept through a prism, converse-curved,
And laid their light, mysteriously blent,
Upon a final mirror, which conserved
Grave, shining characters that neither shook nor swerved.

"These are the sacred Grammata," she said,
"A fusion, in imaginative flame

[285]

Of thought and feeling, radiantly shed
In holy signs, immutably the same.
These are the golden gifts for which you came:
Apart from these, all mortals who draw breath
Are lost forever, both to praise and blame;
They lie in Hell like sheep, and greedy Death
Gnaweth upon them; yea, their portion perisheth.

"Relentless as the malison of Zeus
Is Time's dark judgment on our fleeting days;
All scrutinies of fortune but deduce
Poignant impermanence of works and ways,
Like arrows shot by twilight or like haze
Across the deep. And since these Characters
Share not our mortal nature which decays,
Learn well the Grammata, whose grace confers
A writ to turn back Time's unpitying officers.

"Soon must thou leave our citadel of peace
And penetrate the Mountains of the Seers;
The measure of thy gift shall not increase
Till thou hast clomb there. Traverse next with fears
The Vale of Pain, and from all tragic tears
Learn wisdom without arrogance, to seal
Thy entry to the Kingdom of Dead Years.
For there, at last, pale monarchs will appeal
To thee in silent ways that I may not reveal.

"The dust of daily toil may blind thee oft;
Self-puzzledom of reason blur thy track;
The phantoms of despair may whisper soft;
The faded hand of care may hold thee back;
But guard the Letters, like a zodiac
Whose astrologic power may never fail;
For through their talisman thou canst not lack.
Thou hast a secret nothing can assail;
Against it even gates of Hell shall not prevail!"

II *"The Mountain Glory"*

One summer morning, Desiderius
Set thoughtful forth to seek the mountain'd West.

[286]

Slowly he walk'd; and as he journey'd thus,
He bore on ivory tablets in his breast
The sacred Signs in golden script impress'd.
Above him, sky-borne fleets of myriad sails,
The white clouds drifted onward without rest;
Or floated, vaporous flakes, across the dales,
Sifting the checker'd sunlight through their shifting veils.

All day the cloudland pageantry march'd on
To music of the wind upon the heath—
Sometimes colossal shapes of snow that shone,
Dazzling the eye; sometimes in silver'd wreath
As exquisite as lace; or red beneath
The flames of sunset, cloaks with golden frill;
Or dancing, wither'd leaves, before the breath
Of twilight winds; or, as the night grew still,
Hanging like shadowy hawks above the moonlit hill.

But when the morn return'd crepuscular,
He saw to eastward, o'er the gloaming plain,
Pale columns of white mist that mounted far
And toppled back in drifting dust of rain.
Then through dawn's sombre fabric throbb'd a vein
Of rosy light, as from divine desire;
Then scarlet, purple, crimson lent their stain
Until the welkin, as the sun rose higher,
Was one mad, molten sea of iridescent fire.

To westward lay the Mountains of the Seers,
Across whose calm, high crests, as dayspring came,
The glaciers writhed beneath the sun's bright spears,
Gigantic snowy snakes with scales of flame.
Long avalanches leap'd in bright acclaim
And sent their smoking tribute up to heaven;
Out of the towering rock's eternal frame,
Gold-billow'd cataracts, that flash'd like levin,
Crash'd into dark abysses with deep-bellowing steven.

Blue skies of noon-day found the traveller
High on a mountain-path, beside a brook,
Where moss and flow'r conspired to confer
A mass of jewell'd colour on each nook:
The Alpine rose and hair-bell gently shook;

The gentian sway'd beside them in the breeze,
Bluer than ocean; with exultant look,
Flush'd lilies kiss'd the white anemones
And heather clasp'd narcissus round the shining knees.

Rock-pools, in pattern'd shadow, caught the noon,
And golden flakes of light, like falling leaves,
Sank softly through their depths. In green festoon,
Vines over-hung the branches, emerald weaves
Of jade and chrysoprase, and shatter'd sheaves
Of viridescent wonder, sheen and grace.
Soft as the silver voice of summer eves,
The wind in leafy laughter stole to chase
The drowsy, murmuring bees about the dreaming place.

But steep behind those bright-enamell'd dells
The mountains tower'd upward, height on height,
To one sheer wall of shining sentinels
Above the whispering pinewoods, dark as night,
That mask'd the middle slopes. With strange delight,
Young Desiderius gazed mutely up
In vague and dizzy rapture at the sight,
Feeling as if all glory in one cup
Had been pour'd forth for his ecstatic soul to sup.

Beyond all thought of bliss he e'er had dream'd,
Fairer than Eden's walls of flame forbidden,
Those ramparts rose; majestic, too, they seem'd,
Like those vast walls of Death, to mortals hidden,
Circumvallating Heav'n, on which have stridden
The ever-blessed maniples of God.
And by that sight his heart was over-ridden
As with a hunger, a strong joy that trod
In passion o'er his nature, fierce and fiery-shod.

But as he labour'd upward o'er the pass
By which the road pierced through, he fumbled out
His ivory page, and as he read, alas,
His passion'd moods were stricken through with doubt.
A universal sadness rose to flout
His ecstasy,—a tide, before his feet,
Of cold, grey human sorrow merged about
The circling of the seasons as they beat
In spring and winter, storm and sunshine, cold and heat.

And yet a solemn spirit seem'd to bless
The grandeur and the beauty of those hills,
A chasten'd sense of brooding holiness
As if man's inmost nature, joys and ills,
Were one with some dim Power that fulfils
Its Being through these forms, arrays a stage
Wide as the heavens for weak human wills
To play their tragic parts from age to age,
And mutely moves with joy man's darkling grief to
    assuage.

III   The Vale of Pain

Beyond the pass, the road sank almost sheer
To reach a wooded vale, a dark abyss
From which ascended, to his awestruck ear,
A ceaseless moan, a universal hiss.
Down through those trees a creeping syphilis
Corroded root and branch; brown rot and rust
Ate herb and shrub unsated; unremiss,
The grub and caterpillar fed their lust
Of maw on lacerated leaf and bark's torn crust.

Along his path, upon that lower ground,
As shades of evening darken'd o'er his head,
A herd of antelopes came staggering round:
Their ears dripp'd fungus, thick as clotted thread;
Great festering open ulcers overspread
Their mangy flanks and ringworm-riddled nose;
And inward pus-fat parasites oozed red
Foul flux of phlegm, up-vomited to close
The incontinent, mad mouth with anguish as it rose.

And there were ticks, whose tiny pincers pluck'd
The living skin and burrow'd in the flesh,
And gnats that stung, and savage flies that suck'd
The thick blood from the throat, and turn'd afresh
To lay dark eggs, whose maggots bred a mesh
Of wriggling, feeding torment in the wound.
In vain the suffering victim then might thresh—
Surely as haggard cachalot harpoon'd,
He must endure that swelling torture till he swoon'd.

[289]

By every herb lurk'd serpents, swift to strife;
On every hand he saw their horror stretch'd
With fangs of torture flesh'd in nerves of life.
A screaming frog, half-swallow'd, twitch'd and retch'd,
Held in those reptile jaws; a rabbit fetch'd
Shrill gaspings from a throat that felt the screw
Of scaly-coil'd constriction; terror etch'd
Such piteous anguish on its face as threw
The traveller into shuddering nausea at the view.

A shrike sat spitting sparrows on a thorn,
Alive and shrieking; then a vulture swoop'd
Upon a hare, and raised it, clutch'd and torn,
In greedy talons, while wing'd fellows troop'd
In haste behind, and, snatching as he stoop'd,
Tore at the writhing prey; a-swarm with flies,
A fawn stood, caught in mire, its weak neck droop'd,
And on its head, unmindful of its cries,
Crows croak'd with pleasure, picking out its staring eyes.

A weasel held a partridge by the throat,
Drinking her blood; the trembling brood she left
Were craunch'd alive by hungry rat and stoat;
A vampire bat slid from a rocky cleft
And with its thirsty, unclean muzzle reft
An antelope of life. A wolf howl'd wild
In exultation at his bleating theft
From scatter'd flocks; with blood and flesh defiled,
A snarling grizzly gnaw'd the warm corpse of a child.

Thus was all Nature playing fugues of pain
Upon the nerves of sense. He grew afraid—
Toss'd in a contemplative hurricane,
A meditating reed that reel'd and sway'd—
And saw how tooth and talon had been made
As operative symbols of Design;
Praise to a God seem'd mocking masquerade
As, with profounder fear, he watch'd the line
Of human fate in that dark pattern intertwine.

He could not think of earth as wholly bad,
Like that grim garth of Attalus that held
Envenom'd flowers only. Man was glad
In god-like apprehension, acts that spell'd

The rarest pity, reason that excell'd
In pure nobility, and moods as chaste
As new-fall'n snow. But faith was all dispell'd
As with stark honesty of soul he faced
The unintelligible woes of tragic waste.

Upon a village dung-heap by his path,
A white-hair'd leper damn'd his own sad birth:
"Why is light given," cried his tortured wrath,
"To man, whose way is hidden upon earth?
Is mine the strength of stones, the whale's great girth,
That the Almighty's arrows through me thrust
And drink my spirit up that once had worth?
My flesh is clothed with worms and clods of dust!
Why does affliction come upon the pure and just?"

Another old man's voice, like broken fife
Cried: "Howl, howl, howl! O you are men of stones:
Why should a dog, a horse, a rat, have life,
And thou no breath at all, my daughter?" Groans
From that crazed father mingled with the moans
Of one fresh-hang'd upon a gallows-tree,
A thorn-crown'd carpenter, nail'd flesh and bones,
Who look'd aloft in piercing agony,
And choked: "Why hast thou, O my God, forsaken me!"

Yet as the pilgrim took from out his breast
The shining Script, he felt the sweet relief
Of daybreak after nightmare. 'Twas not rest
From sleep's grey cancellation of all grief,
But passion purged by pain till peace was chief
And captain of his heart. He knew not why
Acceptance came; life had seem'd cruel and brief;
But now he neither wish'd nor fear'd to die.
Out of the Shadow'd Vale he walk'd with head held high.

IV   *Fronting the Infinite*

And after many days the wanderer found
A kingdom by a tideless Western Deep,
Beneath whose waters continents lay drown'd
But on whose shores, grey, solitary, steep,
Old barrow, cairn and cromlech lay asleep;

There myriad mossy sepulchres were spread,
And stones and mouldering epitaphs did keep
The sense of wistful voices of the dead
For him who stood there, meditating, overhead.

High on a hill, a tower'd castle stood,
Facing that boundless ocean, grey and cold;
The marbles of its massive walls held good
Though all their weather'd face was rich and old,
Lichen'd to pale and melancholy gold.
And there the pilgrim sought an inner fane;
And thinking on kings' converse, once foretold,
He lean'd where many a lamb, of old, was slain
Upon an altar, and read out his Letters plain.

Then, strange as fire, his tingling sense divined
Pale kings who smote vain hands upon the door,
Their voice an inner wailing in the wind.
He read again: they throng'd the long, dim floor
In shadowy rank on rank; they stood before
The altar, pleading loud, he knew not what.
Once more he read: and, comprehending, tore
His breast apart, and pour'd his heart's blood hot
Upon the altar, as the sacrifice they sought.

Their voices clear'd. One solemn king began:
"Not without blood, this offering thou hast made,
Couldst thou receive our converse; for a man,
To hear us, must himself be half a shade.
And but through such as thee there is display'd
No wisdom, work, nor knowledge, nor device
Within the grave, nor joy for lovers laid
Dead cheek beside dead cheek—yea, there's no price
Whereby the soul of man may taste earth's glories twice!

"We loved the play of billows in the wind,
The hawthorns with their plumage of white fire;
We watch'd the sunset arras as it thinn'd
To ghostly lace; we saw the day retire,
Borne on the wings of twilight, and the choir
Of starry minstrels issue forth ablaze,
And then at last in dawn's clear flame expire.
But all these things have vanish'd from our gaze,
And silence is the wage of all our earthly ways.

"Dust lies upon our lips; and yet we live
Through these bright Grammata that thou hast learn'd;
By these we speak to him who dares to give
His blood for our dead voices. Thou hast burn'd
To speak with us; and we, whose hearts have yearn'd,
Here, in the ancient stillness, for thy hail,
Shall share the immortal moods that once we earn'd,
Though they from earth have faded as a tale
That childhood hears by evening while the shadows fail."

"Think," said another, "soberly on Death,
And humbly sigh to know thy human peers
A few poor, piteous bones that once had breath.
Thy laughing boasts avail not, nor thy fears,
To check the ceaseless falling of the years
Or stay cold Lethe's currents. Therefore set
All arrogance aside, and shed slow tears,
Tender with pensive pity and regret,
For all the earth's unseeing passion, pride and fret.

"To look, without desire, on women's faces;
To praise, untouch'd by envy, famous men;
To breathe a sigh for stricken grief's embraces;
To sympathize when pleasure comes again;
To thread with candour falsehood's daily fen;
To write thy wrongs in ashes ere the dark;
To accept the call of death, respond Amen
In simpleness of soul, and quench thy spark—
This is true wisdom's bright and sanctifying mark."

"Our thoughts live on, immortal and unmix'd!"
Cried out a third. "In this calm world of ours
They abide as brave, unfading phrases fix'd
With lead in rock forever. Time devours
Life's shadow-show, but cannot touch these towers.
We are not dead, who live in memory!
As long as man's remembrance guards the powers
Of these pure Letters, they will keep us free
And give our poignant longings immortality!"

And there the humble pilgrim knew his heart
A pulse within the spirit of his kind;
He felt all sentiment of self depart;
The living past swept round him, and his mind

Was fill'd with voices, echoes that enshrined
Their beauty, quick and fragrant, in his sense.
With these he lived, and still, as days declined,
Wrought on the rock his Letters as defence
Against the dying present's dim impermanence.

THE WAY OF A SCIENTIST

I The Alembic of Hermes

The Egyptian delta lay, a vast, green fan;
And Memphis, like a jewel at its base,
Glitter'd with tower and temple. But a man
Who strode its streets that morn with youthful pace
Bore on his lean, incalculable face
No sign of exultation at that sight;
Rather he brooded inwardly to trace
The lineaments of some problem, and his sprite
Seem'd scarcely conscious of earth's vision of delight.

Northward a while he fared past pillar'd fane
And gleaming portal and bright-hued bazaar;
Then westward through the palm-trees of the plain
Along a mighty causeway. Angular,
All-dominating even from afar,
A ponderous, sky-pointing pyramid
Glow'd in the sun with buff and cinnabar,
And grew before him; but the quiet lid
Of his dark eye show'd naught of all the thoughts it hid.

He reach'd at last the flanks of that great pile.
Strict at the centre stood a massive door
Of figured bronze, where snake and crocodile
Mingled their scaly forms upon the ore
With owl and scarab, in shrewd metaphor
Of human quest to know whence Being sprang.
Here, with a brazen stylus that he bore,
The young man beat: and the sonorous clang
Went echoing till the inmost chambers chimed and rang.

Slowly, at length, the mighty door swung wide
On griding hinges, harsh and thunderous;

There, in the inner gloom, the youth espied
A tall, white-bearded sage, the genius
Of this majestic place, who, summon'd thus
From his deep haunts, address'd him, curt but kind:
"Who art thou, stranger? What wouldst thou discuss?
Only those enter here who dare to find
An answer to the deepest probings of the mind."

"Ah, Father Nous," said he, "I know in truth
The fame of thy stern arts, and so desire
To learn of thee and spend my questing youth
In scientific search through earth and fire,
Water and air, that I may grasp entire
The cosmic scheme in which all marvels merge.
Teach me, I pray, to probe from high to higher
Until I see upon life's farthest verge
The consummating age-plan of the Demiurge!"

Old Nous stood silent. His unchanging eyes,
Tranquil as time and yet more passionless,
Assay'd the seeker, and esteem'd him wise.
"Come, then," he said, "and share my loneliness!"
But even as the sage did acquiesce,
Two strangers wander'd by, a Chinese bonze
And by his side a Brahman, void of dress,
Each with his gaze, through all his orisons,
Bent on his own umbilicus of sun-burnt bronze.

These, as they heard petition and assent,
Besought the youth, Mathetes, to beware:
"Shun this rash wizard of the Occident!
He wastes his life in measuring out the air
And burning earth, the follies of despair.
But we of Asia know the world is spirit,
And therefore seek Reality through prayer;
Unlike this fool who thinks his acts may clear it,
But in his blinded search for Truth comes nowhere near it."

Said Nous: "Ye speak from ignorance and sloth.
Mine is religion purer than your own.
The truth for me is mind and matter both,
Found, not in soft delight of hymn and moan,

But in those laws, inflexible as stone,
Which high imagination, strictly train'd,
Finds in the universe. By toil alone
And mental honesty is truth attain'd;
But mystics shun a fact as though their heads were pain'd!"

The yogi cursed them long in fervent zeal;
The bonze spat out abuse in cataracts;
But Nous and his disciple turned on heel.
"Come," said the sage, "and enter those high tracts,
Those far, cold worlds in which eternal facts
Are as they are, and not as human folly
Wants them to be. My discipline exacts
The strictest sacrifice; but meet it wholly,
And thy aspiring mind shall ne'er know melancholy."

Within the pyramid, a steep stair led,
Step after step, to reach an inner room;
There flames of chymic fire sparkled red
And mercury lay fruitful in the womb
Of an alembic. In the upper gloom
Was hung an egg, the symbol of that art
And of the First Creator, after whom
The alchemist had framed the subtle chart
By which he sought out truth with all his earnest heart.

Upon the walls were painted moon and sun
And all the wayward planets of the sky;
Strange vessels strew'd the pavement, mark'd each one
With the seal of Thrice Great Hermes. "Thou and I,"
Explain'd the sage, "must seek to magnify
This master of all those who question earth.
Doubt, therefore, all thou knowest, and rely
Only on triple test; all else is worth
Scarcely the fleeting impulse of derisive mirth.

"Men say I change base metals into gold,
And name me greedy; but they know me not.
I seek for truth, not wealth. My vials hold
Fierce questions that grasp Nature, crying hot

For answer to some beauty or some blot.
Slowly I see God's plan unfold itself,
Evolving from one primal stuff each jot
Of varying substance on his cosmic shelf;
Thus search I after comprehension, and not pelf."

II   *The Cave of Demogorgon*

Near the abode of Nous, an androsphinx,
Colossal granite, couch'd upon the sand
And eyed the orient sun, as one who thinks
So deeply that he lives in shadowland.
Inscrutable, men call'd it, vaguely bland
Yet terrible and ruthless; and none knew
What ancient sculptor hew'd it, nor who plann'd
The silent temple, visited by few,
That lay beside it in the dust, half hid from view.

Hither came young Mathetes and the sage
One autumn day and eyed the mighty beast.—
"Knowest thou, Father, from what hand or age
This mystery comes, set here by king and priest?"—
"My grandsire told me (but I marked it least)
That once his grandsire's sire had found a shaft
Beneath the temple-pavement, near the east,
And entering, saw strange sights. But all men laughed
And said he had been drunk, delirious, or daft.

"I know no more than that. Perhaps the tale
Was sooth in very deed."—"Shall we not test,
As in our chymic art, that ancient trail?"—
And so, with spade and lever, they address'd
Themselves to probe the flagstones where they guess'd
Some subterranean way might open under.
Six days they toil'd; at last their curious quest
Laid bare a depth that proved their search no blunder.
Down a descending stair they went in speechless wonder.

The dust of ages lay upon those steps,
Stirred only where two feet had come and gone

Long centuries before; nor asp nor seps
Crawl'd hissing; bat and spider were there none;
Though here and there a serpent skeleton
Lay white and crumbling on the ancient stair.
Each with a flaming torch, the friends went on,
Watching the winding way with every care
Lest peril unforeseen should take them unaware.

A thousand fathoms down the walls grew dank;
The staircase ended; and before them spread
A subterranean hall, whose black floor sank
To far, slow depths, whose roof rose overhead
Past vision. And Mathetes almost fled,
Seeing in that dim place a monstrous throne,
Bearing a vast form, silent as if dead;
On him, from head to foot, long moss had grown,
Long hair and beard of fungus trail'd upon the stone.

But Nous invoked that spirit with a spell:
"Hail, Demogorgon! Hail, dread deity!
Awake, by all the powers of heaven and hell!"—
The great eyes open'd: "What wouldst thou of me?"—
"The secrets of the Sphinx, the lost decree
That rear'd its temple, and this deep domain!"—
From that recumbent form, that seem'd to be
A moss-enveloped pine-trunk, words of pain
Sigh'd forth like forest winds through branches before rain:

"Alas, has earth then lost the primal plan
That wrought the Sphinx to typify thy kind,
Symbol of that duality in man
Which mingles beast and reason in one mind?
This was the hand to which God once assign'd
The task of moulding matter into life
And shadowing forth his nature. Are men blind
That, in a world where evidence is rife,
They slash away their ancestry with hasty knife?

"This is the rock from which man first was hewn,
The pit from which he rose. But come and gaze
Upon my kingdom, where old bones are strewn
With which I labour'd once in far-off days!"

His deep eyes slowly kindled to a blaze;
He raised his hand, and phosphorescent light
Shone soft from every cranny of the place.
He stood erect, a figure of affright,
His misty hair and beard about him trailing white.

Along the shelving floor they wander'd down,
Ever descending. Bones of bear and ape
Lay mouldering by old weapons, dull'd and brown.
The path sank deeper. A great stream took shape.
Suddenly there Mathetes paused agape.
Huge as the frame of some abandoned galley,
A lizard's skeleton, from tail to nape,
Lay white-ribb'd in the subterraneous valley;
Near it, an eyeless nightmare head bore teeth to tally.

The trunks of mammoth ferns stood thick and black;
A giant cycad leaf, like some vast feather,
Fused with the fraying rock across their track.
Deeper they plunged in galleries dark and nether,
Until at last bones vanished altogether
Save for the husks of crab and trilobite
And snail and oyster; and they ponder'd whether
Forms such as these, so senseless and so slight,
Had once been sole companions of the Eremite.

At last they reach'd a low basaltic pool,
Mantled with sheeny gloss of greenish scum.
"Here is a spot where human pride may cool:
Up from this humble crypt all creatures come.
Yet what more wonderful than that the sum
Of all things known to life since that first age
Sprang from my magic here! That day was dumb
As to the glories of their final stage,
For I myself knew not the forms they would engage."—

"Lowly indeed," said Nous, "are these beginnings;
But all the more I prize the high estate
That we inherit from thy subtle spinnings."—
"I gave thee life, but reason, uncreate,
Crept somehow into man."—"By what strange fate?"—

"Ask of the stars!" the grisly Spirit cried
And vanish'd. Then in puzzle-brow'd debate
Over his words, they turn'd without a guide
And mounted slowly upward to the world outside.

III   "Spinoza's Eye"

South from the pyramid of Nous there rose,
An evening's walk away, a kindred mass
Ascending by great steps, that all who chose
Might reach its level crest. With tube of brass
That bore in it huge lenses of clear glass,
Mathetes came one eve and scaled the slope
To the high summit, where he wish'd to pass
The night in gazing through his telescope
And questioning the mystery of heav'n's starry cope.

Westward the desert lay, a sea of blood,
For sunset crimson flooded all its dust
And drifting sand. Mathetes idly stood,
Awaiting night, and idly did adjust
His glass upon that waste. Strange forces thrust
Each shining grain asunder as he gazed;
Each sand-speck grew a star that shone robust
In infinite star-companies that blazed
Across a boundless sky. Mathetes linger'd, dazed.

So long, indeed, he watch'd, that when the dark
Led out the stars across the firmament,
It seemed to him that each celestial spark
Was but a sunlit sand-grain, with assent
That the vast star-host equall'd in extent
The sands on all the shores of all the world.
Still pondering what Demogorgon meant,
He ranged his glass where star-mists swung impearl'd,
Or sought the mighty orbits where the comets swirl'd.

Then, as when Glacial man, with panic frown
Each year saw bergs of ocean grow more steep—
Mute shapes of ancient terror drifting down
The inexorable currents of the deep,

[300]

Eternal cold and vastness seemed to sweep,
Implacable, towards life, intent to freeze
Its puny flame, till all that fly or creep,
Or walk or love, in silent lands and seas
Should merge in cosmic time's chill taciturnities.

He saw the human spirit, fair and fain,
Flit like a flake of snow or fleck of fire
Borne on a tempest; and a worm of pain
Ate at his heart in pitiless desire.
But suddenly he felt his pangs expire,
And all his thought grew luminous and high,
Exultant that man's spirit could conspire
To wrest from stars obedient reply
And storm the flaming ramparts of the eternal sky.

Then light dissolved to waves; the lucent stream
Flow'd through infinities of space with all
The soundlessness and lustre of a dream
Where tides of shadowy splendor rise and fall
Along the ledges of some deep-sea hall;
And still he gazed, and still that glory grew,
Swelling to symphonies majestical,
Music of colour, red, green, gold, and blue,
In fugues of pulsing fancy ever bright and new.

Then, by degrees, the lambent light grew less;
The universe swung ghostlike in its course,
A bubble blown of radiant emptiness;
The worlds had weight no more; the suns, no force;
Dark Time from three-fold Space knew no divorce,
But, misty all, they sway'd in spectral dance,
Baseless, ascending from some spirit-source,
A shadow-show of moving circumstance
Whose essence was of Mind through all its vast expanse.

Then, last, he reach'd across the gulfs of space
To tear aside that vision as a veil
And gaze upon its Weaver, face to face,
But his hand shook, his cheek grew ashy pale,
Gazing on Darkness Absolute. "I fail,"

He murmur'd. "Yet perhaps the fault is mine.
For how can finite intellect avail,
Itself within the Web, to break the line
And know if some Grey Spirit spins in ways divine?"

IV   *The Desert of Denial*

At dawn the watcher left his lofty ledge
And sought again his master's dark abode;
But passing near the teeming city's edge,
He met a smiling priest upon the road.
Remembering the night, the young man glow'd:
"I know that Time and Space are but the dress
Of spiritual power, the hollow mode
Of everlasing Cogitativeness.
This truth I find the least and farthest star express."

The happy parson threw exultant arms
About Mathetes' neck and kiss'd his brow:
"I praise the Lord, dear brother, that the charms
Of Nous, the infidel, have left thee now!
Osiris' hand has raised thee from the slough;
His healing touch can make thy foulness sweet.
Before His frown the pale archangels bow,
The clouds are dust before His shining feet,—
I glory that thy eyes have seen His mercy-seat!"

Mathetes shook his wordy unction off:
"I cannot brook the god thy creed declares.
I know the figure well—and fain would scoff—
Counting the sparrows fall, or numbering hairs,
Or damning little children to the flares
Of endless brimstone. But thou wrongest me,
In hinting I might turn to him in prayer.
When I traversed the stars for Being's key,
'Twas Intellect I found, not Personality!"

As they still talk'd, two dervishes came by,
Old Ivan and young Joseph, cynics twain;
And Joseph smote the parson, hip and thigh,
With insolence, and drove him o'er the plain.
"All mind is matter and all matter brain!"

[302]

He cried in mockery. "Who gives a damn
For babble about souls and sinful stain?
Expel all spirit! *Ecrasons l'infâme!*
I have dissected consciousness and found it sham!"

At him Mathetes frown'd; but Ivan wove
A slow hypnotic spell before his eyes,
And bound his will. In vain the young man strove
To fight that mute mesmeric exercise.
His struggles ceased. "Come with us, and be wise,"
Said Ivan, "for we go this very day
To gain a near-by, unknown paradise
Where all men can make jewels out of hay
By training them from sprouthood in the proper way."

They cross'd the gleaming Nile with febrile glee;
They scaled the eastward heights and boldly faced
A desert plain, as naked as the sea.
Over the burning sand they pass'd in haste,
Only to find, beyond, a wilder waste,
Thick with black fragments of infernal stone
From shapeless jet-black ridges that embraced
Their path like burnt-out slag-heaps, madly strown
To break the cruel sand-sea's glittering monotone.

Hot winds, with furnace-flavour, soon arose
And swept the stinging sand, that cut the cheek
And crack'd the bleeding lip and block'd the nose
And stabb'd the eye, till Joseph with a shriek
Fell headlong and lay still. Too choked to speak,
Old Ivan beat his breast and stagger'd on,
Only to fall in turn, worn out and weak.
As one who wakes when ether's spell is gone,
Mathetes was himself once more, and groan'd anon.

Backward from that appalling place he turn'd,
Lurching, he knew not how, towards life and rest.
All through the torturous afternoon he yearn'd
For Egypt's watery welcome in the West.
Thick dust-clouds hid the sun, yet still he press'd
By instinct towards the River and its bars;
Till, with the night, he stood upon the crest
Of Memphis' cliffs; and wept; and felt his scars;
And gazed again, like Dante, on the steadfast stars.

I The City of Old Dream

A panting youth, dark-hair'd and passionate,
Trod the long ribbon of a southern road
Across the green campagna. Love and hate
Flash'd in his eyes. His ample forehead glow'd,
And ardour seem'd to drive him like a goad
To seek some rendez-vous; while far and clear,
A chariot came to meet him as he strode,
That, wrought of gold, drew radiantly near
With white wing'd chargers and a maiden charioteer.

Two steeds were harness'd to that gleaming car;
Their necks wore manes of mingled murk and fire;
Restive they were, and wilful; muscular,
With mettle that no mastery could tire.
The one, a mare, was older, stronger, higher;
The other, once her foal, more fine of limb.
Only the skill'd and fearless could aspire
To wield the lash and reins, and rule their whim;
Against a weakling they would turn and mangle him.

Incarnate female beauty, samite-clad,
Controll'd them now and held them curveting.
Lucid her brow as dawn; her eyes as glad,
Blue as dream-tarns, more blue than sapphire spring
In deep skies wash'd by rain. Curls fell to cling
In golden grace round her ambrosial breast
And all its budding splendour. Ravishing,
The perfect body breathed a mute behest
That stung him like white fire into wild unrest.

A double thread of scarlet were her lips;
Her throat was pearl; her shoulder shone like snow;
Raising her rosy, slender finger-tips,
She cast her curls behind her back, and lo,
In white virginity from head to toe,
Her beauty gleam'd like satin in the sun.
Reeling, he felt his pulses come and go,
And stammer'd forth his ecstasy to one
In whose consummate grace all nature was outdone.

"Ah, Helena," he sigh'd, "to win thy love,
I'd risk all pain or peril, howe'er wild,
In earth, or lowest hell, or heaven above!"
Soft as Madonna's whisper to her child,
The answer came in accents clear and mild:
"If thou, my Tiziano, wilt but learn
To drive these restless steeds, ill reconciled
To human rule, thine ardent soul shall earn
That marriage of our lives for which thy passions burn.

"There is no other way. I cannot give
To mere desire high beauty's sacrament.
Face like a man the austere alternative
Of toiling discipline, and I assent;
Nay, more, shall share with thee in full extent
The joy of ancient treasures that are mine—
In ruin most, by time and vandal shent,
But glorious in themselves, town, tower, and shrine,
And strong to stir thee up to copy their design."

Loudly he vow'd devotion to that task;
But when he seized the reins, the chargers rear'd,
And his rash spirit was constrain'd to ask
For counsel; yet as his companion cheer'd
With comfortable words, he persevered,
And, gaining strength from striving, stood supreme,
Acknowledged master, and as such, endear'd
To Helena. She kiss'd him with gay scream:
"To-night we slumber in the City of Old Dream."

She pointed out the way; he drove apace
By grass-grown roads deserted long ago
And mouldering mountain-bridges, at whose base
Forgotten waters wander'd to and fro.
With night, he saw the lonely moonlight glow
On broken marble tower and ruin'd gate
And battlements that told of overthrow
In far-off days when iron-handed fate
Smote them to toppling dust and left them desolate.

Majestic, though in wrack, the city stood,
A honey-comb of shadows, dim and sweet.

Wild creepers hid its mansions like a hood,
And grasses cloak'd the cobbles of the street.
Statue and font had fall'n in old defeat;
Pillar and dome lay shatter'd in the dust;
But still one ancient palace stood complete,
High in a terraced garden, where the crust
Of its white marble had been tarnish'd by old rust.

Its walls were milk-white fretwork, rich and round,
By which the silver moonlight, as through boughs,
Cast velvet black embroidery on the ground.
But in the inmost chamber of the house
That night beside his radiant, white-limb'd spouse,
Glad Tiziano, wrapt in slumber deep
After their ecstasy of mutual vows,
Beheld a holy vision round him sweep,
Soft as the silken silence of their nuptial sleep.

II *"The Vision Splendid"*

In that fair dream, he saw a glorious god
Walk, lyre in hand, across a barren waste,
A naked, ugly plain; and as he trod,
He shook his shining head in sad distaste.
A sluggish river, murky and debased,
Flow'd from a place of skulls across the scene;
In its black depths no life stirr'd. And he traced
Its poisonous course, maleficent, unclean,
Along the blighted leagues of all that bleak demesne.

Raising his lyre, Apollo struck the strings,
Lilting a glad Allegro, sweet and gay,
And sang; and at his voice up-burst fresh springs
Of living water from the stony clay;
The menie of the birds made roundelay—
The throstle and the lark blent silver notes
As exquisite as moonlight; and the lay,
Flowing ecstatic from their throbbing throats,
Swell'd with the healing strength of sorrow's antidotes.

He heard the bourdon of glad bees that pass
In search of nectar, and the crickets' trill

Beneath the shimmering dew-bow on the grass;
From opening buds a fragrance rose to fill
The nostrils, and the river of black ill
Now roll'd in golden waves like sparkling wine
Amid bright fields of rose and daffodil;
There trees of topaz spread in glittering line,
And golden blossoms on their branches burn'd divine.

The high song changed: a deep Andante rang
Sonorous as a trumpet, grave and slow;
And city walls ascended as he sang,
With tower and shining temple row on row,
Stately as steepled pines o'erhung with snow;
Within, down vaulted aisles, no person wept,
But tides of diapason there did flow
Majestic, as the festival was kept.
Pure, golden beards of flame from smoking altars leapt.

And there a matchless palace rose to view—
Jasper and porphyry and serpentine,
Green, fleck'd with flakes of snow; blue marble too,
In azure undulation, line by line,
A dream of frozen music in design.
A mighty dome upon the building there
Slept like a crown of radiant opaline;
While minarets of marble, thin and rare,
Soar'd in seraphic splendour in the morning air.

A sudden change came o'er the golden song:
A laughing Scherzo, light as leaping flame,
Broke from the gay Apollo, clear and strong;
And hosts of white-robed revellers, youth and dame,
Girded about their breasts with gold, in game
Of happy health approach'd the golden flood,
That once was black, and drank it, and became
As jubilant as if their very blood
Felt the keen, pregnant power that drives the twigs to bud.

Then lyric song was born, to tell of love;
And jocund dance, for lovers to be gay.
Light-hearted down the highways did they rove
And trip it lightly, making holiday.
And some set up a stage, on which to play;

And some, exultant, chanted tuneful story.
And some spoke jests to drive dull care away,
Fain for light kisses, blithe and amatory,
Or waggishly contemptuous of solemn glory.

The mystic music paused. Then caught once more
The selfsame key in which it first began.
And he who dream'd stepp'd down upon the shore
Of that bright stream; and, stirr'd to some strange plan,
Enter'd a boat; push'd off; and wavelets ran
In fiery ripples round his drifting prow;
Till, as the great song soar'd, he turn'd to scan
The shining city; and beheld it now
Waver mirage-like, lit by bright Apollo's brow.

Then all things merged and melted, sound and sight,
Strange hues, rich odour, attitude and tone.
He seem'd a moving focus of delight
Amid a drift of sense; he pass'd alone,
A solitary wisp of soul and bone
On which the flooding eddies ever beat—
Unstable, flickering, burning forces, blown
Into brief gem-like flame and joyous heat.
And through each perfect mood Apollo's song ran sweet.

Bird-song and flowers, temple, love-song, dance—
All essences of beauty and of art—
Wove and unwove themselves across his trance,
A flux of fleeting rapture through his heart.
"Ah, stay!" he cried, grown conscious, with a start,
Of life's dark brevity; but saw, like smoke,
The river fade, the pageantry depart.
The harp-strings of Apollo crash'd and broke;
And Tiziano, with a cry of grief, awoke.

III   *Towards Realization*

"In this brief human day of frost and sun,"
Said he to Helena, "how dark my fault
Were I, for ev'n an hour, to leave undone
Whate'er my hand may further to exalt
The praise of thy white beauty; Nay, I halt

Even in talking thus, and shall set forth
To amend thy city and beneath the vault
Of purple heav'n and o'er the verdant earth
Proclaim in form and music thy transcendent worth!"

She laugh'd for joy, in notes like silver bells,
And closed his lips with sacramental kiss,
As when soft-bosom'd Spring to Summer tells
Her joy to yield her fragrant days to his.
Then he, in sheer extremity of bliss,
Utter'd triumphant chantings like the lark,
And wrought to raise that dead metropolis
Of wonder to new beauty, striving stark
To re-create wall, palace, statue, tower and park.

Gilt traceries of sapphire rose again,
Lovely as laughing waves gold-lipp'd with light;
The Parian frieze of portico and fane
In living form and fancy glitter'd white;
He forged bronze gates; the battlements shone bright;
And crystal domes, transparent as all space,
Hung over palaces whose rainbow height
Was jasper stone and emerald, ablaze
With beryl, jacinth, amethyst, and chrysoprase.

Mild Helena inspired him to mould,
In loving worship and artistic stress,
From marble, breathing bronze, and chisell'd gold,
A thousand moods of female loveliness;
For though her living grace he might possess,
Her spirit still escaped him, and he sought
To snare in deathless form her soul's excess;
But though the eye might swear that he had caught
That sacred essence, he esteem'd his work as naught.

An infant crown'd their love, a laughing boy
With eyes like dewy pansies, full of peace.
Him they named Jox, to symbolize their joy,
And swaddled him in silk and snowy fleece.
Proud Tiziano's hand could scarcely cease
From painting, upon canvass, that dear elf—
Sometimes with parents twain, or rock'd at ease
On Helen's breast, or sometimes by himself.
The happy father prized him past all dreams of pelf.

[309]

But in Bœotian cities, broad and fat,
Word came at last of Tiziano's toil.
Then oily-whisker'd grocers cursed and spat,
And organized a foray to despoil
The white dream-city: "For its cursed soil,"
They loudly cried, "is poisonous as gall.
Plague swept that city once, and we recoil
To think that, through this knave, disease might fall
On us in resurrected strength and slay us all."

Sanballat led the horde. Unmark'd they came
To Tiziano's halls to seek him out.
They gazed upon his art with rage and shame;
Its naked rapture made them snarl and shout,
Snigger, and sniff, and fling the busts about
With holy anger and abusive word.
With knives they slash'd each canvas to a clout,
For beauty was unseemly and absurd,
A scandal and a hissing to that swinish herd.

When, at that din, the artist's gracious wife
Came anxious in, they spat upon her face.
Almost she perish'd at their hands of strife,
But some of them, transported by her grace,
Turn'd on their blinder brethren and did chase
Their hoggish whines of murderous piety
Out of the city. "Let us stay a space,"
The victors cried, "perchance ev'n such as we
May help to build this vision, thus inspired of thee!"

IV   *The Coming of the Robots*

And so the city grew. But out of Gath,
A town of fat Philistia, there emerged
A peril that left ruin in its path.
A reprobate inventor, who asperged
With cynic laughter every act that verged
On search for beauty, made, for very scorn,
A race of dolls, mechanically urged,
Robots of metal, man-sized, as a thorn
In Tiziano's flesh to make him weep and mourn.

A nickel-plated minstrel, earliest wrought,
Made hideous the morning with its din.
Its metal mind knew no such thing as thought;
Nor could a miracle put music in
Its brazen belly and its tongue of tin,
Its leather lungs, its scrannel throat of quartz;
And when the woodland heard its tunes begin,
A rout of tortured rabbits fled with snorts
Of indignation, and all birds sought new resorts.

A jelly-jointed painter next was made,
A palsied piece of zinc with filmy eyes.
This robot, though it painted in the shade,
Stung every gaping watcher with surprise
By limning forms that moved, albeit in wise
So clumsy that mature minds turn'd away;
But children of all ages learn'd to prize
Its crudeness of portrayal, and would stay
To see it scrawl its dancing daubs the livelong day.

A final apparition issued forth,
And flapp'd on creaking wings across the air.
Betimes a live musician lent his worth
To give the robot voice, but subtle care
Soon match'd its nature with the earlier pair
And sent it, voice and brush, to sweep the world,
Plying its arts at all times, everywhere.
Grimly the lip of the inventor curl'd
To hear the flying robot bagpipes wildly skirl'd.

He turn'd each type of robot out in swarms.
He sent them to destroy the Town of Dreams.
But Tiziano's magic kept their forms
Out of the shining palace. With high screams
Of loud mechanic frenzy, they laid schemes
To starve the proud defenders till they died.
And so they ring'd the town; cut off its streams;
And let no saving morsel pass inside
To feed the unsurrendering Tiziano's pride.

And they of Gath know not the issue yet;
The burghers of Bœotia ken no more

Than that the black blockade has long been set
And hated Helen's halls beleaguer'd sore.
But Gittite spies suspect some secret store
Of deathless food, some hidden living springs;
For when by night they harken at the door,
An easel creaks, hands clap, a chisel rings,
And there, exultant in the darkness, someone sings.

THE WAY OF A WARRIOR

1 The Challenge of Adventure

A tall, strong youth in chain-mail trod a road
Through golden fields before a high-wall'd town.
His curls were fair, his ruddy forehead glow'd.
His blue eyes, stern yet kindly, look'd not down
But ever forward. Though his cheeks were brown,
Broad scars of honour streak'd them o'er with white.
Upright he walk'd, from heel to comely crown
As straight as any pine that fronts the light
Upon the crest of some dark Pyrenean height.

As he approach'd the town, he met a maid,
Fair like himself and clad in armour too.
"Welcome, Achilles!" was her cry. "Thine aid
Is sorely needed, for our troops are few
In present battlefields. We know thee true
To high adventure's spirit in thy heart.
Decisive struggles in the far fields brew.
Our fate will soon be told. Come, play thy part,
And I shall love thee well, serve thee with every art."

"Ah, Brunhild, warrior maid," the man replied.
"I prize thy proud Valkyrie sisterhood.
Like mine, thy spirits lean to danger's side,
And find life's relish in vicissitude
Where death stands close. Existence seems most good
With hazard at its highest, if the deed
Be just and right. If evils are withstood
In this thy war, and innocence has need,
Rely on me to show the courage of my breed!"

"Thanks!" the Valkyrie cried. "Men even now
Are mustering in the city's broadest square
To reinforce the battle. Go, endow
Their weakness with thy strength, and half their care
Will melt away to see thee standing there!"
She kiss'd his manly lips, their arms embraced,
Against his cheek press'd fragrant golden hair
For one brief moment. Then the spot she graced
Was vacant past all gazing that his fain eyes traced.

He turn'd to cross the town with ardent haste
And seek the plaza, but a puffy dame
With cheesy cheeks, and vast, asthmatic waist,
Pale, watery eyes, and dropsied legs half-lame,
In tearful, wheezing panic towards him came,
Two pasty-faced young urchins at her skirt,
And call'd the startled warrior by his name:
"Be not deceived," she wail'd, "By that blonde flirt!
For if thou trustest her, thou shalt be surely hurt.

"All war is hateful," wept the frantic dowd.
"Reason is put to shame when blood is shed.
Fatal pollution must that soul becloud
Which takes man's life. One rather should be dead
Than have another's blood upon one's head.
No claim on earth should cause a man to fight.
Resist not evil. Let the foeman spread
Across the land to rape and burn and smite.
To seek peace and ensue it is forever right!"

Achilles shook his head, and sternly spoke:
"Thou hast misread man's warfare in thy fear.
The very springs of parenthood invoke
Defence of helpless lives we hold as dear.
Should we betray them, as thou urgest here,
Dark shame like deep corruption in the bones
Would damn our lives and we should disappear,
Unpraised, unwept. No casuistry atones
For those self-cozen'd cowards whom the race disowns.

"The soldier is a witness to high faith
Of spiritual essence. Virtue grows

[313]

From roots of truth and honour, springing rathe
In discipline and courage, such as flows
From hazards faced in battles with one's foes.
This is the only character that suits
The plenitude of manhood. When he shows
Stripp'd of these military attributes,
Man's personality is meaner than the brutes.

"And is war worse than horrors of the plague?
War takes its thousands, but the fever's heat
Takes tens of stricken thousands in its vague
Vast-slaying course; and those who chance to meet
With taint of leprous tetter, cholera's gleet,
Or the crazed growth of cancer in the flesh,
Know torture beyond all that soldiers greet.
Though we should perish in war's strangling mesh,
We die a sudden death, with all our pulses fresh.

"The Hebrews tell how Michael and his hosts
Fought with the dragon on the plains of heaven.
The Norse myths crown with praise those valiant ghosts,
Ranged in Valhalla, unto whom is given
The prize of second death when skies are riven
And all the great gods die. Thus war keeps whole
The heart of man, and leaves him pure and shriven,
Ready to give his life to save his soul!"
He ceased, and turn'd once more in silence toward his goal.

II The Wolds of War

Far from that town, for many days they march'd,
Nearing the front of war. That road fulfill'd,
He stood one day, and though his throat was parch'd,
The thronging pulses through him throbb'd and thrill'd
As he beheld the low ridge, billowy-hill'd,
From whose long crest his army's parapet
Look'd down on foes, in myriads brave and skill'd,
Who held the plains below, and struggled yet
To take the summit, though they too were sore beset.

The war had long been fought: at first with spears
And clumsy swords and arrows from the bow.

But brains had changed all that across the years,
And given means of death to friend and foe
In countless ghastly forms of overthrow.
So, when Achilles came, that autumn day,
To join the ranks, he found them crouching low
Beneath barrage, and heard above the fray
The deep, indignant thunder of the guns at bay.

Pulsating fever smote that hill-top, trough'd
With zigzag trenches, and it heaved and tare
As if earth's chest, convulsed with phthisis, cough'd,
Gasping towards death, and spat into the air
Wet fragments of torn bodies, laying bare
In dissolution's pain its nakedness
Of shatter'd, stone-ribb'd slope. Flames flicker'd there
In sudden daggers. Even in that press
Achilles bore his part and showed no weak distress.

Rain from grey skies came mingling grimly down
With that black broth of upchurn'd earth and oil,
Making a slough in which the weak might drown.
Up from the sodden depths where sappers toil
Great mine-bursts ripp'd the bowels of the soil
To thick black pillars of rent earth and spume,
Brief giants of despair, who fell to spoil
All things that hell's combustion could consume,
And left the live air choking with their pungent fume.

Achilles and his comrades drew scant breath,
They felt the shallow line in which they crouch'd
A moaning sand-bar wash'd by seas of death;
But still the worst came not—the attack that couch'd
The war's last issue. Low they lay and grouch'd,
Half swimming in foul clay, or named their wives,
Aught to allay the tension where they crouch'd,
Tension that scraped the spine like notch-edged knives
And made those yellow'd, wasted warriors loathe their lives.

At last, far down the hill, they saw the foe
Rise in long waves of madness to attack.
They watch'd shells rake those ranks, and shrapnel mow
Unnumber'd grey forms down, but still the pack
With howls of fury held the upward track,

Looking like bestial puppets oozing bran.
O'er slippery lumps of flesh and battle-wrack,
Even with splinter'd stumps of legs they ran,
Sans jaws, sans mouth, sans face, sans all that makes a man.

Quickly Achilles' comrades down the slope
Loosed gently moving clouds of blinding gas.
Borne by the sluggish wind, it seem'd to grope
Like jellyfish obscene among the mass
Of those insensate foes who sought to pass;
And all those human forms, too dazed to run,
With blacken'd lips and cheeks of tarnish'd brass,
Fell twitching like grey spiders every one.
The onslaught of the infantry was spent and done.

The foe then launch'd great dinosaurs of steel,
Dragons with mouths that spew'd out leaden wrath.
They churned the embattled earth beneath each wheel;
To them stout palisades were flimsy lath,
And men no more than pismires in their path,
Ants to be squash'd in wallowing on their way
And dimly visible in that wide swath
Which lay behind them in the mangled clay
Like currants in raw batter mix'd for Christmas Day.

Achilles at that sight made haste to rise,
Borne on a plane of fine Canadian fir.
He bomb'd the tanks to wreckage from the skies;
But as he wrought, he heard the mounting purr
Of foes in flight formation and the whir
Of enemy machine-guns. Without boast
He faced their three-score as a challenger—
An eagle-plane against a vulture-host—
And swoop'd in swift decision at the uppermost.

He smote it down in flames. He rose once more,
His own gun barking as he broke their line.
Four times he drove them headlong, but to soar
Triumphantly himself. With Parthian whine
Of parting gun-fire, they at last assign
Vict'ry to that fierce barker of the height.
Then he, too, sweeping down the vast incline,
Landed, unhurt, in evening's waning light.
So, tir'd, he slept, and mix'd his spirit with the night.

[316]

When he awoke, a yellow moon rode high.
Across the earth, a shatter'd oily waste,
Lay pools that glimmer'd like a dead man's eye,
Bloodshot with red, drown'd craters interlaced
With shards and carrion in a greasy paste.
Long streaks of vapor crept from pit to pit,
Weird mists of strangling white, that foul'd the taste
With fetor of decay and made him spit
In choking shudders at the loathsome sweet of it.

The bulging hill was like the bloated form
Of some gigantic corpse; but moans of pain
Arose from scatter'd men whose veins were warm,
Though batter'd breasts and faces torn in twain
Imposed on ebbing lives a fatal drain.
Some writhed in ashen-visaged fortitude;
And some, more cursed with strength, still sought in vain
To crawl, like half-crushed worms, across the mud,
Holding their entrails in their hands, and oozing blood.

A lad lay near him, not far short of death,
His back laid open by a gaping rent
Through which the torn lung pulsed with every breath,
And scarlet foam in bursting bubbles went
Out of his gasping mouth, incontinent.
Enveloped thus in pain on every side,
Achilles uttered groanings of lament;
But at a sudden marvel that he spied
Dumb, icy horror rose about him like a tide:

Flying between the cold moon and the earth
Came silent female shapes on batlike wings—
Things dead, that yet live on without new birth,
Slaking the body's thirst and hungerings
With human blood withdrawn from living springs
Or e'en decay itself. Teeth weasel-keen
Shine in their corpse-rat mouths. Corruption clings
Upon their toadlike lips, that fix obscene
Upon unhappy human veins to suck them clean.

Downward these midnight forms of evil dipp'd
To feast upon the wounded and the dead.

[*317*]

Loathsome as lepers' kisses, carrion-lipp'd
They bit the quivering throat or gnaw'd the head—
Part wolf, part bat, part living corpse that fed.
Closer they drew to where Achilles lay.
One seized the lad whose back so foully bled
And gorged upon his life, nor turn'd away
In pity for the anguished moaning of her prey.

Achilles stayed no longer at that sight,
But leap'd upon his feet and seized his sword.
Swiftly the hellish creature turn'd to fight;
And though her naked breasts and hands abhorr'd
Were sticky with the fresh blood and gouts were scored
Across her livid cheeks, he recognized
The very War-maid he had once adored,
The radiant Valkyrie, but disguised
And to these horried attributes diabolized.

"Brunhild!" he cried. She answered with a hiss;
Then tower'd like a cobra, poised to strike.
And had the startled warrior been remiss,
She would have seized him as a hungry shrike
Clutches a careless sparrow on a dike;
But as she swoop'd, he thrust his glittering blade
To spit her like a wild sow on a pike.
Yet, though she stagger'd back, he saw dismay'd
His weapon, stain'd by her black ichor, melt and fade.

He cast its hilt away, and with his hands
Gripped at her gullet till the fingers crack'd.
Her claws and teeth made ravenous demands
On him in turn, but neither could exact
Supremacy in strife, though sorely rack'd.
Then, in the east, the heavens paled to grey;
Up rose the ghoulish flock from that grim tract;
And as her comrades fled the coming day,
She struggled from him with a shriek and flew away.

Peace, with that dawn, came once again to man.
In far, tumultuous cities rose a sound
Of fevered exultation; courtesan
With priest and merchant gaily beat the ground
In public dance; and generals renown'd,

Who never suffer'd battle, shouted loud
In ardent joy at fame so aptly found.
Non-combatants by millions, fiercely proud,
Wax'd fat and damn'd the vanquish'd in a frenzied crowd.

But in the silent fields of former war
Mute butterflies poised gently on old skulls;
And where a muddy chaos lay before,
Soft spring laid that green carpet that annuls
The wounds of strife with grassy miracles;
And poppies, brighter for the blood once shed,
Bloom'd up the hillside in the noon-day lulls
Of unforgetful summer, flaming red
In their unsleeping watch above the dreamless head.

IV   *The Higher Heroism*

But he who strove with vampires swore an oath
That he would purge the earth of fiends like these.
Yet, though his burning soul was nothing loath,
He knew not where they lodged, nor how to seize
Their weapon-proof invincibilities
And slay them for all time. In zeal to know,
He sought a hermit Sage with courteous pleas:
"Help me, I pray, to find and overthrow
The ghouls who prey on man in battle here below!"

"Thou wouldst embrace life's best and hardest part,"
Replied the ancient man. "For only such
As God has blest with brain and steadfast heart
Dare track these hateful fiends whose fingers smutch
The whole of human life with fatal touch.
They lurk in highest places; power defends
And principalities avail them much.
Yea, thou shalt see thyself and thy brave ends
Despised of men, rejected by thy kin and friends.

"Yet could the spirit of adventure find
No higher task, no nobler work to face.
Seek, and though natural eyes at times are blind
To their dark lurking essence, do but trace
The symbol of the Cross in every place

[*319*]

Where thou dost come, and boldly cry to men:
AN PRO SALUTE MUNDI ISTAE RES?
For at that charm, the grisly denizen
Will be reveal'd, defenceless, to your angry ken.

"Then, since no steel can harm them, drive a stake
Of oak through each foul heart, and they shall die.
Come, I go gladly with thee for the sake
Of unborn generations who rely
Upon this deed for life and destiny.
Quite to forget the horrors of old war
That blasted countless homes, would be to lie
Against our very souls. Come, conqueror
Of unforgotten fights and win one conflict more!"

They sought a church, and heard a fiery priest
Applaud the wars of David, whom God loved,
And Samuel, who butcher'd man and beast
And Agag and all babes, though Saul was moved
To soft compassion. But the priest approved,
And urged that for the faithful and devout,
Stern hatred towards all heretics behooved.
Achilles cross'd himself in anxious doubt:
AN PRO SALUTE MUNDI rang his clarion shout.

Before the words of that bold exorcism,
The stately service vanish'd like a spell.
Instead of nave and chancel, font and chrism,
They saw an ivy-mantled funeral cell,
A mouldering coffin, and a form of hell
That lay within, as bloated as a leech
New-gorged on blood, and heavy with the smell
Of corpse-fat. Then Achilles made a breach
With oak through its dark heart. It died with mandrake-
                                                screech.

With mallet and sharp stakes, the pair pass'd on.
They found a woman's club and heard proud chat
How heroes were in fashion. Each anon
Must have a hero-spouse to match her hat.
Here lurk'd a vampire like saucy rat.
That slain, Achilles turn'd to statemen's rooms
And heard the gunsmith and the diplomat

Plotting to send whole nations to their dooms
For private fame and profit. Here lay vampire tombs.

Achilles and the Sage then sought the halls
Of education, where the sword was praised
And stirring battle-pictures fill'd the walls
And myths of alien wrongs were daily raised
In lessons falsely taught. Not less amazed
Were they to see processions in the street
Of formal factions, dull fanatics crazed
With memories of old feuds that kept their heat.
Cold vampire-souls were marching with the marching feet.

Unceasing vigilance and zeal were theirs,
But still Achilles' task was not achieved
In its completeness. To a thousand lairs
He traced the ghouls and with his oak-staves cleaved
The hearts that plotted death. Mankind received
Unmeasured good. But nothing could abate
The zest of that stout soul who only grieved
In finding life too short to extirpate
The last illachrymable form of human hate.

"Yet grieve not," said the Sage. "The true man's joy
Is found in earnest action day by day.
Happy is he who lives, an eager boy,
With life the Great Adventure all the way.
If reason guide his quests and mercy sway
His ardent spirit, all his jousting fight
Shall lift up life itself, as brave and gay
As one who seeks, with all his reckless might,
The last unconquer'd ice-peak in the glittering height."

THE WAY OF A GAMBLER

1   Crabbed Age and Youth

Across a Thracian hillside April stirr'd
Like some fair babe that wakens with a smile;
Exultant songs of larks were faintly heard
From gulfs of purple air; and mile on mile
Along the white-paved highroad, trees in file

Quite overhung the way with flowering boughs,
Fair spring-kiss'd branches, fragrant to beguile
The murmuring bees to linger and carouse.
Along the highway strode two men with sunlit brows.

One was a youth, a pilgrim by his dress,
Ruddy of countenance and gay of talk,
From foot to curly hair, all comeliness;
And full of swooping fancy as a hawk.
The other, lately met, was slow of walk,
A venerable leech, just overtaken
That very day, who yet had sought to balk
The wayward promptings of the lad, and waken
Some temperance of mind but found his shifts unshaken.

A golden crocus shone beside a brook;
Down sprang the youth, and seized it in his fist;
Then stagger'd back. His aged comrade shook
To see a viper clinging to his wrist;
But smote the scaly-tailed antagonist
So fiercely with his staff that down it fell;
More buffets broke its back; it feebly hiss'd
And writhed to death. But it had left too well
Its poison in that arm, which now began to swell.

The old man suck'd the venom from the wound;
Then sought his simples; mixed a mithridate;
And this the sufferer swallow'd ere he swoon'd.
Anon, revived, he swore affectionate
Devotion to his saviour from vile fate:
"Eubulus, thou art good! I owe thee much!
How shall I thank thee?"—"By a life sedate
And sober," said the leech, whose mood was such
That he affected often the didactic touch.

"True moderation is a law of life,"
Continued he, contented much to preach.
"The reckless and the feckless are at strife
With the Eumenides, who still impeach
All false excess, each hot impulsive breach
Of measure; for to sever from the whole
Swift pleasure without pain is past our reach.
Our lips may brag; the Law is in our soul;
The gambler's hopes are cancell'd by divine control.

"In nature naught is given; all is sold.
Pay but the price in anguish and in sweat,
And what you will is yours. Lore, power, gold,
All have appropriate payment duly set:
The wrestling brain gains learning's alphabet;
The artist grows by labour; rich is he
Who slowly earns his wealth with strain and fret.
All good things must be paid for; naught is free;
God's ledger is still settled with morality.

"The intemperate are vanquished everywhere;
They sow the sea and garner no reward;
They glimpse the mermaid's breast and golden hair,
But not her reptile tail and scales abhorr'd.
The pleasure-jaded throat grows quickly bored
And gulps down sin like water; yet the smart
Of sick satiety at last is lord.
Like rust on iron, care corrodes the heart,
And luxury's licentious ecstasies depart."

But young Cybeutes took the counsel ill:
"Thy talk is dull—though sapient, I grant—
Tedious as toiling up a sandy hill
Or sharing wedlock with a termagant
Whose chidings know not slumber. What I want
Is life, life more abundant, not this prim
Precise, prudential, praise-begetting cant
Of moderation seasoned with a hymn!
Give me red cups of pleasure bubbling to the brim!

"Friendship I also crave, but not for gain.
Philosophers may prate of valued fruit
That friendship bears: a sweet release from pain
By sharing sorrow; counsels where they suit;
And aid in all those acts where tongues impute
Some censure for self-praise. But I confess
I long for friendship pure and absolute,
Good in itself, like mirth and cheerfulness,
Those mothers of all virtue that my mind can guess!"

Eubulus shook his head, yet seem'd to smile.
"Thy mood is noble, but too rash, I fear,
For yonder city's gaiety and guile.
Yet take my blessing and this signet here,

Whose amethyst may tell I cherish dear
A youth whose life I saved. Now are we come
To where my road leaves thine." He shed a tear.
Soon they embrace and part. With care-free hum,
Cybeutes treads the highway to Byzantium.

II   Gamesters Rampant

An August sun, from skies of livid fire,
Beat pitilessly down on tower and dome
And gleaming palace roof and glittering spire,
And most of all upon the Hippodrome,
The glorious marble axis of New Rome
Where rose a myriad benches, seat on seat,
And multitudes in togas, white as foam,
Intent on chariots' victory or defeat,
Sat sweating in the stark, intolerable heat.

To eastward stood the emperor's high throne;
To north and south the crowded benches rose
In league-long terraces of polished stone
That curved at last the westward to enclose.
A barrier built of marble like the snows
Sunder'd the long arena into twain,
And down that gleaming back-bone of the shows
Ranged obelisk and column, trophies' train
Brought hither as the prize of many a far campaign.

But these the crowd saw not; they view'd the east,
Where straining teams were marshall'd to their place;
Fierce factions' colours deck'd both man and beast;
The Blues and Greens stood avid for the race.
And in that shouldering mob one youthful face
Caught fever with the lust of gainful chance
And lost some semblance of its boyish grace:
Cybeutes grew a gambler in his glance,
And burn'd with all a gamester's hot inordinance.

And two sat by who saw his spirits rise:
The one a wither'd man with wrinkled cheek,
Drab as a sun-dried fish, and peering eyes
Like lizards in old walls; the other sleek
And feminine, a beauty with the reek

Of heady musk, her mouth a crimson gash,
And just a hint of vulture in her beak.
These watch'd Cybeutes' eyes, beheld them flash,
And hoped for pleasant plunder from a youth so rash.

"I'll pluck this dabchick," quoth old Pandarus.
"I saw him first" said Cressid, with an oath.
She brush'd against the youth, who, jostled thus,
Looked round; forgave; made converse, nothing loath,
With one so fair and free; the talk of both
Pass'd quickly to the race that should begin;
She praised the Blues, accused the Greens of sloth;
He vow'd the plunging Greens would surely win.
Old Pandarus listen'd with the shadow of a grin.

"A novel bet, fine sir!" suggested she.
"If thou wilt wager with that amethyst,
I'll back the Blue with my virginity—
My virtue 'gainst thy ring! Thou ne'er hast kiss'd
A braver wench. I'll add, if thou insist,
Since odds oppose the Green, this heavy purse,
Contents unseen!" He gazed as through a mist
Into her eyes, and felt all faith disperse:
"I'll take my luck!" It seem'd half promise and half curse.

But even yet he felt his conscience gnaw,
And might have waived such hazardry of stakes
And rescued Friendship's ring. This Pandarus saw,
And whispered slily: "Shame on him who breaks
So sweet a bet! What pause young Joseph makes!
Nice as a nunnery hen, by Zeus!" The gibe
Struck at his male conceit. With virile shakes
Of head and fist, he swore he would subscribe
To this warm risk in face of any threat or bribe.

And now the chariots start. Two four-horse teams
Make growing thunder down the clamorous course.
Far off, in front, the gilded goal-tip gleams
Round which they are to turn. Superior force
Impels the Greens. The shouting mob grows hoarse
To see them draw ahead and skirt the high
Bepillar'd terminus with skill'd resource.
Half-hidden in their dust they gallop by
The spot where stands Cybeutes with excited eye.

[325]

Six times they ran the course with straining strength;
The last and seventh circuit was begun,
With Green still leading by a chariot-length;
But swirling at the turn, they fail'd to shun
The marble rampart; with a crash, they spun,
Upset, and flounder'd into hopeless rout;
The Blues behind them swerved, and lightly won.
Then half the arena gave a deafening shout.
"The amethyst is mine!" said Cressid, with a pout.

"I take my luck" said he. "Accept the ring!
With it go resolutions that I rue,
Which might have saved my soul, but now I fling
Its memories by. Nor would I say adieu
To such a witty wench: I vow it true
Thy gages had no value. But I've still
A hundred golden bezants as my screw.
Be friends and help me spend it!"—"That we will!"—
And arm in arm the three went down the forum hill.

III   The Death of Friendship

So years pass'd by. One autumn afternoon,
As chilling gusts from off the western sea
Moan'd through grey skies wherein a waning moon
Hung like a wraith of old satiety,
A hard-faced man walk'd slowly in the lee
Of certain mansions near the Golden Horn.
At one he knock'd; and as he heard the key
Grate in the brazen lock, a look was born
Within his eyes, of friendship mixed with greed and scorn.

Cybeutes had grown harsher than of old:
Foregathering with wolves, he learn'd to howl;
His appetites increased; his heart turn'd cold;
His merry smile had harden'd to a scowl;
And even his very graces grew part foul,
Like flowers too long upon a dead man's breast
That take the scent of carrion; for the prowl
With predatory gamesters dispossess'd
His soul of countless generous promptings towards the best.

Thus Cressid's venal favour help'd him not;
And Pandarus was mentor but in vice.
Within his darkening soul, the only spot
Of radiant impulse was the paradise
He found in friendship for a man of price,
One Phintias, with whom he often met.
The bond in part was mutual love of dice;
And so today a rendezvous was set
At Phintias' villa for a round of dice and debt.

The bronze door open'd wide; he met the smile
And servile greeting of a Nubian maid:
"The master's yonder in the peristyle,
And waits for you." He sought that colonnade
About the garden where a fountain play'd,
And there embraced a weak-chinn'd, pale-eyed man,
Who paced the marble pavement in the shade
With the glad ardour of a veteran
Impatient till the wonted war of chance began.

Near by, Honora stood, his noble spouse,
Her neck a perfect tower of sculptured snow,
Olympian Juno in her stately brows
And Paphian Venus in the form below.
And Phintias had ready in a row
His dice of crystal, mark'd with Lydian gold,
And beakers of carved ivory to throw
The gleaming dice, and wine-jars manifold
To guard the eager players from November cold.

They cast the little cubes upon the floor.
Cybeutes' fever'd fortune ran amuck
And won so constantly, that Phintias swore
Such marvels of unmitigated luck
Would daunt a man who lack'd the highest pluck.
"I'll lay you ten to one! I'll double that!
The tide will turn!" And guzzling like a duck,
He drank till reason gave no caveat
Against mad stakes that prudence would have cancell'd flat.

"You've all my wealth. I'll wager you this house."
Cybeutes laugh'd, and won it. "Now, by Zeus!"

[327]

Cried Phintias, as drunken as a mouse,
"I'll wager you my wife—hair, hide, and shoes—
For all you've won!" Three mocking sets of twos
Were Phintias' lot. Cybeutes turned up three
Full sixes, Aphrodite's cast. The noose
Of hazard choked his love. His voice of glee
Stank like the kiss of Judas in Gethsemane.

"I'll take my luck!" he murmur'd with a leer.
"And since the night draws on, and rights incurr'd
Crave prompt possession, get you hence from here!"
He spoke no jest, and as Honora heard
She moan'd and falter'd like a lime-snared bird.
Then Phintias' brain cast off its drunken heat,
Yet dared not contradict its plighted word;
Gnawing white lips, he left in chill defeat,
And pass'd in shuddering anguish down the twilight street.

A leprous light still linger'd in the west;
And in that garden-close where friendship died
Weird shadows waver'd as the man caress'd
The shrinking matron, whose insulted pride
Was mute with rage. The robe that veil'd her side,
Fine as a mazy mist of Moslem lace,
Trembled with heart-throbs. Then with steadfast stride
She led him to her chamber; and her face
Show'd sudden resolution and a nameless grace.

"To holy Hermes, guardian of dreams,
I pour this last libation before sleep";
With steady hand she raised the glass, whose gleams
Show'd strangely turbid. Then she drain'd it deep.
Her foil'd assailant gave a sudden leap,
But seized the hand too late; the poison flow'd
To still the outraged heart, and let her keep
Herself unsullied from that base-bestow'd
Dishonorable honour of the gambler's code.

IV   *The Palace of Dishonour*

The autumn chill'd to winter. In that home,
The Villa Vanitas, Cybeutes dwelt.

Musing, he often gazed upon the dome
That crown'd a near-by palace, and would melt
In meditative envy as he dealt
In rumours of an Empress hidden there:
Old, wealthy beyond fable, one who felt,
Even in age, concupiscence most rare,
And shower'd gold and gems on those who used her fair.

But grimmer gossip mingled with the tale:
Men said Eudoxia was a wrinkled hag,
Half crazed and mad, and, should a lover quail
Before her face and let his flatteries flag,
Would cast him from her like a dusty rag,
Or, as the female spider eats her mate
Whom she but now embraced, would bind and gag
The wretched fool, and have him carried late
By night and sunk beneath the waters of the Strait.

Once, as the greedy gambler sat and mused,
Befuddled with imaginings, there came,
Beyond all hope, the messenger who used
To bear the invitations of the dame:
She greeted her new neighbour by his name,
And bade him come that night to sup and stay.
Excitement moved Cybeutes to exclaim:
"I'll take my luck! By night all cats are grey,
All women beautiful. My thanks to her, I pray!"

The servant bow'd and left. Cybeutes turn'd;
Dress'd for the tête-à-tête with arduous care;
And set out through the night. Ambition burn'd
Like ague in his veins. Then, in the square,
His agitated spirit grew aware
A shadow like Eubulus warn'd him back;
And softly by his side, with tangled hair,
Dark Cressid wrung her hands and cried "Alack!";
And Pandarus kept pointing out the homeward track.

But more than these, pale Phintias dogg'd his path,
Glaring upon him like a ghost from hell,
Until Cybeutes, full of fear and wrath,
Cursed at them all, and saw his words dispel
Their forms to darkness; and it seemed a bell

Toll'd in his brain: "Dishonour damns thee dead!
Dishonour damns thee!" And the echoing knell
Beat like the pulse of madness through his head.
His flagging feet seemed shod with sandals of dull lead.

But suddenly these fantasies were spent.
He found he stood before the palace gate.
It opened at his knock, and in he went.
Two eunuchs led him on though halls of state
To where he saw a jewelled beauty wait
Upon a rich divan of snowy silk.
A banquet table groan'd with golden plate,
The candelabra, too, were of that ilk;
High walls were hung with arras, mingled fire and milk.

He came; he sat beside her, in surprise
To see her fair beyond all guess or thought.
"Ah, dear Cybeutes, gaze into my eyes!"
He lean'd and look'd; deep in their depths he sought
For tender glances, but instead he caught
A sudden chill, and saw on the divan,
Instead of beauty driving him distraught,
A naked, jaundiced, white-hair'd harridan,
Who leer'd in mocking lewdness at the staring man.

"Look yet again!" Against his will he gazed.
Corruption smote the hall in which they sat.
The candelabra's fires no longer blazed,
The arras fell and rotted; snake and rat
Slipt softly by on many a mouldering mat;
The slime of ordure stank upon the stones;
And every golden dish became a vat,
Which, girdled round with rusted leaden zones,
Held swill of clotted blood and rotting human bones.

"Now, kiss me!" quoth Eudoxia, grinning wide
With shrivell'd, hairy lip and toothless gum.
"No, never, cursed hag!" Cybeutes cried.
"Too late I see my error; but let come
What fate there may, my soul shall lack the scum
Of that supreme betrayal of my worth.
Give me what form thou wilt of martyrdom!
I once had dreams of honour upon earth,
And shall not wholly shame the manhood of my birth!"

[330]

She clapp'd her hands. Four tongueless negro slaves,
Gigantic mutes with bow-strings, came at call.
Two moved a massive floor-stone; reek of graves
Rose from a yawning well beneath the hall,
Black as the womb of night. Beside the wall
Cybeutes stood with disimpassion'd face,
Nor fought the noose. A muffled splash was all
That told of death, or touch'd with mournful grace
The silence within silence in that shadowy place.

THE WAY OF AN ATHLETE

I *Vis Victrix*

Through high Hellenic hills a roadway ran—
A ribbon of white dust that climb'd and wound
Past jagged cliffs and fissures. There a man
Mounted in mid-morn heat with ardent bound,
Fronting the sunlight. Suddenly he found
A recent avalanche of rocks transgress
The path before him. For a space he frown'd;
Then laugh'd, and casting off his scanty dress,
Strove with vast boulders in majestic nakedness.

His was an Atlantean amplitude
Of shank and shoulder, chest and loin and throat:
Six cubits high he stood. His arms were thew'd
Like many a wrestler's thigh; if boxer smote
His belly with clenched fist, no fatty bloat
Would show, on those bronzed muscles, his malease.
He lacked the grace that makes beholders gloat
O'er athletes sculptured by Praxiteles,
But he had brute immensity far more than these.

His years seem'd scarce a score. His eyes were blue,
Blue with a watery blur as if the whites
Had mingled with the pupils, and their view,
Conjoin'd with narrow brows, habitual sites
Of reason, show'd him one whose slow brain slights
All intellectual play, but finds its joy
In all the range of muscular delights.
No maladies of thought were wont to annoy
This giant with the spirit of a guileless boy.

A scarp rose left, to right a deep ravine
Fell to sheer depths; and here he roll'd the rocks,
One after one, watching each mass careen
And topple down to where far thundering shocks
Roar'd and re-echoed. Like a mighty ox
He struggled with his task until he clear'd
Away the last of those stupendous blocks
That fill'd the road. His sweating face was smear'd
With dust and dirt, but on he strode extremely cheer'd.

An hour more, and in the loneliest part
Of those wild hills he heard a shout for aid
Not far ahead. Giving an eager start,
He sprinted swiftly forward, unafraid.
Rounding a crag, he saw an ambuscade
Where three stout robbers cruelly beset
Two peaceful travellers, one already laid
Unconscious on earth, the other wet
With blood about the head but fighting fiercely yet.

The indignant giant caught them unaware.
He seized the first dacoit, a black-brow'd thug,
And swirl'd him as a flail—so smote him square
Upon the next, and crush'd him like a bug.
Flinging the carcass from him with a shrug,
He faced the third, who saw his foe close in,
And when the huge arms sought a lethal hug,
Struck with brass-knuckled fist upon his chin
And sent the assailant reeling backward in a spin.

The bandit was a man of massive build,
Though shorter by a cubit than the youth.
His sinewy arms and frame seemed rarely skill'd
In all the arts of combat. Without ruth
He smote the youngster's mouth, and shatter'd tooth,
Split lip, shed blood in rillets; while the lad
Maul'd his opponent hard in ways uncouth,
But found the cruel knuckles still forbade
An issue which gave play to all the strength he had.

Superior skill laid busily its mark
In livid weals upon his chest and face;

But still he battled on, and when the stark
Red onslaught slacken'd for a fleeting space,
He leap'd and caught the foe in his embrace:
Then the great biceps, raising him on high,
Two fathoms from the earth, with stern grimace
Hurl'd the thief downward, caught by throat and thigh,
And broke his back upon a boulder standing nigh.

"A noble fight!" a cultured voice exclaim'd,
The comment of the rescued traveller.
"I thought no mortal could have thrown the famed
But base Theagenes; for this, dear Sir,
Was that unbeaten champion who made stir
Three seasons at Olympia with his fists,
But then turn'd robber like a common cur.
I marvel that you dared to take the lists
Against this greatest of all Grecian pankratists."

"I did not know," the victor panted out,
"That this was he. I only knew your need,
Hearing from yonder hill your frantic shout
And coming to your rescue with all speed.
He who has strength has duties. Who, indeed,
Would hesitate to spend undoubted might
Of body such as mine for those who plead?"—
"Well said!" replied the stranger. "You are right.
And I would gladly strive my saviour to requite."

II Porch and Palaistra

As rescuer and rescued, side by side,
Walk'd down to Epidaurus that same day,
The former, Gigas, often turned and eyed
The suave Protagoras, and heard him say
That in his private school he taught the way
For man to grow in selfhood like a king:
"Upon your strength's foundation, I could lay
A life of amplest power, apt to wring
All happiness from earth and shun all ills that sting."

"Gladly," said Gigas, "would I learn of you;
But tell me, would my thews be left to rust?

[333]

My body is my treasure. I pursue
All gifts that sun and air and oil and dust
And exercise bestow to keep robust
The excellence of manhood Zeus has given.
How would your training view that sacred trust?
For no dead lore on earth would I be driven
To sacrifice the strength for which I long have striven!"

"Fear not at all," replied Protagoras.
"Much rather would I have you taught the skill
You lack'd in yonder fight. I have a class
That learns all sleights of craft, all forms of drill
By which the frame is moulded to the will.
Sweat is the doorstep of the virtuous life;
The brain is poison'd if the brawn keep still;
And so we blend our studies with that strife
Of sturdy bodies. In such training joy is rife.

"To sit too long at books is evil sloth;
It melts away the temper of the soul:
The mind itself is hinder'd in its growth,
And when the state exacts its fitting toll
Of warlike service, he whose strength is whole
Rightly despises the perspiring fool
Whose muscles are not harden'd by control
In manly regimen, whom no games school
To noble pose and posture, among men to rule.

"Athletics are essential to my school.
Yet, that once said, things greater lie behind:
The bravest body were a useless tool,
Lacking the crowning culture of a mind
In which all comprehension is refined
By education. Greater difference lies
Between the scholar and the unlettered hind
Than lies 'twixt life and carrion. Seize this prize
Of fuller consciousness! Enrol amongst the wise!"

So Gigas settled down and sought to learn;
But found his greatest joy in naked sport,
When pairs of wrestling lads would roll and churn
The sand of the palaistra, or consort

[334]

In games of ball or leap-frog in the court
Or box'd, or punch'd the bag, or hurl'd the spear,
Or, ranged in pageantry of stately sort,
March'd to the flute in Dorion modes austere
And felt that life was good and virtue very near.

But when he walk'd the shady pillar'd porch
Wherein Protagoras was wont to teach,
And heard him speak of learning as a torch
Committed by the ages, each to each,
And talk upon the mysteries of speech,
The nature of the state, the forms of plants,
Or Cloudland happiness that man could reach—
He listen'd dully in a sort of trance,
With half-glazed eye and tedium in his glance.

He liked the refectory diet even less,
For temperance in all things was a law
On which Protagoras laid urgent stress:
"Eat sparingly. Drink little wine. A maw
Too full is dull."—Such lessons would he draw.
But dates, dried fish and salads seldom stay'd
The giant's appetite; vague pangs would gnaw
At times his empty entrails and persuade
The man of flesh that virtue was a mocking shade.

III The Business Basis

Now Gigas' strength and Gigas' mighty deeds
Upon the mountain road in honour grew
Within that little town; and sundry seeds
Of reputation reach'd a raw yahoo,
Pollux by name, who, skulking out of view
In gallows haunts in Corinth with his son—
One Paul the Pig, who shared his revenue,
A red-nosed sot whose drinking ne'er was done—
Began to ponder whether gain might here be won.

This precious pair sought Gigas out by stealth,
And stress'd the weak unwisdom of his course:
"To hide your strength," said Pollux, "Hoards up wealth.
Your teacher makes you drudge like some blind horse

Upon a treadmill . . . You're his best resource!
If he were wise and left the plans to me,
I'd advertise you, draw in students, force
The town to give him gold by glad decree,
And make his school a prosperous university.

"Put on a business basis, you'd be rich
And this place famous in a single year;
But he's too dull, too stupid; that's the hitch.
His only thought of business is austere
Cheese-paring stint of food, denial of beer,
Economies his lads know all too well.
Come, stay with us in Corinth. Your career
Could open with the Isthmian games, and spell
Wealth for devoted friends and you, if you excel.

"We'd run you as a dark horse. We'd get high stakes,
Long odds—for you as yet are quite unknown—
And when you win, hands down, the clean-up makes,
I'm sure, twelve thousand drachmae. You alone
Would get a cool six thousand as your own,
While Paul and I would salt away the rest."—
"But could I eat in training?"—"Beef and bone,
Stew'd eel and hare and sweetbreads of the best,
Eat till your midriff presses hard upon your chest!"

But as they talk'd, Protagoras came and heard
Young Gigas promise greedily to go.
"Before we part," he bitterly demurr'd,
"Be sure you mark the fate most athletes know—
Slaves of their jaw and belly here below,
Bloated like dew-blown cows with guzzled food,
And rank as he-goats, while their wits outgrow
All liking for the lovely and the good,
Mere beasts with beastlike uselessness and hardihood!"

"All rot!" said Paul. "The belly bears the feet.
You cannot build a man on water-cress.
We get your athlete for his fill of meat,
An ox a day if need be." Forth they press
And take the Corinth road in glib success.

Over the hills they pass'd, beneath a sky
That darken'd in a dim uneasiness,
And as they walk'd along that pathway high,
Around a bend they heard a sudden anguish'd cry.

A stone's cast from the road, an angry bull
Vented his rage upon a prostrate form;
Near by, a mountain torrent eddied full,
And here another wretch in wild alarm
Had stumbled and was drowning. Blood ran warm
In Gigas' veins, but Paul and Pollux pled
The hazards to their project, held each arm,
And argued hotly till at last he fled
With them from that dark spot, shamed, with averted head.

A lonely farm near Corinth was their goal;
And here, conceal'd from subtly prying eyes,
They train'd their man. He ate without control
Vast quantities of meat. His monstrous size
Grew solid and more certain of the prize.
Then Pollux must be absent for a season,
Leaving the work to Paul. "My son, be wise,"
He urged in parting. "Keep your drink in reason.
And lie here close: To show our man were arrant treason."

IV   *The Wages of Brawn*

"'Fore God," said Paul one day. "I'm quite as dry
As any toad, and homesick for the mud!
Let's go to Tim the Taverner's and try
Some toddy for my stomach's sake. God's blood!—
You haven't lived until you've met the stud
Of super-sinners there at Timothy's,
Lapping their booze!" And with another flood
Of thirsty oaths, and many a longing wheeze,
He steer'd young Gigas to the inn to take his ease.

Threading Corinthian slums, they reach'd at last
A basement pot-house, from whose open door
Came husky songs and laughter upward cast.
"Here's Tim's," said Paul. His entrance brought a roar
Of greetings from his cronies, and he swore

They all must meet the youth without delay:
"Here, Gigas, are the rakes that I deplore—
The seven deadliest sinners of their day,
All damn'd, I'm sure, but damn'd good fellows in their way.

"This man with slimy eyes and sloven hair
Is Creeping Crispus, laziest louse on earth.
The next is Wrathful Rufus: mark his air
Of white-eyed rage, his snivelling nose, his dearth
Of courtesy. This cock a-crow with mirth
Is Leaping Luke, as lickerish a lad
As ever served Priapus from his birth.
And Pompous Pete, beside him, grows quite mad
If you suggest that Lucifer is half as bad.

"That tripe-faced blackguard with the triple paunch
Is Gulping Gaius; and that blear-eyed soak,
With dangling dewlap and lean, threadbare haunch,
Is Steve the Stingy. Yonder in the cloak,
Gaping with bulging eyes as if he'd choke,
Is Jaundiced Jason, drunk as David's sow.
Without these topers, Tim would soon be broke.
Meet Timothy himself, my lad! I vow
You never saw a master of his art till now!"

With Tim, Paul, Gigas, and the Seven Sots,
There made the devil's dozen at that inn
Three of the Cyprian sisterhood, whose lots
Made ample profit out of wine and gin—
Chloe the Cat, an ancient piece of sin,
A jade with wincing withers, long since wrung;
Loose Lydia, a wench with wither'd skin,
Toad-spotted and unclean; and stupor-stung
Old Simple Cecily, who had a babbling tongue.

Then rat-eyed Tim, as furtive as a skink,
Made Gigas welcome in that low resort.
"More pigwash, Tim!" said Paul. And with their drink,
They turn'd to jest and oath and tipsy sport,
With much fine fabling of the baser sort.
But Gigas took to tipple like a trout.
If e'er he paused—"Come, just another snort!
Don't hesitate, about it and about!
Sing like a happy hog! Turn to, and wet your snout!"

Then Pete stood up amongst them and was bold:
"Your tadpole, Paul, must drink, to prove his way,
As much as Tim's big measure here can hold—
A gallon and a gill. We in our day
Have each put down the pitcher, dregs and spray.
This is the test no man-sized tup would skimp.
The devil save your prighood! Drink, I say,
Or I abjure you as a yellow shrimp,
A pusillanimous and sanctimonious pimp!"

"God rot your gizzard, Pete, lay off the boy!"
Said Paul in haste. But Gigas' pride was hurt:
"Bring on your wine," said he. "I'll gladly toy
With such small potions, for this stuck-up squirt
Can't stand and hand me contumelious dirt!"
Then, on one breath, the ponderous giant drain'd
The mighty flagon, till the belt that girt
His tumefying belly stretch'd and strain'd.
"Well swill'd!" cried all the crew. "Your honour is
                                        maintained!"

And so all afternoon they sat and lush'd
Their liquor down and guzzled tipsy-blind.
Young Gigas' features slowly grew more flush'd,
And fumes of wassail mounted to his mind.
It chanced they spoke of strength, and Paul opined,
Fuddled past caution, that the Isthmian games
Would get a jolt from Gigas: men would find
That Herakles and Atlas were slight names
Compared with Gigas then. So ran his frantic claims.

"Don't talk such rot!" snarl'd Rufus, in a huff.
"Your stripling's got a brisket like a sheep,
Legs like a pea chick, and such soggy stuff
About his loins that he could hardly keep
A calf at bay. I'm sure you got him cheap;
But he may cost you dear before you've done."—
"Yes," mutter'd Jason. "I could almost weep
To think old Paul has found this shoal-brain'd tun
And fancies that the thing can lift and throw and run!"

"You lie!" said Gigas, with a mighty belch.—
"The strongest man in Greece!" protested Paul.

"Come, name your feat! He'll do it. He can squelch
Your envious gibes and thunderstrike you all."—
"Taken!" said Luke. "Put stakes up, and we'll call
Your precious bluff before the night is black.
Come to the stadium; we'll let him haul
The obelisk of Milo on his back
And walk the full two-furlong limit of the track!"

"You're mad," said Paul. "The little pillar weighs
Two tons at least, and took a hundred hands
With hempen ropes to put it in its place."—
"I've carried more for fun! The challenge stands,"
Gigas broke in. "I'm tough, boys, guts and glands,
Hard as the devil's horns. I'll tote the spike,
Even if you should double your demands.
And if I stagger, may the devil strike
Me dead for keeps. This is the sort of game I like!"

Out of that den and down a labyrinth
Of frowsy lanes the drunken rabble raged
Until they stood beside a five-foot plinth
On which a ponderous obelisk was staged,
Granite, three fathoms long, remotely aged,
Carved with Egyptian signs of strength and death.
There Gigas stoop'd to take the weight engaged,
Made broad his back, drew in his ample breath,
And tightened up his girdle by a twentieth.

But neither he who strove, nor they who asked
To see him strive, conceived in fuddled brain
How easily a man were overtask'd
If overwhelm'd by too abrupt a strain.
The seven topers pushed with might and main
To move the tottering column from its base,
All standing on the plinth; nor push'd in vain—
The tall shaft made a clumsy arc through space
And crash'd where Gigas squatted, waiting, in his place.

It crush'd the skull and spilt the brains abroad,
A sort of bloody porridge on the ground.
The carcass crumpled sideways, gaping-jaw'd,
And sank upon the earth without a sound.
The mighty muscles twitch'd and writhed around,

Held in convulsive death beneath the stone.
A puked-up flux of gore and beer embrown'd
The sand beside his mouth. But life had flown
And left a useless heap of flesh and fractured bone.

The seven sweating sinners stood aghast:
"By God!" said Jason. "That's a sudden end!
He went to meet the devil mighty fast!"
"Come sober" hiccup'd Luke. "I recommend
We do a bunk before the cops descend
And run us in." So coarsely did they spurn,
Save for a hasty search, their quondam friend,
Taking his purse and rings to serve their turn,
And left the corpse as garbage for the town to burn.

THE WAY OF A CAPITALIST

1   *The Mediaeval Marsh*

Beneath dull, boundless skies, a traveler walk'd
Amid a boundless marsh, and sought his way
By faint, uncertain paths. Plants, oozy-stalk'd
And fleshy, sprawl'd upon the miry clay;
Lush marish grasses, green as moist decay,
Lined seepy pools; the vast plain seem'd to be
An endless, viridescent, treeless tray,
A sort of silted-in Sargasso Sea
Where sedge and rush and flag spread to infinity.

Across green puddles, glaucous serpents slid;
Before them fled green frog and emerald newt;
Under a lily-leaf, pale lizards hid;
Deep in the jasper pools, the fish hung mute.
But from the farther fens arose the bruit
Of hollow-booming bittern, wail of snipe,
The mad, unearthly laugh of rail and coot,
And rasping of the reed-bird's rusty pipe—
Bird cries that nearest match their reptile prototype.

The wet slough here and there grew dank and dense,
As clammy, ancient rot of root and stem

Had curdled to a pulp of foul offense,
A slimy mucous paste of pus and phlegm.
This lay in sludgy pits, upon whose hem
The very quagmire shook its shuddering grass,
And no birds nested, lest it swallow them;
Even the cold-eyed vipers dared not pass
Over the clotted poison of the dark morass.

Slowly the traveler probed the sodden swamp,
Now lighting on low spits of sedge-grown sand,
And now on spongy tussocks, crass and damp,
And sometimes sprawling prone, with head and hand
Deep in some slushy sink. But still he scann'd
Undaunted, the vague trail by which he went,
Though myriads of mosquitoes made demand
Upon his throat, and flies wax'd virulent,
Assailing eye, lip, cheek and brow with fierce intent.

Ere evening shadows fell across that waste,
He reach'd a swarm of houses, built on poles
Above the bog, mere stilt-borne nests, disgraced
By midden-heaps beneath them in the shoals
And ill-framed doors that seem'd mere hiding holes
From gnats and marsh miasma and the night.
Men lived like rude, unfeather'd orioles
In these high, reedy huts, secure in spite
Of all that deep-drench'd prairie and its humid blight.

Their leader dropp'd a ladder for the guest
And hospitably lodged him. Bronzed and fat,
The sweating pilgrim reach'd the lofty nest.
"My name," puff'd he, "is Crassus. Like a rat
I've scurried here across this marshy flat
To give you greeting; for I bring a scheme
That can transform your dripping habitat
Into a land of farms and towns, supreme
In wealth beyond the limit of your wildest dream."

His host, a wither'd, fever-ridden man
With nose a sun-dried fig, gaped like a fish
To hear him speak of this prodigious plan.
"Nonsense," he sneered. "Your brains are all a-swish,
Mad as an idiot's nightmare! Pshaw! Pah! Pish!"

Laughter like moonlight play'd across the face
Of undiscouraged Crassus: "Grant my wish!
Come, work with me to drain this plashy place;
And if my venture fail, then slay me in disgrace!"

The dwellers in that hutch debated long;
They call'd to council all the near-by thorps,
And Crassus told his project to the throng:
"If this be false, consider me a corpse!
If you will help with shovels, ropes and warps,
Rubble and riprap, boulder-clay and brush,
In building ditches, dykes, and counterscarps,
We shall obtain, instead of quaggy mush,
A country for which none on earth would need to blush!"

They gave assent, and Polderland had birth.
Colossal dykes cut off the ambient swamp,
And drainage channels dried the fertile earth
To ploughman's use. Unresting pump and tromp
Drew waters where the wildfowl used to romp
Into great reservoirs. And cities grew,
Exultant with all circumstance and pomp,
Out of the former fens. All things were new,
Transform'd by Crassus and his toiling retinue.

And when they spoke to Crassus of reward,
He claimed control of water, the canals,
And all the reservoirs in which they stored
The oozing flood. Said he: "These rising walls
And avenues of your new capitals
Are freely yours, for you have toil'd with me.
Mine is the water-system; yours, these halls
And mansions. May your people happier be
Than when you lodged in damp, despised extremity!"

II The Fabric of Finance

The years passed swiftly on, and Crassus turn'd
His tanks to many uses, in whose course
Water quench'd human thirst when summer burn'd,
And saved the lives of cattle, sheep and horse;
Man's body from the bath drew new resource;

And linen, ample cleansing from its power;
Even the farmer's wheat-fields felt its force
In supplementing heaven's scanty shower
And ripening the full ear from the thirsty flower.

The master of the waters then took heat,
Made steam, and piped its essence through great mains,
To every throbbing factory, where it beat
Like some dynamic pulse in all their veins
Of steel and brass. Lathes, hammers, pulleys, cranes
Moved in unwearied strength at its command.
Light-hearted owners multiplied their gains,
And all gave cheerful blessing to the bland
Fat-paunch'd, long-headed water-lord of Polderland.

But presently the Polderlanders rued
The strictness of the bargain they had made.
Pride is the mother of ingratitude;
And Crassus, growing proud, forgot the aid
That native nerve and sinew, spar and spade,
Had given to his vaulting enterprise;
And so he rack'd his rents, and all men paid
The toll of him who could monopolize,
And not the measure of his service, as 'twere wise.

Once he had dreams of good, but now he wax'd
Bold as Beëlzebub, smug as a smelt;
Ever his smile grew oilier as he tax'd
The toiling state; more ample grew his belt
While he enslaved the men with whom he dealt.
Lolling in luxury, his pudgy wife
Sighed like a simpering kettle as she felt
The tedium of too, too affluent life,
And wheezed out smiling wishes for domestic strife.

But deep in crowded slums the workers lay,
Ground down by his demands to muddy spite.
Industrious as ants, they toil'd by day;
Moody as moulting birds, they moped by night;
Pale housewives stayed the pangs of appetite
By chipping, chopping, paring cheapest cheese;
And puny children, rickety and white,
Shook with the famined palsy of disease.
But Crassus little knew, or reck'd, of such as these.

Rather he came to think of moiling men
As robots, clad in overalls of blue;
And women were not saint or Magdalen
But only factory-fodder, swaddled too
In epicene attire. If danger slew
Or maim'd in some machine their flesh and blood,
He cast them by, replacing them with new;
They were but flotsam on the golden flood
That he had conjured up from out the waste of mud.

Only one problem irk'd him for a while:
Sometimes the water staled, sometimes grew spent;
Nor could he heal the waters that were vile
Until at last, across the whole extent
Of that wide, wet Serbonian continent,
A score of states arose by like device
Of ditch and dyke; and gave their glad consent
To interchange of store, that each might spice
And purify his vats and channels, at a price.

Each nation labour'd strongly to construct
To every other dyke-land round about
A mighty tube, a siphon-aqueduct,
Whose leaden leagues extended like the snout
Of some colossal insect, stretching out
To suck unceasingly. By that fierce flow
The agitated streams, beyond all doubt,
Were rendered pure and able to bestow
More fertile blessings as they blended to and fro.

III   The International Collapse

But one dark year, an earthquake overthrew
All siphons of all countries but his own.
Crassus' incurrent conduits suck'd and drew
Their tribute from abroad, yet gave no loan
Reciprocal to others. Like a drone,
That feeds on unearn'd honey, was his state,
Or like some monstrous squid, that, sprawling prone,
Reaches his greedy tentacles to sate
Gross, guzzling gluttony on all things animate.

[345]

In far-off, suffering cities, water fail'd,
Drain'd by that toll. The toil of factories ceased;
The farms grew parch'd; and little children wail'd
In dry-tongued anguish as their thirst increased.
Their rulers might, by violence, have released
The lands from Crassus' levy, but they said
That honour was involved. They would be fleeced,
Rather than break those aqueducts of lead.
And so their streets were dotted with the thirsty dead.

But Crassus rear'd a towering reservoir,
Wide as a lake, a thousand cubits high,
To hold the burden that his sluices bore
And hoard away the bountiful supply.
Yet even this might flood or putrefy,
And so he flush'd his flumes and dropp'd his tax
Until the poorest Poldermen could buy
An ample store, and were as willing wax,
Consenting to the load he laid on alien backs.

His wife, Dorada, built a lordly park
On her estate, begemm'd with many a pond
On which one sail'd in gay Venetian ark
'Mid lily-pads and white swans, tame and fond.
Bright marble fountains play'd in lawns beyond,
And drain'd in crystal streams across the sward.
But still the crop-full matron belch'd and yawn'd,
And often grew so heavy and so bored
That on her grassy terraces she lay and snored.

The plenitude of water and of steam
Stirr'd up the factories to new endeavour.
Out of their bulging portals came a stream
Of all things, gay and useless, whatsoever
Had been invented by man's brain to sever
Fools and their money: toys of every kind
Made glad the population, dull and clever,
Until all Polderlanders crossly whined
To cease from work forever and to lie reclined.

Their wish had dark fulfilment. Day by day,
The waters in the Reservoir had crept

Up, up, uncheck'd by spending and display,
Until, one night, while all men grossly slept,
The mighty walls by which the flood was kept
Broke with a voice of thunder. Through the land,
By farm and slumbering town, the waters swept
In one vast tidal wave, terrific, grand,
Against whose overwhelming mass no power could stand.

Five million perish'd mutely in that flood,
Caught in the nets of negligence and sleep;
Others, awaken'd by the crash and thud
Of that descending death, had time to leap
For upper rooms and roof-tops, where like sheep
They cower'd for a time, too dazed to think.
Ev'n Crassus almost smother'd in that deep,
While dull Dorada, far too fat to sink,
Went floating, wet but sleepy, stripp'd and pink.

Inside of Polderland's great outer dyke,
When that wild wave was spent, there spread a tide
Two fathoms deep, on field and street alike,
In which all victims lay and putrified.
All factories were ruin'd, far and wide;
All work and weal were strangled for a season;
And as the sunlit waters slowly dried,
The citizens, enraged, sought out the reason
For their distress and murmur'd of high treason.

IV   *The Indictment of Crassus*

After the deluge's slow subsidence,
The people, having call'd a solemn court,
Indicted Crassus for the whole offence.
The first to cite his felony and tort
Was Opifex, a lawyer shrunk and short,
With smouldering eye, like fire in a pit:
"What need have we," he cried, "of long report?
No person in his senses would acquit
A monster who has starved our state and flooded it.

"Long years the workers famish'd through his fault,
Hungry as frost, they huddled, each by each,

[347]

In slums, or stood, his power to exalt,
Like regiments of penguins on a beach
That seamen club to death. His acts make breach,
By inhumanity, of contracts made
For water-work monopoly; I now impeach
This rackrent murderer, thief, and renegade
For triple treason in his uncompassion'd trade!"

But Crassus answer'd nothing, sitting there
In fat amazement, blinking like a toad.
A second barrister, Mercator, tare
His flowing wig: "All commerce bore a load
Most grievous through his toll; for merchants owed
A greater tax to him than they could gain.
All walk'd to ruin by a common road,
Or, seeking food, found only, to their pain,
The shadowy fare that Schacabac enjoyed in vain."

The senior counsel, Sagax, follow'd next:
"The basis of monopoly is wrong.
The price of scarcity unfairly vex'd
This state of Polderland, to which belong
All profits save that part just amply strong
To draw out each man's powers, great or small.
Without the state, no man is worth a song;
The public creates values, and may call
That man a liar, who, as self-made, claims them all.

"This same society that causes wealth
Would seek out waste, and justly, if it took
All of these surplus profits for the health
Of every mind and body. It should look
That no man lack'd his toil of brawn or book
For home and public good; and skilful tax
Should seek out gross excesses like a rook
That feeds her hungry nestlings with all snacks
That vigilance can garner over fields and tracks.

"Were wealth devoted to the common good
And subtle science shared in kindred way,
I wager that the human multitude
Could meet all wants by two hours work each day!
Then could they spend much time in healthful play,

But more at books and science, talk and art,
Culture of flowers, chant of roundelay,
Until life's darker shadows would depart
Before that sunrise of train'd body, mind, and heart!

"But this all-grasping rogue has left our folk
Debauch'd, degraded, destitute, defiled.
Nay more, the burden of his unjust yoke
Has marr'd the lives of woman, man, and child
In scores of distant lands; and now the wild
Unholy waters that he stole break free
And ruin us, too long, too well, beguiled.
Therefore I claim, for his repacity,
Defeasance of his contract, and a gallows-tree!"

"Spare me," said Crassus, "for I once meant well.
Peccavi, I have sinned."—The grim judge bow'd:
"Yea, good intentions pave the road to hell!
We find you guilty, and have disallow'd
Your tainted title. Yet your gifts o'ershroud
Some measure of your injuries, we ken.
Your life is spared for service. Be not proud,
And seek no more to rack the lives of man—
For, by the Lord, you may not do the like again!"

THE WAY OF A JURIST

1   The City of The King

Through olive-orchards on an eastern hill
A thoughtful stranger trod a westward way.
About his feet bloom'd rose and daffodil,
But his cold glance, his eyes severe and grey,
Saw nothing of their beauty, nor would stray
To left or right from that high-tower'd town,
Girt with stone walls, which straight before him lay
Across a sudden valley. With a frown
He paused at last, and ponder'd, gazing darkly down.

Draped across low twin hills, the city spread
Its mingled mass of stateliness and shame:

A maze of tenements, where squalor bred,
Form'd a dilapidate and filthy frame
For gleaming palaces of lofty fame
And solemn temples, overlaid with gold,
That glitter'd in the sunlight like a flame.
Within the watching eye, whilom so cold,
An answering fire bespoke a man volcanic-soul'd.

He moved again at last; he cross'd the vale;
And enter'd through the broad, high-arching gate.
But there two guardsmen stopp'd him with a hail:
"Halt! Go not forward, or we break thy pate!"
Then, in accord with statutes of the state,
They stripp'd him of all monies: "Thus our wise
And sapient Sovereign serves each reprobate
Who comes from foreign parts. This act supplies
A motive for new work and gainful enterprise."—

"But this is theft!" he cried. "What king is this
That beggars me to toil against my will?"—
They frown'd in answer: "Sure thou speakst amiss
Of royal Anax, Heaven's sacred Rill
That nourishes our Sion. Naught of ill
Can come from his mild heart. He is a king;
Kings come from God; and all their acts fulfil
The authority of Heaven, which would fling
On them the governance of every earthly thing.

"Anax, our King, rules by divine decree.
He loves our sacred people, and has built
Proud temples and a vast distillery
To enrich our shrines. Upon him God has spilt
Such wealth as proves his kingship to the hilt;
A thousand wives make quick his hopeful Seed;
The nation calls him Father. It were guilt
To speak against his law. We pray take heed,
For they who measure strength with him are lost indeed!"

But young Seldenius, the stranger, struck
His hand upon his thigh: "What scut's excuse
Can call that rogue a king whose vices suck
The life-blood of the land? Kings have their use
As symbols of that Law (in ways abstruse)

By which alone the commonwealth may live.
When monarchy and church join in abuse
Of drunken exploitation, they can give
No reason under heav'n for their prerogative!

"True justice is the bond of men in states,
The mainspring of all order and all rule;
But every wanton tyrant abdicates
And makes himself more futile than a fool."
Then they who heard this wrath and ridicule,
Pierced by the smiting frankness of his speech,
Bound him with chains and bore him on a mule
To Anax' palace, where they hoped to teach
The glory of the monarch whom they now beseech:

"Delight and Terror of the Universe,
Bright Ornament of Nature, gracious Lord,
Whose Royal Person is above all curse,
Whose Precious Name is everywhere adored,
Fair Occidental Star, Avenging Sword,
Most tender Nursing Father of thy Land,
May all the trembling world with one accord
Accept with joy the Rule, divinely plann'd,
Of thy most sacred, most sublime, most holy Hand!

"And now behold, dread Lord, this Man of Sin,
Who in our ears has made his hatred known
Against our Church, its holy Trade in gin,
But most against thy high exalted Throne,
Calling thee despot!" Anax stood like stone,
His eye a stormy sunset, shot with red;
Then, after silence, cried: "Were this alone
A crime towards Church and Trade, I should have said
My Tower of Oblivion should hide his head.

"But as his words against my Throne have stunk,
Excise his navel, nail it to a tree,
And make him wind his bowels round the trunk,
Driving him deathward!" But fair Clemency,
A queen, bribed guards, and set the captive free
For one brief instant in that judgment-hall;
Then guided him in flight, and saw that he,
Like Rahab's Hebrew spies or Tarsan Saul,
Escaped them through a brothel on the outer wall.

Nine days he fled: upon the tenth he found
An aëry city, perch'd upon a peak
Above the range of clouds. No filth was found
Along its marble lanes; there rose no shriek
To tell of sharp disease among the weak;
No nakedness or sin were noted there.
But they who ruled this state were pale of cheek,
Sad men, with golden crickets in their hair,
And in their solemn eyes a look of grave despair.

The human basis of their polity
Lay in a horde of slaves, as sleek as cows,
Who bore all menial toil in each degree,
And carried on all trade in every house.
For all the freemen claim'd, with scornful brows,
That work and commerce rotted character.
And so each citizen was bound by vows
To educated leisure and the stir
Of martial exercise that warrior-castes incur.

Five thousand fighters and five thousand wives
Were all that shared in freedom; and among
These few all things were common—homes and lives,
Wealth, slaves, and progeny. For Reason flung,
With fixed, impartial, algebraic tongue,
To all a universal change of mate
Each night for fifteen years; and so the young,
From all these couchings inter-permutate,
Were 'bastards rear'd in bureaux' by the kindly state.

Out of this warrior class, the sagest sort
Were chosen as the Guardians of the rest—
A philosophic senate, mild of port,
Who ruled with iron hand and calm behest.
All that their reverend wisdom judged the best
Was forced with ruthless will upon the herd.
Unselfish to a fault, their minds profess'd
No merit in emotion, but averr'd
That reason must have sway, lest man be quite absurd.

Into this city came Seldenius
And sojourn'd many days; but as he learn'd
Its form of rule, he ventured to discuss
Its faults upon the street, where many turn'd
To hear the speech of one whose phrases burn'd
With zeal for freedom. Then the Guardians woke,
And sent their burly sergeants, much concern'd,
To seize this dangerous stranger. "Come!" they spoke,
"And tell the justices what laws thou dar'st invoke!"

The white-robed council watch'd with grave displeasure
The entry of this man who braved their law;
Yet still they waited with unhasting measure
To hear his apologia and to draw
A just decision without blot or flaw.—
"Are thoughts not free of tax? And is not speech
The privilege," he cried, "of ripe or raw,
Learn'd or unlearn'd, that so the mind of each
May help the common wisdom in its upward reach?

"It is the mind that makes us bond or free.
As all man share in reason, you ensure
The highest good of all by liberty
To think and speak. Men otherwise endure
Foul slavery of spirit, past all cure."—
The guardians frown'd, and one, their white-hair'd chief,
Denounced that claim as rashly immature,
Asseverating rather the belief
That uncheck'd discourse was a spring of endless grief:

"Bœotian Gotham gagg'd itself for years
With woolly apophthegms, lest words of men
Should bring the Doom of its perspiring fears;
But the police, who read not, left a den
Of tedious clerks untouch'd, threescore and ten
Dull pedagogues, whose moping owlish lore
Was scorn'd by every active citizen
As dunces' dust, dons' claptrap to ignore:
'Twas clear no clerk could pass as a conspirator.

"Yet even one of these, against his wit,
Spread poisonous doctrine and subverted good

Until the sorry state was rent and split.
You cannot leave unchain'd the hardihood
Of human tongues and pens. We understood
That peril from the first in this high town.
The timber of our laws is perfect wood,
Adzed out of Reason, and if knave or clown
Raise hands of discontent, we smite them harshly down.

"That some should rule and others should obey
Is, of all things, the most expedient.
God mingles gold, from birth, in some men's clay,
But most with brass and iron have been blent.
Intending those to govern, these he meant
Obedient slaves. Only the worst of cheats
Could carp at Heaven, calling Discontent
Noblest of human passions. How he bleats,
Blown like a bladder with the wind of false conceits!"

"Hearken!" Seldenius cried. "Does not the state
Have, as its end, the Good Life for us all?
How can a man know truth without debate?
Or virtue, without chance to err and fall?
Your faultless government leaves man a thrall,
Incapable alike of sin or growth;
So communistic joys of wedlock pall,
And generosity is choked with sloth
When wealth the liberal heart might give is owned by
                                                    both."

Then one by one the pondering sages nodded
Their grave assent, with wonder in their eyes
To feel emotion quicken as he prodded
Humanity, long harden'd, into sighs
For fuller life and ampler destinies.
Then faith engender'd action, and they plann'd
A constitution where all men might rise
Through school and forum and by virtue stand
In highest place to mould the statutes of the land.

III Vox Populi

Leaving their cloudland eyry, most and least,
The New Republic sought the black-soil'd plain

To found that freer city. Slavehood ceased;
All shared in government; and did ordain
Strict monogamic homes without a stain;
And each, according to his skill and whim,
Built lodgings for his household, being fain
To have his proper hearth and teraphim,
And found a family to bear the name of him.

But all these new-enfranchised proselytes
Soon slew the dream of individual grace.
The human atom with a fringe of rights,
That young Seldenius had preach'd, gave place
To corporate ways. The zealous populace
Sought, with its new-found power, to impose,
By penal law or socialized disgrace,
The habits of the Many on all those
Who dared to frame their living as their own minds chose.

A mob of lantern-jaw'd evangelists,
Once slaves themselves, untouch'd by art or thought
But handy with their jaw-bones and their fists,
Headed the public prejudice and wrought
So earnestly and fiercely that they caught
Complete control, and set about to shape
All that the city did, said, ate or taught
By standards narrow-minded for an ape;
And scarcely from their clutches could man find escape.

This force of public piety consign'd
The cornet, flute, harp, sackbut, psaltery
And dulcimer, music of every kind,
To ignominious silence; while to see
A theatre meant death by stern decree.
Games were forbid by solemn ordinance,
And dames who dared, in wanton-hearted glee,
To eddy in the ecstasies of dance
Were branded on the brow with grimmest circumstance.

All paintings of Madonna or the Christ
Were burned in execration by the crowd
As forms of idols. Beauty that enticed
Was subtly used by Satan, so they vow'd.
Fine raiment was a sin that mark'd the proud;

And wine that had made glad the heart of man
Was utterly denounced and disallow'd,
Being hateful to the godly Puritan.
All things that once cheer'd life were brought beneath the
                                                    ban.

As most men lived by toil of hand and arm,
The stronger number ruled that none might get
Reward in field or city, shop or farm,
Except for manual labour; those who set
Their straining brain to work in cabinet
Or office were but pale-faced parasites,
To whom one gave no thought and paid no debt.
Minorities in all things had no rights
Beneath the iron heel of democratic spites.

In vain Seldenius from their rostrum cried
In fine forensic frenzy at this wrong:
"Here is the height of arrogance and pride,
To imagine that the Many, because strong,
Are therefore right. More reason may belong
To those who are but few. All noble things,
All wisdom, science, and supremest song
Have issued from the Few. Your violence wrings
The stubborn neck of genius and breaks freedom's wings."—

"The man's an anarchist!" the audience gasp'd.
"Perhaps an atheist too, for is not God
Heard in the People's voice! This rogue has grasp'd
With reckless fingers after Aaron's rod,
The power of the good to ride rough-shod,
And justly, over sinners. Quench his gab,
And fling the noisy streetling into quod!"
Headlong they rush'd, priest, pauper, drudge and drab,
And cast him into gaol, to lie all bruise and scab.

IV   *This Side Idolatry*

In earlier days, the Guardians had worn
A golden cricket-brooch in their long locks,
Boasting themselves autochthons, nobly born
And ancient as the crickets of the rocks.

But now a shrill-gorged demagogic fox
Set up a pillar in a public square,
A mighty column, reared of marble blocks,
With a colossal cricket, made of rare
Sabean gold, upon it in the sunlit air.

So was a symbol of the nation rear'd;
And windy edicts everywhere proclaim'd
That it must be by every man revered
And worshipp'd with wild ritual, grossly framed.
The children of the schools were all inflamed
To bow each day before the shining pole;
In every church the golden sign was named;
And skimble-scamble scribes prepared a scroll
In which all loyal Cricket-People should enroll.

The test of full allegiance was a vow
To disembowel all foes in case of war.
Then men and women came with beaming brow;
The lecher and the lazar ran before;
The rip, the rakehell and the orator
Came next with piggish punk and smockless slut,
And all the crowd of sin-worn patriots swore
Their keenness to bear bayonets and gut
All alien folk as scullions clean out halibut.

For days the hot enrolment kept its tone,
Till every man and woman vow'd to hate
All nations, for the honour of their own,
And promised gladly to eviscerate
Youth, maid, or baby for the warring state.
Two only scorned the canon of the law;
A gentle nurse named Blanda braved her fate,
And, in his cell, upon the rotting straw,
Seldenius was reason'd ice that would not thaw.

These two were brought to court for speedy trial,
But ere the case was call'd, men haled a third
To join them on the charge of base denial
Of fundamental duties towards the herd.
With kilts, Dutch clogs, a fez, French hosieries,
A stomacher and stays, a sash to gird
His waist. Before this figure of surprise
Judges and lawyers gaped, and gasp'd, and rubb'd their eyes.

"I am a true Cosmopolite," he said,
Mouthing his words like bones. "I own no race.
The wide world is my city. Where my head
Rests for the night, I count my dwelling-place.
I sip from every flower, I cull a grace
From every folk and culture of mankind.
Humanity is one. I would deface
Our common soul and desecrate my mind
Should I accept the oath your zealots have assign'd."

The speech of Blanda follow'd, clear and firm:
"I rather prize the loyalties that link
The life of each poor mortal for a term
To some one land, where loves and hopes may sink
Into his inmost heart. I would not shrink
From serving as a nurse in thickest battle;
But slaughter is a cup I will not drink!
This hand will not dismember men like cattle."
"Tush," said the judge. "Such talk is only idle prattle."

Seldenius spoke: "I stand for law, and pledge
My powers to the welfare of the nation.
But warfare is an axe without an edge,
That crushes without cleaving. Litigation,
Whether for man or folk, solves agitation
By search for truth and right, not might and force;
But battle is a way of desperation.
Why should I join the mob that shouts so hoarse
In furthering the triumph of the baser course?

"I count that man the best who, taking root
In his own people, grows in heart and brain
Until his spreading branches drop their fruit
Not for his nation only but the gain
Of all humanity. Yet this is vain
Unless the rule of law within our lives
Keep the world sweet. To take away the bane
Of ignorance and hate on which war thrives
Is still my choice!" He resolutely shook his gyves.

The jurymen were Gunsmith, Lust and Gore,
Suspicion, Envy, Hatred, Greed, and Graft,

[358]

Age, Anger, Bile, and old Ambassador;
Dark Anger gave the verdict, and he laugh'd
To think them hang'd and aptly epitaph'd
By his loud "Guilty." But the law's redress
Seem'd less than mortal to the judge. "Since daft,
You merit exile only!" Thus, in stress,
They drove them, like God's scapegoats, to the wilderness.

THE WAY OF AN INVENTOR

1 The Priestlike Task

A bearded youth limp'd down an evening road
Between long, new-plough'd corn-fields, moist and black.
Lame was he, but not weary, for there show'd
No sweat on his broad brow; he bore his pack
As lightly as a thought upon his back;
And still he fashion'd in his supple hands—
Hands with long fingers, infinite of knack—
Some fine ingenious toy of links and bands,
And heeded not the setting sun and darkening lands.

At length the work was finish'd, and he laugh'd
With happy sense of skilful mastery;
Then gave his scrip the product of his craft
And slowly gazing round, intent to see
What manner of man's shelter here might be,
Mark'd with his black shrewd eyes a farmer's cot
With milch-cows in the byre and progeny
Of cock and drake and gander; and bethought
Himself how pleasant food and rest might here be sought.

Nor did he seek in vain; well lodged and fed
He slumber'd in contentment till the morn.
His host, Agricola, bull-cheek'd and red,
Found him a clever artisan, once born
In an Egyptian shop, but lately torn
By restlessness to journey far and wide.
Then, since the farm lack'd help, great oaths were sworn
To pay the young man amply should he bide
And labour till the coming of the harvest-tide.

So he, whose name was Tubal, sojourn'd there
And drudged through moiling hours in the field,
Liking it little, ready to declare
That he could wrest from earth a larger yield
With paltry effort if allow'd to wield
His cunning in creating some device
Or tool for every task, and so to shield
His bones from useless aches—within a trice
To change his hell of toil into a paradise.

"You peasants mix emotion with your work,"
He often said. "You till the thistled earth
As if some mystic virtues strangely lurk
In your hard duties; or as if the birth
Of wheat-blades with new harvest for man's dearth
Had some religion in it. Drive it out!
Put steel machines to work. Make farming worth
A cold cash profit; and you'll put to rout
All carking toil along with lunacies devout.

"The fingers made the brain," the youth would say.
"I heard some sages in Bubastis tell
How man was once an ape, but learn'd to play
With sticks and stones as tools, and it befell
That such communion made his reason swell
In pregnant bigness. Tools, my master, tools
Transform'd the beast to man! So do we well
To press the process forward till it schools
All of the race to wisdom, and there be no fools."

"It may be as they say. I think they lie."—
Came back the farmer's angry, rasping voice.
"If man be shaped from beast, I see not why
Moses, throughout his Genesis, employs
Jehovah as creator. Can his choice
Be challenged by their word, or thine, my lad,
Thou vagrant tinkering smith, whose tale destroys
Our sacred scripture's version? Nay, thou art mad!
And all thy dreams of tool-freed man are nigh as bad.

"Toil is our lot since father Adam plough'd
The glebe to east of Eden at the first;

Nor is it evil, for the Lord endow'd
That work with secret blessing when he cursed
Our errant race with appetite and thirst.
All these give life its meaning, dark makes light,
And hunger zest, best issues from the worst;
And shouldst thou banish effort and invite
Mankind to drowsy ease, the gift would be a blight!

"Thou hast reviled the peasant's love for all
The wonder of warm earth and living grain;
Nor canst thou understand the springtime's call
That draws him to a priestlike task again,
The task of sharing with the sun and rain
In conjuring into life man's daily food.
With such a purpose, who would live in vain?
And I defy thy leisured brotherhood
To fashion for our lives a meaning half as good!"

The quarrel grew, till Tubal, full of rage,
Because the peasant ceased not to condemn
His crafts and creeds, resumed his pilgrimage.
Some village might approve the stratagem
Of skill'd artificers to try and stem
The anguish of man's toiling, though this clod
Of rustic dotage drooled with apophthegm
And dusty damn'd ideal, and would nod
In crabbèd evening discourse on the farmer's God.

II   *The Gospel of Labour*

Three days brought Tubal to a little town,
A white-wall'd hamlet in the Hebrew hills
North from Jezreel, most gracious with a crown
Of orchard figs and olives and the quills
Of cactus-hedges; such a sight as thrills
The heart in love with beauty, but not so
The scheming wit of him who only wills
Mechanic consummations and a show
Of wrought arachnid industries for man below.

He lodged that evening with a carpenter,
Joseph Ben-Seth, a calm dark-bearded man

With eyes as grey as twilight, and a far
Infinity of gaze that seemed to scan
Beyond the sky yet often also ran
In loving pride as gentle as a prayer
To smile on wife and sons; the artisan,
All stain'd with travel, found a welcome there,
And tasted hours of peace in kindness past compare.

Yet still the inventive fever in his brain
Drove him to bare his hopes for wondrous tools
That would absolve the toiler from the strain
Of tiring effort; things of springs and spools
And cranks and cogs and copper stands and stools
Would weave and bake and build by subtle ways
That might be trusted to the hands of fools,
And all men should be blest with workless days,
Released from labour to a life of glad amaze.

But Joseph gently smiled, and gently sigh'd
And said: "O man, what shall it profit thee
To loose the bonds of toil? Will not lewd pride
And festering lust and vaunting vanity
Spread like the spotted plague if man be free
To riot on the sunny shores of sense
Amid the surf of Satan? Yea, I see
The discipline of duty a defence
Ordain'd in love by an all-seeing Providence.

"Two men I honour, and no idle third!
The first is he who labours with his hands
In service of mankind; who seeks, unspurr'd
By rowell'd dreams of pride, to till our lands
Or rear our homes or interweave the strands
Of human vesture. Venerable, great,
Is that rude heart that dimly understands
Its primitive nobility of state
In helping with hard hands the God who did create.

"A second man I honour, and still more.
He likewise toils, but toils to give to man
The bread of Life, and sacramental ore
From mines of rock-hewn truth; his worn eyes scan
The universal gulf for hint of plan

That may give meaning to our lapsing lives—
Ready to nourish like the pelican
With his heart's blood the stricken soul that strives,
And happy beyond measure if that soul revives.

"Sometimes my little Joshua has dreams
That he, as such an one, shall die in shame.
But who can tell? I only know thy schemes
Of labour turn'd to leisure would defame
The noblest thing in life, the fairest aim,
And send the human herd in riot hence,
Restless as mercury, unfix'd as flame,
To fill their bellies with the husks of sense,
Passing, confused as shadows, into nescience."

But Tubal's face grew darker as he spoke,
Mantling with anger as a pool with scum,
And hot impatience of a sudden broke
Impulsive forth: "Plague on this burdensome
Exalting of crude hardship's martyrdom!
As though mere toil were great! Who wants to sweat
In some small shop like thine, mole-mad and dumb!
I stand for human freedom!" And an epithet
Of poison fell, as he departed in a fret.

Calm as an eagle when he fronts the sun,
Calm as the loneliness of outer space,
Calm as a frozen lake when autumn's done,
And calm as death upon an infant's face
Stood Joseph then, unsmiling in his place,
And, after silence, turn'd again to work
In quiet diligence with saw and brace
And plane and plumb, nor did a shadow lurk
Of aught within his eyes to tell of thoughts that irk.

III   *The Progeny of Invention*

Slow tides came swelling in to meet a dark
Sea-questing river in a northern isle;
A village faced their foam; gaunt hills lay stark
And sinister behind, in mile on mile
Of sprawling giant flanks, deformed and vile,

Tetter'd with quarried abscess, varicose
With veins of bitumen, sallow with bile
Of seeping sulphur, while deep down, ramose
In darkness, arteries of iron cluster'd close.

Thither sail'd Tubal, still intent to prove
The virtues of invention for mankind,
Certain his cunning could indeed remove
The yoke of poverty, that he could find
By subtle evocation of the mind
Release from all the ills that gnaw the flesh;
And seeing in these hills the means design'd
To transform life, he settled here to thresh
Their metal harvests with an ardour free and fresh.

In that dull village dwelt a homely girl,
Still virgin, for men shunn'd her ugliness.
Thrift was her name; her pale hair knew no curl,
Her eyes no gleam; all threadbare was her dress.
But Tubal's glance in her could wisely guess
Her noble potencies for motherhood:
Breasted like Eve, loin'd like a lioness,
She held the promise of a lusty brood;
And so the artisan paid suit, nor vainly woo'd.

Then from that union sprang a gifted race
To help their sire to mould the world anew.
He built a laboratory as his place
And dwelt in lofty towers, whence his view
Swept round o'er rising factories that grew
In magic swiftness from the murky land;
And there his teeming intellect would pursue
Grave problems as his children made demand
In compassing the issues that the family plann'd.

He fashion'd frames that wove unending cloth;
He turn'd the pools to steam, and drove his mills;
He shipp'd his goods abroad by sail; then wroth
With slow delay, took entrails of the hills
And shaped them into fish with iron gills
And pectorals of steel; these swam the sea
With smoky speed, and bore his tweeds and twills;

While coal-fed stallions, prompt at his decree,
Drew thundering trains by land with giant energy.

He turn'd swift streams to power subtler yet,
Subtler yet stronger, luring it through lines
Of spidery filament, a rivulet
Of cosmic death that toil'd in shops and mines,
And fed a billion lamps, in homes and shrines,
And bore the living voice as swift as light
Across the gulfs of space; yea, his designs
Made rich the soil with essence which its might
Rent from the sightless air, and doubled nature's right.

Almost he triumph'd in his soaring aims:
He saw his sons engross'd with mental zest
In meeting all the challenge of life's claims,
Yet not worn haggard by their work's behest;
And other later children sooth'd his breast
With leisured arts: sweet music, sculptured stone,
The chisell'd gold of poetry, the quest
Of faëry form and colour—these made known
Rare virtues he had caused, yet virtues not his own.

But germs of utter failure lay in wait
To blast the crescent world his brain had rear'd;
For though his wiles had trebled man's estate,
The menace of a fault he had not fear'd
Grew on in silence in the slums that smear'd
The beauty of his cities. It was this:
Lust linked with ignorance obscenely leer'd
At all his gifted toil for human bliss,
And bred relentlessly in poverty's abyss.

For while the sober poor were circumspect
To mete their families by means and food,
Yet feeble-minded vagrants spawn'd uncheck'd
And sodden imbeciles begot dull brood
Predestinate to crime from fetus crude;
And all of Tubal's efforts fail'd to feed
These human gnats, in fertile multitude—
Greedy as hate, improvident in need,
And hungrily insatiate to breed and breed.

IV "The Falsehood of Extremes"

But centuries pass'd slowly to their graves;
And Tubal grew incalculably old,
With beard like wind-swept foam on Arctic waves
And shrivell'd heron hands that seem'd to hold
Dead bones in casts of skin; his blood grew cold,
Though flames within his eyes lay fiercely blank
Like embers under ashes; uncontroll'd,
His laughter, like a vulture's, breathed out rank
Thick reek of rotting flesh till all the chamber stank.

Plain Thrift, his fruitful wife, had died long since,
And sons of children's children now made light
Of virtues of the past, nor would evince
Aught but harsh pride and idleness and spite.
And so their flaunted gold became a blight,
The while the murmuring poor beheld with ire
Their streaming chariots passing down the night
Like shadowy ghosts with eyes of yellow fire,
Bearing their silken selfishness and sick desire.

Then there arose a prophet of revolt,
A lean Elijah of the underworld
With eyes like molten iron and a bolt
Of blistering thunder on a tongue that hurl'd
Its vehemence abroad. His thin lips curl'd
In venom'd scorn at those who, sleek and fat,
Made riot at their ease, begemm'd and pearl'd,
While, housed in sweaty filth, like hog or rat,
Wan workers form'd a famished proletariat.

"Labour alone makes wealth," he told a crowd
Of sullen hearers in a city street.
"Labour shall rise," he prophesied aloud,
"And lay the bloated tyrants at its feet!
We are the worker-bees that build complete
The fabric of that hive they call the state.
Ours is the anguish'd toil that makes the sweet
Thick store of honey, which the drones we hate
Devour at their ease while we must starve and wait.

"Deep as the place of Judas in the pit,
Lower than Lucifer, the brute should lie

Who feeds upon us like a new-hatch'd nit
And fouls our poor existence like a fly.
These purse-proud parasites would rather die
Than dig a common ditch, while we, forsooth,
Must suffer the contagion of a sty
To render possible their gilded youth
Whose useless rotten lives are damn'd in very truth.

"Their idle wives are she-wolves without whelps,
Kept creatures, who abhor the honest pang
Of motherhood, though every paper yelps
About their wasteful weddings, tells who sang,
What silks, maids, flowers there were, with long harangue
About their style and station. Pah! I'm sick
To see these cats, so bright of fur and fang,
Live on in sloth, high-scented, sleek, and slick,
And call it marriage in their simpering rhetoric!

"There is no hope in patience. These are men
With hearts as hard as hate, as cold as crime;
We are but pawns or robots to their ken.
Now is the hour when we must strive to climb
Out of this poison'd gulf of blood and slime;
Now is the hour to end their futile feasts,
Or fate will bear us down the flood of time
Like swollen carcasses of strangled beasts,
Distorted by the shameful fetor of corruption's yeasts.

"Let winds of revolution drive the drifts
Of heap'd-up property across the land
And level them to justice! Strew your gifts
Of confiscated plenty with a hand
That, no more slavish, reaches to command
And crush these idle dastards to the earth!
Beat them as small as dust, as fine as sand,
And vindicate nobility of birth
In men whose mothers shaped them in the midst of dearth!"

They roared applause. But some in secret went
To tell the tyrants, who pass'd on in haste
And told grey Tubal of the dark event,
Who, while he listen'd grimly, granite-faced,
Waken'd a glance of fire, as in a waste

[367]

By night a sudden beacon flames and dies;
Then in slow tones of anger and distaste
He mutter'd forth the malice of replies,
Voicing his scorn of all the rebel enterprise:

"Fools, frantic fools! The workers make the hives;
But drones and queen must give them being first.
Were work the source of wealth, their fretful lives
Had never been; this teeming town they've cursed
Would be plough'd fields at best, a waste at worst,
With only scatter'd hovels here and there
And famished peasants brutishly immersed
In wringing from the clay in dull despair
A toilsome penury no slum-bred slave would share.

"Brains make the modern state, not straining brawn.
Remove the brains, and cities would collapse
To palsied dissolution before dawn.
Though honest faithful toil may help, perhaps,
Yet restless radicals, these hungry chaps,
These lice, these locusts, are a bowel-worm,
A brainless, ravening mouth whose sucking saps
The vigour of the state and makes infirm
The nation's virile strength ere its appointed term.

"And now, be not dismay'd, though foes may lie
Knotted like wintering snakes where thousands sleep
In pits of scaly horror. We shall try
What brains can do to terrify the deep
Base heart of envy that would darkly leap
And rend us. I shall frame some new device
Of gun or gas to render them like sheep."—
He ceased, and blithe as men who win at dice
They left, nor mark'd how senile slumber seal'd his eyes.

V   Götterdämmerung

And so he sat asleep. And through his brain—
Tired, unquiet—restless visions pass'd.
He had been reading how the gods were slain
In those old Eddas where the Norse forecast
The doom of shining Asgard in the last

Fierce fight of all; and these old legends kept
His thoughts in anxious thraldom, for like vast
Distorted shadows on a wall they leapt
Phantasmic through his slumbers as the old man slept.

He seem'd to stand with Odin, where he gazed
From Lidskjalf on the universe, and saw
The silver roofs of heaven, the fires that blazed
In tropic Muspellsheim, the fogs that draw
Across the world of Dead Men in the raw
And frozen north; the plains of Midgard, too;
The dwarfs and dark elves in the mines' deep maw,
And gloomy Jotunheim, where giants brew
Their plots against the gods and rally their huge crew.

And Yggdrasil he saw, that mighty tree
Sustaining heaven and earth and even hell:
It seemed to him like that sagacity
Which he and his had used to order well
The state their brains had built, a citadel
Of intellect, a shining tree whose fruits
Brought healing strength wherever souls might dwell,
Supporting life throughout for men and brutes,
Though snakes of greed and envy gnaw'd its gnarl'd grey
                                                    roots.

Then swiftly gather'd in the burning south
A host of black-skinned enmity and hate,
Ugly as misborn monsters, with a mouth
Like some mad maelstrom at the height of spate;
And out of Niflheim rode fire's mate,
Cold death, dress'd like a Cossack; by his side,
The dragon of Destruction writhed, dilate
With Slavic anger, and the wolf of Pride
Howl'd in his senseless wrath till heaven itself replied.

And at the menace of that gathering storm,
The idle gods of Asgard ceased from sloth;
The heroes in Valhalla did reform
From beer and boar's flesh, faithful to their oath
That Odin in that Twilight might have both
Their soul and valour. Though they knew the night
Of that great issue meant an end of growth

[369]

For all the universe, yet would they fight
And perish with high honour in all hell's despite.

Fiercely the foemen rallied to attack,
Implacable as fire and just as doom'd
To perish with their fuel into black
Cold ash of ruin. Like red clouds they loom'd
To east, west, south, and north; their swords consumed
All living things beneath the lurid sky
Until they compass'd Asgard's walls and spumed
Like rivers of live lava surging high
Against the marble battlements they sought to scorify.

The heavenly rampart quiver'd like a cliff
Smitten by waves, as the besiegers rose,
Flaming like Phlegethon. Resistance stiff
Flash'd back in valiant fortitude from those
Who lined the walls. But their incessant blows
Were unavailing on that vast array
Which, when its foremost fell, would simply close
Its myriads in. Yet still the gods held play
And strove like stricken tigers in the unequal fray.

The Fenrir-wolf slew Odin, but his son,
Brave Vidar, slit the monster's dripping throat.
Loud-thundering Thor made fierce attack upon
The Midgard-serpent, but although he smote
Its head to writhing pulp, he could not gloat
In victory, for its breath destroy'd him too.
Thus the defenders' hopes grew more remote,
And still the encircling armies closer drew
To crush them as a python coils its scaly screw.

The gods were ill prepared for that fierce hour;
For ever since the day when Baldur died,
Baldur the God of innocence, the flower
Of gentle piety, their ways pass'd wide
From pristine strength and wisdom. Vices plied
Their easy lusts among them; hence they fail'd
To meet the testing of a time that tried
Their utmost virtue. Now at last they quail'd,
And with a horrid shout the enemy prevail'd.

So ran old Tubal's dream; and through it stole
The whisper of a menace, moans that spoke
Of rising winds, and rivers past control,
And tidal waves that swept in roaring smoke,
And grew in volume, till at last there broke
Across the stillness of that slumbering room
A cry like dawning madness, and he woke,
And through his window heard in outer gloom
Red revolution raise its splintering shout of doom.

THE WAY OF A LOVER

1 *Flesh without Spirit*

With heat of rocky highway underfoot
And heat of sultry skies above his head,
Strode Andrikos, a youth, who sought to put
Long leagues behind him ere the daylight fled.
A virile sweat on his dark curls lay spread;
The ruddy flush of strength was on his cheek;
His dark eye flash'd; like panther's was his tread;
And oft his nostril quiver'd at the reek
Of heavy musk that haunted every pass and peak.

The eager pilgrim trod a canyon road
That breach'd grim mountains through a labyrinth
Of blood-red gulches, where hot altars glow'd
On many a summit by some phallic plinth
Of rugged stone, or rough-hewn terebinth
In hermic form be-garlanded with green
Or smear'd with gore to match the hyacinth,
While all about in attitudes obscene
Dark Edom's congregations plied their rites unclean.

Anon the lured cliffs drew slowly back
In solemn order, and disclosed a plain
Floor'd with smooth marble of infernal black,
Upon whose darkness, like a double stain,
Two savage temples lay. The horrid twain
In praise of passion stood, one large, one small.
The greater sanctified the virile reign
Of Tyrian Baal; the less, the animal
Excesses of horn'd Ishtar and her wanton brawl.

[371]

Before the mightier fane two pillars blazed,
Parents of those in Zion once begun,
Boaz and Jachin named, which Hiram raised
To satisfy Bathsheba's subtle son
(Himself the fruit of lust, surpass'd of none
In harem revelries) what time he made
A shrine to Israel's god. Of these, the one
Was pure smaragdus, green as Kansu jade,
The other polish'd gold, with wandering gems inlaid.

About them danced a ring of naked boys
With nameless baubles on their bosoms hung,
While, from the temple, timbrels made a noise
Of frenzied fanfare to an anthem sung
In those dark halls, where clouds of incense clung
In maddening murk above the ministrants,
And drunken mullahs, to the marrow stung,
Moist-eyed, fierce-breathing, raised their impious chants
Or sway'd in hot embraces in the carnal dance.

A gross and oily priest, Priapus' kin,
Goat-bearded, pandar-mouth'd, and lewdly bland,
Came sidling from the temple with a grin
And took the youthful traveler by the hand:
"Well met!" said he. "Young stranger, come and stand
Beside the altar of the Lord of Life!
We worship here the god whose great command
Moves all who gender flesh in fertile strife,
And stirs the mood of man wherever lust is rife.

"The Hindus of Benares hail him chief,
As Visvesvara, Siva, sovereign lord;
Ten thousand cities, in devout belief,
Before his potent symbols have adored;
Ten thousand shrines his puissance record
From Egypt to Peru and Yucatan;
And Balkan peasants, lest some blight abhorr'd
Should smite their harvests, plough his talisman
Of sex upon each field, the sterile curse to ban.

"Even in far-off Britain, man and maid,
After a night of revel in the wood

On May-Day Eve, with wanton masquerade
Bring home with tumult of the neighbourhood
A mighty Maypole (wherein virtues brood
From Baal himself) which two-score oxen draw,
Their horns with flowers bound; and pleasant food
Of wine and milk and cakes delights the maw
As folk in dance adore, obedient to his law.

"Yet there are powers that bend him to their will:
He is the seeker, but the service sought
Goes to the softer sex that rules him still,
And to the woman's lure his strength is naught.
If then, indeed, some weakly scrupled thought
Impede thee from my counsel, turn aside
To yonder shrine of Ishtar, and be taught
By daughters of the dark voluptuous bride
Of my strong lord, who o'er its sacred cells preside!"

He ceased; and from the porch a nautch-girl came:
A sloe-eyed slut with wanton-swaying hips,
And cheeks that kindled with a lawless flame,
And dewy rose of passion on her lips.
Her full-orb'd breasts, a-tremble to the tips,
Peer'd from the hiding of her open dress,
As when the sun, light-cleft by half-eclipse,
Dazzles the gazer; and her comeliness
Begg'd with a thousand voices that he should possess.

She cast her velvet arms about his neck,
His mouth was musk with perfumes of her hair,
Her lips were at his throat, not could he check
The kisses that the temptress planted there;
While all the burning ardour of her bare
Bold breast and clinging body warm'd his own,
As she bent back her subtle head to stare
In voiceless speech, petitions without tone,
Deep, deep into his eyes that ne'er such gaze had known.

Then, as in summer, when the noon is hush'd
In sultry expectation, and cloud-giants rise
In silent menace towards a zenith flush'd
In sombre passion, till at length the skies
Crash into sudden crazed ferocities,

So did that pilgrim's soul grow overcast
With stormy heat, and fever'd with replies
To all her importunity, he caught her fast
In sudden rage of lust and to the temple pass'd.

II *Spirit without Flesh*

A sadden'd Andrikos pursued his way;
His flesh was sated, but his soul was sick—
Sick nigh to death from sty-fierce months of stay
With Ishtar's priestess, tireless and quick
In all the arts of passion. Choleric,
With wormwood on his tongue, he left behind
Her dark abode, and journey'd on through thick
Vile villages in yearning hope to find
Far to the north some love that did not mar the mind.

His road pass'd onward through a land of dunes
Like breasts upon a harlot, broad and full,
And still the curves of those soft plenilunes
Haunted his eyes and made his vision dull;
So that at first he wist not, as a gull
Swoop'd snowy past him and a litany
Of salty winds arose, that all the mull
Of murky spells was past, his soul set free
By shining waters of a great unsullied sea.

He bought his passage in an Attic ship,
A trading trireme fill'd with amber grapes
And purple fabrics; and his love-bit lip
Grew dry and manly as by rocky capes
They swept along past dreaming sunny shapes
Of marble islands in the wine-dark deep,
Until one dawn the swift resounding swapes
Drove on the bark past Sunium's templed steep
To where upon green plains a City lay asleep.

A theatre of mountains rimm'd it round,
Hymettos, white Pentelikon, austere
Kithaeron and dark Parnes, but the ground
In miles of flowering meadows spread with sheer

Enraptured colour of the opening year
To break in billows of sweet-blossoming mirth
Beneath a cliff, with snow-white temples, dear
To radiant Athens, Beauty's fairest birth,
Enwreathed with violets, the envy of all earth!

Then as the stranger trod the fragrant street
That ran from port to city, he beheld
The coverts of Colonus, where the sweet
Deep-hidden choir of nightingales out-swell'd
Among the berried ivies where they dwell'd,
Unvisited by sun, unvext by storm;
While, where the springs of Kephisos up-well'd,
The crocus and narcissus strew'd a swarm
Of breathing buds in gold and jewels multiform.

Within the stately town he lodged betimes;
Where, soon companion'd with the eager sort
Who sought the secrets of man's hopes and crimes,
He shortly learn'd to offer humble court
To one gross bare-foot Satyr, whom report
Declared the shrewdest midwife of man's thought—
All who laid bare their pangs to his retort
Were from their travail into reason brought
With offspring of clear intellect surpass'd by naught.

One day he sat with Socrates alone
Beneath a plane-tree, by Ilissos' brook;
The grass was soft; cicadas' silver tone
Blent with leaves' whispers as the branches shook
In rippling melodies; then without book,
The golden-tongued Silenus spoke of love
Until the former anguish quite forsook
The spirit of the youth, that rose above
The errors of the past and hasten'd to approve.

"Love is a madness of the nobler sort!"
So spake the teacher, on his task intent.
"Like prophecy and poetry, in short,
It shows a frenzy of divine descent.
Our souls crave wings; they feel a power pent

Within imperfect flesh, and yearn to rise
Toward beauty, wisdom, goodness so are rent
With soaring passion when in mortal guise
They see these virtues shadow'd forth before their eyes.

"Another tale has Aristophanes,
A fable that he told us yesternight
When with good Agathon we took our ease
In feast and talk. He said that once in spite
The gods cleft man, then double, into slight
Unhappy halves, the humans whom we know;
Hence comes the piteous hunger to unite
The sunder'd moieties of man below,
And so to lose awhile our loneliness and woe.

"But this he said in jest; it smacks of flesh
Too much to meet my judgment of the truth;
The beauty of the body is a mesh
To snare the eye. Learn even in thy youth
That beauty of the mind is less uncouth,
And spirit's beauty fairer than them all.
Accept this preaching as in very sooth
A chart to truest joy, when thou shalt fall
In love with that in man which is not temporal."

So through the solemn hours the talk went on,
And oft the youthful questioner address'd
Some quiet query, till the sun was gone
Behind Aegina's shark-fin to the west
Across the gulf. Then even speech had rest.
And side by side they sought the town once more—
One pleased with discourse, but the other blest
Beyond all telling with the shining store
Of fair philosophy he ne'er had known before.

The years sped by. And on the Aegean isle
Of Melos, to the south, he urged his plea
Of friendship to a maid, whose artless smile
Was eloquent of grace and purity;
And when one shore-spent evening, knee by knee,
They sat in darkness, and a white moon rose
Like Aphrodite's shoulder from the sea,

He whisper'd out his story to the close
And found her spirit ready for the ways he chose.

There follow'd months of tranquil happiness:
They roam'd the orange orchards, hand in hand,
Or pinn'd arbutus blossoms on her dress,
Or, on Mount Kalamos, their faces fann'd
With sun-sweet zephyrs, tried to understand
The absolute of beauty and of faith,
Eternal in the heavens, purely plann'd;
And said the body's beauty was a wraith,
Lovely, no doubt, and good, but perilous of scathe.

With wisdom's eye they scann'd the circling hills
That held the harbour like a Titan's cup,
And said: "How good, that living beauty fills
This ancient crater, where the abyss stirr'd up
Of old a flaming drink for hell to sup!
Ev'n so the spotless worship of our minds
Leaves dead the scalding rut of ewe and tup
That marr'd man's creature past; the spirit finds
For slopes of human life new forms of fairer kinds."

But, with the end of summer, discontent
Drew shadows o'er her face, and sometimes wild
Strange moods of silence caught her; or she bent
Aside in sudden grief, and oft her mild
Blue eyes were wet. At first her lover smiled;
Then paled; then ask'd her wish; and on his ears
Burst her desire; "Thy passion, and a child!"—
All overcome with shame, and hopes, and fears,
She broke into a storm of hot, hysteric tears.

As one who, tripping barefoot through the grass,
Perceives a rainbow viper, angry-eyed,
Hiss in the flower'd space he thought to pass
And sees its fatal beauty toward him glide,
And runs in pallid panic, terrified,
So did the youth, in agony of fright,
Start from the weeping woman at his side,
And in a coasting galley that same night
Set sail for distant Egypt in his virtuous flight.

An empty tomb of crumbling limestone lay
In far Thebaïs near the Nile's black bank,
By rocky deserts where the bats held play
And carrion-mouth'd hyenas came and drank.
Here, where the mouldering ruins reek'd and stank
With reptile writhings on their filthy floors,
A haggard hermit enter'd, wild and lank,
And, having chased the vipers out of doors,
Slept dully on the stones, unmindful of his sores.

For Andrikos at Memphis had been met
By certain monks, to whom he bared his woe;
And they with bitter words had sought to set
His ardours towards a final overthrow
Of what he fear'd; "Thy body is thy foe!
No drop of virtue dwelleth in thy frame;
But in thy veins the foulest passions flow
That would infect thy soul with hellish shame
And set thy life on fire with a satanic flame.

"Thy appetites are carnal, sold to sin!
The motion of thy members worketh death!
Only by cleansing penance canst thou win
Salvation for thy soul. Our prophet saith
That man must struggle to his latest breath
To mortify his body and its lust.
Then purge thy flesh, be one who sojourneth
In penitence amid the desert dust,
And thou shalt know the peace that sanctifies the just!"

Hence came at last this refuge in the waste,
And here with fierce austerities he tried
To tame his erring body and be chaste.
Once only every day he would provide
His maw with dates and water, and would chide
The hungry throat that begg'd for ampler food;
His voice grew fervent as he vilified
The deep abiding rancour of a mood
That still stirr'd undefeated in that inward feud.

He wound a rasping rope on legs and loins,
Twisting the coils so tightly that they cut;
And wore that anguish till his flanks and groins
Were rotten with great ulcers; then he shut
His face from sunlight, and for days would glut
His frenzy with prostrations past all count,
Smearing his features with the noisome smut
That strew'd the floor, in madness to surmount
The pride that kept his flesh a foul unfailing fount.

But as he lay in pale exhausted sleep,
His mind's imaginings grew more intense,
For Ishtar's priestess evermore would creep
Within his arms, and wild concupiscence
Shook him with epilepsy's vehemence;
Sightless obscenities would make his brain
A pit of slimy adders, and offence
Seem'd past endurance when he woke in pain
And in the dark began his penance once again.

Upon the walls, within that sepulchre
Where he was lodged, were scenes of ancient time
Painted in vivid truth of character,
And still at noon, in spite of gloom and grime,
Presenting to the eye a breathing mime
Of vanish'd men and deities of old
That subtle Egypt fashion'd in her prime
Of deep-eyed wisdom, when her priests were bold
To probe all mysteries that nature might enfold.

And Andrikos grew ware, one sadden'd hour,
That Isis, with young Horus on her arm
And crown'd Osiris near her, stood in power
Depicted on that wall in breathing charm
Of bosom'd motherhood. A strange alarm
Beset the hermit as she seem'd to move;
Then came a voice that hush'd all fear of harm,
And, like the gentle murmur of a dove,
Spoke in the pitying accents of upbraiding love.

"Cease from thy wicked struggle, and be wise!
False is thy task, and futile all thy strife.

Rather let fall, repentant, from thine eyes
The scales that blind thee to the grace of life!
For I, a goddess, and the faithful wife
Of heaven's king, proclaim thy celibate
Devotions a vile error, harshly rife
With foul infection of despair and hate,
And treacherous most of all towards man's divine estate.

"Know then, indeed, O man, that thou hast not
Two natures, soul and body. Both are one.
Both in a bestial past were once begot
When all creation's life was first begun;
And form and spirit were together spun,
So interwoven that, like warp and woof
Or light and darkness, they are all undone
To senseless nullities if torn aloof.
This is most true, though monks may gabble in disproof.

"Thy single life has destinies that blend
The flesh and spirit in a holy plan;
Both are co-operant to a mighty end,
For thou, once beastlike, art become a man
To do thy work as beauty's artisan
And rear the palace of all human grace
With glories for eternity to scan.
In this great scheme the body has its place
In the devout begetting of the coming race.

"Wise beyond all were those who painted here
The holy infant and the two that fused
Their bodies for his birth; the wise revere
This trinity of parenthood, suffused
With pious knowledge that when breasts are bruised
In wedded passion, they are not their own
To wanton lightly on a bed abused,
But still must seek to pay again the loan
Of golden life they drew from years now overthrown.

"Cease then, O fool, from this thy daily death,
And learn the living lesson marriage speaks;
That, when at last thou yieldest up thy breath
And with white hair and wanly wasted cheeks
Thou sinkest into night, the Melian peaks

May look in beauty down upon some child
Who carries on thy ardour, though time wreaks
Its vengeance on thyself. Be reconciled
Through love to life and death, and be no more defiled!"

The soft voice ended. From the ancient tomb
He stagger'd wildly out into the light,
And knew himself, and cursed the loathsome gloom
And all the torments of his savage rite.
Then, as a homing pigeon, thrown to flight,
Flutters a trembling minute o'er the earth,
And then departs; so waver'd he one slight
Distracted moment ere he started forth
And ran, and fell, and ran, with frenzy toward the north.

IV   The Symphony of Life

An ageing man, with children at his knee,
Sat in a cottage, where old Kalamos
Looks down in silence on the Myrtoan sea.
And there the happy father gazed across
His orchards and his vineyards with their gloss
Of greening leafage and abundant fruit,
And held all other blessings were but dross
Compared with his, and gave a glad salute
To her who had not left his passion destitute.

Yet, one must add, to give the truth its due,
The sun of his content was often hid.
The little wife was something of a shrew;
And cries of cradled infants would forbid
Sweet slumber after toil; his children chid
By all their very helplessness the sloth
With which he sometimes faced the tasks he did;
And countless worries warr'd against the oath
That held the man and wife to ways that burden'd both.

But Isis ruled. He was not vainly scourged.
The tiny hammers of the cherish'd home
Upon a daily anvil slowly forged
A life of finer temper. Each young gnome
Drew him to virtue, made him loath to roam,

[381]

Working through daily duty heart's true ease
Deep-based in gentleness and frolicsome
Good nature, meekness, temperance, and increase
Of all the sober discipline of inward peace.

Forgetting self, he found it more and more;
And saw his lavish'd gifts return'd in gain
Of more abundant life, in ampler store
Of growing satisfaction's richer grain;
And knew himself devoted to maintain
In his small way a universe of soul
That wrought with body, working on with pain
And consecrated passion toward a goal
Of wisdom, beauty, love, incarnate in the Whole.

THE WAY OF A PHYSICIAN

1 *The Call of Suffering*

The Attic night looked pitilessly down
On city streets that writhed in hot dismay
As a young stranger stray'd into the town.
His glance was grave and thoughtful. Eyes of grey
Spoke the pure mind where all the moods obey
The temperate purpose. Dignified and calm
Yet sympathetic, seem'd his gracious way,
A personality as sweet as balm
And strong and healing as a penitential psalm.

"Fly, from this city!" cried the folk he met.
"The pestilence is slaying man and beast!"—
"Nay," said the man, Hippocrates, "ne'er yet
Have I turn'd back where even in the least
Degree I might give help. Here is a feast
For one who thrives on ministry to others!"—
And so he labour'd there, and never ceased
To wait upon his suffering human brothers,
Unscathed himself, but baffled by the Pest's dark smothers.

For nothing could withstand the brooding plague.
On men in health, the blow fell swift and sore:

The eye grew glazed and red; the voice was vague;
The livid throat bred ulcers, oozing gore;
Infection fill'd the breast, which forth did pour
A fetor as if corpses lay and rotted;
Deep in the maw, vain retching strain'd and tore;
The channels of the mind grew dark and clotted,
And with the bitterest melancholy soon besotted.

Red fester scarr'd the skin and marr'd the sight,
But fire within the body burnt the bones
And sear'd the flesh, till nothing was too light
To clothe their anguish, and they loosed their zones,
And naked, sought for water, uttering moans
Of flaming thirst. Some reach'd the river's brink;
Some leap'd down open wells, and still'd their groans
With mouth agape head-foremost; but no drink
Could satisfy that all-consuming thirst that bade them sink.

In voiceless fear the victims mutter'd low;
They toss'd in sleepless torment, staring-eyed;
The ears were fill'd with ringings; and the slow
Large breath would quicken and again subside.
Sweat glisten'd on the neck; harsh coughs supplied
Thin flakes of salty spittle, saffron-tinged;
Up from the twitching feet a frosty tide
Of shivering mortality infringed
Upon life's innate heat till ev'n the midriff cringed.

Then, at the end, the shrinking eyes fell hollow;
The temples sank; the nose was sharp and thin;
A warping coldness of the ears would follow;
Upon the swollen brow, the scabrous skin
Stretch'd tense and parching; and a skull-like grin
Grew on the gaping mouth. The greenish face
Was like the pale clay of its origin;
And presently held no more tepid trace
Of life than the cold earth, its final resting-place.

And if, by chance, some sufferer should escape
The doom of speedy death, there still remain'd
Foul after-fate in many a noisome shape—
Fecal discharge of ulcer'd blood soon drain'd

His wither'd strength; or, from a forehead pain'd
With purulence, great gouts of blood gush'd black
Through the gorged nostrils; or the pest profaned
Some limb or organ, and the man would hack
The gangrened member off and hold destruction back.

The corpses of the dead lay everywhere,
Alike in pillar'd fane and peasant's hovel:
Decaying carcasses defiled the air
In city streets where men had sought to grovel,
Drinking at fountains. And it rank'd as novel
That neither hawk nor vulture, wolf nor dog,
Would eat that flesh to further its removal;
Or if one tasted, the disease would clog
His greedy throat, and leave him lying like a log.

The worship of the gods was disregarded,
And if devoted Habit sought to grant
The dead sepulture, honour was discarded:
The rites were hasty, without funeral chant;
Some shriek'd, but in them fear was dominant;
Some wept a space, for children or for sires;
And some, through desperation and sheer want
Of faggots, flung their dead on others' pyres
And held all off with bloodshed while they lit the fires.

But young Hippocrates was wrung and torn
To see the torment of that pestilence;
And in his soul a high resolve was born
To seek the cause of sickness, and defence
Against its rage; that in benevolence
He might slay pain and give man perfect health,
A priceless blessing. Thus he question'd whence
Those powers came that ravaged man by stealth
And stole all meaning from his science, art, and wealth.

II   *Seeking the Invisible*

Years pass'd. Upon a sunlit mountain-top
He kept a hospice that his hands had rear'd
To tend the sick, and by research to stop
The suffering of man. Such throngs appear'd

That he chose out disciples, who revered
The cause he loved and join'd him in the quest;
But though they all in patience persevered,
The ultimate beginnings of the Pest
Evaded every scrutiny and every test.

As unremitting servants of the sick,
They sought to know the body's every part;
In diagnosis, laying brick to brick,
They work'd through observation towards an art.
They found that rest and quiet heal'd the heart;
That sunlight and inunction help'd the frame.
They learn'd that baths and diet conquer'd smart;
That Temperance and Health were oft the same;
And sickness, Vice and Folly by another name.

Yet still their patient vigils by the ill
Fail'd to unmask an ever-lurking foe
That, all-defiant, worked its fatal will.
When hands, tools, beds were clean, its pace grew slow;
And sunlight often slew it. But to go
Beyond that point of knowledge seem'd in vain.
Ever the feverish onslaughts brought their woe,
Racking the breast and torturing the brain
With fierce, immedicable forms of death and pain.

"Yet be not downcast!" said Hippocrates
To his disciples. "Though our life is short,
And this our Art is long, and fell disease
So hastens in its course that to extort
Its meaning is most hard, yet we must court
These mysteries for ever, for on us
Depends all welfare of the human sort
So long as suffering like an incubus
Weighs heavy on all life and ravishes it thus.

"Each sentient soul in lonely grief has lain,
Lonely above all else when in distress;
And none but we can truly share with pain
Its incommunicable loneliness.
Words cannot penetrate by any stress

The sightless cell in which each sits apart;
He cannot tell his hurt, nor others guess;
But healing acts have holy power to thwart
Those cruel crystal walls encompassing the heart.

"Thus, though we have not yet o'erthrown disease,
We have a charge to keep, a cause to serve:
To tend all seizures and infirmities
Even beyond our strength, and not to swerve!
We live by faith, and, that we may ennerve
The virtue of our mission, let us bind
Physicians who come after to observe
All sanctities of body and of mind
Framed in this Oath, a contract of the strictest kind:

"I swear by Apollo and Asklepios,
Hygieia, and each listening deity,
To keep this Oath regardless of all loss;
Holding the man who taught this Art to me
As dear as those who bore me; wholly free
Shall I impart this knowledge to his son,
As to my own, and take no warrantee
Save this strict Oath, as by our cult is done,
Who teach disciples who make promise, and no other one.

"I pledge my word to seek my patient's health;
To abstain from every act that worketh doom—
Giving no poison, though man plead with wealth;
Helping no woman purge the pregnant womb.
I swear to weave my life upon the loom
Of purity, to stain no home I serve,
And keep all counsel of the inner room.
And if from this high promise I shall swerve,
May I be shamed and outcast, as I shall deserve!"

III   The Odour of Sanctity

But as the good physician labour'd there
With his disciples, suddenly there came
A cassock'd multitude with greasy hair
And slimy cheeks like corpse-rats. Fierce as flame
They seized the little band, and without shame

Carried them off to their monastic den—
A monstrous mountain cave of pious fame,
Cut in the flanks of Hinnom's flagrant glen
Where worms die not and fire consumes the waste of men.

Mephitic fetor issued from that cave—
An odour as of swill and sickly swine
And rancid carrion bones without a grave
And rotting fish and carcasses of kine,
A stench like phallic fungus and a fine
All penetrating stercoraceous steam,
A loathsome choke-damp—all these did combine
To set the prisoners puking, as at cream
Drawn from the Devil's dairy by some ghoulish scheme.

But when they enter'd in, they only saw
The filth of human bodies at their worst.
Women were there whose fly-blown chests were raw,
With breasts hack'd off; and men forever cursed
With mutilation; all, it seem'd, immersed
In ritual fonts of dirt that darkly stank.
And still the monks in putrefactive thirst
Clung to the scummy reservoirs and drank,
Urged to defilement by a gross-paunched Mountebank.

For, to this rout, the Abbot of Unreason,
Gilbert by name, extoll'd a life of dirt;
And gave example, in and out of season,
Dress'd in a lousy cowl and livid shirt.
Huge as a tun he was, yet malapert
As some lewd boy, and full of paradox.
When'er he laugh'd, the mighty belt that girt
His bloated belly creak'd. Strong as an ox,
He bellow'd out his views on fevers, pains, and pox.

"The dirtiest body hides the holiest life.
A cleanly body means a hell-stain'd soul.
Sweet Athanasius, that prince of strife,
Was right to praise Saint Anthony's control
Of his proud flesh, in that throughout the whole
Of his last years he never wash'd his feet.
Others lick lepers' sores and thus console
The poor in heart; or find their peace complete
In grovelling in filth upon the reeking street.

[387]

"Ours is an age of faith, when hogs and hens
Sleep calmly by the hearth in every house.
Saint Francis bids us love earth's denizens
In fur and feathers—raven, dove, and mouse;
And shall we not include the flea and louse?
What nonsense to want aqueducts and sewers!
I'd take all sanitary sots and souse
Them in their wells: then bid them fill their ewers
With good beer from the best of convent brewers!

"If fever ask for drugs, the best receipt
Is pestled dung and spiders, mix'd with milk.
Soft syrups made from herbs might be more sweet,
But pleasant remedies are made to bilk
Dolts, dullards, fools, and others of that ilk.
All should be freely bled from time to time,
Whether they dress in sackcloth or in silk,
Or else the blood grows thick and full of slime
In spite of every change of regimen or clime.

"The inspirer of disease is still the Devil,
Who works through witch or wizard, or direct
By demonized possession, prompting evil
Within the very veins his powers infect.
Who would not be exultant to detect
The guilty witch, and killing her, work cures!
Who would not, as an exorcist, eject
The serpent from the soul! Such work allures
Devoted spirits while the universe endures.

"More things are wrought by prayer than this world
                                        dreams of!
Our orisons bring health from all the saints!
Their shrines drive out the fiends that this earth teems of,
And free a million lives from morbid taints!
Here is a glory stifling all complaints:
Lepers are cleansed, dumb speak, deaf hear, lame walk.
Shame on the weak in faith, who falls or faints!
The saints can stay all maladies that stalk."—
So ran the tyrannizing current of his talk.

Hippocrates cried out: "Behold there lives
One only evil, namely Ignorance!

I cannot think a Deity forgives
The muddy minds that fester in this trance."
But Gilbert grew more fierce of countenance,
And call'd down Heaven's wrath upon the curs
Who dared blaspheme the Faith: "I'll make you dance,"
He cried, "you reason-sucking scavengers!"
Then flung them into dungeon-pits like sepulchres.

IV   The Blood Stream

After long days of dark, and evil smell,
One, Friar Bacon, cleanlier than the rest,
Took them in secret to an outer cell,
In whose stone floor a well was manifest.
Down through its subterranean depths, a nest
Of lambent lenses sank in wondrous wise,
So that, in light beyond, small things possess'd
Incredible proportions, and the eyes
Ached at the unfamiliar increment of size.

"Some prisoners sank this shaft in other days,
Seeking escape, but Gilbert found them out
And burned them," said the Friar. "By what ways
They would have gone, has puzzled the devout,
Who think this of the Devil, past all doubt,
Yet vague in use. But I've a brazen head,
A magic toy that speaks and loves to flout
The brethren, and its tongue has often said
That herethrough lies a land where monkishness is dead.

"My vows prevent my passing. If you will,
Leap through this shining well to liberty!"—
With gratitude they stood upon the sill
Of that deep orifice, content to flee
By any hazard from the tenebrae
Of Gilbert's cave. And as they leapt, the lenses
Parted like mist to let them pass through free
To radiant sunlight, where their dazzled senses
Gazed on a world of wonders and wild differences.

For there a river ran, a scarlet pulse,
Through myriad oozy channels with a tide

That flooded marshlands, only to convulse
Its waves in canyons on the other side
And sweep full circle. On the stream did glide
Masses of clotted weed and driftwood waste,
And millions of red coracles, inside
Whose rounded gunwales stores of food were placed:
And floated down the current with unceasing haste.

Amid the marsh a mighty city stood,
Fed by the freight of this untiring fleet.
Grey ramparts reared their height above the mud
Through which the crimson channels throbb'd and beat;
Here grey-hair'd sages mused on every street,
But took no notice of the distant skies
Where high fantastic storm-clouds form'd complete
Shapes of mosquitoes, ship-rats, fleas, and flies,
Vast and repellent in their thunder-headed guise.

The storm broke far away; but from the womb
Of those dark vapors, living pests descended—
Billions of black-toothed otters, that brought doom
To all they met, and bred as they contended,
Until their teeming multitudes transcended
The river swells by which they swam apace.
But lo, they found the city-wharfs defended
By great white monsters, ravenous to embrace
And swallow down the whole abominable race.

Larger than blue whale or diplodocus,
They wallow'd in red waves and gulp'd their foes;
But these spat out black phlegm so venomous
That mists of strangling poison quickly rose
And drifted through the city, where they froze
The dreaming citizens to icy pain;
Yet still they knew not that they must oppose
An all-consuming army or be slain,
Such was the inattentive blindness of the brain.

Hippocrates caught fire at that sight:
"Come, let us rouse the town, for if we fail,
These friendly monsters will be put to flight
And all those hellish legions will prevail!"—
Into the streets he rushed with frantic hail:

"Death! death! Come, line the ramparts, or you die!
Bring fire and sword! Bring pitchfork, ax, and flail!
The battalions of Beëlzebub are nigh!"
And all the city startled at his clarion cry.

Beyond the battlements the fight grew warm;
Over the flagging monsters surged the foe.
But now the city rose to meet that storm
In serried ranks through which no power might go.
With torch and glaive in hand, they wrought stern woe
On those fierce swarms and drove them from the wall;
But in the very hour of overthrow
They saw the great Physician reel and fall,
Dragg'd down to sudden martyrdom before them all.

Scales fell from off their eyes at that disaster:
They knew again the old familiar earth,
And mourn'd beside the death-bed of a Master
Who had died to give men life instead of dearth,
Transforming filth and pain to light and mirth
By slaying sightless legions of disease.
Above his body there, they swore his worth
Should never die. Men wept his exequies:
"Here lies a Saviour. Bare thy head to such as these."

THE WAY OF A WORSHIPPER

I   The Animistic Jungle

A tropic night lay deep upon the track
By which a youth ran fearfully along
Amid gigantic trees; a living black
Envelop'd all the jungle with a strong
Insensate weight of horror, like a throng
Of giant incubi that crush the breast,
Strangle the panic throat with clutch of wrong
And cold inhuman ravage, and invest
The citadel of life with death's most foul unrest.

Lianas sway'd like pythons o'er his path
And wound their clinging coils about his arm;
Legion'd mosquitoes shrill'd their febrile wrath
And lurking shapes of ravine crouch'd to harm;

Ever the man's heart sicken'd in alarm
As stumbling in the dark he touch'd aghast
Rank lumps of fleshy fungi, huge and warm,
Like rotting lungs and liver from some vast
Dismember'd monster, slain in combats of the past.

He sensed a hidden presence in the trees,
He felt a spectral power in the stream,
The language of a thousand mysteries
Spoke to his senses in the heavy steam
Of decomposing mould and pools a-team
With ferment of hot growth and spawning grass,
And every voice of midnight fed his dream
Of spirits in the sinister morass
Who hover'd there to slay him or to see him pass.

Then like the pulse of fear, far off, came throbbing
The beat of frenzied tom-toms through the night;
The maniac iteration of their sobbing
Grew in the darkness like the appetite
Of some blood-hungry beast; the wandering wight
Paused in dismay, but terrors of the gloom
Drove him to master down this lesser fright
And with a haggard spirit to resume
His course across the dark to shelter or to doom.

Soon fierce light led him; and he ran and came
Where countless mud-built kraals were spread around
And livid camp-fires lifted beards of flame
And paint-smear'd Zulus squatted on the ground
About a hideous fetish, to the sound
Of tom-toms. These beholding his dismay
(In horror at the welcome he had found)
Laugh'd like the fiends of that infernal bay
To which the dead ships come at dying of the day.

At last a tall witch-doctor rose to speak,
A ghastly wraith (with dagger at his thigh)
Lipp'd like a leech, with carrion-yellow cheek
And eyes like poison'd jewels, hard and dry.
With twitching tiger-nostrils he drew nigh
To where the shuddering stranger stood agape:
"Behold the victim!" shrill'd his condor cry.

"Our potent charms, the fetish's dark shape,
Have drawn him here to us and he shall not escape!

"His blood shall heal the sickness of our land,
Wipe out our sins and win us food again;
Come, and while he is bleeding let a band
Of famined wives and warriors warmly feign
The rites of passion that the seed of grain
May sprout once more from earth!" Then, though the
                                                    youth
Scream'd like a choking fowl, he scream'd in vain:
His cries were drown'd in bellowings uncouth
And dark hands dragg'd him to the altar without ruth.

That stone of sacrifice, two fathoms long,
Lay darkly circled by a colonnade
Of atlantean marble, sarsens strong
As those of Ammon-Ra, but rudely made
And cross'd with ruder lintels, firmly laid
On cyclopean shoulders. Horseshoe-wise
The solemn triliths spread, and left a glade
Between their ranks to face the eastern skies
Where presently the summer sun would fiercely rise.

And there, to eastward, stood a dial-stone,
Darker than death's lean finger; and the priest
Withheld his dagger till the dawn had thrown
Its shadow on the altar. Uproar ceased
Among the throng as slowly light increased
Throughout the empyrean; and a hush
Of waiting seem'd to throttle man and beast;
Till all at once in heavenly vaults aflush
With blood-red flame the sun shot upward with a rush.

But as it rose, a battle-cry rang out
From hosts of tall, blond strangers who had crept
Unnoticed while the Zulus crouch'd about,
In cruel expectancy of slaughter kept.
Wild chaos broke. The fierce assailants leapt.
"Great Mazdah lives!" they shouted. "Yea, is nigh!"
All irresistible as seas they swept,
Smiting the shrieking savage, hip and thigh,
And saving past all hope the victim doom'd to die.

[393]

With corpse-cold eyes, unstirr'd by reason's gleam,
He watch'd his foes depart like wind-blown hosts
Of autumn leaves or as a drifting dream
Of harpies put to flight and panic ghosts,
Shrieking towards hell at cock-crow. At their posts
No blacks abode the onset. All gave way,
As Persians, too austere for cheers or boasts,
Hack'd at the flying remnants of the fray,
Or strove the frozen terror of the youth to allay:

"Thy name, lad?"—"Obed."—"Then a son of Shem.
What dost thou here?"—"I sought to worship God;
But stray'd; grew lost; became the prey of them
Whom here you saw, who bow to every clod,
Salute the sun, yet soak the greedy sod
With blood, like mine, and join in rites impure,
Knowing not virtue!"—"Ay!" the Persians nod,
"Ay, thou hast spoken sooth, we know them sure,
And shall not let their foul iniquities endure!

"For God is One, the Lord of Truth and Light,
Ahura Mazdah, ever wise and just.
He wages against Ill an endless fight;
And, for the vanquishing of lies and lust,
Has made man's soul, that dwells in sentient dust,
An image of his own eternity,
Immortal flame, here honor'd with a trust
To choose the right, unfetter'd by decree,
And having purged itself to find its nature free.

"Angelic hosts, the shining attributes
Of God's own mind, effulgence of His thought,
Stand ever ready, as the Lord deputes
To aid us when we struggle; and we ought
To live as men who shall at last be brought
Before the judgment-seat of life and death.
There shall a man be judged as he has wrought,
Against that Day, when, as our prophet saith,
All Evil shall be swept away by Mazdah's breath."

Now had the mighty earth, austere and old,
Cast off the coverlets of shadowy night;
And hills of ivory, bright-edged with gold,
Rimm'd the horizon with a new delight
As Obed join'd the victors of the fight
In their triumphant marching towards the west.
His heart seem'd free as air, his thought as white
As foam or snow; there kindled in his breast
The sweet exultant ardour of an ageless quest.

Then Obed loved the leader of that band,
Shamash by name, a paragon of friends,
Who often clasp'd the stranger by the hand
And spoke of peace that flower'd when the ends
Of human life were love. "For love transcends
All pangs of suffering and grief and shame!"
So spake he, and his face, that lack'd amends
Of form and comeliness, shone white as flame,
And in his eyes unutterable glory came.

All morn they journey'd on with ardent joy;
At noon they join'd a troop who swore that dreams
Were pregnant with man's fate, and would employ
Strange figures drawn of stars to prove their themes.
Then, as the long day waned, these uttered screams
Of horror as they recognized their road:
"Yonder's the Fen of Fiends, whose murky steams
Bear countless unseen devils as their load!"—
"March on!" their leader cried, and mutely on they strode.

Along the highroad lay a marshy waste
With whispering reeds and scum of black and red.
Strange visions vex'd them as they pass'd in haste—
Dragons with seven crests, and on each head
Fantastic horns, wild eyes, and mouths that said
Words wild past thought; four-headed leopards, too;
Lions with eagles' wings; and steeds whose tread
Struck fire from the firmament and slew
The trembling stars. But all was frenzy, and untrue.

As evening shadows fell, a monstrous hill,
Domed like a skull, lay dark across their way;

Twin death-caves grinn'd like eyes; one vaster still
Open'd its maw, a chasm of decay,
To swallow up their path. With cold dismay
They started back, in fear of hidden doom;
Then saw the cave a portal, by the ray
One shaft of sunset shot across the gloom
In brief Shekinah-glory on that empty tomb.

EXTRA THEURGIAM NON SALUS EST—
So read a writing o'er that grisly gate
That none could understand. But chill unrest
Beset them closely, for the hour was late,
And vampires brush'd their brows with wings of hate,
And diabolic gnats, a seething mist
Of voice and venom, grew reverberate.
So driven by the foes that round them hiss'd,
Each entered with the firmness of a fatalist.

III   The Place of a Skull

Above their heads the gloomy archway rear'd
Its portals strangely wrought with forms of fright;
And now, instead of darkness, there appear'd,
Vast as some wave that gathers out of night
Beside a beetling cliff, a tide of light
Amid gigantic shafts that upward soar'd
To shadowy vaults above; to left and right
Of this great nave stretch'd cloisters richly floor'd;
High o'er far altars gleam'd a mitre and a sword.

That was the grandest temple of all time,
To which the shrines of Nineveh and No
And all the massy fanes of Mizraim's prime
Were boxes built for dolls or huts of snow
Set up by children. Yet the courts below
That atlantean roof were void and still,
And fierce before the altars leap'd a glow
From pits aflame with sulphur, swift to fill
The shrine with fire from hell and incense thick with ill.

Guided by that bright flame, down cloistered aisles,
Seeking for hope and rest the travelers spread,

Till wandering in a maze of crumbling piles
Young Obed lost his friends; yet trudged ahead;
Heard distant chants; descended stairs that led
To deeper crypts; and there beheld at last
A choir of naked boys, and priests that read
Long formulas from books by which to cast
From each initiate all evil of the past.

One blew upon his face and made a sign
With consecrated oil on lip and ear;
One exorcised some salt with holy whine
And touch'd his tongue; another, more austere,
Spat gravely on his finger-tip to smear
The boyish mouth and bid the devils pack;
Another smote a cesspool standing near,
Drove out more unseen fiends, and dripp'd the black
Unhealthy ritual drops on each small head and back.

And others Obed saw, with rising scorn,
Who gazed in worship at a massive scroll,
A miracle of parchment, patch'd and torn,
Most of it palimpsest thrice o'er, the whole
A maze of golden script with blots like coal;
And frenzy seized the shamans as they read:
"Who calls this book not perfect, let his soul
From diptychs of the living and the dead
Be stricken utterly, with curses on his head."

Then Obed turn'd aside from that low grot;
And passing farther on, beheld a den
Where sweating godsmiths labour'd, each with hot
Dogmatic confidence that in his ken
Lay all essential truth. Gods shaped as men
They moulded out of ectoplasmic ooze;
For passions fused their intellects, and then
Out of the psychic plasma, each could choose
To form the god that he himself would wish to use.

So gaping Obed mark'd, who walk'd unseen
And listened to their lore. But soon he stood
And watch'd a turban'd youth with ruddy mien,
Who slew a bull, and dabbled in the blood,
And cried: "Come wash your garments in this flood,

And be forever clean! Come, be ye saved!
Naught ye yourselves can do can make you good.
'Tis blood, blood, blood will cleanse you; and if laved
In this, ye live forever!" Obed thought he raved.

From one dark cell, set deeper than the rest,
A fetor rose that sicken'd all who came.
The denizens of this foul pit profess'd
The body was a mass of lustful shame.
These flogg'd themselves with whips, in hope to tame
The unregenerate flesh; wore shirts of hair;
Unmann'd themselves with knives; and rack'd the frame
With nameless tortures; words can scarce declare
The age-long, unwash'd horror of their wild despair.

And Obed saw where, in a brimstone ditch,
Men held a shrieking beldame in the dark,
And stripp'd her harshly, swearing her a witch,
And probed with awls to find the devil's mark,
And took the wrinkled breasts beneath her sark
And tore them with hot pincers, nor would shun
To clamp her in the hand-screw's mangling cark
And crush her agèd fingers one by one,
Chanting to drown her agony: "God's will be done!"

Now down these winding catacombs there trod
Two sudden mobs of zealots, seeming foes;
These bore three-headed idols, those a god
One-headed only, and a fight arose:
Each damn'd the other's fetish; each with blows
Made most prodigious slaughter, and the floor
Ran ankle deep in blood; until repose
Came like a weeping lull amid the roar
Of madden'd wind and wave upon a wintry shore.

Then wrath soon surged afresh; no war it sought,
But torture of the prisoners of their zeal.
On hapless nakedness their frenzy wrought
All anguish known to water, oil or steel,
Or rack or rope or ripsaw, ax or wheel;
And if some spark of spirit yet remain'd
In that torn flesh, capacity to feel,

It was with faggots to a pillar chain'd,
And burn'd, that God be praised and piety maintain'd.

"Stop, in the name of Reason!" Obed cried,
Moved beyond measure at the hellish sight.
Then, for a startled pause, the tumult died,
Only to burst in cries of bellowing spite:
"An infidel! An infidel! Come, smite
This man who calls on Reason! Slay him! Slay!"
As famish'd dogs beneath the Arctic night
Behold a hare and rush to rend their prey,
They ran at Obed then, who fled in swift dismay.

The rabble neigh'd like horses at his back.
From every grimy cell and slimy crypt
The indignant mages rallied to the attack:
There ran the exorcist, whose finger dripp'd
With sanctified saliva; scorpion-lipp'd
The scroll-priests ran; with them, the flagellants
With the maim'd horror of their bodies stripp'd—
Swinging their scourges with Satanic prance,
They vow'd to whip him small enough to fed the ants.

There ran the godsmith with his plasmic joss;
The witch-hound with his pincers and his awl;
The lectors ran with tablets torn across;
The blood-priest left the slaughter'd ox's stall
And ran to choke poor Obed with its gall;
And all the torturous host of rack and stake
Ran arm'd with rope and saw and ax and mawl,
Shouting in ardent zeal to overtake,
Whooping in clamorous tumult in their victim's wake.

Upwards he sped, and reach'd the temple nave;
Behind him the Walpurgis rabble came;
Then, when it seemed no power on earth could save,
He heard a gentle whisper breathe his name,
And saw the sweet face of a holy Dame.
Quoth she: "Above the altar look, and see
A mighty mirror in an ageless frame.
Come, through its crystal surface pass with me.
Forsake Illusion here; there find Reality.

Like a bright silvery mist the glass made way
And melted like a dream about their feet;
Celestial silence still'd the pursuer's bray;
The tumult vanish'd, with its angry heat;
A sense of holiness, serene and sweet,
Envelopp'd him, no longer sore distress'd;
"Peace," said the Lady, "reigns in this retreat.
But lift thine eyes, and see this place of rest
The same sublime cathedral thou hast first address'd."

He look'd, and saw the truth of what she said.
Around him stood the pillars of the fane:
Colossal columns arch'd above his head
In solemn majesty, without a stain;
While shadows that had once upon it lain
Were banish'd by the glory of the sun
Streaming through great rose-windows to ordain
A holy sign, a pattern'd orison
That spoke its praise to God for glories thus begun.

Then sound join'd prayerful hands with sight; a great
Missa Sollemnis, on an organ blown,
Proclaim'd a sacrifice that conquer'd fate
With the deep diapason's urgent tone:
"*Kyrie eleison!*" came its moan.
"Lord, in Thy saving mercy, pity us,
Quoniam tu solus sanctus, Thee we own."
Then "*Sanctus, sanctus, sanctus dominus!*
How dark our doom, hadst Thou not sav'd us thus!"

Onward they walked to where a sunlit door
(Not the black cave through which he had reach'd the
                                                    shrine)
Open'd its portals to the day once more
Where flowers and a paradise of vine
Deck'd shady bowers of most rare design.
High round that garden stood a wild, rank press
Of strangling jungle tangle; but a line
Of sundering beauty hedged the fruitfulness
And order of that Eden from all outward stress.

As Obed gazed in wonder at the grace
Of that retreat, an ancient sage drew near,
With high, bald head and hoary-bearded face,
Serene, gray eyes, and accents trumpet-clear:
"Young stranger, thou art warmly welcome here!
The labourers in this garden are but few;
And earnest are our duties year by year
To guard the garden's fairness, yea, and hew
Its borders ever outward into pleasaunce new."

"What is this spot" ask'd marvelling Obed then.—
"The Garden of the Soul," the sage replied.
"Here grow the budding lives of struggling men,
Hemm'd in by primal lusts on every side;
And we must ever work to stem the tide
Of greedy cosmic growths the saints call sin.
Uncheck'd, their seeds and shoots would soon preside
Along these paths, and grow a waste for kin
Of savage wolves to gorge and apes to lecher in.

"I know the road thou cam'st by, and the herd
Of those who would have slain thee, making vows
Of high devotion to the Holy Word.
The dullard does more ill than dogs or sows;
Blind zeal is worse than sin, and oft allows
Hot deeds of hell; the zealot may remain
A pious weasel in a poultry-house,
That slays, and prays, and slaughters yet again,
Invoking heaven's blessings on his deeds of pain.

"Such cannot understand that God transcends
All figments of a Person, howe'er great.
No body, parts, or passions mock his ends
By bounding the infinitudes of Fate.
But man must still be itching to create
A God in his own image, at the best
A fictive, man-sized Father who will wait
To give the childish spirit that soft rest
It craves since parted from an earthly father's breast.

"Yet must the soul of man encounter God,
Confront the Infinite as Thou and I,

Humble his spirit there before the rod
Of the sheer holiness of the Most High;
Repentance then his soul shall sanctify
To faith in One who has redeem'd mankind;
Faith to commitment shall its zeal apply
In service to the Highest, and shall find
Its life made strong and with th' Eternal intertwined.

"Thus dedicate thyself! Be strong, not weak!
A peace naught else can give or take away
Shall fill thy heart, and thou shalt gladly seek
To build a heaven on earth from day to day
And help the Divine to live in human clay.
Hereafter cometh night, that blots out bliss
But labourers in this garden flout decay.
This is our portion and our lot it this.
Who treads in peace life's pathway has not walked amiss."

So spoke the Ancient, while his deep eyes shone
Like lamps of fire, his shining hands and feet
Grew bright as brass, and his great voice march'd on
As stern as marching armies in the street.
Then Obed's stalwart heart went out to meet
The challenge of that gospel of the strong,
Pledging his service there with ardent heat,
Vowing to labour on, his whole life long,
In building up the good and warring with the wrong.

And One in shining raiment stood near by
Whom he supposed a gardener, till He turn'd
And show'd His face; and Obed raised a cry
Of "Shamash! Master!" Then as yet he yearn'd
To clasp the friendly hand, his thought discern'd
The likeness of Another in that gaze,
Mix'd with the tenderness he once had learn'd,
And knew the sacred mystery of ways
Transfigured by pure purpose to the end of days.

From Canada to Iceland

ALTHING, 1930
(Alliterative Alcaics)

O ancient court of reverend counsellors,
That, calm with sense of longeval destiny,
   Here, throned in earth's most solemn senate,
     Sittest in silence of convocation,

Take now our tribute, comity's offering,
Our toll of honour, grandsire of parliaments!
   In this thy day, mankind acclaims thee,
     Kingdoms and commonwealths call thee blessed!

A thousand years look yearningly down on thee,
Old yesterdays yet cling to these terraces,
   Where age by age new generations
     Answered thy call at the dawn of summer.

Yet art thou young, for age hath not vanquished thee;
Thy ardour kindles, asking new victories;
   The beams of dayspring flush thy bosom,
     Brighten thy brow with the gold of morning!

From The Tide of Life, and other Poems

LINES NEAR GIZEH, A.D. 1921

The morning sun beats warm upon the sands
That spread, a yellowing ocean, to the west;
In gaunt decay along their borders stands
A line of giant tombs that here attest
This planet's most majestic place of rest:

The mighty mounds that Memphian monarchs raised
South towards Sakkâra on the desert's crest
In cyclopean majesty that has amazed
A myriad beholders, nor is yet unpraised.

A hundred thousand hands upreared the stone
In these memorials mounting to the sky;
But sixty human centuries have flown
Above their soaring summits; yonder lie
The mouldering causeways that could once supply
These atlantean ashlars; past all rust
Have vanished mawl and chisel, plumb and pry;
Only these monuments their peaks upthrust
While those that wrought so well are rendered into dust.

A modern avenue, with lebbeks lined,
Leads to the city of ascendant Mars;
Across the ancient stillness harshly grind
The sullen wheels of sand-worn tramway-cars;
Far off, above a din that faintly jars,
There soar aloft a thousand shafts of white
In pure, aspiring perpendiculars
That lift the Muslim spirit toward the bright
High heaven of Allah and his paradise of light.

These things are new; but eastward, as of old,
The gleaming Nile flows on in solemn flood;
The steep Mokattam shines, a cliff of gold,
And Gebel Ahmar is a hill of blood;
On shaded mounds, across the delta mud,
The fellah's hamlets swarm like hives of ants;
The ibis haunts the bars; all this has stood
Untouched by time through all the ceaseless dance
Of days and years and sundering circumstance.

Pensive, like me, Callimachus once walked
About these sands and pondered on the past,
Weeping awhile because no more he talked
With Heraclitus; here beside these vast
Memorials stood Herodotus and cast
A wondering eye upon their soaring sides,
And listened, as I do, from first to last,

To all the glib palaver of his guides,
Who mouthed a thousand myths, with modern lies besides.

Fair women lingered here: Zenobia came,
A conquering queen, to gaze for one brief day;
The exquisite Hypatia did the same
Before mad Cyril's monks arose to slay;
And passioned Cleopatra walked this way
One golden evening in those far-off years
And told her Antony their love would stay
As timeless as this tomb, that still uprears
Its passionless rebuke to human vows and tears.

The masters of the world have known this spot.
Here Bonaparte first fledged his eagle wings;
Here Selim stood, who left the land to rot,
And Saladin, who smote Crusading kings;
The Caliph Omar came; and yet there clings
A gash in the foundations whence men stole
Vast marble booty in their ravagings,
Yet hardly seemed to mar the mighty whole
By all the demolition of that wanton toll.

The godlike Julius trod this quiet place;
Young, ardent Alexander bowed his head
Amid this silence; and Cambyses' face
Grew graver in this garden of the dead;
Stern Assurbanipal calm tribute said,
With Esarhaddon, to the royal ghosts;
And Rameses and Thothmes fought and bled
That all the pride of their imperial hosts
Might match their ancient fathers and these matchless boasts.

What sights, if you could speak, O mounds of death,
Could you recount of days when thus increased
The proud arrays of men whose fleeting breath
Has chilled to mute inanity and ceased!
But in that list of days, one far from least
Was that, I think, when, wandering exil'd,
A tired man led here a tired beast
Bearing a Mother, with a little Child
Who gazed upon your haughty majesty, and smiled.

[405]

THE WOUNDED DOG
(On reading Canon Streeter's *Reality*)

The writhings of his anguish haunt me still,
That wounded dog I found long years ago;
The crazed eyes, slavering mouth, and moanings shrill
Proclaimed his fierce extremity of woe.

And shall this unctuous cleric have me hold
That these bespoke no suffering in the brain?
That in this best of worlds the manifold
Dumb sufferers have no consciousness of pain?

Must I believe that nature is a quack,
Who works legerdemain of unfelt smart?
That man alone is sentenced to the rack—
And through it gains the chastening of his heart?

The moans of stricken sentience, bird and beast,
Rise like a strangling mist by night and day;
Earth, air, and sea, north, south, and west and east,
Are tense with torture and convulsed dismay.

The voice of suffering clamours at my ear,
The face of torment pleads with me to see.—
I cannot choke my sympathies, I fear,
To justify a sleek theodicy!

FAITH WITHOUT HOPE

I raised the tinted amphora, and lo,
Amid the red wine floated flecks of curd
And yeasty gobbets, pulpous growths that blurred
The ruddy depths that should have sparkled so.
I poured the liquour on the channeled stone
And sniffed the burning reek, yet caught a keen
Cruel stench of evil, nauseous, unclean;
The ashes sputtered as I stood alone.
I leaned against a marble pedestal,
And though a soughing wind, half curse, half kiss,

Oozed from the sanctuary, and the hall
Writhed in the dusk, I watched, calm courage mine,
Unmoved, as one who makes the future his,
The smouldering altar and the wailing shrine.

BOYHOOD

The blue horizon fades far, far away;
Shrill sea-winds falter; purple hills grow dim
In memory; great ships near the ocean's brim
Melt in the magic of a summer's day.
The rocky ramparts soften to a dream,
Pine-darkened; and the laughter of the shore—
Waves lapping, lisping, plashing evermore—
Is fainter than the rippling of a stream.
And so, like summer clouds, the visions fade,
Passing beyond our ken, as all things pass
And are forgotten, till the vows we made
Are silent; dusk comes, for the sun has set;
And rarest hours of happiness, alas,
Are but a yearning and a vague regret.

FORT HENRY REVISITED

October moonlight floods the barren hill
With mellow magic, and the silvery way
Gleams whiter, winding up to walls of grey
Old stone upon the summit, slumbering still
As sepulchres by antique tribes designed,
Except for one strayed cricket's elfin tones,
A dog's far howl, and, on the mouldering stones,
Dead grasses whispering to the sighing wind.
Strange shadows form and vanish on the wall;
Wraiths of departed sentries, peering; gaunt
Uneasy captives seeking flight; and all
The restless visions with which fancy teems,
Vague as the wistful memories that haunt
The crumbling ruins of our youthful dreams.

HIGH WINDS

Winds, and far voices wailing, threnodies
Of timeless ages ere man was, make chant
Above the sea in accents dominant,
Over the shapeless rocks and naked trees.
Dirges of wild regret for worlds o'erthrown
Sob in shrill anguish down the winter sky.
Aeons rush by me, raising as they fly
A hollow echo from the empty stone.
My flesh is cycles old, my scaly lids
Shroud eyes that feel the pulse of primal time,
The swaddled Pharaohs are ephemerids
Compared with me, whose soul is cased in rime.
For still the winds wail over land and sea
Hoarse lamentations of eternity.

Selected Verse Translations

European Elegies

In Memoriam Conjugis Meae Pulcherrimae, Dulcissimae, Fletissimae

1 TO CALVUS, ON THE DEATH OF QUINTILIA

If we may breathe the faint belief
That on the silent dead
The tributes of our human grief
A gracious influence shed,

And they find tender comfort in
Our longing sighs and tears,
As we lament love that has been
In desolated years,

Then to thy sweet dead bride, my friend,
With woe at hapless fate
The knowledge of thy love shall blend
And bless her sad estate.

From the Latin of C. Valerius Catullus

AUTUMN

2 ANIMAE RERUM

As I survey the landscape's shadowy gloom
And feel a deepening night within my heart,
My anguish seems dark nature's counterpart
And nature seems my misery to assume.

I watch the driving rain this sombre eve
And feel my eyes aflood with bitter tears,
Until I know not, all confused with fears,
Whether I weep from grief, or, weeping, grieve.

As melancholy shades the valley claim
In murky dark, and o'er all outlines roll,
My unforgetting lips call one dear name—

And in that tortured silence infinite
I know not if the darkness blots my soul
Or if my Stygian soul makes black the night.

From the Spanish of Francisco Villaespesa

3 GREY HOURS

Grey hours of grieving, grey as falling night,
    Enfold my brain . . . cold, livid snake-coils cleaving
    Clammily round my heart and with their weaving
Waking old wounds of weariness and fright
And stifling hope and faith with slimy might—
        Grey hours of grieving.

    Sombre as storm-wrack o'er bright plains upheaving,
Blotting the blue from out the gleaming height,
They bring my life its cup of aconite—
        Grey hours of grieving.

    I loved with untold love, and fate's bereaving
Leaves me to mourn to-day untold delight:
Crushed daily by a serpent parasite,
    Dazed daily by a poison past relieving—
        Grey hours of grieving.

From the Polish of W. Nawrocki

4 DARKNESS

The sun sets; and before the saddened eye
The waning light fades wearily away;
While night's dark hand, as it resumes its sway,
Sows clouds in sorrow down the sombre sky.

The village roofs have vanished utterly,
And the swart cypresses are lost in grey;
All things are still, save where in yonder bay
Upon the sands the full waves slowly die.

With hand on brow, I sadly gaze among
The shades that deepen round my darkened brain
And teach my tears their passion to prolong;

And if I could command relief from pain,
It would be that the night should last so long
That dreary day would never dawn again.

From the Portuguese of João Xavier de Mattos

5 LACRIMAE RERUM

Alas, my dear! Throughout this cottage small
Your vanished form haunts all familiar things;
To the little mirror and the pictured wall
The recollection of your beauty clings.

Something of fairy fragrance, faintly shed,
Floods the poor dwelling with a sweet unrest,
And your dim phantom steals beside my bed
To thrill with silent touch my throbbing breast.

Without, a deep-voiced spirit of the waste
Wails round the roof-tree; while from couch and chair
The sobbings of each corner you have graced
Blend in one anguished outcry of despair.

And, from his place, a comrade in the dark,
Our old clock speaks, my comforter-in-chief,
Whose measured dirge o'er dying time will mark
The endless iteration of my grief.

From the Romaic of Lambros Porphyras

6 MY TRAGIC MUSE

Alas, your lovely fingers touched
    A tragic lyre;
To veil your sad lament in verse
    My lines aspire.

There in faint quaverings of fear
    Your low voice grieves,
Like a night wind through withered flowers
    And fallen leaves;

Until in darkness side by side
    Once more we sleep,
And whisper to each other still,
    And mutely weep.

From the Romaic of Miltiades Malacassis

7 IN THE CEMETERY

I sought the cemetery, where the sod
Shrouds with its green the symbols of decay—
The mounds where Age lies quiet in the clod
And Beauty is forever laid away.

I gazed upon a newly opened grave,
Three feet across, a fatal fathom deep,
The last cold bed that tired mortals crave,
Where human thought is stilled in endless sleep.

My heart sighed bitterly in sick dismay;
My clenched hands beat my bosom with a groan;
My plaint paid ghastly tribute to Decay,
And the dank tombs gave back a hollow moan.

From the Slovene of Simon Jenko

8 PEARL

It was a pearl to kindle kings,
Chastely mounted in mellow gold;
Never in Orient journeyings
Did I its priceless peer behold.
There lurked within its lambent springs
Soft, lustrous magic manifold;
And when I judged of precious things,
Its beauty paramount I told.
Alas! One day it slipped my hold:
I lost it in the churchyard grass
And groan because the graveyard mould
Mars graces that the world surpass.

Yearning with many a bitter sigh
In that green waste I wait; and long
The lost delights of days gone by
Before black sorrow choked my song
Arise in anguish to my eye,
And through my memory's chambers throng;
Till underneath that quiet sky
There stabs a dolour doubly strong
That her fair flesh should lie among
The sullen depths of sodden clays—
Ah earth, dank earth, you do me wrong
To rot the roses from her face!

From the Middle English

9 THE UNENDURABLE

My broken spirit cannot bear
That, as of old, the sun is gay;
That, as when life was still your share,
The clock ticks on upon the stair
And day comes calmly after day;

That, when the twilight shadows flit,
And fireside circles form anon,
The place where you, dear, used to sit
Is filled with others' smiles and wit,
And nothing seems to know you gone;

While far across the quiet night
The pallid, flickering moonbeams pass,
And with indifference infinite
Lay bare in wavering ghostly light
    Your gravestone in the churchyard grass.

From the German of Theodor Storm

10 A LITTLE DUST

The eyes that stirred my passioned eloquence,
    The arms that held me fast, the hallowed face
    That made my heart ecstatic by its grace
    And walled me round with dream's circumference,
The golden ringlets' soft munificence,
    And the angelic lips whose laugh could raise
    The joy of paradise in this poor place
    Are but a little dust, forlorn of sense.
I linger on; despising life, I lie
    Without the light that once made day so fair
    And by withdrawal darkens every sky.
My songs of love are mute: in this chill air
    My veins of poesy grow void and dry,
    My numb hand harps the discords of despair.

From the Italian of Francesco Petrarca

11 THE WITHERED LEAF

The sere leaf from the bough to-day
Drops swiftly to the autumn clay,
And moves the meditative mind
To mark a moral for mankind.

For once she laughed with emerald thrill
To watch the dawn dream up the hill;
Or minuetted in the breeze
Mid countless leafy companies.

But now the dew too heavy clings
Upon her faded flutterings
In this chill air whose flagging breath
Bears her companions to their death.

No more may suns bring warm delight,
Nor glad moons solace her at night,
Nor can the gentle breezes bring
Once more the tender strength of spring.

She lived but to express in grace
One happy smile in nature's face,
Until October cried "Destroy!"
And slew her beauty and her joy.

From the Welsh of "Alun"

12 ON THE HEATH

Over dank moorlands I wander slow;
Hollow earth-echoes repeat my woe.

Autumn is come now; spring half forgot—
Can I remember the things that are not?

Menacing mists are about me to-day,
Frost-blackened leaf and sky iron-gray.

Woe's me to think that we kissed here last spring!
Young life and love—ah, how soon they take wing!

From the German of Theodor Storm

13 LOSS

The spring has gone. And I have lost the flowers
  I might have gathered from its meadow-grass.
I merely marked the sudden spring aspire
Up through the turf in white and golden fire,
  And, as I dallied, saw that glory pass
As swiftly as the rainbow of June showers.
  Ah, maiden beauty, fleeting are thy hours!

Summer has gone. And I have missed the gleaning
  I might have gathered from its harvest-field.
I merely marked the flaming wheat-waves swaying
Across the leas where summer winds were playing;
  But as I gazed, time seized that yellow yield
And fate forestalled my frantic intervening—
  Ah, love, at last I know thy tragic meaning!

Autumn has come. Bare stubbled prairies taunt me
  In my sad brooding on what might have been.
Across the sky the haggard mists are weaving
A fog-shroud for the dying sun's receiving;
  And fears of these dark days, bereavement's keen
Heart-hunger and deep thirst of spirit haunt me.
  Alas, the terrors of love's winter daunt me!

From the Slovak of Hviezdoslav

14 AUTUMN DIRGE

Autumn begins
With violins
Of lament,
Wounding my breast
With dull, oppressed
Discontent.

Roused by the shocks
Of stricken clocks
From pale sleep,
I think upon

Sweet nights now gone;
And I weep.

And my heart flies
Down wailing skies,
In my grief
Blown here and there
As down night air
The dead leaf.

From the French of Paul Verlaine

15 AUTUMN

The wailing wind of autumn sobs in pain
By wet untrodden paths that thread the night;
In heavy eddyings its vapors smite
Strange swaths of gloom across the sodden plain.

Disconsolate and shadowless it rends
The ragged yellow garments of the trees,
Pausing in grief above each lifeless glade,
Helplessly savage over hope's decease . . .
Its writhing length upon the earth is laid,
And then once more in moaning it ascends.

By lonely paths among the haggard hills
It lays the pallid leaves in humid heaps;
Sleepless it wanders till its wailing fills
The world with clamour of a thousand deeps.

From the Bulgarian of Sirak Skitnik

16 NOVEMBER

The gloom of grey November
On field and copse is shed;
Life can no laugh remember
While the cold earth lies dead.

No more come robins calling
From branches by the door:
Only the sere leaf falling
From the pale sycamore.

And the slow drops unceasing
Dripping from barren boughs,
Tears that for sorrow's easing
Fall on your last, dark house.

From the Plattdeutsch of Fritz Husmann

17   AUTUMN LAMENT

Gone is the grace of summer! Gone at last,
  Its laughter lies behind me.
Gone is the summer: that its grace is past
  Mountain and vale remind me.

Gone is the song of summer; hushed and still
  Is birds' melodious chanting;
No more brave madrigals adown the hill
  The shadowy dells are haunting.
Only a far-off echo seems to thrill
  Forsaken glades enchanting
Where in July beside the forest rill
  Our valiant hearts were vaunting.

Gone are the loves of summer, and the morn
  When we went sweetly friended
And gaily by thatched hut and hillside thorn
  Our white-fleeced flocks we tended.
And as the deepening autumn shall adorn
  The slopes with snow, transcended
Shall be my autumn woe, my heart forlorn
  Know even autumn ended.

From the Basque of Tene

18 BIRD SONG

I was a tree in blossom, whence there sang
The sweet bird of my youth—too quickly flown.
And even ere he left his leafy throne
His plaintive song betrayed an inner pang.
    His mourning was so soft and piteous
That in my bare unpeopled solitude
The listening bushes at his misery rued,
The ancient oak shed tears to hear him thus.
    Now all is still and dead. That music lost,
I spread bare branches to November skies.
Dull groans betray a heart that breaks with frost,
    Yet steadfast in the gloom my head I raise
Until the fatal Raven to me flies
To croak the last black chant of winter days.

From the French of Charles Augustin Sainte-Beuve

19 SEA-ANGUISH

Billow on billow is breaking
Shrill on the iron shore;
Sorely the ocean is shaking,
Sweeping the surf before.

Leaden there lies an all-clothing
Incubus of despair—
Nightmare of formless loathing,
Pestilent everywhere.

Waves on the wan, cold shingle
Batter their broken breasts,
Fall back and meet and mingle
Moaning that never rests.

Out of the west comes wailing
Inconsolable woe,
Born out of infinite ailing,
Endlessly, always, so.

[421]

Winds to the shore come throbbing;
Spume sprays the rocks a-lee;
Grey waves in sorrow are sobbing;
Sobbing the earth and sea.

From the Finnish of Aaro Hellaakoski

20   THE DEAD MISTRESS

Alas, my love is dead,
And dead my dearest hope!
My happiness is fled!
Forlorn and faint I grope!

Farewell to youthful dreams—
For all their hopes and joys
One bitter hour blasphemes,
One fatal day destroys!

The sweet familiar tones
Of oft remembered words
Mix with my own wild groans,
Pierce my weak heart like swords.

The music of the rill
We kissed to in the grove
Haunts my sad spirit still
With bygone hours of love.

My heart is like a plot
Of flowers choked with tares,
All happiness forgot,
O'ergrown with dank grey cares.

Like a doomed ship that steers
Upon a sudden reef,
My torn heart fills with tears
And founders in its grief.

From a Breton folk-song

My distrest spirit
Reels in the rushing
Whirlpool of crisis
Greedy and crushing.
Life's fragile shallop
Hurries me tragic
On through the stormtost
Darkness pelagic.
Vast seas appal me.
Ah, to sail shoreward!
But in wild thunder
Winds thrust me forward.
Surge-serpents hiss us;
Ship-thews are shaken;
Low in the green gulfs
Lurks the foul kraken.—
Sweet stars in heaven
Guard from disaster!
Great wind of mercy
Be my mild master!

From the Slovene of Simon Jenko

22 THE STORM

Rent sail and rudder, roar of wind and wave,
Outcry of stricken crew, and spent pump's groan:
The last worn cable severs with a moan,
The wild sun sinks in blood, and naught can save.

The tempest howls in triumph; on the deck
Grey shapeless breakers raise appalling crests,
And Death's grey spirit the doomed ship invests
Like soldiers storming through a breached wall's wreck.

Some sailors lie half-dead, inert with fear;
Some cross themselves and take a last embrace;
Some pray, that their last words may conquer death.

But one, a traveller, sits in silence near
And thinks: "How happy he who faints, or prays,
Or bids a friend farewell with pious breath!"

From the Polish of Adam Mickiewicz

23 MY GALLEY

Rage, tempest! Rage, and let my galley's sail
Strain in a sweeping hell of hail
And swirling, snarling snow!
Yet will I tack
While jib and jack
And helm and mast
Alike hold fast,
Though the fiend-waves dash
And hiss, and lash
Their spume against my prow!

From the Swedish of Karl Jonas Love Almqvist

WINTER

24 WINTER SONG

Hark to my song:
The cold comes on;
With winter's snow
The summer's gone;

The winds are snell;
The sun is low;
Its life is short;
Fierce sea-tides flow;

Deep red the fern,
Long dead and dry;
The phalanxed geese
Make loud the sky;

Warned by the frost,
The birds depart;
A winter dirge
Wails in my heart.

From the Old Irish

25   WHERE ARE THE SONGBIRDS?

Where are the songbirds of the summer vanished?—
They fled o'er southern surf-capes long ago.
Where are the blossoms of the June fields banished?—
They lie in their dark graves beneath the snow.

Hushed is all song, except the chill wind chanting
Over the snowy hills and on the shore,
Stirring the silent seafowl with its ranting,
Rocking the headlands with its hollow roar.

Gone are all flowers, except the death-pale petals
Painted by frosts upon the frozen pane,
And, where blue ice-plains gleam like mirrored metals,
Flowers of magic in a moonlight-lane.

Far to the south the absent songbird lingers;
Deep under snowy shrouds dead flowers lie;
Within, hearth-huddled, man warms tortured fingers;
Without are dreary drifts and iron sky.

From the Icelandic of Steingrimur Thorsteinsson

26   THE FOREST

The forest green, the forest green
Too soon in autumn garb is seen,
    And down its deep aisles glancing
    Dead leaves are madly dancing,
Till hoary winter howls about
And blots the woodland beauty out.

And man's green strength must slowly die
And waste to grey senility,
    All happiness forgotten
    Amid the dank leaves rotten,
Till in the forest's frozen woe
His bones lie dead beneath the snow.

From the Rumanian of Dimitrie Petrino

27 WINTER WOODS

Fair sylvan solitude, belov'd retreat
Of my bewildered spirit, tired out
These dark, short days, when north winds wrap about
The earth and sky frost's hoary winding-sheet,
Thy ancient, green-dark tresses, touched with sleet,
Are grown as white as mine, and all throughout
Thy open glades the snow has put to rout
The scarlet flowers that made the springtime sweet.

Here, in the misty light of this brief day,
I meditate upon my mortal pain
And feel my mind and members turn to ice;
But more than nature's is my frost's stark reign;
My winter brings a wind more sharp to slay,
A longer night, a day with darker skies.

From the Italian of Giovanni della Casa

28 SLEEPLESSNESS

I cannot rest. Around me lie
Cold darkness and uneasy sleep.
Only the clock's dull accents keep
Their vigil's cadenced dignity.
But still a sense of whispered things,
Or mice in their meek scamperings,
Comes haunting the husht hours of night—
What art thou, spirit of affright?

[426]

Whisper incessant, wearisome,
Art thou my guilt? Or art thou come
With by-gone grief my heart to smite?
Speak! Tell me thy mysterious will!
Mean'st thou my past or future ill?
For my pale spirit waits, unstrung,
The strange demands of thy dark tongue.

From the Russian of Alexandr Sergeevich Pushkin

29   TO SLEEP

O Youthful Sleep, thou gentlest of the gods,
Let not my wretched eyes alone lack rest!
The beast in lair is silent, bird in nest,
And the bowed mountain-crest in slumber nods;
The torrent's voice is hushed, the sea-waves dream
And cease from moaning on the drowsy shore—
I, only I, thy absence must deplore
And toss distressful till the dawning's gleam.
Alas! If somewhere in the long, dull night
Some lover throbbing in the arms of love
Shall flout thee, Sleep, turn hither thy soft flight!
Nor do I ask thy sweet wing's full embrace;
Give but a wand-touch, hovering above,
Or trail thy airy train across my face.

From the Latin of Publius Papinius Statius

30   A VAIN APPEAL

O Sleep, thou gentle son of shadowy Night,
Dewy and silent, thou that bringest peace
To fevered mortals and serene release
From the harsh tyranny of life's mad might,
Help now my heart, that sickens with the blight
Of sleepless hours, my limbs whose pains increase;
Fly hither, Sleep, to bid my sorrows cease;
Brood with thy dusky wings upon my sight!

Where now is silence, fugitive from day
And sunshine? Where are the light dreams that sport
With hesitating feet about thy way?
Alas, in vain I call and vainly court
These vague and chilling shades! Sleep has no sway
O'er my hard couch, my nights grim past support.

From the Italian of Giovanni della Casa

31 UNHAPPINESS

Night makes my grief more tense and tragical . . .
Disquiet haunts the darkness like a ghost,
And writes with shadowy fingers on the wall,
A menacing reminder of things lost.

The flooding tears that from my sorrow start
Wash down the silted miseries of the past;
Black clouds envelop and suffuse my heart,
And freeze my dreams, and leave my hopes aghast.

Yet, oh that some great Hand's transfiguring rites
Would set soft roses where rough thorns now are,
And with the touch of peace transform my night's
Egyptian anguish with a paschal star!

From the Spanish of Juan Ramón Jiménez

32 NIGHT

The day has gone; and with the night
The gathering gloom confounds the eye;
With all its torches set alight
The moon is marching up the sky.
In dusk I sit, forsaken quite,
No loving heart, no friend is by—
Only a song of far delight
Comes throbbing through my memory.

Who's there? What face peers through the leaves?
Who floats before me but to fade?
What white-clad figure flits and weaves
A haunting horror through the shade?—
'Tis but the night my eyes deceives,
And yet my spirit is afraid.

From the Finnish of Eino Leino

33   TIME

Nestlings are husht in sleep. Without a sound
Night folds the faint earth in her dewy breast;
Her brooding bosom wraps its darkness round
Save for dim starlight in the drowsy west.

Yet in her midnight veins throbs vaguely dark
A mystic, speechless sense of fate and crime,
For in that sleeping present pulses stark
The ineluctable intent of Time

From the Serbo-Croatian of Mileta Jakšić

34   MEMORIAL STANZAS

My sad mind, when night harasses,
Will with wakeful resolutions
                Contemplate
How poor human life soon passes,
How approaches dissolution's
                Silent fate;
How soon stilled are joy and laughter
And their loss in retrospection
                Gives us grief,
How the past appears long after
Brighter in our recollection
                Past belief.

Each man's life is but a river
Rushing onward towards the ocean
Of the dead:
Thither empires must deliver
All their glories with commotion
Lurid red;
There the rich man's golden torrent
And the pauper's rill are tending;
Great and small
Equal face their fate abhorrent,
Equal meet the dark impending
Doom of all.

From the Old Spanish of Jorge Manrique

35 DEVOURING TIME

Devouring time drags all things down,
And leaves no beauty in its place;
Years, like a sponge, all joys erase;
Ages, like waves, all memories drown.

The rivers fail; the seas retreat;
High mountain summits melt and die.
Mere trifles these. The glorious sky
Itself shall pass in fervent heat.

Death claims all things at last, for death
Is a grim law to all that is;
Till the whole universe and his
Vast vaults shall vanish like a breath.

From the Latin of L. Annaeus Seneca

36 THE GRAVE

The grave is deep and sunless,
An orifice of fright
Through which our loved ones enter
Strange lands of naked night.

No nightingale sings round it
Soft lyrics of the south;
Only love's bitter tear-drops
Bedrench its mossy mouth.

Here raven-weeded widows
Wring hands in fruitless pain,
And children's wailing voices
Invoke the dead in vain.

Here living mourners suffer
No solace or release;
But through these doors of darkness
The dead have passed to peace.

For hearts in earth's wild desert
Attain no calm retreat
From cruel storms of sorrow
Until they cease to beat.

From the Flemish of Karel Lodewyk Ledeganck

37 THE HATEFULNESS OF DEATH

Go, lovely woman, haste and prove
The features of the man you love,
Watch earnestly his ardent air,
His quiet eyes and shining hair,
Till you can hold the happy grace
With which he smiles down in your face.
For sudden silence stills the voice
Forever, that declares its joys
In proudly praising you to-day.
Alas, a fathom deep in clay
That tongue is rotting in his mouth
Wherewith he sang your radiant youth
In his light-hearted gaiety:
No longer may it form with glee
The words that made your bosom throb.
Recall, too, with a choking sob

The bearded chin and lips you won;
For now the vile earth lies upon
The tender arms that held you fast
And guarded you from every blast
In happy days, forever past.

From the Middle High German of Heinrich von Melk

38 MEMENTO MORI

Man and woman, meditate
On your unrelenting fate!
Though you love this fragile clay,
Hoping to prolong its day
In the light of Beauty's eyes
And her fleeting paradise,
All the prayers of passioned breath
Cannot stay the hand of Death.

No man's wisdom can avail
To complete the broken tale.
Death will steal our every grace,
Leaving nothing, fame or face;
Death comes soon to small and great:
No man is of such estate
Nor of such possessions vast
He may cozen Death at last.

Though you linger here below,
Youth and Age alike must go.
All must die; your lives are vain;
Nothing of you shall remain.
Briefer is mortality
Than the winking of an eye.
Thus I view my life's distress
Gulfed in Death's forgetfulness.

From the Old High German (Anonymous)

39 DEATH

Death passes no one by; all men must go.
Even from infancy he flutters nigh;
Faintly, as through thin fog, his footsteps grow;
    He passes no one by.

Through his grey mask, flame flashes from each eye,
And gleaming shin-bones in the darkness glow;
His hands hold suffering and senility.

Sometimes he lays a toiling traveller low,
Smiting him, hawklike, from an open sky;
And sometimes, cat with mouse, his play is slow.
    He passes no one by.

From the Czech of Jaroslav Vrchlicky

40 TOMORROW

—What of tomorrow, tomorrow?—
Vespers are tolling the doubt,
Voicing my heart in its sorrow,
Seeing the sun blotted out.

—What of tomorrow, tomorrow?—
Beats the panged pulse of my heart . . .
"Nature next morning will borrow
Sun-tints transcending all art."

—But, is that all?—comes my mutter.
"No, nature blossoms and grows;
Yesterday's rose-bud," you utter,
"Opens tomorrow a rose."

—But, is that all?—I say, chiding.
Swift is your answer in scorn:
"Lured into life from its hiding,
See the white butterfly born.

"All through the rare summer hours,
Ravished, for nectar it roves,
Resting on fresh rosy flowers,
Happy through gardens and groves."

Likely you think my doubt shaken.
But I insist, in my sorrow,
Knowing the dead do not waken:
—Ah, but we have no tomorrow!—

From the Czech of Robert Lev Novak

41 THE CALENDAR

Deciduous as life is, day by day
The dead leaves flutter from the calendar;
And drop by drop, fading in deeps afar,
Time drips into eternity away.

Swiftly I pass upon my pilgrimage,
Leaving the wanton fields of youth behind,
And still lamenting each new day to find
More evil, darker grief, and harsher age.

In silence, noiselessly, the cold leaves fall
From the dark trunk of time, that darker grows
Against the grey brow of senility.

Leaf after leaf, the fluttering funeral
Of days and deeds into the darkness goes,
And nought on earth can bring them back to me.

From the Portuguese of Conde do Casal Ribeiro

42 THE CLOCK

Clock! dull, dread, passionless divinity,
Whose finger writes "Remember" with a threat,
In thy pale heart are quivering sorrows set
Like arrows that in mortal quarries lie.

For thee, the shadowy joys in pleasure's mime
Dance swiftly from the stage like choral sprites;
Each moment slays a share of the delights
Granted each man for his appointed time.

Three thousand and six hundred times each hour
Thy tickings lisp "Remember"—Insectlike,
The present's buzzing voice says: Still I strike
And with my unclean beak your days devour.

Remember time insatiate casts his die
And wins without deceit or word gainsaid.
"Remember!" The day wanes. The shadows spread.
The thirsty gulf still gapes. The glass runs dry.

From the French of Charles Baudelaire

43   THE OLD BRIDGE

About the bridge's crumbling piers
The quiet river ripples by.
We lean to hear its liquid sigh:
Its ancient story fills our ears.

It tells of lovers long ago
Who loitered on this parapet,
And learned, as we do, how to let
Love sway them like the stream below.

It tells how, with the years that glide,
Matrons, once maids, passed here again,
Pale with maternal care and pain,
Their tender children by their side.

It tells how centuries unguessed
Have rolled by slowly since the day
It saw them, hearse-borne, take their way
Across the bridge to their last rest.

Alas, how soon we too are gone!
That babbled message chills the blood:
Man fades down time's lethean flood;
Earth's crumbling arch lasts dully on.

From the Catalan of Emili Guanyavents

Life is a moment's maze,
Life is an anguisht cry,
Life is a shifting haze,
A shadow that flutters by;
Life is a fugitive dream
That melts like snow in a stream
Or like mists in the morning sun;
Life is surpassing brief
And tenous past belief,
For life is a falling leaf
That the winter winds have won.

Life is a flower by a stream,
Life is a breath quick-drawn,
Life is a comet's gleam,
Life is a lark at dawn,
A cloud by the wild wind tost,
A wave on the wild sea lost
In the pathless ocean's spume;
Life is a bird's frail feather
Wing-torn by tempest weather
And drawn to dark gulfs nether
On the plangent winds of doom.

From the Portuguese of João de Deus Ramos

45 FATE

The sole memorials of the faithful band
Are frescoed fragments of a fortress wall.
The strength of spears has slain the host, and all
Have died proud deaths with hungry sword in hand.

Bleak blizzards beat upon the shattered keep
In the dread winter, when the daylight ends
In bitter night, and the snell north-wind sends
Harsh hail to crush man's spirit in its sweep.

The kingdom of the earth is full of woe,
For time's iron edicts grimly overturn
All tenures under heaven: riches go,

And friendships fade, and kinsmen yield to fate,
And all the lives of men to ashes burn,
Leaving the earth's foundation desolate.

From the anonymous Anglo-Saxon poem, "The Wanderer"
Lines 97–110

46 SAHARA VITAE

Above the level waste the heavens reel
A boundless arching vault of lucid fire,
Whence the inexorable sun in ire
Riddles the sea of sand with shafts of steel.

There, far across the blazing wilderness
Of dust and ruthless flame, the eye with bliss
Sees the green palm-fronds of love's oasis
Off'ring illusive hope to man's distress.

But death's sirocco swirls about the sky
Its dark dust-pillars, overwhelms all life,
And satiated sinks in lethargy.

Then the sun flings once more clear shafts of red,
And o'er the hidden graves of futile strife
The unmarked sands lie passionless and dead.

From the Portuguese of Olavo Bilac

47 THE LAMENT OF ADMETUS

How shall I enter, O my shining hall?
How shall I enter, since foul fortunes fall
And desolation has confounded all?

I entered once when torches were aflare,
Exultant bridal chantings rent the air,
And a sweet spouse was all my tender care.

Clamorous revels were our escort then,
And every voice acclaimed my bride and me,
Both sprung from noblest of heredity
And made one flesh to the delight of men.

But now a dirge has stilled the marriage song;
Tenebrous grief has robbed our robes of white;
And silent escorts lead me back to-night
To lie alone where love was once so strong.

From the Greek of Euripides' "Alcestis"
Lines 911–925

48 FUNERAL SONG

The years of youth
Speed yearning on;
Hope's happy thoughts
Are hid and gone.
The mind of man
Has many a dream,
But memory's
A misty gleam,
And soon his corpse
Grows stiff and stark
In the cold embrace
Of his clay-bed dark.
The man we mourn,
The monied son
Of a substanced sire,
Too soon is gone.
Swift ships at sea
Set sail for him;
Fat beeves in byre
Brought wealth to brim;

The loveliness
Of a loving wife
Then crowned his joy—
But crushed from life,
He lies behind the graveyard hedge
Bereft of all love's privilege.

From a Lappish folk-song

49 WRITTEN IN A NEW CEMETERY

A little fenced-in field of fine-clipt grass,
A carven cross as sacred sentinel
Amid young willows: a new plot, alas,
Planned all too well.

So is it, and shall be, while year by year
The round earth sees in soil fresh hollows made
In season by the farmer's plough, and here
The sexton's spade.

From the Czech of Josef Kálal

50 THE STRANGER

His youth was over, for his hair was grey,
And his bent figure told of burdens borne;
Life from his cheek had stol'n life's bloom away
And time upon his brow deep lines had worn.
Ever his withered lips were folded fast
As if to guard a sorrow of the past.

Sometimes he wanly smiled as if to cloak
A grief whose pangs consumed his tortured heart,
But through his eyes his cold despair still spoke:
My life, alas, has passed from joy apart.
My ship is burnt, my weapons shattered lie,
I live, indeed, but live in days gone by.

From the Swedish of Gustaf Fröding

[439]

51 THE SONG OF GRIEF

My brothers, blame me not because I sing
A doleful song;
If I aggrieve you with my sorrowing,
Forgive the wrong!—

For when your transient joys and happiness
Have turned to dust,
And sorrows curse your midnights with distress,
As sorrows must,

Then, since grief's slavery is sung by me,
To seek relief
Your lonely lips will whisper wistfully
My song of grief.

From the Ukrainian of Ivan Franko

52 MOURNING

Everywhere I pass to-day
Cold rocks wall my wretched way;
Down the granite wastes a-wing,
Winter winds have slain the spring,
As my frosts of grief have done,
Marring May when scarce begun,
Nor can showers of my weeping
Rouse 'that dead joy from its sleeping.
Could I be the grave's dark guest,
I would gladly take my rest.

From a Romany folk-song (Gypsies of Hungary)

53 CHURCHYARD-FLOWER

The winter, with its wilting will,
Brings blossom-birth to bareness;
Sometimes its frosts, unpitying, kill
The flower's unfolding fairness;

And, as the living gems rejoice
In fragrant gratulation,
Sudden breaks in the blighting voice
Of icy death's afflation.

With spring, rare buds will re-appear,
And earth renew her dower:
But, ah, I weep for you, my dear,
My pale, young churchyard-flower!

From the Frisian of Pieter Jelles Troelstra

54   INFINITY

I love to linger on this lonely hill,
And lie behind this hedge whose gloomy yew
Blots out all distant vistas from the view;
For here the air is so profoundly still,
Time seems so merged into eternity,
That in the mystic silence all my brain
Is flooded with a mood where fear and pain
Are lost in a strange peace, serene and free.
And as I hear from every branch the wail
Of vast wind-voices, waves of passion sweep
From out old ages, and my senses fail;
Until dead years and moments speak once more,
And my dazed heart, lost in a misty deep,
Swoons towards oblivion on its endless shore.

From the Italian of Giacomo Leopardi

55   THE DAY IS DARK

A day has dawned, a day of strangling darkness;
The tears of angels drench the fainting earth;
A cloud has blotted heaven, and cold starkness
Of grief and fear has stilled the voice of mirth.

The heaven in anguisht gloom is overclouded,
In anguisht gloom the livid landscape lies,
The sun and moon are lost and overshrouded,
Cosmic convulsion racks the dying skies.

For life has lost, and death is darkly leading
Fear and despair behind the stricken rout,
And on that field of carnage, crushed and bleeding,
Beauty and trust and love are trampled out.

From the Albanian (Tosk dialect) of Naim Be Frasheri

56 THE SUN-DIRGE

I saw the sun sink, blotched with blood;
My fainting spirit almost failed;
All former solar glories paled
Beside that lurid plenitude.

I saw the sun sink, while it shed
Such fire that I swooned, and sore
A seething river, thick with gore,
Bellowed from dark depths of the dead.

I watched that sun with anguisht eyes;
In fluttering, fearful joylessness;
My very heart in its distress
Dissolved away in clotted pain.

I watched that sun with anguisht eyes;
Impending death began to freeze
My tongue as taut as winter trees,
And utter frost congealed the skies.

Then my sun sank to rise no more,
For waters of the wild waste hills
Went wailing o'er me, and my ills
Were washed to nothing down death's shore.

From the Old Icelandic, eleventh century

57 THREE SPRINGS

In this terrestrial wilderness, three springs
Gush forth mysterious in the boundless gray;

The spring of youth, with passioned murmurings,
Sparkles and boils on its rebellious way;

The spring of poesy exalts the blood
Of wanderers in life's desert sands apart;

But chill oblivion's spring in soothing flood
Alone can cool the fever of the heart.

From the Russian of Alexandr Sergeevich Pushkin

58 UNREST

Happy is he whose days are full of peace,
Who sits beside his hearth in warm content,
Who even in reverse is reverent:
For him life's paths have no asperities.

But hapless they who chafe at fate's caprice,
Whose souls in bitter sorrowing are spent,
For if life's cup with slime and gall be blent
The groans of black disgust bring no release.

Like the eternal birds that change their skies
And in this land have no abiding-place,
My spirit burns in longing to depart.

Long since is dead my faith of other days,
And yet on restless wings my yearnings rise
In vague and hopeless hunger of the heart.

From the Rumanian of Alexandru Sihleanu

59 LOVE KNOWS BUT LOSS

I was upon that high and hallowed hill
    Where at a sacred grave I yet adore
    Her vanished beauty, fall'n in anguish o'er
    The marble slab where the engraver's skill
Has carved the honour, virtue and sweet will
    That earth closed over when death from me tore
    My bride as fit for heaven, and loudly swore
    No further grace could her perfection fill.
Then I cried out to Love in sorrow's throe:
    "Sweet Deity, tell death to draw me deep
    Into the darkness where my heart lies low."
But Love, not understanding, turned to go
    And called for my lost lady down the steep,
    And made the hill re-echo with his woe.

From the Italian of Cino da Pistoia

SPRING

60 HEART, MY HEART

Heart, my heart, be not o'ershaken!
Bravely bear thy bitter fate!—
Suns of April surely wait
To restore what winter's taken!

And how much survives thy sorrow!
See how fair the world is yet!
Heart, my heart, fail not to set
Love's last hopes to meet the morrow!

From the German of Heinrich Heine

61 APRIL

Wav'ring remembrance of bright, far-off days
And spring scents moves me, like the fading face
Of buried beauty that with tears I trace
In baby features and their blue-eyed gaze.

Up from the past in flames of memory start
Passion-sweet midnights in the vanished years,
When mellow moonlight music filled our ears
And golden hair lay soft against my heart.

This is the message that this April morn
Has breathed upon me with the breath of spring
From far, familiar gardens, till forlorn

I falter as the shadows come across
That fugitive delight, and backward bring
The eternal poignancy of love and loss.

From the Catalan of Miquel S. Oliver

62 THE CUCKOO

The cuckoo's call rings loud and gay
Down Cuawg's vale at break of day:
For dawn demands a lavish melody.

By Cuawg stream the cuckoos sing
On blossomed branches of the spring;
Ah, let their full notes pour forth ceaselessly!

The cuckoos chant by Cuawg stream
Where spring's bright-blossomed branches gleam:
Their happy notes bring back the tears to me!

By Cuawg stream the cuckoo's song
Awakens memories doubly strong
Of one who hears no more their gaiety.

And while the clamorous cuckoos call
From ivied trunk and branches tall,
My heart renews its old, mute misery.

From the Old Welsh (Red Book of Hergest)

[445]

The lull of night is laid o'er lane and lea;
The wind is mute; but moonlight's minor key
Keeps faltering faint romances.
How strange on such a night to sit alone
When May is sweet and moonbeams' silver tone
Is tuned to elfin dances!

The lull of night is laid o'er lane and lea;
Low music murmurs, but the melody
I cannot quite discover.
It is a dream long dead that comes and goes,
A dream of vanished seasons, and a rose
Reft from a lonely lover.

And so my sorrow vibrates to earth's verge;
The farthest darkness echoes back the dirge
In stress of yearning shaken,
Sighing in pine-tree tops, in sallows sobbing . . .
Ah, God, on this May night how sorely throbbing
Is my sad heart forsaken!

From the Norwegian of Vilhelm Krag

64 A NIGHT IN MAY

Across the clearing sky the soft clouds go,
Slow-fading; thus
The sickle moon reaps their last sheaves of snow
Diaphanous.

They pass, and from the stars strange power of spring
Breathe down to bless
My heart in this vain earth with whispering
Of happiness.

But still the shades of time such visions blight;
As clouds, alas,
Into the vacant vastness of the night
We too shall pass.

From the Russian of Afanasi Fet

65 SPRING NIGHT

O gentle night, sweet night of spring,
Thy quiet spell enchants me still!
The soft May breezes, whispering
Of youth and love, my spirit fill.

How often on such nights the bay
Of friendly watch-dogs used to greet
My wooing footsteps to the gay
White cottage in the village street!

How light my feet, how light my heart!
How clear the carol that I sang
As I fulfilled the lover's part
And youth flamed bright without a pang!

Alas, young nights, nights far and fair,
Heaven of love, where have you fled?
My eyes are flooded with despair:
Harsh moon, ah hide thy mocking head!

Yet holy still to some is fate's
Twin happiness of love and youth;
But me a wifeless bed awaits—
Dark grief, for God's sake, show me ruth!

From the Slovene of Josip Stritar

66 TEARS OF SLEEP

Fair, fragrant morning, bring release from dreams
And drive the phantoms of my sleep away!
Dissolve my restless phantasies in day,
And cleanse my troubled mind from night's extremes!

For corpses, pale and wan as withered limes,
Have haunted the strange chaos of my brain:
Shades of mute Hecuba and all the slain
Sad sons of Priamus of olden times.

And there the mother, stricken beyond tears,
Made futile sacrifice without a moan
And hid her sorrow in her ancient breast.

[447]

But thou, my heart, that grief has turned to stone,
Hast wept in sleep for her, as dim appears
Stalactite-drip far down a cave's dark rest.

From the Romaic of I. N. Grypares

67 "PULSE OF MY HEART"

Before the sunrise, in the early dawn,
I watched her radiant grace upon the lawn,
    Her cheeks where flame and snow
    Strove and bade beauty blow,
Her slender body like a stream-girt swan—
Pulse of my heart, what shadow makes you slow?

Her voice was soft and gentle; not more sweet
Was Orpheus' tongue, that could wild beasts entreat;
    Her song was clear and low
    In that loved long ago,
Like dew-kissed meadows round our morning feet—
Pulse of my heart, what shadow makes you slow?

From the Erse of O'Carroll

68 DEATH, THE REAPER

Flowers in the flush of sunrise,
Starring the meadowy lawns,
Fresh in their fecund beauty,
Sweet in the dewy dawns,
Wither and waste in a moment
Cut by the scythe's keen knife;
Gay jewelled petals perish—
Emblems of human life.

Death is the master mower,
Swift is the scythe's fell sweep

Swung by his unseen fingers,
Reaper of all who reap.
Grasses and flowers together
Fall to him as he goes,
Ruthless to rank stalks ripening
And to the soft new rose.

From the Icelandic of Hallgrimur Petursson

69   MORNING

From wide, star-woven curtains
The heavens are released,
And the flusht dawn flings open
The portals of the east.

Forest and vale are flooded
With birds' melodious chant,
And mountains' echoes answer
In songs exuberant.

Fair as for birth or bridal,
All nature breathes with bloom—
And man takes blindly onward
One step more towards the tomb.

From the Rhaetoromanic of Gian Fadri Caderas

70   CLOUDS OF SILVER

Clouds of silver, clouds of silver
Ride and race and soar
On beyond the blue horizon
And return no more.

Fair they flash and gleam and glitter,
Laughing in the light,
And behind far golden portals
Vanish from the sight.

[449]

So bright days of perfect pleasure
Pass and disappear,
Leaving the cold hail of sorrow
To its task austere.

From the Finnish of Lauri Pohjanpää

71 ON THE OLD BRIDGE

Upon the old bridge, marred with moss
And lichens' red corrosion, here
Two whispering lovers leaned across:
    'Twas we, my dear!

He, urging tenderly his plea,
Laid all his life before her feet
And pledged her his fidelity:
    'Twas I, my sweet!

And she seemed hesitant and pale,
Trembled yet did not disapprove,
As listening to a far-off tale:
    'Twas you, my love!

On the old bridge two lovers pass
Once more to hold sweet rendez-vous.
He tells his love; she smiles: alas,
    Not, not we two!

From the French of Auguste Angellier

72 MAY ROSES

With the sweetest hours of May
Come the wild red roses;
Thick throughout the meadow-hay
Wine-bright bloom uncloses.

Yet my heart is sorrowing,
Full of grief unsleeping;
In a green hill-plot in spring
I have sat a-weeping.

For the tears I shed to-day
Fall upon the roses
That, in sweetest hours of May
One grave's grass encloses.

From the Dutch of Didericus Dorbeck

73   TO ADOLPHE GAIFFE

Sweet youth, with face sunlit and jolly,
Let not cold-reasoned melancholy
Extinguish thy delightful folly;

For it is wisdom. Love good wine,
Fair women, April days divine—
They are enough. The rest, decline.

Smile, even if black bereavement come!
And, when the gay primroses bloom,
Scatter their blossoms on the tomb.

For to the body lapped in clay
What message matters but to say
Love ruled indeed for one brief May?

"Let us seek truth in life's brief hours,"
Cry dull old men, with frown that lours.
Words! Empty words! Let us pick flowers!

From the French of Theodore de Banville

74   BY THE GRAVE OF THE COUNTESS POTOCKA

In pleasant gardens in the land of spring
You died, sweet rose! For memories of the past
Into your pure, soft-petalled bosom cast
The maggot of nostalgic suffering.

[*451*]

Thick through the northern sky a myriad stars
Mark a bright highway to the land you loved;
Ah, did your homesick eyes, that thither roved,
Burn that high path as you escaped life's bars?

I, too, am fated to an exile's end.
Strangers will lay me here in alien earth.
But when some wandering poet shall attend

Your grave with tribute in the tongue of home,
Dreaming some lonely lyric into birth,
My dust will wake and call to you to come

From the Polish of Adam Mickiewicz

75 "AS THE ROSE BLOSSOMS ON HER VERNAL SPRAY"

As the rose blossoms on her vernal spray
In the first flower of her beauty new,
Rivalling the heavens with her living hue
When watered with the dew at dawn of day;

Her petals breathing grace and loveliness
Perfume the garden-walks and orchard air,
But suddenly she dies in wan despair,
Extinguished by rough rain or sun's excess.

So in the freshness of your maidenhood,
While heaven and earth smiled in your happy eyes,
Fate crushed you down. Now at your grave I've stood

To bring as tearful tribute of past hours
This wreath of roses, that there may arise
Even from your dead lips the breath of flowers.

From the French of Pierre Ronsard

SUMMER

76 TO MEMORY

Spirit that wakest when the weary wind
Sleeps on the ocean and the moon is low,
Son of the silent night, serene and slow,
Thou art the sole soothsayer of my mind.

Faint as a far-off song thy light lip sighs,
Low as a lute and lingeringly sweet,
Lulling my fluttering bosom's fevered heat,
Laying thy peace upon my panic eyes.

Thou canst discern the dream that broke my rest,
Flooding the darkness with a fierce desire
To seek dead joys in ghosts of long ago;

Thou canst discern the sorrow of my breast,
Its nameless fester and consuming fire,
And thou alone canst heal its haggard woe.

From the Portuguese of Anthero de Quental

77 TO ISABEL

Ah, golden-haired young Isabel, I miss
Your cheek's red rose, the apple of your kiss,
And your soft, seraph mouth that used to greet
My homeward steps with music passing sweet.

Your mien was ever womanly and pure;
Like blushing fruit your countenance demure;
Your eyes, calm pools of peace and gentleness;
All sweet humility your shy address.

Your likeness was the swan upon the lin,
Like swan's-down the white softness of your skin,
Your breasts like snowy castles on a lea,
Your throat the sun, your flesh fair ivory.

The yellow ringlets of your braided hair
Were coiled and filleted with gracious care,
Plaited with ravishing yet simple art
Like strains of music to enchant my heart.

From the Gaelic of Duncan MacIntyre

78 HER PICTURE

O sweet familiar cheeks
And dear blue smiling eyes,
Face where each feature speaks
Of love 'neath happier skies,

Can you not change to flesh
By some mad, magic chance,
And put in words afresh
The message of that glance?

Ah, can you never tell
Glad things she used to say?—
Alas, I hear too well
Dead words of yesterday!

From the Norwegian of Theodor Kjerulf

79 A NAME

In an old note I found it—
The name my heart is keeping.
No mourning-border bound it,
But I fell to weeping.
Ah, I fell to weeping!

The hopes of happy hours
She wrote with heart up-leaping;
Her thoughts were sprays of flowers—
But I fell to weeping.
Ah, I fell to weeping!

That signature should settle
All sorrows into sleeping:
Each stroke a soft rose-petal—
But I fell to weeping.
Ah, I fell to weeping!

No cry from her was riven,
Only a promise sweeping,
Only a sweet pledge given—
But I fell to weeping.
Ah, I fell to weeping!

From the Magyar of Mihaly Szabolcska

80 HER FAITH

She lifts her eyes to the eternal stars,
Sincerely hoping down each fleeting doubt,
And still believing, against every fact,
That hidden in the sky's vast sterile tract
A living Spirit guards the worlds throughout.

She feels at every moment an abyss
Gaping beneath her as she works and prays—
A black abyss of gloom, a heaven of bliss,
A hell of shuddering, a gulf of grace—
And treads life's common pavement all her days
With a hushed reverence in her dreaming face.

From the Danish of Johannes Joergenson

81 HER INFLUENCE

Little star on which I gaze,
Tangled in the moon's mild rays,
In thy golden splendour strays
She whose loss makes dark my days.

Doubtless God desired to raise
Her to be in evening haze
Such a star to light our ways.
Yet my heart devoutly prays
That I may but reach the blaze
Where afar her spirit stays,
There but kiss her longed-for face,
Though thereafter fate conveys
Me to a more hateful place.
Teach, O teach me, thou, to praise
Love that conquers death's dismays,
Star of my life!

From the Old French

82 HER LEGACY

Sleep, little sons, my heart's delight!
Close little blue eyes to the night!
Silence broods on the churchyard hill;
Softly sleep, I'm beside you still.

Angels of God, whose loveliness
Is fair as yours, draw near to bless;
Gladly their gracious vigils keep,
Lulling your sorrows into sleep.

Life is all beauty to your eyes.
Sleep, little sons! too soon it flies,
Bringing the fate of human years,
Pillows that know not sleep but tears.

Hush, little sons, my heart's delight!
Love watches by you all the night.
While through the dark the clock's hand creeps,
My heart, that loves you, never sleeps.

From the Lithuanian of Rutu Lapelei

83   GRIEF

I saw a little child to-day
A child that sang about his play;
He hailed me straight, he came to me
And perched in pride upon my knee.

But, ah, what chokes my laugh with tears?
What grief comes calling down the years?
And how do present joys but fill
My cup of sorrow fuller still?

From an Estonian folk-song

84   FALLEN LARK

Sweet summer songster, fall'n from glad ascending,
Dead in the dust, your wings no more aspire.
"How did she come to die? What was her ending?"
I hear my children's lisping lips inquire.

High in the heaven you rose with chant unresting,
Seeking the raptured crown of love's endeavour,
And in the anguisht heights of that high questing
The body broke, the song was stilled forever.

From the Finnish of Veikko Antero Koskenniemi

85   GRIEF AT DAWN

When I behold the lark that soars
In fluttering joy athwart the sun,
And poised in lyric peace outpours
The rapture of a day begun,
The sight of his pure happiness
Makes my dark grief once more awake:
Ah, strange, that in such sore distress
My longing heart should fail to break!

Alas, how much I thought I knew
Of human pain—how much more now
When love has said its long adieu
And fruitless is each tender vow!
My joys were hers, we felt a free
Sweet love from others set apart;
And passing, she has left to me
Her memory and an aching heart.

From the Provençal of Bernart de Ventadorn

86 AFTER RAIN

Ah, how fair the sunlight seems
When the dark cloud passes!
Ah, what soothing fragrance streams
From the deep-drenched grasses!

Little birds in airy flight
Flit, forgetting showers;
Bury faces in delight
Deep in breasts of flowers.

All along the laughing brook,
Bees lurk through the clover;
But, for tears, I scarce can look—
My heart's day is over.

From the Serbo-Croatian of Jovan Grčić-Milenko

87 THE CLOUD

Last of the rain-king's retinue,
Alone thou marchest through the blue!
Alone thou darkenest our way!
Alone thou saddenest the day!

But, now, thy night shut heaven out;
Stern lightning wound its coils about;

Thy thunders shook the trembling hours,
And drenched the avid earth with showers.

Enough, begone! Thy time is sped.
The earth revives; the storm has fled;
And gay winds, tossing tree-tops high,
Expel thee from the placid sky.

From the Russian of Alexandr Sergeevich Pushkin

88   BROKEN PINES

The wind has rent the soaring pines
That towered by the ocean-side,
Reaching strong arms towards far sea-lines,
Cleft but unconquered in their pride.

"Thou breakest us, unpitying foe!
Yet hast not had the victory:
Horizon-yearning still, we throw
Hissed hate from every branch to thee!"

The shattered pines lie spent no more;
Wrought into ships they sail the sea;
Proud-breasted o'er the waves they soar,
Scorning the wind's dark perfidy:

"Fling howling billows, hateful foe!—
The terrors of thy tumult cease:
Thy strength could break us, yet we know
Through death a far, still dawn of peace."

From the Lettish of Janis Rainis

89   THE SAIL

A lone white sail on the blue sea soars,
Far away on the misty foam.
What is it seeking on far-off shores?
What has it left in the ports of home?

Over waves winging the wild winds shrill,
Making the wrack'd mast groan in stress.
Ah! It must look for wares of ill,
Nor was its last freight happiness.

But still before it the sea gleams blue;
Still on the sail shines the golden sun;
Still the defiant heart throbs true,
Fearless in faith as the gale is run.

From the Russian of Mikhail Yur'evich Lermontov

AUTUMN

90   EVENING PEACE

Be wise, my grief, and let your sobbing cease.
You asked for night: and now it darkens down
In grey enfolding shadows o'er the town,
Bringing to some pale care, to others peace.
    And while the common multitude of men
Beneath the lash of pitiless excess
Sow their remorse in weak licentiousness,
Give me, my grief, thy hand; come hither then,
    Far from their path. See how the dead years lean
In faded garments from the galleried sky,
And glad regrets rise from the watery deep;
    Beneath the vault, the sick sun sinks to die,
And, like a long shroud drawn in grief between,
Comes the soft silence of the night, and sleep.

From the French of Charles Baudelaire

91   THE BURDEN OF THE NIGHT

Weary, beyond the crest
Of mountains in the west,
The sun sinks down to slumber,
While in the darkening blue

The light comes glimmering through
Of star-eyes without number.

Earth's features fade away,
And colours of the day
Are swallowed up in shadows;
Silent the marsh-bird flits
In sleepy search of its
Soft nest among the meadows.

Now the returning night
Has touched us with its blight
Of grief too deep for tears:
Man, whom the fates shall kill,
Must first with groans fulfil
Life's black predestined years.

But slumber breaks the blow
That else would overthrow
The shaken heart of sorrow;
Through the still hours of sleep
Returning life-tides creep
And rally towards the morrow.

From the Catalan of Emili Guanyavents

92   FIAT NOX

Now let night's still extinction lend release
To those who sat in sorrow through the day
And felt that all life's cares around them lay
Like billows of grey universal seas.

Noon was a sultry torment; tears' increase
Made morning seem a century away:
Ah, night, sow thy cool shadows soon, I pray,
And hush my restless heart in drowsy peace.

My spirit has consumed itself in strife
And futile brooding over passion's stress,
The tears of loss, the galling chains of life.

But see, the night and nothingness draw near,
Deep yawns the gulf of dark forgetfulness,
And gladly into silence we fall sheer.

From the Finnish of Veikko Antero Koskenniemi

93 WANDERER'S EVENSONG

Over all peaks slow peace
Descends;
In every branch the breeze
Now ends
Its sighing sweep.
The birds in the wildwood are sleeping.
Cease, heart, thy weeping!—
Thou, too shalt sleep.

From the German of Johann Wolfgang von Goethe

94 TWILIGHT

The mountains sleep;
Ridge and ravine and valley lie a-dream;
In earth's dark seam
The writhing reptile slumbers; and the gleam
Of feral eyes grows drowsy down the steep;
Bee-murmurings cease;
Over the blue brine comes release
For slow sea-monsters, and to birds surcease
Of stress for fluttering pinions in forgetful peace.

From the Greek of Alcman

95 IN A CEMETERY

Elusive melodies of lips long dead,
Long since dissolved to cemetery dust
And the damp exhalations of their bed,
Blow from the graves in soothing tones of trust.

Sad, quiet strains of deep tranquillity
Falter and tremble to the dying sun,
Falter and tremble o'er the dewy lea
In haunting harmonies of days long done.

From the Czech of Jaroslav Havlicek

96 AUTUMN SONG

Flame forth, pale hidden moon
Behind the dark clouds shining
And lighting them with silver lining!
For all the river-rushes breathe a plaintive tune
And night-winds are repining.

Another night in autumn haunts my heart:
Across the waves is bound
A belt of golden beams that dart
From the bright moon; along the languid stream,
The wind soothes sedges into slumber sound;
And swaying rushes seem
To make faint hidden harp-strings fitfully resound;
Low lisper
A-whisper,
The wind croons to the drowsy reeds around.

Flame forth, pale hidden moon
Behind the dark clouds shining
And lighting them with silver lining!
For all the river-rushes breathe a plaintive tune
And night-winds are repining.

From the Finnish of Yrjö Weijola

97 NOCTURNE

The windmill's pinions no longer flutter,
The river mirrors the eyes of night,
Soft flower-lips their orisons utter,
Tree-tops whisper in hushed delight.

[463]

Priests now kindle their tapers pale,
Grey-robed sisters meek vespers sing,
Kneeling children fold fingers frail,
Swans hide their bills in a snowy wing.

Soon comes rest to all the weary,
Heavy heads are pillowed deep;
All released from their grey griefs dreary,
Slumber and sleep and dream and sleep.

From the Norwegian of Sigbjörn Obstfelder

98 "ALL TIRED THINGS"

All tired things of earth now find
    Relief in sleep,
While gently the great shepherd wind
    Herds home his sheep.

All through the day he drove them far,
    From east to west,
And now behind the star-fold bar
    Brings them to rest.

In silence from the sight are borne
    The snow-fleeced flock;
And the great shepherd drops his horn,
    Lays down his stock.

Softly he bars the skyey gate,
    With drowsy croon,
While o'er the bridge of heaven strides late
    The watchman-moon.

Light flooded all the moorlands lie,
    Slumbering and still,
Save for the dark waves' stifled sigh
    Beneath the hill.

All tired things of earth now find
    Relief in sleep,
For the great shepherd of all living kind
    Has lodged his sheep.

From the Danish of L. C. Nielsen

Hush, my heart, the sun sinks restward;
    Drowsy cattle seek the town;
From the crimson heath to westward
Solemn storks drop softly nestward—
    Hush, my heart, the sun goes down!

Silence steals across the lea,
    Silence floods the highway; none
But a belated humble-bee,
Murmuring, mars tranquillity—
    Peace, my heart, the day is done!

Lapwings haste in lonely flight
    O'er the wold to seek their nest;
Mid the matted leaves alight;
Fold their pinions for the night—
    Hush, my heart, you, too, shall rest!

Far-off eastward windows blaze,
    Sunlit, into crimson clear;
Moorland tarns in twilight haze
Mirror back the failing rays—
    Peace, my heart, the night is here!

From the Danish of Jeppe Aakjaer

L'ENVOI

100 A MAN'S LAST WORD TO A WOMAN

I followed, flushed with hope, thy path of roses
In springtime's radiant dawn and showery stress;

The record of our summer love discloses
Noontides of passion past all power of guess;

And in the autumn gloom, when the act closes,
I give thee thanks, who wert my happiness.

From the Swedish of Verner von Heidenstam

From The North American Book of Icelandic Verse

THE BALLAD OF THRYM

Thor was wild when he awoke
For he missed his mighty hammer;
Shook his beard, and tossed his brow,
And felt about him in his fury.
This the speech that first he spoke:
"Hearken, Loki, hear an outrage
Yet unheard-of in earth or heaven;
Thieves have stolen Thor's great hammer."

They went to beauteous Freyja's bower.
This the speech that first he spoke:
"May I have your suit of feathers
As a help to find my hammer?"

Freyja speaks:

"I would give it were it gold;
Grant it, even if 'twere silver.

Then Loki flew and the feather-suit whirred,
Till he left behind the home of the gods
And reached the distant realm of the giants.
On a mound sat Thrym, the giants' master,
Braiding halters of gold for his hounds
And trimming the heavy manes of his horses.

Thrym speaks:

"How do the gods fare? How do the elves fare?
Why come you alone to the land of the giants?"

Loki speaks:

"The gods fare ill. The elves fare ill.
Pray, have you hidden the Thunderer's hammer?"

Thrym speaks:

"Yes, I have hidden the Thunderer's hammer
Eight miles down in the depths of the earth.

No man shall bring it back to its place
Unless he fetches me Freyja as wife."

Then Loki flew and the feather-suit whirred,
Till he left behind the home of the giants
And reached the distant realms of the gods.
Thor it was greeted him at the gate:
"Have you tidings for all your toil?
Tell me now your news from the sky,
For he that sits often trips in his story,
And one lain down often deals in lies."

Loki speaks:

"Yes, I have tidings for all my toil.
The king of the giants is keeping your hammer,
And no man may bring it back to its place
Unless he fetches him Freyja as wife."

They went to beauteous Freyja's bower,
And this was the speech that first he spoke:
"Bind on, Freyja, your bridal-veil.
We two must ride to the realm of the giants."
Freyja was wroth and snorted with rage;
The hall of the gods was shaken greatly;
She burst the necklace the dwarfs had braided:
"Sure I would look the most lustful of women
If I rode with you to the realms of the giants."

Then straightway the gods together met
And all of the goddesses gathered in council;
The great ones plotted a plan to find
By which to get hold of the Thunderer's hammer.
Then up spake Heimdall, the whitest of gods,
Wise he was like the other Wanes:
"Let us bind on Thor the bridal-veil;
Let him bear the necklace the dwarfs have braided;
Let house-keys rattle around his waist,
And petticoats billow about his knees;
Fasten brooches upon his breast,
And tie a bonnet about his brows."

But doughty Thor made haste to differ:
"Surely the gods would think me shamed
If I were bound with a bridal-veil!"

Then answered Loki, the son of Laufey:
"Tarry, and say not so, O Thor!
For the giants will dwell in the gods' domain
Unless you have your hammer back."

Then they bound on Thor the bridal-veil;
And gave him the beads that the dwarfs had braided;
Let house-keys rattle around his waist,
And petticoats billow about his knees;
Fastened brooches upon his breast,
And tied a bonnet about his brows.

Then up spoke Loki, the son of Laufey:
"I will go in a bridesmaid's guise;
We two shall ride to the realms of the giants."

Then goats were brought with the greatest speed
And hitched to the shafts for a hasty journey.
The rocks were rent and the hot earth reeked
In Thor's mad ride to the giants' realm.

Then muttered Thrym, the giants' master:
"Stand up, giants, and strew the benches!
They bring me Freyja to be my wife,
The daughter of Njord from Noatun.
I keep in my stables gold-horned kine
And jet-black oxen, the joy of giants;
Gems are mine, and treasured jewels;
I lack for nothing but Freyja's love."

Early that evening the bride-guests entered.
Ale was brought of the giants' brew.
Thor swallowed an ox and several salmon;
Ate all the sweets set aside for the women;
And then guzzled down three casks of grog.
Then muttered Thrym, the giants' master:
"Who ever saw bride that bit so boldly!
I never saw bride with a broader bite
Or a maid that drank so deeply of mead!"

The wily bridesmaid was sitting by,
And found response to the giant's speech:
"Freyja for eight long days has fasted,
Yearning to lie in the land of the giants."

Then he peered 'neath the veil, for he panted for kisses;
But backwards he lurched the length of the hall:
"Why are Freyja's eyes so fearful,
For they flash with flames of burning fire?"

Then the wily bridesmaid, sitting by,
Found response to the giant's speech:
"For eight long nights she has slumbered not,
Through yearning to lie in the land of the giants."

In came the giant's agèd sister,
Begging bold for a bridal-fee:
"Take off your rings of reddest gold
If you would win my willing love."

Then muttered Thrym, the giants' master:
"Bring me the hammer to hallow the bride!
Let Mjollnir lie on the maiden's knee
That Vor may bless our marriage vows."

Thor's heart bounded in his bosom
As he held his iron hammer.
First he maced the giants' master;
Then he crushed his crew of fellows,
Smashed the giants to a jelly;
Slew the giant's agèd sister
Who had begged a fee of bridal;
Gave her "pounds" instead of pennies,
Hammer-strokes instead of bracelets.

Thus did Thor regain his thunder.

Translated from the Old Norse (Anonymous)

THE BALLAD OF TRISTRAM

Tristram against the heathen hound
   The battle set;
Many a man got bloody wounds
   When there they met.—
To the lovers it was shapen but to sunder.

Back was he borne upon a shield,
    That brave young knight;
Many a leech sought leave to heal
    His body's blight.

But all their leechcraft he refused
    And swore a vow;
"Only Iseult, that lady fair,
    May heal me now!"

Tristram sends his messengers
    And three men leap:
"O go and tell Iseult the Fair
    My wounds are deep."

Tristram sends his messengers;
    Five take his plea:
"O go and tell Iseult the Fair
    To come to me."

"And bid her as I shall command
    Prepare her trip:
Let all the sails be dyed with blue
    Upon her ship."

His messengers to Cornwall came
    O'er waters dim:
"Young Tristram, lady, bids you come
    To visit him."

Then went Iseult into the hall
    And sought the king:
"O may I not to this knight, thy friend,
    Some healing bring?"

The king made answer in angry wise
    And stern did say:
"He spurns the healing of all the rest:
    He must be fey."

Iseult the Fair with softest speech
    Pled piteously;
Her arms about the monarch's neck
    Made earnest plea.

"I'd gladly let thee heal this knight
    Of his sore wound,
Could I but know thou wouldst return
    Both safe and sound."

"With God must rest my safe return,"
    The lady quoth.
"I may not in this journey now
    Forget my troth."

She cast on her a sable fur
    With sigh and tear;
Then went the jewelled lady out
    Upon the pier.

"I must as Tristram did command
    Prepare my trip,
And let the sails be all of blue
    Upon my ship."

They wound the sails as the lady bade
    To the masthead high;
To Tristram she will not fail to come,
    So like to die.

Iseult the Dark went from the hall,
    And said not true:
"Black are the sails upon the ship
    Instead of blue."

Into the hall Iseult the Dark
    Returned once more:
"Black are the sails upon the ship
    That nears the shore."

Tristram turned his face to the wall,
    And naught he spake.
Three miles away a man might hear
    That great heart break.

They brought the blue-sailed ship to shore
    On the cold black sand;
Retainers bore Iseult the Fair
    The first to land.

Long was the way they had to walk;
   The road was wide;
But ever she heard the sound of bells
   That clanged and cried.

Long was the way they had to walk;
   It marred the feet;
And ever she heard the sound of bells
   And chanting sweet.

Then said Iseult, the lady fair
   From o'er the foam;
"Tristram, alas, should not be dead
   When I come home."

Iseult came into the solemn church
   With a hundred men;
The priests were chanting their last farewell
   O'er his body then.

Iseult o'er his coffined body bent,
   Like a rose-bud bright;
The silent priests in the chancel stood
   By candle-light.

Iseult o'er his coffined body bent;
   Scarce seemed alive;
The silent priests in the chancel stood
   With candles five.

Many a heart in this weary world
   With woe is fed.
Iseult o'er his coffined body bent,
   And lay there dead.

The bitter soul of Iseult the Dark
   With grief was torn.
Two bodies then from the ivied church
   Were straightway borne.

Iseult the Dark in anger spoke,
   And took her troth:
"If I can help it, death shall fail
   To join them both!"

Hastily, quickly they were laid
   Beneath the mould;
To north and south of the church they lie
   Alone and cold.

And from their graves two birches grow
   That mutely strain
Across the roof of that dark church
   To meet, in vain.—
To them it was not shapen but to sunder.

From 14th century Icelandic

REMEMBRANCE

Though you have trodden in travel
All the wide tracts of the earth,
Bear yet the dreams of your bosom
Back to the land of your birth,
Kin of volcano and floe-sea!
Cousin of geyser and steep!
Daughter of downland and moorland!
Son of the reef and the deep!

High over heaven and landscape,
Haunting your thought as it strays,
Torrents and towering summits
Tremble once more to your gaze.
Far in the outermost ocean
The isle of your heart is awake,
Shining in shadowless summer,
Showered with light for your sake.

Vivid that Icelandic vision
Viewed in your dreams as they run—
Granite rocks growing with flowers,
Glaciers warm in the sun,
O kin of volcano and floe-sea,
Cousin of geyser and steep,
Daughter of downland and moorland,
Son of the reef and the deep.

From the Icelandic of Stephan G. Stephansson (1853–1927)

I SAIL IN THE FALL

I

Summer is dying, is dying,
 And cold is the breath of fall.
The waves are beginning to labour
 And beat on the ocean-wall.
The leaves are blown from the branches.
 The children have frost-reddened lips.
The birds are departing. Keen strain at
   their cables
 The storm-hearted ships.
I yield to a mighty power.
 I am drawn by a hidden hand.
And the sea—the sea is calling
 In tones I cannot withstand.
I am the bird that passes,
 The ship that the tempests blow.
My song is a song of parting.
 I came, and I go.

II

The storm leads away from harbour.
 Surf beats the ocean-wall.
I came from the south in summer
 And sail in the fall.
Prayers cannot hope to hold me.
 I hack through the holiest ties—
Abandon the woman I worship,
 The land of my boyhood skies.
I turn from the ship a moment
 To speak the farewells I owe.
But my song is a song of parting.
 I came, and I go.

III

I envy all that can scorn thee,
 Thou wave-driving wind of the deep!—

The sun that glitters in glory,
 And the lands that lie asleep;
The peaks in their crystal beauty,
 Silent and heaven-high;
And the sphinx that keeps its secret
 While the myriad years go by.

IV

I am borne by breeze and billow
 From land on to land.
I ask not the people for praises
 Or honoring hand.
I long to be blest with friendship,
 But am everywhere ever alone,
Ever a man without country,
 A vagrant in every zone.
But my song is a song of parting.
 Surf beats the ocean-wall.
I came from the south in summer
 And sail in the fall.

From the Icelandic of David Stefánsson (1895–1964)

From The Magyar Muse

A FLAG

Just a stick and some linen,
Yet not stick and linen
But a flag.

Ever it speaks.
Ever it waves.
Ever it is restless.
Ever in unconsciousness
Above the street
It soars aloft,

Untorn in the sky,
And proclaims something
Eagerly.
If men grow used to it and heed it not,
If they slumber also
By day and by night,
So that it is wholly wasted away
And stands, like a gaunt apostolic orator,
On the peak of the roof,
Still, alone,
Wrestling with the calm and the storm,
Fruitlessly, ceaselessly, ever majestically
It waves,
And speaks.

My soul, be thou too, thou too—
Not stick and linen—
But a flag.

From the Magyar of Dezsö Kosztolányi (1885–1936)

THE VICTOR

The loot the legions sent embraced these three:
Treasure, and slaves, and slips of cherry-tree.

The treasure sank like mercury from sight
Amid the orgies of the city's night.

The slaves were slain to make a holiday
With blood and flame and gladiatorial fray;

Or nail'd to crosses by the highway's side
In endless choking lines they writh'd and died.

But still, across the gardens, fires of spring
Burst from the cherry-tree's white burgeoning,

Until my little son in wonder stands:
"Ah, pretty, pretty!" And he claps his hands.

From the Magyar of Louis Aprily (1887–   )

FOR JUST ONE NIGHT

Send them along for just one bloody night—
Your zealous heroes spoiling for a fight.
For just one bloody night:
Their former boasts within our memories ring
As rending shells of shrapnel scream and sing,
As mists of strangling poison slowly rise,
And leaden swallows swoop across the skies.

Send them along for just one bloody night—
Your men of gross, gargantuan appetite.
For just one bloody night:
When thundering cannon start their revishment,
And red Earth groans with belly gouged and rent,
And bursting bullets break in glittering hate,
And ancient Vistula flows red in spate.

Send them along for just one bloody night—
The money-sucking leech, the parasite.
For just one bloody night:
When shell-volcanoes' fire the mud upheaves
And flings torn bodies eddying like leaves.
To crumbling earth the crisping corpses thresh,
Mere blacken'd heaps of bones instead of flesh.

Send them along for just one bloody night—
The unbeliever and the uncontrite.
For just one bloody night:
When hell's hot jaws in paroxysm expand
And vomit blood and horror on the land.
In tatter'd tents, the wounded pass from life,
And sigh across the wind: "my son . . . my wife . . ."

Send them along for just one bloody night—
The patriots of the tongue, of speech and spite,
For just one bloody night:
That, as the blinding star-shells leap the dark,
And cheeks reflect the terror of their spark,
And reeking mists are made of Magyar gore,
They may scream out in tears: "My God, no more!"

Send them along for just one bloody night—
That they may call their mothers in their fright.
For just one bloody night:
That they may cower low in fear and cold
And grovelling gasp their guilt so manifold;
That they may rend their clothes, and beat their breasts,
And cry: "My Christ, what are thy dread behests?"

My Christ, what dost thou ask? My blood demands
That they shall vow to cleanse their greedy hands
Which now oppress these lands:
That brazen infidels who blindly trod
May trust in Christ and put their faith in God,
And never more the Magyar nation blight.
—Send them along for just one bloody night!

From the Magyar of Géza Achim Gyóni (1884–1917)

WHAT BECAME OF CHRIST'S BLOOD

When the Roman soldier thrust
His sharp spear in, and through His back
Out came the cold steel, pushing and tearing
The red shreds of His heart;
When the beating stopp'd
And the Blood flow'd:
Oh tell me, for the love of God,—
What became of that Blood?

 —No doubt the dry sand drank it in,
 Just drank it in,
 As is its manner with all other fluids.

But yet He was the Son of God,
And on His shoulders rested
The starry vault of heaven!

 —The earth, it is not enthusiastic,
 The earth does not bother with the clouds,
 The earth is not enthusiastic about anything,
 But just drinks, just drinks the Blood,
 Drinks, drinks the Blood!

From the Magyar of Pál Gulyás (1899–1944)

THE LOST HORSEMAN

One hears the sound of the blind galloping
Of a lost horseman from the long ago,
And echoing hearts of vanish'd forests ring,
And ancient marshes waken, full of woe.

Where here and there the coppices are choked
With ancient thicket, and the brake is rife,
From winters' tales of long ago invoked,
Unnumber'd spectres, rouse to sudden life.

Here is the thicket, here the coppice lies,
Here is the dull, old tune the wraiths pursue,
Here in the deaf, white mists there swells and dies
Sad martial music that our grandsires knew.

Weird to our eyes grows Autumn; fewer yet
Are men in number; and across the plain,
Whose dreary leagues the dreary hill beset,
Encloaked in fog, November comes again.

Half-naked is this prairie, where persist
Only the rotting marsh, the leafless trees;
Here, in the murk of the November mist,
There lurk the ghosts of by-gone centuries.

What blood outpour'd, how many mysteries,
What ancestry and impulse here must lie!
What forests and what marshes before these!
What gallant madmen in the years gone by!

A straying horseman from the long ago
Takes a strange road o'ergrown with brush and blight,
But there's no spark, no ray of lamp a-glow,
Nor trace of any village in the night.

The villages are lapt in silent sleep;
Coldly they dream of other times and cares;
And from the foggy forest rush and leap
Wolves, bisons, and infuriated bears.

One hears the sound of the blind galloping
Of a lost horseman from the long ago,
And echoing hearts of vanish'd forests ring,
And ancient marshes waken, full of woe.

From the Magyar of Endre Ady (1877–1919)

THE SORROWING HUSBAND

In Szatmár there's a little inn,
A wife named Trézsi lived within:
Dark-eyed, with midnight in her hair,
And round of limb, surpassing fair.
But she, though beautiful, is curst;
Her rosy lips for quarrels thirst.
One day she'd just begun to scold,
Abuse, and beat both young and old;
Her husband crouch'd, expecting harm,
When from without came the alarm:
"Here come the Tartars!"
People in horror run and hide,
But Trézsi pertly steps outside;
She's not afraid of any male,
Not least when tongues may turn the scale.
The flame of battle's in her cheeks;
Quick heave her bosom's snowy peaks;
An ugly Tartar, full of ire,
Comes, loot in heart and eyes on fire;
Fair Trézsi suits his taste, of course;
He wastes no time, but spurs his horse,
Picks up the woman by the waist
And throws her on his horse in haste;
Then gallops off; and, fiercely gay,
Gloats often over this his prey.
The grieving husband lingers on,
And gazing after her that's gone,
He sorrows as from sight they pass,
And wrings his hands, and sighs: "Alas,
Poor Tartar!"

From the Magyar of Károly Kisfaludy (1788–1830)

[480]

From Canadian Overtones (1935)

FRAGMENTS FROM "EN ROUTE"

I

By prairie and slough-side the train that we rode
  Drove ever relentlessly north.
To our left the great River lay turbid and red
  And sprawled itself sullenly forth.
Its breast never quickened in rapid or fall,
  Its dull, heavy waters were fain
To waddle forever with arms full of mud
  And the slummocky clay of the plain.
The landscape unchanged and unchangeable stood,
  Save only where dryads of grace
Had woven on edges of wandering brooks
  A leafy embroid'ry of lace;
But the land itself lay like an infinite board,
  Unslivered, unknotted and clean,
As if all of the stuff of Creation were smoothed
  And stained an ineffable green.

III

(The prairies by night)
Out on the platform that coupled the cars,
  I drank-in the night-air alone;
For drugged in the thick, heavy vapours within,
  Each passenger sat like a stone.
On through the vastness and darkness the train
  Kept ever its shadowy way,
With no halt in the heat of its thunderous haste,
  No hesitant falter nor stay.
Far out in the infinite vault of the sky,
  The stars in their courses looked on
To mock the machine and its stertorous breath
  With flames that for eons had shone.

But the prairies flowed by like an ebony sea
  Of boundless and billowless black,
Where our train, a long Doomship, with belly of fire,
  Sought Asgard with death in its track.

From the Icelandic of Stephan G. Stephansson (1853–1927)

THE OLD HOUSE

Wasted by time and every sort of weather,
Still on its old foundation-stones it stands,
Deep scarr'd on sides and gables altogether
As with the gnarl of aged cheeks and hands;
Its roof-tree grey with countless nights of frost,
The sills on which it totters warp'd or lost.

Still streams the sunlight through the broken sashes,
As bright and gay as in the years now gone;
Age has not turned that old content to ashes
Nor cancelled days on which a glad sun shone.
Still through its southern door, though shatter'd, sing
From radiant skies the breezes of the spring.

Visions borne thither from the vast, far distance
Throng to my eyes, with never a hint of pain;
As in a dream of earlier existence,
Friends who are dead are standing here again;
And old fidelity, old laughter, grace
With holy peace the long deserted place.

As on a monument, there here is written,
Plain to my gaze, an epitaph of hope:
Body and spirit might with care be smitten—
I read it in worn plank and floor a-slope—
But through the darkness of despair and dearth
Shone ever the clear flame of love on earth.

Life, warm and true, abounded in the fulness
Of heart's affection linking friend to friend,
For joy in small things bridged the deeps of dulness
And even death gave speech no palsied end:

In darkest hours, a helping hand or word
Guided to peace a spirit sadly stirr'd.

Here where the land lay empty to the westward,
Fronting the crimson tents of evening light,
We watch'd the sun down stairs of fire turn restward
And pause upon the threshold of the night;
There to embrace the earth before he pass'd
In gentle radiance to his place at last.

Cherish'd remembrance and dilapidation
Brood with join'd hands in this deserted spot;
Old dreams, old memories, without cessation
Roam through these haunts the heart has ne'er forgot;
While, through burst panes, there beckons from the west
That evening sunshine that They loved the best.

My heart grows strangely warm whene'er I wander
Beside this house I knew so well of yore;
And oft could vow, however much I ponder,
That time stood still, that at this empty door
I linger listening to glad words of trust
From lips that now are silent in the dust.

From the Icelandic of Kristinn Stefánsson (1856–1916)

THE CARE OF THE BEES

Honey-bees of my high ideals
Have I imprisoned in this my winter,
Night and day in the chilling darkness
Down in the cellar beneath my spirit.

Honey had grown too hard to gather.
Ghastly and pallid, the flowers had withered;
Burdensome snowdrifts had bent them under:
Blizzards lay deep on my fields and orchard.

Honey-bees of my high ideals
Had to wait for my life's warm summer.
Freely they'd rouse at the first spring sunshine,
Fly from the cellar beneath my spirit.

[483]

Then they would cling to the fragrant clover,
Clammy cells of exceeding sweetness,
Harvesting honey of praise and honour,
Happy in breezes of golden springtime.

Spring came at last, but the lingering winter
Levell'd its snows on the frozen farmlands.
Ere the fields were ploughed and planted,
Pinching hunger assailed their vitals.

Time went by, and I raised the trap-door,
Took to the ladder and sought the cellar.
Stygian voices I heard distinctly
Stir in the subterranean darkness.

Savage hunger and sullen rancour
Sang in the clouds of that dim inferno;
Borne from the depths like a blast of brimstone
Buzz'd the rage of their venomous cursing.

Bees that were pang'd to the point of murder
Prick'd at my flesh in the soul's deep shadows;
Stabb'd me in rage and install'd their poison;
Stung, I scream'd like a wolf half-scalded.

Scars are my due till my day is over,
Deep-sunk eyes and a throat all swollen.
Loathsome I feel in my mutilation,
Less like a man than a fallen angel.

From the Icelandic of Guttormur Guttormsson (1878–   )

THE CLOSE OF SUMMER

Funeral tollings are heard to-day,
Murmuring coldly through woods a-sway,
    Swept by the winds of ocean.
The skies in the mourning of grief are drest,
All haggard and wan with a wild unrest
    And a heavy heart's commotion.

[484]

The beacons of summer are burning out—
Flaming birches are put to rout
   In the waves of the wind's deep thunder.
Its organ-tones of autumnal Doom
Announce the coming of frost and gloom
   To trample the pale leaves under.

Sorrowing ever, the human race,
That seek in vain for a resting-place,
   Waver in that pale hour;
Their eyes are glassy with doubt that grieves,
And they read their fate in the yellow leaves
   That fall in a drifting shower.

All things pass with expiring breath,
Songs of the future and songs of death
   Blend in the doomsday weather;
The strange, vast drift of the autumn sky,
The sighing plains, and the hill-tops high,
   And the dead trees, march together. . . .

From the Icelandic of Einar Páll Jónsson (1881–1958)

IN WARTIME

In Europe's reeking slaughter-pen
They mince the flesh of murdered men,
While swinish merchants, snout in trough,
Drink all the bloody profits off!

From the Icelandic of Stephan G. Stephansson (1853–1927)

From A Golden Treasury of Polish Lyrics

TO HIS LADY

Thy name, sweet lady, that my glad lips love,
That my pen joys to celebrate in rhyme,
Shall in my lines a lasting honour prove
And proud preëminence in future time.

Should men high porphyry in tribute raise
In sculptured grace, adorn'd with molten gold,
To give your worth and beauty fitting praise,
Yet would the lustre of that work grow old.
Nor pillar nor Egyptian monument
Can ward off ineluctable decay,
For fire and deluge all their rage will vent
And time's harsh envy waste their stones away.
Only my deathless verse your fame uprears
Above the rapine and the wreck of years.

From the Polish of Jan Kochanowski (1530–84)

CLEAR MATUTINAL LIGHT . . .

Clear matutinal light
And cool nocturnal shade,
Come, chant omnipotent your deep devotion!
Praise God, thou mountain height,
For all that He has made;
Praise Him ye fields and forests, streams and ocean!
For Master of all motion
In fountain or in flower,
He grants the bud its rainbow grace,
The crystal spring its sparkling face,
Yet shuts and opens heaven by His power,
And, vast and awful, hath
Drawn us to Him, remembering not His wrath.

From the Polish of Sebastjan Grabowiecki (1540–1607)

TO HIS MISTRESS

Your sweet eyes are not eyes, but radiance of the sun
Before whose dazzling light all reason is undone;

Your sweet lips are not lips, but coral, soft and red,
That binds our every sense with bonds of crimson thread.

Your sweet breasts are not breasts, but shapes divinely bright
That capture our warm will in fetters of delight.

Thus reason, sense and will are slaves to the behests
Of light and hue and form in eyes and lips and breasts.

From the Polish of Andrzej Morsztyn (1613–93)

LIBERTY

Straiten'd am I, O Lord, upon a pillar
Of lonely pride, with scarcely room to stand:
Stiff as a corpse long cabin'd in a coffin
    Are neck and knee and hand.

Beyond all else I thirst for greater freedom.
With prairies broad, I pray, my feet endow:
That I may kneel, and in the dust before Thee
    Press homage with my brow.

From the Polish of Leopold Staff (1878–1942)

From The Rhaetoromanic Tradition

THE MARCH OF THE DEAD

I dream'd a dream; I seem'd to wait
In some wild spot where all things wept;
The face of earth was grey as fate;
Grey clouds along the sky-line slept.

And through the midst of that dim land
There march'd in vision endless hosts—
With pallid brow I stood and scann'd
A dark processional of ghosts.

Their visages were veil'd, but still
Like gold beneath black silk did dwell

[487]

Mysterious eyes, ablaze yet chill
With agonizing hints of hell.

They pass'd before me like a breath,
Their glittering glance was cold and dry—
As indefinable as death
That gazes from a dead man's eye.

At last I woke in broken tears,
Unable to endure their tread,
And sadly saw my human years
Pass darkly like the marching dead.

From the Romansch of Peder Lansel

From A Scald in Canada

LUKE 16: 22

A widower read long in Holy Writ,
Then sent aloft a frantic prayer-o-gram:
"I'd rather that my wife in hell should sit
Than warm the bosom of old Abraham!"

From the Icelandic of Guttormur J. Guttormsson (1878–   )

From Poems by Adam Mickiewicz

TO MY RUSSIAN FRIENDS

Do ye remember me? When musing traces
    My friends' deaths, banishments, and baffled schemes,
Ye also gather, and your foreign faces
    Have right of citizenry in my dreams.

Where are ye now? Ryleyev's noble shoulders
  That once I clasped, now by the tsar's decree
Hang slowly rotting where a gibbet moulders;
  A curse on folk that murder prophecy! . . .

If far to northward, from a new, free nation,
  These sad songs come to you on soaring wing,
Above your land of icy desolation
  They'll herald freedom, as the storks the spring.

Ye'll know my voice! For while I was in fetters,
  I duped the despot, crawling like a snake,
But shared my thoughts with you, who as abettors
  Shielded my dovelike frankness, for my sake.

Now to the world I pour this poisoned chalice—
  A bitter tale sucked forth from burning veins;
My country's blood and tears compound its malice;
  Let it corrode—not you, friends, but your chains! . . .

From the Polish of Adam Mickiewicz (1798–1855)

From The Quebec Tradition

THE WORKER IN THE FIELDS

Behind two oxen or two heavy horses,
The man walks, stooping, in the lonely field;
His great hands, clasped upon the handles, wield
The plough that rends the earth with channeled courses.

Beneath a green hill drench'd in sunlight holy,
His eyes fix'd on the soil his labours hallow,
Drunk with the heavy fragrance of the fallow,
He draws his furrows peacefully and slowly.

Dreaming, he sometimes smiles. Perhaps he hears
In fancy a great sea of golden ears,
Wheat ripening on this soil that he has trod;

He sees his barn, in fancy, cramm'd with wheat,
He dreams an angel guards his plodding feet,
And that his task collaborates with God.

From the French of William Chapman (1850–1917)

BEFORE TWO PORTRAITS OF MY MOTHER

Painted in days when she was but a lass,
In this old portrait is my mother seen
With brow of lily white and glance serene
As dazzling as a bright Venetian glass!

And here, my mother is no more the same:
Wrinkles have scored the marble of her brows;
Gone is the grace of days when maiden vows
Like merry carols at her marriage came.

And so to-day with sorrow I compare
That brow joy-halo'd and that brow of care—
The sun, and mists at setting of the years.

But a strange mystery my spirit grips:
How is it I can smile at those pale lips?
And at that face that smiles, why gush my tears?

From the French of Emile Nelligan (1882–1941)

HYMN TO THE NORTH WIND

North Wind, my country's wind from fairyland,
Who blowest most by night, and by whose hand,
After the sun to other skies has fled,
The milky blizzard o'er the ground is spread;
O monster of the fierce, blue sky, whose roars
Stir us as in cathedrals when up-soars
A trumpet at the raising of the Host;
Thou eagle, deafened on the Hudson coast
Amid the slavering growls of Polar bears;
Sublime adventurer of the stellar airs,

Where thou art driving far foul Evil's scent;
O thou whose shouting shocks a continent,
And by whose mighty breath the stars are stirred;
Who rendest trees like garments by thy word;
Vandal and modeller of dazzled sites,
Giving my land the grace of starry nights,
I sing thy heart, which none can comprehend.

Thou o'er the dead a cloak of snow dost send,
So that the charnel's memories of decay
Shall not, O slandered wind, bring us dismay!

Thy force unfailing knows no treacheries:
Not thine the sickening languor of the breeze
That comes to us with fever from the East
And smiles to see it slay us like a beast;
Nor art thou the vast cyclone of the South
Spewing Atlantic billows with his mouth,
Whose breath is hoarse with a volcano's heat;
No cyclone's bastard, no sirocco-cheat,
Who comes and goes, no man knows whence or whither,
Thou dost not, at thy advent, make life wither;
Thou dost not need, like winds of summertide,
To feel the strong-leashed thunder at thy side
Bay at the lightning-flash in anger loud;
O epic wind, rare painter of the cloud,
When thou wouldst come, thou castest on the skies,
Out where the numb, great North's white summits rise,
As faithful heralds of thy coming on,
The blazing banners of the Northern Dawn.

Thou comest then. Woe to the traveller
Whose heedlessness no warnings can deter!

For thou who art to pass to cleanse the world
Canst not restrain thy legions, onward hurled:
They blot the hapless traveller out unblest,
Yet, while the life-blood freezes in his breast,
Thou straitenest for him the boundless plains
And murmurest unceasingly the strains
That rise from Arctic gulfs to greet the skies;
Thou settest the mirage before his eyes:

[491]

He sees a campfire where the cedar burns,
And death upon him like a rapture turns.
Tomorrow, when the sunlit ice shines fresh,
The glory of a star shall touch his flesh.
No, thou North Wind, thou hast no evil goal:
Thou livest, and like us thou hast a soul.
Like roses' perfume in the days of spring,
Thou spreadest love when frosts are lingering.

For in thy voice such pangs of pain vibrate
That, at the sound, the heart forgets its hate;
And through the long months when the days are brief
Thy song makes love expand in warm relief.
Thou singest the strange sorrow of an earth
That suffers under skies of gloom and dearth.
None better knows the awful loneliness
Of exile from one's friends, the shroud no less
Spread o'er the waters by the bitter floes
And the thick winding-sheet of Arctic snows,
The seas' cries of despair, moans as if lost
Uttered by forests tortured by the frost,
All of earth's yearning through the Arctic night
To feel the sun, the warmth, to see the light,
To know the water, and the sportive flocks,
All of thy longings, that the winter mocks,—
All of this sighs and sobs in thy sad song,
And with mad hope its passions are so strong
That none can wholly grasp it as they hear
And all our feeble being thrills with fear.

Without thee, love were lost throughout these hours
When winter keeps us in home's dungeon-towers.
The tête-à-tête grows irksome and half-dead
Unless some terror swoops above its head.
Without thee, smiles of love would turn to scowls,
But when thy mighty voice in torment howls
Fear joins the lovers' bodies, bored no more,
The heart feels pity that was dead before,
Shoulder seeks shoulder with a grace unplanned,
The trembling hand is stretched to touch a hand,

And flesh feels novel rapture when caressed;
The mother warms her child upon her breast;
Husband and wife whom years have dulled to love
In their embrace a sudden ardour prove.
With heady fragrances the bed is filled,
From flowers of long-dead evenings once distilled.
Vanished away are clouds of former cares,
And in embracings where the spirit shares
As well as flesh, a fuller life is born.
O liberating wind, if some in scorn
Curse thee for driving off the irksome hour,
Our hearts with secret vengeance still are sour
And what we hate in thee is hate dispelled.

*   *   *

Like a vase tinctured with the wines it held,
O wind, whose violence I often drank
In the warm days of adolescent prank,
I feel that in my body's fierce sensations
Thou minglest with the blood of generations!
For my forefathers, through long ages urged,
Felt with such zest thy blows upon them scourged
That thy strong rage into their souls did flow:
Thus we became blood-brothers long ago!
Beholding them erect before thy face,
Thou knewest them the makers of a race,
And thou hast given, by strange, magic charms,
The vigour of thy breath to nerve their arms!
The double fierceness pulses through my veins,
And when my soul some futile task sustains,
O wind that often in my play hadst part,
How thy fierce call re-echoes in my heart!
From thee as from my fathers comes this force
That makes me hate all hindrance to my course,
And, spite of all the years that dog my track,
My love of looking forward and not back!
Alas! The City's bricks now thwart thy spell
And I no longer know thy songs so well

[493]

Since I submitted to its slothful reign.
Into my being creeps the fear of pain,
And softness mars my soul, as flowers put
To grow mid paving-stones are soiled with soot.
I feel a laxness gnawing at my nerves,
And glorious speech that thrilled me once now serves
Only to mark a grace that from me slips;
A smile of cynicism thins my lips;
Sometimes I fear that when I wake tomorrow
My heart will lose its power of joy and sorrow.

O wind, transport me towards the mighty Quest!
I wish to drink harsh Nature's eager zest
Far, far away beyond the narrow pale
Of smoky houses where our spirits fail!
For I would sleep, when snowy peaks are crossed,
Upon a bed of branches, white with frost,
There lull'd to slumber by thy angry growls
And by the famish'd wolf-pack's lonely howls!

And when I close my eyes, in slumber prone,
I shall take on the semblance of a stone.
Thou immortal wanderer, as old as time,
I shall no longer feel the pain and slime
Of souls imprisoned in a mortal frame,
Where less than grains of sand the lives that came
Fall with the years into Eternity!
And when the waves of light once more flow free
And dawn shall rudely burst upon my rest,
I shall shake off the snow that cloaks my breast,
And rise, and take cold air upon my tongue
And let its cleansing power fill the lung;
Then through the vault of heaven, where dawn takes fire,
My voice, like thy white blizzard's mighty choir,
Shall in hoarse eddies thunder to the plains
And flood the hives of houses and their stains,
That, mastering the world's shrill blasphemy,
I may declare, O Wind, my love for thee!

From the French of Alfred Des Rochers (1901–   )

OUR LANGUAGE

Our speech was born upon the lips of Gauls.
  The words are tender but the rules austere.
Fashioned to sing old glories in our halls,
  It learns from troubadors to thrill the ear.

Its tone is like the Latin, full and fine,
  It has the charm and sprightliness of Greek,
The radiance of enamels Florentine,
  The gloss of porcelain, serene and sleek;

The mellow voice of an Aeolian lute,
  The murmur of the wind through wheat and rye,
The radiance of heaven, the lightning's bruit,
  The sighs of doves, an eagle's wings to fly.

It sings throughout the world to praise the Lord,
  And scattering the night where error lurks,
It is the deathless angel of His Word,
  To bear His holy light to all His works.

It was the first to name the Name on High
  In the Canadian forest, strange and lone;
It lifted first to our Canadian sky
  Our hymns of love, our prayers to God's great throne.

It was the first, on Mississippi's flood,
  To make the boundless forests on its shore
Tremble and bow in rapture where they stood
  As if that blessed language to adore.

Language of fire, its torch has hitherto
  Kindled the arts, illumined science' page;
It serves the Good, the Beautiful, the True,
  And casts its light across the entire age.

Stern sailors brought it, men we yet revere,
  Out of the land of heath and Druid-stone;
Our mothers' lullabies have made it dear,
  Sung in old Norman ballads, sad of tone.

We keep the speech that to our sires was sweet,
  Spoken by brave men under westering sails,

And though at times it seemed to know defeat,
    Beneath the British flag it still prevails.

Henceforth let no one any more oppress
    This language still so strong and full of grace. . . .
Its executioners find no success,
    And it shall live as long as does our race.

To try to stop it, is to check the flower
    From opening its buds when Night's withdrawn;
To try to slay its beauty and its power
    Is to conceive of cancelling the dawn.

Shine then forever in God's holy sight,
    Speech of our forebears! As the years expand,
Be for us still the cloud of fire and light
    Guiding the Hebrews towards the Promised Land.

From the French of William Chapman (1850–1917)

THE "SANCTUS" AT HOME

One sees, by the open windows, flowers in bloom.
'Tis the hour of mass. Far off a steeple gleams.
All have departed but a girl, who seems
Left to the housework in the humble room.

A black cross hangs upon the home's white wall.
The child is pretty, dressed in new attire.
The water boils, steam rises. By the fire,
A sleek cat roasts himself at flames that crawl.

Then the bell chimes from out the little town:
"Ah, Sanctus, Sanctus!" . . . The young girl lays down
The cabbage on a bench, puts cup away.

"Sanctus!" . . . Before the bell is silent there,
She kneels down, and with arms upon her chair,
Fingers her beads and bows her head to pray.

From the French of Pamphile Lemay (1837–1918)

From A Little Treasury of Hungarian Verse

THE TAVERN BY THE LITTLE TOWN

The tavern by the little town,
Along the Szamos nestling down,
Would be reflected in the stream
Did not the twilight reign supreme.

The night draws on across the plain;
The stirring world grows still again;
The ferry rests; they moor it fast;
Dark silence holds the scene at last.

But in the tavern, what a noise!
A gypsy plays to please the boys.
The village bumpkins leap and shout
And almost break the windows out.

"Come, madam hostess, fair and fine,
Bring here the best of all your wine!
As old as granddad let it be,
And hot as my young lass to me.

"Then strike up, gypsy, louder yet!
On dancing, all my mind is set:
I'll dance away my money-roll,
I'll dance away my very soul!"

Then someone at the window raps:
"Be quiet now, you noisy chaps!
You vex my master, who has said
That all of you should go to bed."

"The devil with your master dwell,
Or take the pair of you to hell!
Come, strike up, gypsy, all the more!
I'd give my shirt to see him roar!"

Another knock disturbs them then:
"God bless you all, good gentlemen!

I wonder could you play less shrill?—
My poor old mother is quite ill."

A silence greets the mild request.
At once the music sinks to rest;
They drain their cups, then softly creep
Across the night to bed, and sleep.

THE FOUR-OX CART

The event I tell of happened not in Pest:
Romance is there a thing at which men scoff.
The members of our noble company
Mounted the cart, and then they started off.
They went upon a cart, an old ox-cart;
Two pairs of bullocks were their team bizarre.
Drawing the cart along the highway white,
The four great oxen plodded on afar.

The night was luminous, the moon was high;
Pale in the midst of clouds it wandered there
As when a widow in a cemetery
Seeks for her husband's grave in wan despair.
The wind—a merchant from the nearby fields—
Had bought their sweetest scent for his bazaar.
Drawing the cart along the highway white,
The four great oxen plodded on afar.

I, too, was one of that glad company;
By little Erzsebet I sat that night.
While all the other members of our band
Chatted aloud and sang in their delight,
I dreamed in silence—then said suddenly
To my sweet neighbour: "Shall we choose a star?"
Drawing the cart along the highway white,
The four great oxen plodded on afar.

"If we should choose a star," I whispered on
To little Erzsebet, "the star some day,
If destiny should separate us two,
Will serve to lead us back, where'er we stray,

To a remembrance of the happiest time."
And she was willing, and we chose a star.
Drawing the cart along the highway white,
The four great oxen plodded on afar.

From the Magyar of Sándor Petőfi (1823–49)

From Miscellaneous Periodicals

THE WOOD

The springtime wood was flooded deep with the mellow
   Light of the bronze-bright hours;
The thickets of willow flamed with a vernal yellow;
   The ground was starred with flowers.

Along the tree-trunks crept the caterpillars,
   And on their track untiring
Came the shy cohorts of their feathered killers,
   Flicker and thrush conspiring.

A Sabbath hush kept radiant and sleeping
   That wood; while, like flood-water,
A tide of struggle, through the far fields sweeping,
   Reddened their grass with slaughter.

From the Serb of Jovan Dučić (1874–1943)

HORACE, ODES, IV, 7

The snows have fled, and living green
Transforms the meadows and the trees;
Earth works her ancient alchemies
And lessening rivers flow serene.

The nymphs and sister Graces dare
To dance in sylvan nakedness.

But hour and year still onward press
And joy's sad brevity declare.

The frost of winter yields to spring;
June tramples April under foot;
Too soon comes autumn with its fruit,
And winter with its perishing.

But though swift moons regain the light
They lose in waning, when we go
Where all the great ones lie below,
We are but dust and shade of night.

Who knows, indeed, if fate will add
Tomorrow's hours to to-day?
Or if a greedy heir will prey
On all that makes your spirit glad?

When you are dead and gone, my friend,
And gods below have claimed you theirs,
No rank nor righteousness nor prayers
Can free you from your certain end.

For Dian cannot free the chaste
Hippolytus from nether gloom,
Nor Theseus break the lethal doom
Of chains about his comrade cast.

From the Latin of Quintus Horatius Flaccus (65–8 B.C.)

ON THE BIRTH OF CHRIST

The earth is dewed with nectar from the Skies
     And honey in pure streams. A golden rose
That rapt the saints in meads of Paradise
     Into a Virgin's bosom softly goes.
Thus from her maiden charm, her modest eyes,
     A flower angelic radiantly grows—
A rosy flower, seraphic, holy-fresh,
Is clothed in grass; our God becomes our flesh.

Thus into flesh descends the Father's Word.
     A maid becomes a mother, without man.

His Godhead through His birth no loss incurred;
    Here is the Virgin's grace for all to scan.
Clouds hid the sun; grass, flowers; the seed was burr'd;
    Honey was lost in wax; when Christ began.
Here Heaven and Earth are like a brooch, to place
Discordant kingdoms in a blest embrace.

From the Latin of Hildebert of Lavardin (1055–1133)

THE GLOOMY FOREST

Despair besets me in the gloomy wood;
Bereft of joy, my thoughts can find no rest.
This place so hostile to all Nature's good
Has robbed me of all gifts I once possessed.
I cannot frame a song as once I could;
Whenever I begin, I grow depressed;
And I have lost the Gaelic's wonted ease
I once knew in the land beyond the seas.

My restless thoughts from all due order fly,
Though I could once endite a tuneful strain.
My sorrows are increased, my pleasures die,
Without some friend's good talk to soothe my brain;
Each day and night, at every task I try,
My heart turns ever back to seek in pain
The land I left beside the long salt sea,
Though in a glen my dwelling now may be.

It is no wonder that in grief I shiver:
Upon a mountain's back I dwell in care,
Deep in a wilderness on Barney's River,
With only scant potatoes as my fare,
Before my tillage can a crop deliver,
The wood must be uprooted from its lair.
The strength of my right arm will soon be seared
And fail before my family is reared.

This is a country in which toil is vast:
A fact to those who came here quite obscure.

Evil have mischief-makers on us cast,
Persuading us to come, by lying lure.
If they make profit thus, it will not last,
It will not help them greatly, I am sure.
From every quarter where their victims spread,
Each wretch will send his curse upon their head.

It will be grand, the story they will say:
This place's reputation will wax great;
They will be bragging that your friends are gay,
Wealthy and unrestricted in estate.
Every deceitful story of our stay
Seeks to allure you on to share our fate.
If you arrive here safely, you shall see
New hardships worse than ancient poverty.

When agents come, prospective settlers seeking,
It is with lies their project will be sped;
Without a word of truth they will be speaking,
The heart condemning what the mouth has said;
Everything here with praise they will be sleeking
As the most rare on which the sun is shed.
Yet when you come here, little will you spy
But soaring forests shutting out the sky.

When winter comes, the season of rough weather,
The snowdrifts towards the boughs mount ever higher;
Over the knees you sink in altogether;
Though trousers may be strong, they still require
Thick double stockings, moccasins of leather,
And leather thongs to tighten such attire.
A wild beast's fur completes our new-style suit,
Torn yesterday from off the slaughtered brute.

If I am careless in my dress of winter,
My nose and mouth are frozen without fail
By the North Wind, a bitter blast, imprinter
Of wounds upon my ears, grown chill and pale;
In such a fearful frost, the axe will splinter;
The sharpness of the steel will not avail;
Unless one warm the head, its use is through;
The smith must mend it or it will not hew.

When summer comes, and in the month of May
The sunshine's sudden heat my strength impairs,
It stirs up ardour in the beasts of prey
That drowsed all winter in their savage lairs.
Amid my hapless flock now come to slay
Black, hungry brutes of just awakened bears;
While the black fly, envenomed, fleet of wing,
Wounds me unceasingly with sharpened sting.

Their bites upon my face grow worse and worse;
I cannot see the ground on which I tread;
My eyes are swollen by this insect curse,
So potent is the poison that they shed;
I cannot tell the number in my verse
Of each obscene new beast that rears its head.
As many plagues are in this country found
As once with Pharaoh, till at last he drowned.

The world sees many changes, much distress;
Back home of old, the fact escaped my grip.
It was my thought, on fire for success,
That I should prosper if I came by ship.
With every change, I profited the less;
I crossed the sea on a mistaken trip
To the dark forest where I am not free,
Cowless and sheepless in stark misery.

In many a step I shall be deeply mired
Before I own the land I work for now;
With hopeless toil my body will be tired
Before I make a clearing for my plough;
Piling burnt log on log, I have perspired
Until my very loins are racked, I vow,
And every part of me is grimed so deep
That I am brother to a chimney-sweep.

Fine tales they told the Scot who might migrate
But in experience they prove untrue.
I shall not see blue dollars circulate,
Though they are here supposed to greet the view;
When we would sell, in vain for coin we wait;
They will not even name the money due;

If in the shops a bargain should be made,
The settler is with flour and butter paid.

I shall not see a market nor a fair,
Nor driving forth of cattle on that day,
Nor anything that might our loss repair;
The people are in hardship every way.
When they must sell their holdings in despair,
Their grievances no comfort can allay;
While creditors expect, with heart of ill,
To jail the man who does not pay his bill.

Before the cases come before the court,
So that in justice double may be spent,
The law allows, by jurymen's resort,
The plundering to proceed with dark intent.
Through all the land the sheriff may extort,
Pursuing and demanding settlement.
I am most anxious lest he come to me:
He would not pity my extremity.

My griefs the measure of this verse exceed;
I cannot in poetic form devise
All that of which I'd have my friends take heed
Back in the land that heard my infant cries.
Understand reason, all of you who read,
And do not listen to the boasters' lies.
For tales to tempt you, by false prophets told,
Are careless of your good. They seek your gold.

Although I should be diligent in writing,
I should require a month of toil or more
Before my mind could finish its enditing,
Before my mouth could empty all its store.
A secret sadness is my spirit blighting,
Far harder to express than aught before.
In this dark wood, I little know but pain,
Where no man calls on me to sing a strain.

Far other was it when my days began,
When I could join in jest at every table:
A hearty, courteous company I'd scan
And all the chorus rang with carefree babel.

Alas, I left you all, a wistful man,
And to control my tears, I was not able,
On Thursday morning, beyond Caolas going,
With sails set and the off-shore breezes blowing.

From the Gaelic of John MacLean (1787–1848)

THEY WALLED UP EVERY WINDOW

(Europe! To you in this verse our voices come; to you we call, we
tens and hundreds of thousands of Hungarians who sojourn in the hell
of prisons! Our tongue falters too much in our dungeon and millions
do not know what the poet says. Foreign poets, our brothers! Translate
us into the language of your peoples, so that our message may reach
you! While in 1955 in Pest the Communists were spouting about
legality, in the Vác prison they sealed up the windows with sheet-
metal so as to take away even that much air and light.)

Of life without, only this gleam was left,
A tiny patch of stars, a glimpse of sun.
In daily gloom, within dim walls bereft,
We watched the vent for this as day was done.
This too they stole, this streak of sunlight thin,
They've walled up every window tight with tin.

With memory's eye, I mark the azure sea
At Naples, and beside the shining shore
Vesuvius waits and smokes. Can you, like me,
See happy, sun-browned swimmers by the score?
We live in night like men who blind have been:
They've walled up every window tight with tin.

Our ten mouths gasping for the missing air,
Ten of us lie, in one close kennel pent,
As fish-gills on the bank might gasp despair.
To eat the food, which stinks of excrement,
Our stomachs lack the power to begin:
They've walled up every window tight with tin.

From the bright fragrance of the Alpine peaks
The west wind wafts the freshness of bouquets;

[505]

Of virtue to the soul that distance speaks,
And smiling summits swell the hymn of praise.
But phthisis grips my cell-mate, dark as sin:
They've walled up every window tight with tin.

For us no more the steamer's whistle blows;
All maiden laughter from our sense is wiped;
No pleasure in our ears sonorous flows
No summer plays an organ, myriad-piped.
Our cells are deaf, all sound is dead herein:
They've walled up every window tight with tin.

By Barcelona, in a garden fair,
The warm voice of a tawny woman croons;
The streets are pied with dances here and there;
A gay guitar gives dusk its tinkling tunes.
Our leaden days flow silent in chagrin:
They've walled up every window tight with tin.

We probe in darkness towards the velvet skies
As if within a coffin we were nailed;
We only touch our rags and agonize,
Or feel our hands by vermin-hosts assailed.
We once caressed the sunlight, like soft skin.
They've walled up every window tight with tin.

There is a ball in London; like a rose
A girl glides in her silks, on floors that gleam;
In all the bloom of lustrous hair she glows,
Soft-mirrored in the wainscot, like a dream.
The West is dancing. Has it Magyar kin?
They've walled up every window tight with tin.

Our tongues recall the pleasant taste of spring
Then swallow with a groan our morsel dank
Whose fecal horror chokes its entering
And turns our bellies sick, our reason blank;
Yet even this our famine forces in.
They've walled up every window tight with tin.

Sleep locks our hungered bodies in its spell
And there I sate a gourmet's appetites
On all that Paris offers—see as well,
Climbing above the city's neon-lights,

The Silent Ghost—but here no dawns begin:
They've walled up every window tight with tin.

The radios shout hoarsely of new deals,
Of freedom and of justice due to man.
But here my dungeoned body only feels
The million lashes of foul Stalin's plan.
From Vác to far Peking his slaves make din:
"Beware! Beware! Or through the entire world
They'll wall up every window tight with tin."

From the Magyar of Tibor Tollas (1920–   )

The poet is a young Hungarian patriot, who escaped from Vác prison, and from Hungary, during his country's brief interlude of freedom in November 1956. He had composed this poem in prison and committed it to memory for lack of pen, paper, and light.

From Pan Tadeusz

THE SENESCHAL BLOWS HIS HORN
IV, 769–816

Then the old Seneschal his horn did take,
Strap-hung, long, spotted, crooked as a snake,
And pressed it to his lips with either hand.
Like some out-blown balloon his cheeks were spanned;
His lids were lowered; bloodshot grew his eyes;
He drew his belly in to half its size,
Transferring to his lungs his breath entire,
And blew. The horn, a cyclone swirling higher,
Bore far into the woods his ardent strain,
Whence echoes soft repeated it again.
The sportsmen hushed, the hunters were amazed
At the sweet power of the notes he raised.
The old man was exhibiting once more
The art that made him famous long before;

Straightway he filled the woods with living notes,
As if he led there, with their vocal throats,
A kennel all entire and launched the hunt.
He told the whole chase over. Brisk and blunt,
In perfect mood and speech professional,
Rang out the summons of the morning call;
Then yelp on yelp whined forth—that was the hounds;
Then harsher thunder spoke of muskets' rounds.

Here he broke off, but still he held the horn;
You'd swear he played—while echoes smote the morn.

Once more he blew. You'd think the horn was changing.
In form, now thick or thin, as subtly ranging
It mocked the cries of beasts: a wolf's long throat
Gave to the trembling air a piercing note;
Then broadening its pitch, it roared, a bear;
A bison's bellow next salutes the air.

Here he broke off, but still he held the horn;
You'd swear he played—while echoes smote the morn.
Hearing this masterpiece of trumpet-speech,
Oak echoed it to oak, and beech to beech.

He blew again. There seemed within the horn
A hundred bugles summoning the morn;
One could hear mingled outcries, as men set
The dogs on; wrath and terror bursting yet
From men and pack and beasts; last, for those crowds
A crowning hymn of triumph smote the clouds.

Here he broke off, but still he held the horn;
You'd swear he played—while echoes smote the morn.
There seemed to be a horn for every tree;
Each to another spoke continually
As though they spread it on from choir to choir.
And on the music went, still farther, higher,
More gentle, pure and perfect, till it dies
Upon the very threshold of the skies.

From the Polish of Adam Mickiewicz

JANKIEL PLAYS THE DULCIMER
xii, 897–1036

He said his hands were stiff, he dared not play
Without due practice; and so great a day
Embarrassed him with men of mighty station;
With many a bow, he shunned their exhortation.
When Zosia saw this, she ran hastily
And with one white hand offered, as her plea,
The hammers that his skill was wont to use
To sound the strings; and lest he should refuse
The gentle courtesy for which she pled,
She stroked his old grey beard, and curtsying said:

"Jankiel, be kind; this is my wedding day;
Play for me, Jankiel. For you used to say
That at my wedding you would play with pleasure."

Jankiel loved Zosia greatly, beyond measure,
And bowed his beard in token of assent.
So to the centre of the throng he went
And on his knees the dulcimer they slide;
He gazed upon it with delight and pride,
Like some old veteran whom new battles call,
When his small grandsons take down from the wall
His heavy sword: the old man laughs to heft it;
Though many years have gone since last he left it,
He feels his hand will not betray the blade.

Two of his pupils meanwhile gave their aid,
Knelt by the dulcimer, tuned fresh the strings,
And twanged them as a test of readyings.
Jankiel with half-closed eyes in silence lingers
And holds the hammers sleeping in his fingers.

He lowered them in a triumphal beat,
Then smote the strings again with brisker heat,
As with a shower of rain: all were amazed,
Yet this was but a test that he had phrased;
He stopped, and raised both hammers up aloft.

He played anew; the strings now trembled soft
With motions light as though a fly's faint wing

Sounded a gentle buzz upon the string.
The master gazed intently at the sky
For inspiration; with a haughty eye
He looked down at his silent instrument;
Then raised both hands, dropped them with firm intent
And with both hammers all the strings coerced.

Then all at once from many strings there burst
A sound as though a janissaries' band
With cymbals, bells and drums made glad the land.
The *Polonaise* that marked *the Third of May*
Came thundering forth! The rippling notes were gay
And in one's ears they poured a breath of joy;
Girls wished to dance and each impatient boy
Could not stand still—but thoughts of older men
Into the blessed past were borne again,
Those happy years when Deputies and Senate
On that great day saw Liberty's proud tenet
Made perfect in the reconciliation,
That Third of May, between both King and Nation;
"Vivat our King!" then sang the dancing masses,
"Vivat the Diet, people, and all classes!"

The master kept on quickening the time
And ever played with power more sublime;
But suddenly a false note sounded crass—
A snake's hiss or the screech of steel on glass—
A shudder through the listeners wandered free
And mingled with the general gaiety
An ominous foreboding. All alarmed,
Men pondered if the instrument were harmed
Or if the player's hand had made a blunder.
With such a master lay no cause for wonder!
He purposely kept touching that foul chord
To mar the music with its note abhorred;
Louder and louder still its angry moans
Make plot against the harmony of tones;
At last the Warden understood the master,
Covered his face, in sorrow of disaster,
And cried: "I know, I know those notes too well;
They speak of *Targowica*, foul as hell!"
And suddenly the bad string hissed and broke;
The player to the high strings swept his stroke,

Confused the measure, left the treble race,
And hurried with his hammers to the bass.

A thousand noises ever louder warmed,
Of measured marching, war, a city stormed;
One heard reports of guns, and children's groaning,
And mothers in the rape and slaughter moaning,
So well the master all these crimes dissembled
That all the village girls in terror trembled,
Calling to mind, with teardrops not a few,
The Massacre of Praga, which they knew
From song and story; they were glad at last
When the great master from those horrors passed,
Thundering on all the strings a blast of dearth
As if he crushed all outcries in the earth.

Scarce had his startled hearers grown estranged
From wonder, when once more the music changed;
First there were only light and gentle hummings;
A few thin strings mourned jointly in their strummings
Like flies that strive to leave the spider's web.
But more strings mounted upward from that ebb;
Now scattered tones were blended in the flood,
And legions of rich chords united stood;
Now they advanced with measured steps and strong
In the sad music of that famous song
About the wandering soldier who must travel
Through woods and forests as his days unravel;
He often faints with woe and hunger's need,
And falls at last beside his faithful steed,
Who with his hoof paws out his master's grave—
A poor old song, yet very dear to brave
And wistful Polish troops. The soldiers knew it
And crowded round the master to ensue it;
They hearkened, and remembered that dread season
When by their country's grave they had with reason
Sung that same song and joined the exile's train;
They called to mind long years of wandering pain,
Mid foreign peoples, over sea and land,
Oppressed by winter frost and burning sand,
When by this song they had been comforted.
As thus they thought, they sadly bowed the head!

But raised it straightway as the master's fire
Blazed out in music that was stronger, higher;
He changed his measure and proclaimed a theme
As different as daylight is from dream.
Once more his eye looked down, the strings to note;
Then suddenly he joined his hands and smote
With both the hammers: such a skilful blow,
So powerful, that from the loud strings flow
Great brazen trumpet-tones in which is given
A well-known song that mounted to the heaven,
A march of triumph: "Poland's not yet dead;
March, march Dombrowski, at our legions' head,
To Poland!" And all clapped and cried in chorus:
"March, march, Dombrowski, to our land, before us!"

The master seemed amazed at his own song;
He dropped the hammers from his fingers strong
And raised his arms aloft; his fox-skin cap
Was tumbling all unnoticed to his lap;
His beard uplifted waved in majesty;
A flush upon his cheeks glowed strange to see;
His zealous glances showed a youthful blaze.
But when at last the old man turned his gaze
Upon Dombrowski, he must hide those spheres,
And through his fingers gushed a stream of tears.

From the Polish of Adam Mickiewicz (1798–1855)

From The Ukrainian Poets

THE HIGHWAY-BUILDERS

Strange was my dream. Before me lay a plain,
A boundless waste beneath a leaden sky,
While I stood there, fast in an iron chain,
Before a granite mountain's vast domain
With other countless thousands such as I.

On each man's brow his grief deep furrows makes,
In each man's eyes the flame of love has glowed,
And each man's hands the chains entwine like snakes,
And each man's back to earth obeisance makes,
For all are burdened with the same dread load.

There each man's hands a heavy hammer hold,
And from the peak a voice bursts forth like thunder:
"Shatter this rock! Let neither heat nor cold
Arrest you! Bear your torments manifold!
It is your task to crush this mountain under!"

Then, as one man, we raised our hands aloft;
Thousands of hammers crashed against the stone;
The battered fragments lashed at us as oft
We smote the mountain; at despair we scoffed;
And broke that stony brow's primaeval bone.

Like a loud cataract, like battle's din,
Our sledges' blows incessantly resound:
And foot by foot a further space we win,
And splinters gashed at many a cheek and chin—
But nothing stayed us in our ceaseless round.

Each of us knew no fame would crown his head,
No grateful thought from men salute his toil;
That no one on this highway broad would tread
Till we had crushed the rock, the ballast spread,
And laid our bones to rest beneath the soil.

But we have never longed for people's praise;
We are no heroes, and no warriors we.
A voluntary serfdom crowns our days:
As builders of this highway that we raise,
We have become the slaves of liberty.

We all believed, with these hands of our own
We'd crush the granite and the rock down-hurled;
That, having sacrificed our blood and bone,
We'd lay a solid highway floored with stone—
New life, new weal, would come into the world.

We knew that somewhere, in a tract afar
That we had left to endure this toil in chains,
Tears hail us where our wives and mothers are

And friends and foes in jealous anger jar
And curse our high resolve and noble pains.

We knew all that; release from pain we'd ask;
Our hearts were broken and our nerves on edge;
But grief and sorrow played in vain their masque,
No imprecations drew us from our task;
Not one of us let fall his battering sledge.

Thus we go on, chained in a single mind
By holy faith, with hammers in our hands.
Let us be cursed, forgotten by mankind—
A mountain-road to justice we will find
That, though we die, will bless our sacred lands.

From the Ukrainian of Ivan Franko (1856–1916)

THE GUILDSMAN KUPERIAN

The Poles a city once besieged
    In days of long ago;
They smote with hate each wall and gate
    And mined them deep below.

Cossacks were bold in their defence,
    Nor did the burghers sleep;
By day and night from cannon throats
    Came roars of anger deep.

Kuperian, the guildsman good,
    Was staunchest of them all;
And to his fellow guildsmen
    He gave this secret call:

"Fellows, for long enough we've sat
    Like owls on parapets;
Let's show that we, the burghers,
    Are not a hare's begets.

"We'll strike by night against their camp
    Out of that steep ravine!
Let's either die or crush those Poles
    To shreds of snuff unclean!"

His plan was turned to action,
　　And luck was on their side;
They smashed the forces of the foe
　　And off the remnants ride.

Then shouts of victory resound!
　　All seek the city square,—
Cobblers and tailors, guildsmen all,
　　In countless numbers there.

They welcome bold Kuperian
　　With his victorious powers;
He is a hero: all his path
　　They gladly strew with flowers.

And in the square the Council grave
　　Began in sombre thought
To plan Kuperian's reward
　　As they most truly ought.

Some say: "He has a guildsman been!
　　He should be something vaster.
Now, for his service to us all,
　　Let's make him burgomaster!"

But others say: "Why make him mayor?
　　We will not vote for that.
Our fire brigade a captain needs
　　And this would suit him pat."

Still others say: "No, gentlemen!
　　Your plans we're thunderstruck at!
Let every household in the town
　　Give him a golden ducat!"

"Oh, no! no! no!" the indignant crowd
　　Cries out in angry chorus.
"Dull cash for high heroic deeds
　　Would shame him here before us!"

A hubbub rises, discord reigns
　　As projects they contest;
And every plan that some approve
　　Is scoffed at by the rest.

Then the pot-bellied burgomaster
    Leaped on a bench, and stood,
And cried: "Long live our matchless friend,
    Kuperian the Good!

"God has Himself this hero sent
    Our foemen to destroy;
But has not given us the wits
    Fit honour to employ.

"To give him cash is rude and rash;
    Besides, we all are poor;
And yet, to give him some great post
    Envy could not endure.

"So long as he remains alive,
    His case will vex the town,—
And so, my fellow citizens,
    Set my opinion down:

"Yes, let us kill him with despatch,
    And nicely here impale him!
After his death, we'll all lament
    And as a saint we'll hail him.

"And high above his holy grave
    A tumulus we'll rear;
And for him chant memorial prayers
    Twice each returning year!"

"How marvellous! A counsel wise!"
    All shouted in devotion;
But failed to ask the saint-elect
    To second the Great Motion.

From the Ukrainian of Ivan Franko (1856–1916)

TREACHERY

Swift is the horse I ride by secret ways
Through the night's ashes and the flaming days;
Only a song behind my saddle hums,
After me comes

A band of friends, eleven young and bold,
Eleven moons they seemed, with miens of gold.

A lofty rock its watch is keeping.
Beneath the rock the earth is sleeping.
And in that earth a tiny chamber lies
And there a lizard lives in woe
Who once had been a princess long ago.

—"Come, lads, and let us fight like lords!
Out from their scabbards draw your swords!
The captive princess let us free
From the dark spell of sorcery!"
The lads all stopped without ado,
And from the sheath their swords they drew.
The captive princess they set free
From the dark spell of sorcery.
She came forth like a flower, fair and white,
But timorous, most timorous with fright.

She asks me: "Do you love me?"—"Yes, I do."
—"Give me your joy, to show your love is true."
I gave it to her.

"And do you love me even now?"—"I do."
—"Give me your strength, to show your love is true."
I gave it to her.

Once more: "Do you still love me?"—"Yes, I do."
—"Give me your courage; show your love is true."
I gave it to her.

She lifted up her eyes
That shone with peace profound;
She pointed to herself;
Slowly I looked around,—
And my eleven friends were lost to sight;
Amid the shadows of the deepening night
Eleven little pillars stood in woe,
Some of them crooked, others putrefied;
Upon each was a tiny cap of snow.
The mysterious princess mounted then my horse:
—"Why do your eyes cold tears of sorrow strew?
Will it not be most wearisome for you:

Day after day,
Year after year,
Ever and aye,
To pace by these small pillars here;
Will you not sing sad songs
That you are stripped of what to you belongs
And never can forget your wrongs,
And still your anger cannot fail to die
Under so blue a sky!"

She showed her teeth: like fearful fangs they shone.
She laughed at me, and whistled, and was gone.

From the Ukrainian of Volodimir Svidzinsky (1885–1941)

From THIRST

You are all thirst, and you are all aflaming,
You—bow, and arrow, and the string tight-drawn,
A vision for the centuries' proclaiming,
My shining, universal star of dawn!

Many a time your lips, O heaven's daughter,
Held tight the secret of your darkest dearth,
When to procure the vivifying water
You went, O holy wanderer of the earth.

When you were coming homeward from your questing,
Having attained the iridescent source
And bringing on a solid beam unresting
Two golden pails, salvation to endorse—

A robber smote you from around a corner;
Shattered the golden vessels; crucified
Your youthful body, as an obscene scorner,
And mocked the immortal form in which you died.

You, there uplifted with your arms outspreading,
Looked down in silence at the rabid horde
Trampling your tender children with their treading,
Looked at the knife that slashed, the cutting cord,

Looked at the buildings and the towers falling
From their proud height to crumble into dust,

[518]

At conflagrations like fierce serpents crawling,
Consuming pale-blue houses in their lust,

At cherry-trees that blackened in the burning,
At the stampeding flocks and frenzied herds,
And at a world to hellish darkness turning
In fields that groaned with malediction's words,—

And your mute glance, O gentle mother, ran on
In thunder that outdid the hostile guns,
Deafening all the arrogance of cannon,
Uniting all the spirits of your sons;

Then the great deed had ripened to beginning,
The designated time at last had come,—
Though yet the wizard had not forged our winning,
Nor quill had trimmed for our exordium,

No scroll has been unrolled, of noble features,
On which might be inscribed, in colours warm,
How, in a duel with inhuman creatures,
The host of men began to rage and storm.

High on the cross I see you, foot and finger
Swathed in white flashings and in suffering rife,
But know that while the sun and stars shall linger
Justice will not be lost from human life,

And I believe, O mother, till I perish,
That ray of justice that all men must cherish
Will be a golden sword to make an end,—
And at the final hour, by God appointed,
In the blue calm for which you were anointed
You, my own love, will from the cross descend!

From the Ukrainian of Maksim Rilsky (1895–1964)

VERGIL

A Mantuan peasant, easy-paced and brown,
From childhood cradled in a village realm,
He praised the staff, the plough, the copper helm,
And rose to heights of unsurpassed renown.

For through the fire and smoke of martial hate
He saw a better age and sang a psalm
How Caesar's eagle would at last bring calm
In the mild yoke of the immortal state.

That age has passed—To Rome and Caesar's deeds,
Through history's hand, lo, dusty death succeeds
Where crowns and ghosts of all the ages sleep.

Yet Vergil lives. His epic's loud narration
Still fills our dreams with Dido's lamentation,
The sound of arms and triremes in the deep.

From the Ukrainian of Mikola Zerov (1890–1941)

THE AMULET

In ancient times some savage in a sweat,
Being priest and hunter with a poet's sight,
Once, from a roe's hoof, made an amulet
To save him from the spectres of the night.

While he was carving with his unskilled hand
That fragment of the hoof, could he forsee
That from his leisure and this work he planned
His times would mingle with futurity?

That somewhere, in some century unknown,
The master of the seas who sought new shores
'Mid bellowing tempests and the mast's deep groan
Would blaze the trail of the conquistadors,

And would direct his battered brigantine
To islands where the buried savage lay,
From whose rough beach the wind had washed out clean
Even the traces of that far-off day!

And as his custom was in seeking gold
He'd pick up a few pebbles from the ground—
And there within his wind-blown hand would hold
The shining, speckled amulet he'd found!

And when the Spaniard stuffed into his coat
That paltry legacy of savage faith,
Could he suspect a future age would gloat
On what primordial genius left a wraith?

That his descendant, home in old Castille,
Forgetting all the glory of his line,
His country's woes would often cease to feel
In gazing on that amulet's design . . .

That later the barbarian's artifact
Would pass through many countries, towns and hands—
So full of meaning in its sculptured tact,
So deathless in creative deodands!

An alchemist, a learned bachelor,
A marquis and an antiquarian,
London, Berlin and Paris—none forbore
The witchcraft of the amulet to scan.

And later still on velvet it would rest
In a museum, that in dust would mew it
Until the wheel of time made manifest
The moment when a poet bent to view it.

All deep in thoughts, beyond the power of speech,
He sailed as in a dream, light-blue and vast,
'Till the communion of his soul could reach
That crude barbarian of the unknown past.

From the Ukrainian of Evhen Pluzhnik (1898–1936)

LOVE UKRAINE

Love your Ukraine, love as you would the sun,
The wind, the grasses and the streams together . . .
Love her in happy hours, when joys are won,
And love her in her time of stormy weather.

Love her in happy dreams and when awake,
Ukraine in spring's white cherry-blossom veil.
Her beauty is eternal for your sake;
Her speech is tender with the nightingale.

[521]

As in a garden of fraternal races,
She shines above the ages. Love Ukraine
With all your heart, and with exultant faces
Let all your deeds her majesty maintain.

For us she rides alone on history's billows,
In the sweet charm of space she rules apart,
For she is in the stars, is in the willows,
And in each pulse-beat of her people's heart,

In flowers and tiny birds, and lights that shine,
In every epic and in every song,
In a child's smile, in maidens' eyes divine,
And in the purple flags above the throng . . .

Youth! For her sake give your approving laughter,
Your tears, and all you are until you die . . .
For other races you'll not love hereafter
Unless you love Ukraine and hold her high.

Young woman! As you would her sky of blue,
Love her each moment that your days remain.
Your sweetheart will not keep his love for you,
Unless he knows you also love Ukraine.

Love her in love, in labour, and in fight,
As if she were a song at heaven's portal . . .
Love her with all your heart and all your might,
And with her glory we shall be immortal.

From the Ukrainian of Volodimir Sosiura (1898–   )

THE RAINY NIGHT

The windows weep with rain. The wind is gusty.
All conversations dwindle to an end.
And this remains: a half-dream, grey and dusty,
That I in loneliness must apprehend.

The rain continues, and the leaves are falling.
My heart from recollection cannot stop.

The pressure of the twilight is appalling,
As time is sinking, drop by bloody drop.

I dream or think—and grief, no longer banished,
Fills up your hours with pain, O rainy night.
A distant flame has darkly flashed and vanished.
To-day there is no time for living light.

With leaves against the glass the tempest blows.
And all that was is branded deep with pain.
Dark reminiscence in a gloomy doze
All lonely visions of today has slain

And I recall our first flight, as of old:
An autumn wind in rainy darkness grieves.
The trampled grass, the puddles and the cold,
Blend in the tumult of the fallen leaves.

A man's form by the window-pane I saw;
He whispered—what a word our peace to pillage:
"Tonight . . . with children . . . to Siberia . . .
Flee quickly. But keep clear of all the village."—

So unexpectedly this message came,
It seemed that something snapped within one's soul.
For such a flight no warning could we claim
And tasty dumplings winked within my bowl.

What shall we leave behind? What shall we take?
Where shall we seek for shelter? Whither go?
My father and unmarried brothers make
A silent survey of the arms they stow.

That we must leave thus did not most annoy;
Another feeling then my spirit spanned:
I felt a painful urge, though but a boy,
To clutch a steel revolver in my hand . . .

O Lord! Our lands . . . our house . . . our hearts'
                                       delight . . .—
Was it forever? . . . Could we not return?
The darkness seemed appointed for our flight:
None in those shadows could our path discern.

[523]

Against the window panes the raindrops beat;
The wind is tearing through the garden black.
. . . Two loaves, a goodly portion of salt meat,
Had now been tossed into a haversack.

The property a lifetime had acquired
Remained for anyone to take at will.
Out of our wardrobe, what we most desired
We snatched in haste, due service to fulfil.

We walked out quietly and closed the door
And vanished in the gloom as we were able;
And bowls of untouched supper as before
Remained to steam upon the lonely table.

Behind the storehouse then, our footsteps mash
The clods of sticky earth the garden gird.
Out on the highroad something seemed to flash,
And angry voices from afar were heard.

Quick! Quick! Already at the door one pounds.
We hear them: "Do the reptiles hope to lock it?"
Quick! Quick! We are the quarry of these hounds—
My brother pulls a pistol from his pocket.

The village, to the right, has homes in ranks,
Where evening windows are a row of lights.
To leftward lie the steep slopes of the banks
Down to the river. There our path invites.

Entreating the Last Judgment from the sky,
We plunge to meet the night, the wind, the rain;
I vow I'll not forget until I die,
Nor yet forgive, that hour of mortal pain.

Through reeds and utter darkness lay our road . . .
The door from off its posts we heard them jar . . .
The gloomy river pool by which we strode
Bore no reflection of a single star.

From the Ukrainian of Ihor Kachurovsky (1918–   )

From The Poetical Works of Taras Shevchenko

IT IS ALL ONE

It is all one to me indeed, if I
Live in Ukraine or live there not at all,
Whether or not men let my memory die;
Here in an alien land, mid snows piled high,
It will not matter that such things befall.

In serfdom, among strangers was I reared,
And unlamented wholly by my own
In exile I shall die, in grief uncheered,
And to my nameless grave shall pass alone.
No trace of me, alas, will then remain
To see in all our glorious Ukraine,
In all that land of ours that is not ours.
No father will commend me to his son,
That prayers for me to God he might confide:
"Pray then, my boy! For us his course was run.
For our Ukraine he suffered and he died."

It is all one to me indeed, I say,
Whether or not that son for me should pray . . .
But while I live I cannot bear to see
A wicked people come with crafty threat,
To lull Ukraine, yet strip her ruthlessly
And waken her amid the flames they set—
By God, these wrongs are not all one to me!

GOD'S AXE

Behind the door in God's own dwelling-place,
An axe lay. (God at that time walked the earth
With Holy Peter, working miracles.)
And a Kirghizian, to his misfortune
(And what a great misfortune!), stealthily,
Without attracting notice, stole that axe
And to the green oak-forest straightway went

To get some kindling wood. He chose a tree,
He gave it quite a chop, and, as he did,
Out of his hands the axe then tore itself
And went about the forest mowing trees!
It was a horrible and fearful sight:
The oaks and every other kind of tree,
However ancient, were cut down like grass
And laid in swaths; while out of the ravine
Arose a conflagration; clouds of smoke
Covered the blessed sun, and darkness followed.
From Ural to Tinghiz, up to the Aral,
The water in the lakes was boiling over.
Villages, towns, and cities were ablaze,
People lamented, wild beasts howled and hid
Beyond Tobol, far in Siberian snows.
For seven years the axe of God continued
To mow the woods, the conflagration raged,
And God's bright world grew murky in the smoke....

    In the eighth summer, on a Sunday morning,
Like a child's doll in a white tunic dressed,
The blessed sun arose. The wilderness
Still looked as black and ugly as a gypsy:
Wherever once a town or village stood,
No brand was left to smoulder, and the ashes
Were scattered by the wind; no blade of grass
Was left, and but a single tree stood green,—
All, all alone, in the vast steppe it swayed.

    Throughout the wilderness the ruddy clay
And the baked shards showed red, the prickly grasses
And weeds and random feather-grass with sedge
Blackened in a ravine beneath a mountain;
And sometimes came a wild Kirghizian
On his decrepit camel up the slope.
Mysterious things then happen there: it seems
As if the very steppeland spoke to God,
The camel weeps, the nomad droops his head
And at Kara-Butak and the steppe he gazes.
Singich-ahach the Kaizak then recalls,
Then slowly down the mountain slope he comes
To vanish in that wilderness of clay.

All, all alone in that forgotten valley
Amid the flatland, by a highway bare,
Stands that tall tree, abandoned there by God;
Untouched by axe or flames, it whispers low
And tells the valley of that fatal hour.
And the Kirghizians will never pass
That hallowed tree, but down into the valley
They come to marvel at the miracle;
Then to the tree they pray, and offer gifts,
Beseeching it to spread its branches wide
Above the desolation of their land.

PRETTY KATIE

A BALLAD

To pretty Katerina's house,
    That stands so rich and stately,
From all the Zaporozhian realm
    Three wooers came but lately.

And one was Semen Bossiy named;
    The second, Ivan Holiy:
Young Ivan Yaroshenko, third,
    Was a Cossack far from lowly.

"We've been through all of Poland's towns
    (They said) and all Ukraine,
But no such beauty have we seen
    As Katie, we maintain!"

The first one said: "If I were rich,
    My brothers, I aver,
I'd give the whole of all my gold
    For one brief hour with her."

The second said: "If I were strong,
    My comrades, I aver,
I'd give at length my utter strength
    For one brief hour with her."

The third man said: "No thing on earth,
    My fellows, I aver,
Would I eschew to give or do
    For one brief hour with her."

Thoughtful grew Katerina then,
  And to the third says she:
"An only brother do I mourn
  In dread captivity.

"In far Crimea he must lie.
  Who brings him to my house,
That man, O Zaporozhians brave,
  Will then become my spouse!"

They all rose up together straight
  And saddled their three steeds
And rode in haste to liberate
  Her brother by their deeds.

And one the Dnieper's flood did drown,
  The Poles impaled another,
But one from Bakchisaray-town
  Brought back the captive brother.

Full early at the lordly house,
  Knocks at the door entreat:
"Wake up, wake up, my maiden fair,
  Your brother come to greet!"

Then Katie glanced upon the pair,
  And Katie smiled and cried:
"This is no brother, but my love—
  My sweetheart—for I lied."

"You lied to me!" His sabre flashed,
  And Katie's pretty head
Fell down and rolled upon the floor.
  Then to his mate he said:

"Out of this wicked house, my friend,
  Let us make haste to go!"
The Zaporozhians rode off
  Swift as the winds that blow.

The black-browed Katerina's corpse
  Men buried on the plain;
And on the steppe the Cossack lads
  Were reconciled again.

From the Ukrainian of Taras Shevchenko (1814–61)

Bibliography of Published Verse

I. ORIGINAL VERSE

1. *The Tide of Life and Other Poems.* Ottawa, 1930.
2. *Canada to Iceland.* Lindsay, 1930.
3. *The Eternal Quest.* Winnipeg, 1934.
4. *To Horace.* Winnipeg, 1935.
5. "A Manitoba Symphony," in *Manitoba Essays,* ed. by R. C. Lodge. Toronto, 1937.
6. *The Bridge Builders.* Winnipeg, 1938.
7. *Lyra Sacra.* Winnipeg, 1939.
8. *A Western Idyll.* Hamilton, 1940.
9. *The Flying Bull and Other Tales.* Toronto, 1940.
10. *The Crow and the Nighthawk.* Hamilton, 1943.
11. *Christ and Herod, and Other Poems.* Hamilton, 1947.
12. *A Rime of Glooscap.* Halifax, 1950. Offprint from *Dalhousie Review.*
13. *The Mod at Grand Pré: A Light Opera.* Wolfville, 1955.
14. *The Primordial Church of Horton.* Wolfville, 1963.
15. *Sixteen Decades of Parsonages.* Wolfville, 1964.

II. TRANSLATED VERSE

16. *An Outline of European Poetry.* Winnipeg, 1927.
17. *European Elegies.* Ottawa, 1928.
18. Contributor to *An Anthology of Czechoslovak Verse,* ed. by C. A. Manning, New York, 1929.
19. *The North American Book of Icelandic Verse.* New York, 1930.
20. *A Magyar Miscellany.* London, 1931, 1938, 1943, 1945 (offprints from *Slavonic Review*).
21. *The Magyar Muse: An Anthology of Hungarian Poetry, 1400–1932.* Winnipeg, 1933.
22. *A Polish Miscellany.* London, 1935 (offprint from *Slavonic Review*).
23. *The Death of King Buda.* With Lulu Payerle, Cleveland, 1936.
24. *A Golden Treasury of Polish Lyrics.* Winnipeg, 1936.

25. *The Poetry of Ady.* Budapest, 1937 (offprint from *Hungarian Quarterly*).
26. *New-Canadian Letters.* Toronto, annually 1935–1964 (*University of Toronto Quarterly*).
27. *A Skald in Canada.* Ottawa, 1939 (Transactions, Royal Society of Canada).
28. *Endre Ady: Selected Verse.* Cambridge, 1944 (*Slavonic Review, American Series*).
29. *The Quebec Tradition.* With Séraphin Marion, Montreal, 1946.
30. *A Little Treasury of Hungarian Verse.* Washington, 1947.
31. *Prince Ihor's Raid Against the Polovtsi.* With Paul Crath, Saskatoon, 1947.
32. *Avitus' Epic on the Fall.* Quebec, 1947 (*Laval Théologique et Philosophique*).
33. *John MacLean's "Gloomy Forest."* Halifax, 1948 (offprint from *Dalhousie Review*).
34. Contributor to *Poems by Adam Mickiewicz.* New York, 1944.
35. *The Celestial Cycle.* Toronto, 1952.
36. *Pan Tadeusz.* Toronto and New York, 1962.
37. *The Ukrainian Poets, 1189–1963.* With C. H. Andrusyshen, Toronto, 1963.
38. *The Poetry of Taras Shevchenko.* With C. H. Andrusyshen, Toronto, 1964.
39. *Selected Poems of László Mécs.* DePere, Wisconsin, 1964.
40. *That Invincible Samson.* Toronto, 1964.
41. Some 31 poems in *Modern Polish Literature*, ed. Gillon and Krzyzanowski. New York, 1964.

III. PERIODICAL PUBLICATIONS (partial list)

Some hundreds of fugitive poems, original and translated, have been published in the following periodicals: *Acadia Bulletin, Amethyst, Canadian Bookman, Canadian Forum, Canadian Jewish Review, Canadian Poetry Magazine, Chronicle-Herald* (Halifax), *Crucible, Czas, Dalhousie Review, Eastern Chronicle, Engadine Express, Evening Telegram* (Toronto), *Evening Tribune* (Winnipeg), *Gazeta Katolicka, Heimskringla, Hungarian Quarterly, Icelandic-Canadian, Jewish Standard, Kanadai Magyar Ujsag, Life and Letters Today, Lögberg, Manitoban, Maritime Baptist, Messenger, National Home Monthly, Norge-Canada, Queen's Journal, Queen's Quarterly, Regina Leader-Post, Saturday Night, Slavonic and East European Review, Slavonic Review* (American Series), *University of Toronto Quarterly, Vox, Vox Wesleyana, Warsaw Weekly, Western Baptist, Western Home Monthly, Winnipeg Free Press, Young Magyar-American.*